War Crimes, Genocide, and the Law

Recent Titles in
Contemporary Military, Strategic, and Security Issues

The Process and Politics of Defense Acquisition: A Reference Handbook
David S. Sorenson

International Crime and Punishment: A Guide to the Issues
James Larry Taulbee

Serving America's Veterans: A Reference Handbook
Lawrence J. Korb, Sean E. Duggan, Peter M. Juul, and Max A. Bergmann

Military Doctrine: A Reference Handbook
Bert Chapman

Energy Security Challenges for the 21st Century: A Reference Handbook
Gal Luft and Anne Korin, editors

An Introduction to Military Ethics: A Reference Handbook
Bill Rhodes

War and Children: A Reference Handbook
Kendra E. Dupuy and Krijn Peters

Military Justice: A Guide to the Issues
Lawrence J. Morris

Military Space Power: A Guide to the Issues
Wilson W.S. Wong and James Fergusson

American Missile Defense: A Guide to the Issues
Victoria Samson

Private Armed Forces and Global Security: A Guide to the Issues
Carlos Ortiz

Women in the United States Armed Forces: A Guide to the Issues
Darlene M. Iskra

War Crimes, Genocide, and the Law

A Guide to the Issues

Arnold Krammer

Contemporary Military, Strategic, and Security Issues

PRAEGER

AN IMPRINT OF ABC-CLIO, LLC
Santa Barbara, California • Denver, Colorado • Oxford, England

Library of Congress Cataloging-in-Publication Data

Krammer, Arnold, 1941–
War crimes, genocide, and the law : a guide to the issues / Arnold Krammer.
p. cm. — (Contemporary military, strategic, and security issues)
Includes bibliographical references and index.
ISBN 978-0-313-35937-8 (hardcopy : alk. paper) — ISBN 978-0-313-35938-5 (ebook) 1. War crimes—History. 2. War victims—Legal status, laws, etc. 3. Prisoners of war—Legal status, laws, etc. 4. Prisoners of war—Abuse of. 5. Torture. 6. Genocide. 7. War (International law) I. Title.
K5301.K73 2010
341.6'9—dc22 2009051995

ISBN: 978-0-313-35937-8
EISBN: 978-0-313-35938-5

14 13 12 11 10 1 2 3 4 5

This book is also available on the World Wide Web as an eBook.
Visit www.abc-clio.com for details.

Praeger
An Imprint of ABC-CLIO, LLC

ABC-CLIO, LLC
130 Cremona Drive, P.O. Box 1911
Santa Barbara, California 93116-1911

This book is printed on acid-free paper ∞

Manufactured in the United States of America

To the newest members of the Krammer clan, Nathan Douglas *and his older sister,* Avery Lorraine, *in the deep hope that they will grow up in a world in which war crimes are to be found only in history books,*

and to Erin Channing Buenger, *age 11, who left the stage too soon.*

Contents

Acknowledgments

A study of war crimes and genocide is difficult to read. It is frightening and depressing to be confronted by the horrific acts that people do to one another during conflicts. Since wars began, humans have hacked, stabbed, burned, and shot helpless enemy prisoners and civilians and killed unwanted citizens in their own country. Such a book is also difficult to write. First, it requires researchers and archivists of a special quality: they need to ensure that the history they relate is accurate; take care that their empathy for the victims and hatred for the perpetrators does not influence their interpretation of the records or their level of research interest; and have the optimism to see the possibility of a brighter day in the future. To this end, I have had the great good fortune of meeting some of the best researchers in the business.

I am particularly indebted to Dr. Tamara Haygood, Ph.D., M.D., who is preparing a book of her own on the medical treatment provided to prisoners of war during World War II, and Professor Robert C. Doyle, of Franciscan University, in Steubenville, Ohio, a leading expert on prisoners of war, whose book on the history of America's enemy POWs is about to see publication. I am indebted to Dr. Alicja Witalisz, English department, Pedagogical University of Cracow (Kraków), Poland for her impassioned analysis of the Katyn Forest massacre; Dr. phil. Joachim Neander, also in Kraków, a world-class expert on the Holocaust; and Captain Regan Turner, USMC, a decorated veteran of Afghanistan and Iraq, for valuable insights into the complexities of combat. Help in assembling facts and locating the proper volumes or quotes was the purview of two wonderful and tenacious researchers: Rebecca M. Eaton, of the Bush School of Government and Public Service, and Kathleen Barr, of the history department of Texas A&M University. The best researchers and bibliographical sleuths, I find, are passionate about the topic and clever in locating new sources of information. Leslie McDonald, another graduate of the Bush School of Government and Public Service and currently at Texas

A&M University's department of political science, is an excellent writer in her own right and is, as in the past, my first line of editorial defense.

All translations from French have been provided by Professor Gérard Chètrit, in Paris, whose fluency in several languages has been enormously helpful.

A major source of modern military information may be found in the U.S. Army Heritage and Education Center in Carlisle, Pennsylvania, under the direction of Dr. Conrad C. Crane, where knowledgeable historians like Dr. Richard J. Sommers and Arthur W. Bergeron, Jr., and photo experts like Clif Hyatt, all of whom have spent years immersed in the records, are standing by with keen archival expertise and helpful advice. For the legal side of the issue of war crimes, one can benefit hugely from a visit to the Robert H. Jackson Center, located in the Jamestown, New York, home of the Chief American Prosecutor at the Nuremberg Tribunal and Justice of the U.S. Supreme Court. His archives are maintained in a quaint, mid-1800s mansion, adding to the personal touch one receives while reading his correspondence and legal decisions on rights guaranteed to war criminals and definitions of their acts.

A surprisingly beneficial source of information appeared in a small county public library in West Virginia. The Brooke County Public Library, in Wellsburg, West Virginia, a local cultural center hard on the banks of the Ohio River, happens to hold an impressive collection of documents related to the Japanese bombardment of Corregidor and the Bataan Death March in the Philippine Campaign during World War Two. Built around the original collection donated by survivor Edward Jackfert, the library is watched over by its very competent director, Mary Kay Wallace, MLS.

Finally, a book of such emotional demands requires a network of friends and family: the endless tolerance of my wife, Jan, whose encyclopedic knowledge and editorial skill have provided answers and corrections at every turn; the irrepressible humor of our son, Adam, in San Francisco; and the sage advice of brother Steven, and his wife, Marleen. When the gloom of man's horrific acts settles over us, we cast our attention to our younger son, Douglas, a paramedic saving lives, a calling that offers us hope for the future.

CHAPTER 1

War Crimes in History

"All is fair in love and war," as the old adage goes. But, is that true? Is everything fair in war? What about the rape and murder of helpless women or children? What about the slaughter of wounded or the torture of innocents? Is it acceptable to murder disarmed prisoners of war or religious captives? What about the modern use of napalm, cluster bombs, and land mines, all of which kill and maim more civilians than enemy soldiers? What about soldiers who sneak up to their enemies under the protection of the Red Cross or a white flag? Nearly every nation in history has committed such heinous acts during wartime, even those that glory in their democratic ideals and seek to export them.

For example, at the end of the American Civil War, the North's triumphant General Sherman led his army of 62,000 vengeful veterans to burn and loot a swath from 25 to 60 miles wide across the state of Georgia from Atlanta to the sea. "Forage liberally when in need of food or fuel," Sherman authorized his units. To his men, the euphemism "foraging liberally" meant that the enemy's property was at their disposal and that any discussion of "rules of war" would not be taken seriously. An Illinois sergeant recalled that "The men worked with a will, seeming to take savage delight in destroying everything that could by any possibility be made use of by their enemies."[1] Another veteran remembered that "We destroyed all we could not eat, stole their niggers, burned their cotton and gins, spilled their sorghum, burned and twisted their R. Roads [railroads] and raised Hell generally."[2]

War crimes on a massive scale are certainly not restricted to any particular century. In a later war, in February 1945, with the end of World War II merely two and a half months away, the United States and Britain firebombed the strategically unimportant German city of Dresden, waves of bombers circling overhead around the clock and killing some 70,000 civilian inhabitants.

War crimes can occur years after the war itself is over. Long considered an integral defense weapon, mines are inexpensive to manufacture and impervious to weather, and they remain deadly for decades after the smoke of battle disappears. Consider the huge number of landmines that have been scattered in desert battlefields and tropical jungles across the globe. Millions of forgotten deadly mines lurk beneath the surface from Afghanistan to Angola, from Congo to Cambodia, from North Africa to South Africa—wherever civil strife has raged over the past half-century. Farmers working in their fields, children playing, and women searching for firewood regularly step on landmines and lose their legs or their lives. According to the International Campaign to Ban Landmines' *Landmine Monitor Report 2000* (p. 23), there were new landmine and unexploded ordnance victims in 71 countries in the 14-month period from March 1999 to May 2000![3] Surely these acts of war can't be fair.

The fact is that, since the beginning of time, conflicts have evoked acts of inhumanity that shocked even hardened soldiers. Such conflicts and their atrocities have littered the landscape of history as tribes, religious groups, and kingdoms have fought for economic, religious, or territorial dominance. Violent acts against noncombatants, women, children, the wounded, or prisoners, as well as the burning of crops and the senseless slaughter of livestock, have been viewed as a part of war. Worse still, these atrocities nearly always fail to influence the flow of events in the slightest.

The murder of prisoners after battles is perhaps more common than any other war atrocity. Turning back the clock to biblical times, the Assyrian Ashur-nasir-pal wrote after one engagement:

> 3000 of their combat troops I felled with weapons. . . . Many of the captives taken from them I burned in a fire. Many I took alive; from some of these I cut off their hands to the wrist, from others I cut off their noses, ears and fingers; I put out the eyes of many of the soldiers. . . . I burnt their young men and women to death.[4]

Even the Greeks, with their historic contributions to the philosophy of democracy, generally killed captives who were of no immediate use. One of the Greek world's greatest philosophers, Aristotle, dismissed the fate of Greece's war prisoners with the simple dictum "Those vanquished in war are held to belong to the victor."[5] Aristotle's student, the great philosopher Plato (427–347 B.C.), warned the soldiers of Greece that if any of them fall alive into the hands of their enemies, they could expect neither mercy nor concern.[6]

Nor were the deaths of these prisoners particularly pleasant. During the Peloponnesian War, in the late fifth century B.C., the Athenians and the Spartans—all Greeks—murdered each other with abandon for 27 years. Battles were fought to the bitter end with no quarter asked or given. If prisoners were taken alive, and the odds were against it, the captives were treated as cruelly as those who suffered in the notorious Confederate war prison at Andersonville, Georgia, or in the Nazi concentration camp at Dachau. The plight of Athenian prisoners after the Syracusan defeat, for instance, saw the prisoners crammed into an open quarry, starved, and left to die. At the battle of Corcyra, prisoners from the Spartan side were shut in a large building, and groups of 20 were tied together and forced to run between two lines of heavy infantrymen from the Athenian side to be whipped and stabbed. None survived.[7]

The early Romans were no more humane. While it is true that the Romans conquered and ruled much of the known world for 500 years and created wonders of architecture, literature, and political stability that would not be equaled for more than 1,000 years, their treatment of helpless war captives was harsh. In warfare, the ancient Romans were as ruthless as the barbarians they fought. Generally, an enemy soldier captured by the Roman legions knew his days were numbered. He was led through the streets of the Roman town or village in celebration of victory or to entertain the public and then used for target practice or as a gladiator in the arenas. Most, however, were simply strangled in nearby cellars.

In the city of Rome itself, after a parade, war prisoners were usually strangled in dark underground passages at the base of the Capitoline Hill (ironically now located below the church San Giuseppe dei Falegnami), where burly servants waited with leather ropes to stand behind the kneeling prisoners.

> Sometimes the war crime could be minor, such as the inexcusable killing of a herald during the battles between the Britain and France in the fourteenth century. Heralds wore distinctive dress and were trusted messengers, diplomats, and recognized experts on the code of chivalry. During his invasion of Flanders, according to a chronicler, Bishop Spenser of Norwich sent a herald to the troops of West Flanders to enquire whether they were supporting Pope Urban, as did Bishop Spenser, or Pope Clement, but the rude people, not understanding what appertained to the law of armes [*sic*], ran upon the herald at his approaching of them, and slue [*sic*] him before he could begin to tell his tale. The herald's killing was an appalling breach of the rules of war of the time and, in fact, triggered a major English retaliation.[8]

On other occasions, the atrocities involved millions of victims. More than a million Armenians were murdered by the Turks during World War I, and at least six times that number of European Jews were murdered by the Nazis during the Second World War.

Sometimes atrocities are shockingly sadistic. Around 840 to 980 A.D., the Danish Vikings, for example, came ashore in search of prisoners and booty along the Irish coast, as well as in northern France and on the southeastern coast of England. The Danes scoured the landscape, wielding heavy axes and broad swords, protected by little more than brightly painted circular shields and leather helmets, killing Christians and pillaging farms and villages. Curiously, the roving Viking bands were often repelled, but when they did take prisoners, the captives were in for a horrible end. The Vikings had a predilection for a brutal punishment called "pitch-capping" or "blood-eagling"—a grisly ritual in which the prisoner was tied facing a stake and his ribs hacked away from his spine with a sword and pulled outward like wings, revealing his lungs, which were pulled out like balloons. Being an aristocrat or a rich prize did not always protect an individual. Consider the fate of King Edmund of East Anglia in 870 A.D. at the hands of marauding Danes, who offered him peace on the condition that he would rule as their vassal and forbid the practice of Christianity. Legend has it that he refused and was then "blood-eagled" by the Viking chieftain Ivar the Boneless (a rather transparent reference to Ivar's impotence) in 869. His defiance on behalf of his faith earned him sainthood.[9]

Regardless of the size of the horrors involved, war crimes are defined in the following ways:

1. War crimes must occur during war. Atrocities committed during peacetime are violations of civilian laws and, consequently, are punishable by the peacetime judicial systems of each country according to its jurisdiction and carefully crafted laws.
2. War crimes directed intentionally against a racial, ethnic, or religious group are considered a separate class of war crimes, constituting genocide.
3. The most important determinant whether atrocities will be prosecuted as war crimes is *who wins the war.* The classic adage applies: the winner writes the history of the war and thus determines what constitutes a war crime and which side committed it.

The side that triumphs rarely views its own actions as unjustified violations of accepted agreements, customs, or laws. Only the enemy—the evil, ungodly side—commits war crimes. Very rarely does a winning side concede the commission of an unnecessarily brutal atrocity against the enemy or its citizens. Yet, the temptation to actually commit additional atrocities increases if such atrocities are viewed as helping bring victory, since victory will allow the winning side to erase or minimize the very atrocities that helped ensure its success. Conflicts are rife with such double standards, and one need only reach back to any random conflict to find examples. During the American Civil War, for example, the notorious Confederate prison camp, Andersonville, where

> Northern captives lived and died by the thousands in the mud, disease, and starvation, is the very definition of a war crime. Indeed, Confederate Captain Henry Wirtz, Andersonville's notoriously cruel Interior Camp Commandant, was tried after the war and hanged.

Yet, history has paid little attention to the northern POW camps at Alton, Grant, and Douglas, in Illinois; Morton and Rock Island, in Indiana; Johnson's Island and Chase, in Ohio; Point Lookout, in Maryland; Fort Delaware in Delaware Bay; and Elmira, in New York. Conditions in Union camps were certainly grim, although not as bad, generally, as in the Confederate camps.[10] The real difference, however, is that the North won the war and thus determined what constituted a war crime and what did not.

In World War II, following the Battle of the Bulge, in December 1944, the melted snow revealed the bodies of 115 murdered American prisoners. More than half a century later, the very name of the Belgian town of Malmedy recalls for many the oft-cited Malmedy massacre war crime. Yet, history seems to have overlooked the story of the outraged American soldiers who reacted to the Malmedy revelations by murdering a substantial number of German prisoners. *Again, everything depends on whether or not you win the war, since the winner defines the war crimes.*

Motives for War Crimes

Every war, every conflict has witnessed war crimes, sometimes cultural violations like the destruction of churches, sometimes the more heinous torture of prisoners and civilians, sometimes massive acts of genocide. Except for the crimes created by psychopaths, who find enjoyment in tormenting others (such as the subterranean minions of Adolf Hitler's Gestapo agents, Josef Stalin's blow-torch-wielding NKVD secret service, and Bosnian Serbian prison guards like Dǔsko Tadić, who ordered his Bosnian Muslim prisoners at knife point to bite off the testicles of other prisoners), war crimes are usually committed for a reason. There are rare exceptions, however, when there is simply no explanation for the atrocity, such as occurred in the Polish hamlet of Jedwabne during World War II, when the Jewish half of the population was brutally murdered, drowned, and burned to death by their non-Jewish neighbors "because," in the ominous words of political philosopher George Will's excellent review of Jan Gross's shocking exposé of the event, "they could."[11] Otherwise, with occasional exceptions, of course, war crimes fall into the categories described in the sections that follow.

War Crimes Committed Because Prisoners Were Simply Too Much Trouble to Bring Along

After the historic battle of Agincourt, in 1415, Henry V of England ordered all French prisoners killed expressly so that their guards could be released for combat duty. The 16th-century English chronicler Holinshed described the cruelty this way:

> When this dolorous decree, and pitiful proclamation was pronounced, pitie [*sic*] it was to see how some Frenchmen were suddenlie [*sic*] sticked with daggers, some were brained with pollaxes, some slaine [*sic*] with malls, other had their throats cut, and some their bellies paunched, so that, in effect, hauing [having] respect to their great number, few prisoners were saued [saved].[12]

Five hundred years later, during the Second World War, American soldiers in the Pacific routinely killed Japanese prisoners to reduce the drag on their forces as events moved quickly around them. While the Japanese rarely surrendered voluntarily—and those who were captured were either unconscious or on the verge of starvation—few made it back to the rear lines alive. American, British, and Dutch soldiers despised their Japanese captives, a loathing that was reciprocated by the Japanese. Realistically, however, combat in the jungles of the South Pacific did not lend itself to the care of prisoners by either side. Once behind the lines and headed for POW camps, the majority were treated decently, if with exaggerated security, and were shipped to camps in Australia and New Zealand, as well as to distant Camp Clinton, Iowa, and Camp McCoy, Wisconsin. (Their greatest punishment lay ahead: the terrifying prospect of returning to Japan at the war's end, back to an unforgiving culture that saw war prisoners as soulless).

On the European side of the war, the Germans occasionally murdered their American, British, and Canadian prisoners. For example, in the wake of the Normandy invasion, in June 1944, the morning sunrise revealed groups of Allied dead, many shot execution-style with their hands wired behind their backs. None appeared to have been tortured, and, since it had been only a short time since they landed, one assumes that they were murdered to enable the enemy to retreat speedily and without encumbrance. The Russians were no better. During the Second World War, Brigadier Fitzroy Maclean, head of the British military mission to Yugoslavia, asked a Russian officer how they dealt with prisoners. "If they surrender in large groups," replied the Russian, "we send them back to base; but if there are only a few of them, we don't bother."

War Crimes Driven by Plunder

There has scarcely been a conflict in history when the soldiers from either side haven't stolen or plundered, often torturing or murdering civilians to get what they wanted. Society's laws are suspended during war, after all. Besides, most soldiers believe they have earned the loot with their blood and that they are entitled to the enemy's valuables, especially when their hatred of the enemy is fueled by propaganda or the loss of comrades. Soldiers commit atrocities out of greed or simple opportunity. History is replete with reports of the beating and occasional murder of helpless civilians and prisoners for nothing more valuable than a watch or a cigarette.

The Thirty Years War, 1618–1648, fought in part between European Catholics and Protestants, probably takes the prize for having the most aggressive thieves on any side. For instance, when Swedish soldiers thought their prisoners were hiding gold, they turned to

> exquisite torments to make them confess. They wound and tied about their heads strong . . . cords, and twisted them until blood came out of their eyes, ears, and noses, yea, till their eyes started out of their heads. They tied burning matches betwixt their fingers, to their noses, tongues, jaws, cheeks, breasts, legs, and secret parts. . . .The mouths of some they have opened with gags, and then poured downe their throats water, stinking puddle, filthy liquids, and pisse [*sic*] itself, saying: This is a Swedish draught.[13]
>
> The invading Swedish army was far from the only culprit in that conflict. "When troops from Saxony marched into the area they ravaged it," recalled an eyewitness named Grützmann, destroying all the grain in the fields and driving off the cattle.
>
> Soon the Imperialists came, the Lüneburgers, in fact a medley of nations, French and Spanish, so that Germany became nothing but a looting ground. . . . Churches, parsonages and schools were wrecked along with farmhouses. Church services were forgotten, the land laid waste, and so many fir trees were growing in the fields that from a distance many a village looked like a wood.[14]

War Crimes Committed on a Whim

When Napoleon invaded Russia, in 1812, and retreated after pillaging Moscow, he reduced more than 3,000 Russian prisoners to eating dead horses by the side of the road and, legend has it, eating their own dead, as well. The

Russians, for their part, buried French prisoners alive, used them for target practice, and cut off their tongues, ears, noses, and genitalia. While various Russian generals treated their prisoners differently, some with almost medieval chivalry, others personally ordered that prisoners be bayoneted. Polish soldiers found among the French were treated with special ruthlessness because they were despised as traitors to the Slavic cause.

Captives throughout history have often been murdered on a whim. During Napoleon's catastrophic retreat across the frozen steppes of Russia, in 1812, for example, Russia's Grand Duke Constantine and his senior officers happened to see a distinguished French officer among the prisoners. Appearing to ignore the mutually accepted rules protecting war prisoners, Constantine asked the officer if he would prefer death to his current humiliation. According to eyewitnesses, the officer answered, "There are those in France who would lament my fate—for their sake I should wish to return; but if that be impossible, the sooner the ignominy and suffering are over the better."[15] To everyone's horror, the Grand Duke drew his saber and killed the man.

A hundred and fifty years, later in the Philippines, in 1942, Japanese soldiers bayoneted, stabbed, and brained 77,796 ragged and starving Filipino and American prisoners in the notorious Bataan Death March. Thousands of limping, emaciated survivors were marched the length of the Bataan Peninsula to waiting Japanese ships and years of starvation, disease, and brutality in Japanese prison camps. Once in captivity, 1,500 American prisoners who had survived the march across Bataan died within 40 days; 25,000 Filipinos had been murdered by the Japanese by July 1942. Those in Japanese captivity never knew what would cause a Japanese guard to shoot or stab them; they often beat a frail prisoner unconscious for the tiniest infraction or for no infraction at all.

Similar savagery was evident in the European theater during the same war. The ordinary German Army—not just the sinister and oft-responsible SS—murdered some 3.3 million Russian POWs out of the 5.7 million in its hands, routinely working them to death and tormenting them in horrific ways, for example, subjecting them to medical experiments and using them to test the Zyklon-B gas, later used in the Nazi death camps.

During the Vietnam War, Lieutenant Sam Bunge, a 101st Airborne platoon leader, recalled how much the commission of war crimes depended on whims.

> When I first took over my platoon, we were on a sweep action and we received a couple of rounds of sniper fire from a village in an area that we knew had a lot of VC. . . . I asked [the advice] of the squad leader [who said] that "the other lieutenant (referring to my predecessor) said that if we ever get sniper fire from a village we were supposed to burn it down."

> So after we got the village secure, I called all the squad leaders together and changed the policy. The point here is, that in a war like Vietnam where the small unit commanders have such autonomy (lieutenants and captains to a large degree ran the show), an individual can make a big difference. If a man wants to burn villages, he can do it.[16]

General Matthew Ridgeway recalls that "in World War I [some American GIs] would cut off the ears [of the Germans] and string them around their neck." One doughboy promised to bring his mother a necklace of "German's teeth."[17] World War II saw American soldiers committing a wide spectrum of war crimes. For example, at the Battle of the Bulge, in December 1944, a company in Colonel James Woolnough's regiment captured 50 Germans after a fierce firefight. The company commander was shot by one who had not surrendered, and the angry men shot the other 50.

On the Pacific side, U.S. Navy and Marines recalled that shipmates mutilated the bodies of drowned Japanese kamikaze pilots. "One of the Marines cut the ring off the finger of one of the dead pilots . . . one of the fellows had a Jap scalp. . . . One of the men on our gun mount got a Jap rib and cleaned it up; he said his sister wants part of a Jap body. One fellow from Texas had a knee bone.[18]

The conflict in South Vietnam was dense with war crimes. One can reach for nearly any memoir of the conflict and read of an almost casual disregard for the internationally agreed-upon rights of enemy civilians or, for that matter, for their lives. In June 1968, a company of Americal Division troops swept through part of the Dragon Valley. It took some casualties and captured two NFL nurses. "The company commander . . . and platoon leader stood by as the two women were repeatedly raped and sodomized. Aware that they might be in trouble if their behavior was reported, they murdered one of the two."[19] Veterans often recall incidents when they or their buddies "killed a gook and cut off the corpse's fingers and ears." The nonchalance of the senseless and random mass murder was reflected at the very top. The journalist Neil Sheehan questioned General William Westmoreland, the American commander in Vietnam, about "whether he was worried about the large number of civilian casualties from the air strikes and the shelling. He looked at me carefully. 'Yes, Neil, it is a problem,' he said. 'But it does deprive the enemy of the populations, doesn't it.' "[20]

War Crimes Committed to Send a Signal to One's Enemies

One of the most striking instances of committing a war crime to taunt the enemy is the act of the Byzantine Emperor Basil II (958–1025 A.D.), remembered as Basil the Bulgar Slayer for his behavior at the Battle of Kleidion in

July 1014, as he fought to extend the influence of the Byzantine Empire over the Balkans, Mesopotamia, Armenia, and Georgia. Basil II triumphed over the Bulgarian Czar Samuel's army and, although Samuel managed to escape, captured some 14,000 Bulgarian prisoners. He used his prisoners, all 14,000 of them, to send a message that the Bulgarians wouldn't forget, saying, in effect, "This is what happens to anyone who rises up against the empire." Basil had 99 out of every 100 blinded. The 100th man in each group was blinded in only one eye so that he could lead his sightless comrades home. The column of almost 14,000 blind soldiers conveyed an unmistakable message to Czar Samuel and the Bulgarians. According to legend, when his blinded soldiers returned to Macedonia, Czar Samuel collapsed and died at the sight (although his official biography notes that he actually died 11 years later).[21]

Lest one think that such gory events are products of the cultures of Eastern Europe and the Balkans, bubbling with centuries-old ethnic hatreds, the Spanish army turned on its Aztec hosts in the midst of a joyful fiesta in the Aztec kingdom of central Mexico at the temple of Tenochtitlan in 1521.

According to one chronicler,

> At a moment of the fiesta, when the dance was at it loveliest, and when song was linked to song, the Spaniards were seized with an urge to kill the Aztec celebrants. . . . They closed the entrances and passageways, all the gates of the patio: the Eagle Gate in the lesser palace, the Gate of the Canestalk and the Gate of the Serpent of Mirrors. They posted guards so that no one could escape and then rushed into the Sacred Patio to slaughter the celebrants, . . . stabbing them, spearing them, striking them with swords. . . . They attacked the man who was drumming and cut off his arms. They cut off his head and rolled it across the floor. . . . Others fell to the floor with their entrails hanging out; some attempted to run away but their intestines dragged as they ran, tangling their feet in their own entrails. No matter how they tried to save themselves, they could find no escape.[22]

War Crimes Committed to Preempt Problems

Tragically, people are sometimes murdered to prevent future problems. For instance, early in World War II, after Poland was divided between the Germans and the Russians, 25,700 Polish military officers and intellectuals were rounded up from various prisoner-of-war camps and, with their hands tied behind their backs, transported deep into the Katyn Forest, 12 miles west of Smolensk, Russia. Once there, the seemingly endless river of captives was herded toward deep pits surrounded by bored gunmen cradling automatic weapons. For days, the captives were shot in the head and their bodies stacked in layers, sometimes 12 layers deep. Thousands more were taken away to three notorious Russian prisons, where, after confirming their identities, they were tortured and executed. A scant 395 prisoners survived the slaughter, and the crime was covered up and forgotten.

The military and intellectual loss to Poland was staggering and included an admiral, 14 generals, 24 colonels, 79 lieutenant colonels, 258 majors, 654 captains, 17 naval captains, and 4,022 warrant officers and NCOs, not to mention 300 physicians, 100 writers, priests, lawyers, and thousands of intellectuals and sons of intellectuals. In the continuing chaos of the war, with the Germans and the Soviets advancing and retreating across Poland, no one knew who had committed the murders, although, given the Wehrmacht's murderous treatment of Jews, Poles, and Russians, the world assumed that it had orchestrated these killings, as well. Each side blamed the other, and responsibility was debated for decades.[23]

The argument about the Katyn Forest massacre became increasingly strident during the Cold War, with both Polish and Russian scholars pointing an accusing finger at Moscow. After nearly half a century of denial, on April 13, 1990, the 47th anniversary of the discovery of the mass graves, Russia reluctantly admitted that its soldiers had done it after all and formally expressed "profound regret."[24] It turns out that Russian dictator Josef Stalin had assumed that Poland would fall under Russian control at the end of the war, and he wanted to rid his future colony of the Polish officers and intelligentsia that might someday work to oppose him. Thus, whether by Byzantine emperor or Soviet dictator, the murder of helpless prisoners is sometimes used to solve future problems.

Another example of the murder of men, women, and children to send a message and to eliminate future problems may be seen in the actions of the Mongol hordes. The Mongols under Genghis Khan breathed vengeance; any act against them was answered with immediate and overwhelming violence. The Mongols prided themselves on their ruthless treatment of captured enemies and their suspected friends. A revolt in their empire was the greatest betrayal of all. When Khan learned of just such an uprising in 1218, an arm of the terrifying Mongol army was instantly dispatched to subdue it. A garrison town of more than 100,000 armed civilians in the Khwarizm region—what is today Uzbekistan—had risen up against his rule. Khan ordered his commander to "strike their heads from their bodies." Khan's orders were never taken lightly, and, after the garrison was taken, in 1220, every single living thing was killed. But, to be absolutely sure that the Khan's order was fully carried out,

> the Orlok [commander] already on the return journey, stopped to send back 2,000 men to make sure that there was no one alive among the ruins. Those emissaries actually found 3,000 survivors, who were promptly

> slain. When the Mongol forces had withdrawn for the second time, from the last lurking-places in the city there crept forth 16 persons, who were joined, after a time, by 24 more from the suburbs. These 40 were all that were left alive.[25]

Chroniclers have determined that each of the Mongols slew an average of 24 people. Other regions would doubtless think twice about provoking Khan's wrath in the future.

One of the most chilling descriptions of war crimes committed to prevent a future problem was the testimony offered by defendant Otto Ohlendorf at the Nuremberg Trial after World War Two. When asked how many Jews his troops had killed in the Crimea and Ukraine, a former leader of one of four notorious *Einsatzgruppen* armies of Nazi killers that followed the German Army into Poland and Russia calmly replied, "Ninety thousand." But, he continued earnestly, the killings were necessary. "I believe that it is very simple to explain if one starts from the fact that [our actions] did not only try to achieve [immediate] security but also a permanent security for the reason that the children were people who would grow up and surely, being the children of parents who had been killed, they would constitute a danger no smaller than the parents."[26] The American prosecutor, Telford Taylor, remembers Ohlendorf's casual ruthlessness. The courtroom was stunned by the eerie chattiness of his admission, he recalled, as well as by the fact that the killer before them had been a well-known economist and, like many of his fellow defendants, a cultured European, not a primitive barbarian. Murdering thousands of Jewish children was, in his opinion, an economical way to prevent the appearance in the future of people who might return to take revenge.

War Crimes Committed to Extract Information from Prisoners

Intelligence information is the lifeblood of any war or battle. To know your enemy's plans in advance is to gain a major advantage. But, intelligence has a limited shelf life: once the battle is in motion, the information has less, if any, value. Thus, every group strives to penetrate the security of the other side as early as possible, to intercept messages, and to interrogate prisoners. The timely use of enemy intelligence might well save or cost lives. Increasingly, through the 20th century and into the current era, the value of information has increased to mythic proportion (a "ticking bomb" scenario), especially since the failure to learn the enemies' plans permitted events like the attack on Pearl Harbor and the attack on the World Trade Center in New York City and on the Pentagon, in Arlington, Virginia, on September 11, 2001. It is now an article of faith in every intelligence community that forewarned is forearmed.

The drive to obtain military intelligence has increased as the ability of military technology to inflict greater and greater damage has grown and as the value of life has cheapened. When the cost of an intelligence failure was a minor unexpected attack, efforts to extract enemy intelligence were restricted to threats, beatings, starvation, and execution. As the stakes increased and technology became more deadly, the torture of enemy combatants by more fearful atrocities became accepted and expected. During World War II, the blinding of French Resistance fighters by the Germans and the tearing out of fingernails by the Japanese, as well as starvation and summary execution by all parties, were very real parts of capture. The Korean War saw the introduction of mind-altering drugs, so-called brain washing, and soldiers hoped, usually in vain, that their refusal to divulge more than the proverbial "name, rank, and serial number" would be honored by their captors. With the appearance of nuclear and biological weapons, the cost of an unexpected enemy attack increased dramatically, and consequently, the desperate drive to learn the enemy's plans reached new levels of intensity. Torture became commonplace and sophisticated, clashing, eventually, with the accepted values of nations' political and religious institutions. As will be seen later in this study, when the demand for enemy intelligence becomes obsessive and the hard-won network of laws is swept aside, questions arise about the legality of the resulting atrocities, and it becomes important to categorize some as "acceptable" and others "unacceptable."

This is becoming especially true in the 21st century. The so-called war on terror has completely changed the paradigm of war. War has become asymmetrical: neither borders nor nationality matter any longer. Combatants now move effortlessly across frontiers by foot or helicopter and blend in with any local population. Passports and military papers are laughably absent in modern war, and citizenship rarely matters if the cause is deemed just—and no war is considered more just than a religious struggle. Terrorist actions are random and horribly costly to innocent citizens and bystanders, and the need for accurate and timely intelligence about the enemy's plans becomes urgent. Torture and other war crimes now pave the road to maintaining national security.

The issue of reciprocity works both ways, however. What one side does to its prisoners in pursuit of intelligence at, say, secret CIA prisons like Guantanamo or rendition centers in foreign countries will be done by the other side, as well. When Major George "Bud" Day's F-100F was shot out of the North Vietnamese skies by a SAM missile on August 26, 1967, he could not know that he would spend the next five and a half years in enemy captivity. With several broken bones, one protruding from his arm, a blind eye, a dislocated knee swollen like a purple football, terrified, starved, and trussed up with ropes and wire, Bud Day was considered a source of information to his undisciplined enemies. They knew that, as a pilot, he would know about his plane's electronics and about roads, landing strips, and unit dispositions. He was beaten senseless, threatened by crazed guards, starved, and tortured. When Day refused to answer military questions—the name of his outfit, the type of aircraft he flew, where he was based, his mission—the serious interrogations began.

> When Day refused to talk, a rope was tied around his ankles and the other thrown over a beam. He was hoisted into the air and hung there, head down, feeling the bones in his broken arm being pulled apart, then forced together, then pulled apart. In agony, he was left for hours as flies and mosquitoes crawled on his exposed skin, as sweat coursed down his body onto his face and into his nose and mouth. The hemp rope stretched, and after awhile, Day's head touched the ground. For the next hour or so he thought his neck would break as the full weight of his body pushed down on his head. . . . The next day, the beatings began.[27]

The nightmare finally ended when the peace process required the release of all prisoners; Bud Day and the remaining POWs, including John McCain, were returned to the American hospital at Clark Air Force Base in the Philippines and then flown on to the United States for an emotional reunion with their families. Like all the American prisoners in North Vietnamese hands, Bud Day was a physical and emotional wreck.

> Emergency dental work was done to repair the front teeth broken by a guard. Doctors found that he was riddled with hookworms, whipworms, and something called "gatamoeba coli." He was deaf in his right ear from countless blows to his head. His right arm was bowed. His eyesight was dimmed. And doctors bit their lips when they saw his buttocks and backs of his legs, still red and inflamed almost three years after his summer of hell.

Although nations at war regularly torture prisoners for what they believe is crucial information, usually until a scandal exposes the government's participation in such war crimes, the home government rewards those who have resisted similar treatment from the other side. Bud Day was awarded the Air Force Cross "for failing to give jailers any information during the sustained torture in the summer of 1969"[28] and was later awarded the Congressional Medal of Honor.

War Crimes Motivated by Boredom

In Vietnam, helicopter gunships often hovered overhead during an operation, waiting to be called in if enemy troops were flushed out. One American soldier recalls that

> the gun ships got bored. So they made a gun run on a hootch with miniguns and rockets. When they left the area we found one dead baby, which was a young child, very young, in its mother's arms, and we found a baby girl about three years old, also dead. Because these people were just bored; they were just sick of flying around doing nothing. When it was reported to battalion, the only reprimand was to put the two bodies on the body count board and just add them up with the other dead people. There was no reprimand; there was nothing.[29]

War Crimes Motivated by Frustration

In Vietnam, those units that were sniped at, ambushed in apparently tranquil terrain, harassed by booby traps and mines, and so forth tended to be more frustrated and aggressive than other units that faced a more conventional war. Add bad weather or snakes, and you have soldiers with a short fuse. The 1st Marine Division in Vietnam was largely involved in counterinsurgency operations against irregular North Vietnamese units and had substantially more courts-martial for violations of the rules of war than did the 3rd Marine Division, for instance, which fought a more conventional war against the regular North Vietnamese Army units.[30] That same aggression born of frustration, notes expert Peter Karsten, was behind the savage attacks on German-speaking Poles by irregular Polish soldiers after the collapse of the Polish defenses in 1939. It was behind the massacre of the Greek village of Distomo, in 1944, by a German unit that had just been mauled by *andartes* (partisans). And it was behind the brutal behavior of many Soviet troops as they advanced into Eastern Germany, in 1945.

In August 1966, a Marine Lance Corporal in Vietnam had just lost two close friends in combat. Unable to trap any enemy soldiers by morning, he moved into a nearby village "to kill a gook," took a man from a home, tore up the man's identification card, and shot him. At his trial, he explained, "I had to kill him. I had to kill a VC. . . . I had to help those guys that were dead. I had to do something for them."[31]

War Crimes for Use of Labor

Slavery was a staple of ancient warfare, and captured soldiers or conscripted civilians could easily find themselves living out the remainder of their lives in a quarry or behind an oar. Sometimes the misuse of civilians, often simple bystanders, has taken a particularly repugnant turn. Such was the experience of the so-called comfort women at the hands of the Japanese military during World War II. As early as 1932, an estimated 140,000 young women, mostly teenagers from Korea, were forced into serving as sex slaves for Japanese troops. These girls report that they were "raped and beaten at the outset before having to serve as many as thirty soldiers a day while living in what were euphemistically called 'comfort stations'." The Japanese military relied on these women to reduce the incidence of sexually transmitted diseases among the soldiers, by monitoring the health of these government slaves. The importance which the Japanese military placed on the sex slave program may be deduced from the fact that the "comfort women" would "frequently arrive at newly conquered territories or battlefronts along with provisions and ammunition."[32] As one could imagine, the agony never really ended for these women, even decades after liberation.

War Crimes Motivated by Vengeance

In December 1941,

> a German sailor threw a hand grenade at Lieutenant Colonel J. F. Durnford-Slater, missed and raised his hands. A sergeant advanced on the sailor, rifle at the hip. "Nein, nein," cried the sailor. "Ja, ja!" replied Sergeant Mills, and shot him. "Yeah, well, Mills, you shouldn't have done that," said Durnford-Slater.[33]

On a far larger scale, Britain's very successful naval blockade of Germany during the First World War is still debated as a possible war crime. Germany was heavily dependent on imports, and the funnel through which these imports entered Germany through the North Sea was relatively easily closed by a picket line of British ships.

In fact, the Hague Convention allows the blockade of war contraband, such as guns and ammunition. Britain's Prime Minister, Sir Edward Grey, in a legal maneuver worthy of Machiavelli, interpreted "contraband" to include foodstuffs. His logic went as follows: since the German people had surrendered their protected status by accepting food rationing from the government, they were no different from combat soldiers in the trenches. In other words, the public had now allied with the enemy government and must take its chances with it. The British embargo was directed not at soldiers but at ordinary civilians, and the "contraband" they were denied was food. Estimates indicate that some three-quarters of a million German civilians starved to death or became too weak to fend off diseases like tuberculosis, influenza, and pneumonia. Live births declined sharply, as did average life expectancy. (The noted psychohistorian Peter Loewenberg traces the emotionally and often physically stunted children from this period to the ranks of the Hitler Youth a few years in the future.)[34]

The intentional starvation of women, children, and the elderly could be considered a war crime, but one could argue that Britain's blockade against Germany should have been expected. One thing about which there is no doubt, however, is the fact that the British blockade did not end with the war. The war was ostensibly over on Armistice Day, November 11, 1918, and the next six months were spent hammering out the peace treaty at boisterous committee meetings and backstairs negotiations at Versailles. Yet, Britain continued the naval blockade for more than half a year after Armistice Day to punish the vanquished Germans. Not until the endless debates and negotiations at the Versailles Peace Conference yielded a final document, in July 1919, was the blockade finally lifted. In the interim, thousands of German civilians, already weakened by four years of war, died of starvation and disease. German history still regards the so-called Hunger Blockade as a war crime. The British, of course, do not.

Other war crimes abounded during the First World War. One of the curious new tactics, created by the clever British, was what were called "Q-Ships," fat freighters flying neutral flags or seemingly abandoned ships that lured German submarines to surface attacks to save scarce torpedoes. Once on the surface, the Germans were stunned to see the British "decoy ships" drop their sides to reveal rows of deadly guns. Not surprisingly, the Germans considered this practice to be unfair and added it to the lengthy list of war crimes being committed by all sides. Of serious consequence in this case, the German submarines became more wary and sank unarmed ships by silent torpedo attack, increasing the loss of life. During the Great War, the British deployed 366 disguised Q-Ships and are credited with sinking 11 U-boats. The definition of a war crime depends largely on whether your side wins the war—in the view of the British, the blockade was not a crime, while, to the Germans, the use of disguised Q-Ships was.

During the next war, the U.S. Marines of Charlie Company on Guadalcanal in 1942, found two missing buddies who had been beheaded by the Japanese and whose genitals had been stuffed into the mouths of the severed heads.

> The sheer barbarity of the thing swept through C-for Charlie like a cold water shock. A cold knifing terror in the belly was followed immediately by a rage of anger. These men they were fighting were veterans of Burma, China, and Sumatra. That they professed to hate all white men was well known. That they had perpetrated this sort of outrage in China and the Philippines on their own dark-skinned races was known, too. But that they would do the same sort of thing to civilized white American infantry . . . was almost too much to believe and certainly too much to be borne. There was a storm of promises never to take a prisoner. Many swore they would henceforth coolly and in cold blood shoot every Japanese who came their way, and preferably in the guts.[35]

In the Pacific campaign, Japanese soldiers committed suicide before allowing themselves to be taken prisoner or, if they were too weak from hunger or wounds to escape being captured alive, were often killed by Allied soldiers.

Live Japanese prisoners were so rare that U.S. Army intelligence continually suffered for lack of enemy information. Out of exasperation when orders and pleas failed, the U.S. Army offered a quart of ice cream to any American soldier who brought in a living Japanese prisoner.

War Crimes Committed to Win the Battles at Any Cost

Winning the battle and, consequently, the war is worth any price. National pride hangs in the balance and often the very sovereignty of the state. The population and the military have been inflamed by propaganda, and negotiation is no longer an option. Winning is now everything. Whatever the era, every war has a moment when the leaders are presented with the opportunity to utilize a "devastating new weapon," be it a huge trebuchet, which hurled boulders and dead bodies into warring civilian centers; buckets of flaming pitch, called Greek Fire, to be poured on approaching strangers or enemy soldiers; or diseased blankets to be introduced to American Indians. In modern wars, some weapons are utilized in battle that certainly border on war crimes; the United States has used, for example, fuel-air explosive bombs, cluster bombs, napalm, and liquid phosphorous, biological agents, and so-called Daisy Cutter landmines and bombs that explode outward and sever everything within a large radius at midleg level.[36]

Despite the intention to restrict the use of such horrific weapons to battles against enemy soldiers, the civilian population is often targeted, as well. The atomic bombing of Hiroshima and Nagasaki virtually vaporized perhaps 200,000 people. The line between a military weapon and a major war crime is often blurred.

War Crimes Committed in an Effort to Obtain Valuable Military Information

Since the beginning of warfare, it has been the goal of each side to fathom the plans of the other. Traditionally, spies have infiltrated the enemy's ranks, or defectors have been sought and convinced or paid to change allegiances. History sneers at the Nathan Hales, the Benedict Arnolds, the Mata Haris, Bella Boyds, and Alger Hisses. Monuments are erected to the winners, however they managed to win.

As technology has improved and the speed of warfare increased, knowledge of the enemy's plans has become critical. It is no longer possible to treat a captive like a valued guest, as the British High Command did with German airmen in World War One, in the hope that they would reveal information colleague-to-colleague. Today's warfare is asymmetrical, in that one side may not wear uniforms or maintain the so-called rules of war. Prisoners may be routinely kidnapped for months or years, tormented, even shot or beheaded.

Weapons have changed dramatically, as well. No longer are they confined to killing soldiers, with, perhaps, regrettable collateral damage to a limited number of civilians; modern conflicts, whether declared or not, now involve the very real possibility that weapons of mass destruction, which kill thousands or more without warning, will be used. Time is now critical. Motivated by the "ticking bomb" scenario, captors view their prisoners as a source of desperately important information, to be extracted quickly and by any means available. Torture, humiliation, even execution—war crimes all—have become acceptable tools of warfare.

Circumstances That Influence War Crimes

Whatever the motivation behind the conflicts in history or the type of horrible atrocities inflicted on captives or bystanders, we human beings have hacked, poisoned, drowned, and tortured one another since recorded time began. The elimination of such acts is probably a vain hope. We do know, however, that a number of things influence the likelihood of a war crime.

1. The professionalism or a lack of professionalism within an army often determines the commission of war crimes. In conflicts throughout history, with genocidal exceptions, excessive brutality can most often be found among the untrained fighters, the volunteers, the guerrillas, the new recruits, or the lower-class combatants. In medieval England and France, the feudal armies often contained large numbers of murderers seeking pardons, ex-brigands, freebooters, mercenaries, and sadists. What better place for sociopaths to hide—in fact, to succeed—than in a collection of rough men whose reason for existence is violence? They are free to pillage and murder whenever the opportunity presents itself. As a random example, many of the knights who offered their services during the Albigensian Crusade were uneducated mercenaries who hoped to profit by the conflict around them. Unruly or poorly trained soldiers are more likely to mistreat civilians, the more so if they have experienced the recent death of a fellow soldier. Well-trained soldiers are usually better controlled than their more rebellious comrades, and the enforcement of military law and a cultural sophistication are the best safeguards against the torture or murder of civilians.
2. A second key to the commission of war crimes concerns the presence of an authority figure. If a senior officer or respected comrade legitimizes the approaching atrocity, it will likely happen. The best dramatization is the classic experiment by the psychologist Stanley Milgram,[37] in which American college students were persuaded to apply crippling doses of electricity to other students when authorized and prompted to do so by a looming authority figure. Every conflict is strewn with untold numbers of war crimes that are committed because someone nearby was

willing to accept responsibility for the action—soldiers such as the infamous German SS troops in Eastern Europe during the Second World War or the Japanese military's horrific Unit 731, which conducted medical experiments on Chinese and American prisoners of war, including open-chest surgery without anesthesia.

A more contemporary example of the circumstances that lead to war crimes was the thunderous blood-and-guts speech to his men in current-day Iraq by a respected and feared commander, Colonel Michael Steele. Talking to his men of the 101st Airborne Division, on the eve of Operation Iron Triangle, on May 9, 2006, at the base outside Tikrit, the legendary Steele reminded the anxious men gathered around him that, according to the rules of engagement, "they were to shoot all military-aged males." "Steele told his men to think of themselves as apex predators ('If you mess with me, I will eat you') but he also insisted that they act lawfully."[38] Here was a war crime in the making.

3. It appears that the fewer people present, the greater the potential for a war crime. Perhaps it would be more accurate to state that the larger the group, the lower the odds of its committing a war crime. The presence of more people means that there is a greater possibility that the group includes informants or that some people will hold opposing opinions. Yet, all that is required is one authority figure and, if necessary, a single participant willing to act.

   There are times when individual responsibility or leadership is unavailing: when crowds are caught up in mass hysteria and commit an atrocity, such as a mob of outraged Vietnamese peasants descending on a now-helpless bailed-out American pilot floating to earth. There is no question at all that such behavior is a war crime—the only question concerns responsibility and our theory that war crimes are influenced by the number of perpetrators and witnesses involved.

4. Emotional distance from one's enemies influences the type of atrocity, as well as its frequency and its severity. In other words, the more different from oneself one perceives the enemy to be, the greater the chances of war crimes. Every nation at war demonizes its enemies. Modern conflicts have pitted Western armies against enemies that have been nicknamed "Krauts," "Jerries" or "Huns," "Japs" or "Nips," "Gooks," "Zips," "Russkis," and other nasty epithets—the marginalization of the Other. Assigning a pejorative label makes already-suspect strangers "things," rather than people. The greater the demonization of the enemy, the easier it is to hate him and to commit atrocities outside the accepted parameters of warfare.

5. If the driving force of the conflict is an internal division, such as a civil war, the treatment of noncombatants and their homes and crops is particularly brutal. When countrymen fight countrymen, whether in Korea, Northern Ireland, Spain, or the United States—or in any of the dozen civil wars brewing at any one time in the world—the conflict brings out the worst in both sides, a situation that only degenerates when the war is protracted. By the end of America's bloody four-year civil war, for instance, General Sherman's infamous march across Georgia to the sea deteriorated into the random destruction of southern plantations and the arrest and murder of Confederate prisoners and civilians. Spain's three-year civil war, which began in 1936, was equally bloody, as Catholic priests were

murdered by one side and women and children were bombed by the other. An estimated 1 million Spaniards died during the war.[39]

However, if a civil war is brief, such as the relatively short civil war in Austria, which lasted from February 12 to February 16, 1934, hatreds do not have enough time to solidify or amplify, although even in Austria's short uprising between the socialists (represented by the Social Democratic Party of Austria) and the conservatives (Christian Social Party), which took place principally in the cities of Vienna and Linz, several hundred people died in the armed conflict.

The best civil war, in terms of prisoners' or civilians' ability to survive, is one that reaches a conclusion, any conclusion, as quickly as possible. Unfortunately, history leans toward prolonged civil wars, producing hurts and hatreds that extend for generations.

But can we really call these acts "war crimes"? These horrors are atrocities, to be sure, but they cannot be called "war crimes." People have slaughtered, raped, and tortured innocents in every conflict, but, as repugnant as such acts are, they cannot be considered war crimes unless they were committed after laws against them were passed. *In brief, a crime becomes a crime only when a law is broken*. To be considered a crime, an atrocity must have violated some law, agreement, or religious understanding. Thus, the history of war crimes is the history of the painfully slow creation of the rules of war.

Notes

1. Joseph T. Glatthar, *The March to the Sea and Beyond* (New York: New York University Press, 1985), pp. 135–136.
2. Mark Grimsley, *The Hard Hand of War: Union Policy toward Southern Civilians* (New York: Cambridge University Press, 1995), p. 169.
3. See the excellent book by Lydia Monin and Andrew Gallimore, *The Devil's Gardens: A History of Landmines* (London: Pimlico, 2002), pp. xvi–xvii, 201. See also John Ryle, "Mines," in *Crimes of War: What the Public Should Know*, ed. Roy Gutman and David Rieff (New York, London: Norton, 1999), p. 256.
4. H.W.F. Saggs, *The Might That Was Assyria* (London: Sidgwick and Jackson, 1984), p. 261.
5. Aristotle, *Politics*, trans. by Ernest Barker, 2nd ed.,(1948) line 1255a, pp. 6–7.
6. Plato, *Republic*, vol. 5, p. 468.
7. Helen H. Law, "Atrocities in Greek Warfare," *The Classical Journal* 15, no. 3 (December 1919): 132–147.
8. R. Holinshed, *Chronicles* (New York: AMS Press, 1965, 1807), ii, 758.
9. A. H. Smith, ed., "Anglo-Saxon Chronicle," in *The Parker Chronicle 832–900*, 2nd ed., Exeter Medieval English Texts (Exeter: University of Exeter Press, 1980). It has been suggested that the name Ivar the Boneless was a not-so-veiled reference to his impotence.

10. James M. Gillespie, *Andersonvilles of the North: The Myths and Realities of Northern Treatment of Civil War Confederate Prisoners* (Denton: University of North Texas Press, 2008).

11. George Will, "The Last Word: Jedwabne," *Newsweek* (U.S. edition), July 9, 2001, p. 68.

12. Holinshed, "Chronicles," (London, 1808), III, 81–82, cited by Henry J. Webb, "Prisoner of War in the Middle Ages," *Military Affairs* 12, no. 1 (Spring 1948): 48.

13. Geoff Mortimer, *Eyewitness Accounts of the Thirty Years War, 1618–48* (New York: Palgrave, 2002), p. 168.

14. Ibid., pp. 174–175.

15. Dubrovin, N., ed., "Otechestvennaia Voina v Pismakh Sovremennikov," in *Zapiski Imperatorskoi Akademii Nauk*, vol. 43, St. Petersburg 1882, cited in Adam Zamoyski, *Moscow 1812: Napoleon's Final March* (New York: Harper Perennial, 2005), pp. 384–405. See also, Sir Robert Thomas Wilson, *Invasion*, (London: J. Murray, 1960), pp. 257–258.

16. Vietnam Veterans Against the War, *Winter Soldier Investigation* (Boston: Beacon Press,1972), p. 63. See also Jonathan Schell, *The Village of Ben Suc* (New York: Knopf, 1967), p. 25.

17. Ridgeway Oral Interview, pp. 1, 113, Senior Officer Debriefing Collection, Military History Research Collection, Army War College, cited in Peter Karsten, *Law, Soldiers, and Combat* (Westport, CT: Greenwood Press, 1978), p. 42; Dixon Wecter and William Matthews, eds., *Our Soldiers Speak, 1775–1918* (Boston: Little, Brown and Company, 1943), p. 336; General Frank Percy Crozier, *The Men I Killed* (London: Michael Joseph,1937), p. 121.

18. James J. Fahey, *Pacific War Diary, 1942–1945:The Secret Diary of an American Sailor* (New York, Boston: Houghton Mifflin Company, 1963), p. 225.

19. Cited in Karsten, *Law, Soldiers, and Combat*, p. 74.

20. Neil Sheehan, *A Bright Shining Lie: John Paul Vann and America in Vietnam* (London: Picador, 1990), p. 621.

21. Sir Steven Runciman, *A History of the First Bulgarian Empire* (London: G. Bell and Sons, 1930).

22. Miguel Leon-Portilla, ed., *The Broken Spears* (Boston: Beacon Press, 2006), p. 74.

23. *The Road to Katyn : A Soldier's Story/Salomon W. Slowes*, ed. Władysław T. Bartoszewski, trans. Naftali Greenwood (Oxford, UK, and Cambridge, MA: Blackwell, 1992).

24. "Chronology 1990: The Soviet Union and Eastern Europe," *Foreign Affairs* 70, no. 1 (1991): 216. See the press release online, Warsaw, November 30, 2004: http://www.ipn.gov.pl/eng/eng_news_high_katyn_press.html.

25. Michael Prawdin, *The Mongol Empire: Its Rise and Legacy* (London: G. Allen and Unwin, 1967), p. 193.

26. International Military Tribunal, *Trial of the Major War Criminals* [Nuremberg IMT, 1947], vol. 4, p. 206, cited in Peter Maguire, *Law and War: An American Story* (New York: Columbia University Press, 2000), pp. 178, 117.

27. Robert Coram, *American Patriot: The Life and Wars of Colonel Bud Day* (New York: Little, Brown, 2007), p. 142.

28. Ibid., p. 281.

29. *The New Yorker*, September 4, 1970, p. 39; Vietnam Veterans Against the War [author], *Winter Soldier Investigation*, (Beacon Press), p. 78.

30. Major W. H. Parks, "Crimes in Hostilities," *Marine Corps Gazette* 60, no. 8 (August 1976): 16.

31. Karsten, *Law, Soldiers, and Combat*, p. 68.

32. Jeffrey Kingston, *Japan in Transformation, 1952–2000* (New York: Pearson Education, 2001), p. 50.

33. Quoted in Richard Holmes, *Acts of War: The Behavior of Men in Battle* (New York: Free Press, 1985), pp. 382–385.

34. Peter Loewenberg, *Decoding the Past: The Psychohistorical Approach* (New York: Knopf, 1983), pp. 254–258.

35. James Jones, *The Thin Red Line* (New York: Charles Scribner's Sons, 1962), p. 151.

36. See James M. Broughton, "U.S. over Iraq: High Tech and Low Culture in the Gulf Conflict," in *Genocide, War, and Human Survival*, ed. Charles B. Strozier and Michael Flynn (Lanham, MD: Rowman and Littlefield, 1996), p. 105.

37. Stanley Milgram, *Obedience to Authority: An Experimental View* (New York: HarperCollins, 1974). For reactions to Milgram's experiments, see Arthur G. Miller, *The Obedience Experiments: A Case Study of Controversy in the Social Sciences* (New York: Praeger, 1986).

38. Raffi Khatchadourian, "The Kill Company: Behind a War Crime in Iraq," *The New Yorker*, July 6–13, 2009, pp. 44, 50.

39. However fictional the situation, José María Gironella, in *One Million Dead* (Garden City, NY: Doubleday, 1963), dwells on the effects of the lengthening civil war on the casualties and vice versa.

CHAPTER 2

Searching for the Law

The very idea of creating rules in the midst of the mayhem of killing has always seemed preposterous. The contradiction was considered by Prince Bolkhonsky in a celebrated passage in Tolstoy's *War and Peace*, when the Prince says to General Bezhukov:

> They talk to us of the rules of war, of chivalry, of flags of truce, of mercy to the unfortunate, and so on. It's all rubbish. . . . War is not courtesy but the most horrible thing in life; and we ought to understand that, and not play at war. . . . The air of war is murder; the methods of war are spying, treachery, and their encouragement, the ruin of a country's inhabitants, robbing them or stealing to provision the army, and fraud and falsehood termed military craft.[1]

Cicero put it more simply, writing that "*inter arma silent leges*"—"in time of war the law is silent."[2]

Rules during wartime? The prospect of rules during wartime was brushed aside by Ernst Jünger, a former German officer who was wounded and decorated countless times in front-line action during World War One. Frankly, said Jünger, neither side should have any expectations of falling into enemy hands without cost.

> The defending force, after driving their bullets into the attacking one at five paces' distance, must take the consequences. A man cannot change his feelings again during the last rush with a veil of blood before his eyes. He does not want to take prisoners but to kill. He has no scruples left; only the spell of primeval instinct remains. It is not till blood has flowed that the mist gives way to his soul.[3]

More to the point, in the direct eloquence of Winston Churchill, "A prisoner of war is a man who tries to kill you and fails, and then asks you not to kill him."[4] How can one possibly develop rules to prevent particular acts of aggression in the middle of a war—where killing is the goal?

Developing rules was going to be an uphill struggle. The Old Testament's "Principles Governing War" (Deuteronomy 20) is irreligiously sanguinary on the topic of war, commanding that, following the surrender of a town, "you shall strike every male in it with the edge of the sword" (20:10), "all its spoils you shall plunder for yourself" (20:13–14), and "you shall let nothing that breathes remain alive" (20:16). In short, the Bible contains few admonitions about behavior in war, except to wisely forbid the destruction of things that would be useful after the war was won.[5]

One of the first codes of wartime behavior, known as the Code of Manu, appeared around 500 B.C. in India. It was surprisingly humane for the era. Under the Code,

> The king [was] advised to ravage the enemy's territory, "and ever spoil his fodder, food, water, and fuel"; to "burst tanks, enclosures and trenches"; to "assail him and terrify him by night"; yet "one should not, fighting in battle, slay enemies by concealed weapons, nor with barbed or poisoned [weapons], nor with fire-kindled arrows. Nor should one [mounted] slay an enemy down on the ground, a eunuch, a suppliant, one with loosened hair, one seated, one who says 'I am thy prisoner'; nor one asleep, one without armour [*sic*], one naked, one without weapons, one not fighting, a looker-on, one engaged with another, nor one who has his arm broken, a distressed man, one badly hit, one afraid, one who has fled: remembering virtue, one should not slay them."[6]

The next codified restrictions came as early thinkers like Cicero endeavored to separate "just wars" from ordinary conflicts. A so-called just war, fought in response to an unprovoked attack or because of a religious principle, was warranted, and so were any atrocities committed in its name. According to early Christian thinkers, such as St. Augustine in the fifth century A.D., any war fought on behalf of or commanded by God was a just war.[7] One can claim that any war is being fought in God's name and is therefore a just war. In short, it is the adversary's wickedness that makes a cause just. Moreover, wrote Augustine, if a state observes Christian teachings, "even war will not be waged without kindness."[8] According to this philosophy, the side fighting the just war is engaged in a lawful war and is not bound by the law of war, whereas the adversary, fighting an unjust war, is restricted from acting equally barbarously.

The hollowness of the philosophy is clear since most leaders claim to receive divine guidance. From earliest times to the present, successful leaders have implied that their representation of a higher power empowers them to speak in its name. If leaders or governments, supported by a majority of their citizens, believe they are following God's instructions in declaring war, the conflict is considered a just war, and all atrocities committed in its name are excusable. St. Augustine pointed out that the opposite of a just war, one based on love and charity, is an evil war. The evil side is driven to war by the basest of motives: "the love of violence, revengeful cruelty, fierce and implacable enmity, wild resistance and the lust of power."[9] Atrocities of war are committed only by the evil side; the other side, driven and commanded by God as it is, can do no wrong.

Lest the matter not be taken seriously, the Bible requires a pledge: "Oh Lord, my God, if I have done this: if there is iniquity in my hands; if I have repaid evil to him who was at peace with me; or have plundered my enemy without cause; let the enemy pursue me and overtake me; yes, let him trample my life into the earth, and lay my honor in the dust" (Psalm 7:3–5). Given the assurance that both sides were fighting in a righteous cause, the pledge could be taken with the greatest sincerity by both sides.

Sometimes, the matter was left up to God, as in 1209 at the Siege of Beziers. During a battle of the Albigensian Crusade (the only crusade to turn on Europe's Christians instead of waiting to kill Turks and Jews in Jerusalem), a crusader asked the papal representative how the crusaders were to distinguish the heretic Cathars from their fellow Catholics. Armand Amalric surveyed the town before him, choked with thousands of terrified people, and famously said: "Kill them all—the Lord will know his own." The crusaders went on to slaughter all 20,000 inhabitants of the town and then burned the city to the ground.

Accuracy requires that we also note that the Cathars, a rather peaceful Christian sect under attack by the Catholic Church, occasionally turned against the crusaders sent from Rome. For example,

> [d]uring the siege of Moissac in September 1212, the Cathar defenders regularly mutilated crusaders' corpses. Two years later, in 1214, the ruling Cathars in the Dordogne, Bernard of Cazenac and his wife Elise . . . conducted a reign of terror that left 150 mutilated men and women in the Benedictine Abbey of Sarlat with hands cut off, feet amputated or eyes put out. Elise specialized in removing women's thumbs to prevent them from working and ordering the nipples of the poorest peasant women to be ripped off.[10]

The unsparing cruelty of war and the indiscriminate violence in pursuit of plunder and expansion during the greater part of the Middle Ages was gradually modified through the influence of Christianity and chivalry.

Christianity was represented, in this case, by Pope Gregory IX, a strident champion of the Church and the founder of the Papal Inquisition. In the early

1230s, the pope created the first authoritative list of people who should be protected in war. Understandably, the pope demanded immunity for priests, monks, friars, and religious pilgrims. Aristocrats and merchants were also off limits. The pope's motives were singularly selfish, of course, since his enemies needed to be reminded that his church was protected by God. Interestingly, this same Pope Gregory IX, a deeply religious personal friend of St. Francis of Assisi, issued a papal decree in 1232 calling for the death penalty for heretics. It was the responsibility of every Catholic to torture heretics without scruple. In fact, any prince who did not burn heretics as charged by the inquisition would be excommunicated himself and go before the same tribunal for heresy. During the next 20 years, Christians in southern France who did not bow to the Church's demands would be burnt.

But, Christians had to be in conflict with another Christian nation for the rules to work. When the war involved non-Christian opponents, such as the Turks during the crusades to liberate Jerusalem, any concerns for regulations were swiftly jettisoned. In battles between chivalrous knights of the realm or friars of the Church, honor was prized even above survival—but honor that lost all meaning when, for instance, Christian and Turk crossed swords.

Chivalry was a knightly code of honor that had developed during the Middle Ages across Western Europe. "It was a way of life, closely associated with war, and critical economic interests of the knightly class through booty and ransom. Chivalry emphasized the notions of duty, honour [*sic*], and glamour [*sic*], and involved such humane and noble principles as aid for the weak and the helpless."[11] The rules of chivalry were issued and adjusted by the kings of England, as well as by rulers of other countries; surprisingly, considering the brutality of the era, "most knightly rules protected noncombatants, innocent civilians, and helpless bystanders. The mortar holding chivalry together was fear of dishonor, cowardice, or public reprobation."[12] Such dishonor was displayed by the reversal (placing upside down) of a knight's coat of arms. Like the Bushido Code in Japan, the rules of war were established in medieval Europe—at least for the aristocratic classes.

In retrospect, it seems astonishing that so little was accomplished in the protection of innocents during warfare for so many centuries. One would have thought that by the time of the Reformation and Luther and Calvin, in the mid-17th century, more elaborate rules protecting civilians and defenseless prisoners would have been formulated. But there had been surprisingly little progress over the past centuries. Luther, in particular, minced no words when he actually praised certain wars, writing that it is "both Christian and an act of love to kill the enemy without hesitation, to plunder and burn him by every method of warfare until he is conquered." Almost as an afterthought, he added: "except one must be aware of sin, and not violate wives and virgins."[13]

Calvin was more obtuse on the matter of forbidding atrocities, warning against imprudent leniency and quoting a Latin proverb that states "it is indeed bad to live under a prince under whom nothing is permitted, but far worse under one by whom everything is allowed." There wasn't much comfort there for those who hoped that the safety of the helpless was somehow being considered. Only on broad principles did Luther and Calvin generally agree:

1. Every effort must be made to resolve differences by peaceful means before resorting to the use of force.
2. The innocent must be immune from direct attack.
3. The amount of force used shall not be disproportionate.[14]

That was it! So much for the first 17 centuries of history after Christ.

It was not until 1625 that Europe took the first huge step in the protection of innocents during wartime. It came from the quill pen of a Dutch legal scholar named Hugo Grotius, a towering intellect and prolific writer, who systematically codified and, for all purposes, created international law. Grotius was shocked that his Christian world had no greater scruples about going to war or about the methods it used than the pagans above which Christianity claimed to have risen. In his words,

> Throughout the Christian world I observed a lack of restraint in relation to war. . . . I observed that men rush to arms for slight causes or no cause at all, and that once arms have been taken up there is no longer any respect for the law . . . it is as if, in accordance with a general decree, frenzy had openly been let loose for the committing of all crimes.[15]

Grotius's legal conclusions were far-reaching for their time and were published across Europe as *De Jure Belli ac Pacis Libris Tres* (On the Law of War and Peace).[16] Grotius leaned heavily toward moderation and the avoidance of conflict and maintained that violence beyond what is necessary to secure the military goal should be avoided. But, he insisted that if nations did go to war, their actions should be governed by a strict set of laws. The use of poison, for example, was expressly forbidden, as were deliberate terrorism and the harming of a hostage. During a truce, all acts of war were unlawful, and the harming of innocent bystanders was unacceptable. More than four centuries later, his views of war are mainstream, if idealistic. Military lawyers and diplomats in the centuries since his death are indebted to his work.

Yet, however brilliant the legal argument or progressive the foresight, the overwhelming majority of the public was illiterate, and Grotius's published views reached only a small circle of philosophers and legal scholars. For the next two centuries, war captives continued to be tortured, enslaved, or slaughtered.

The history of the English Civil War, fought during the 1640s between supporters of absolute monarchy and supporters of the Parliament who were determined to bring the monarchy under its control, is peppered with atrocities. Prisoners were routinely skinned or burned; some had large amounts of urine forced down their throats through a funnel or had a rope twisted around the forehead until the victim's eyes burst from their sockets. Yet, for all the deplorable torture and executions endured by both sides, halting steps were taken toward the protection of prisoners and noncombatants. Parliament's often-violated rule that "None shall kill an Enemy who yields and throws down his Arms" was vaguely matched by the Royalists. However, both sides spared prisoners who willingly swore an oath to cease fighting; other prisoners saved themselves by swearing an oath to fight on the side of their captors. Prisoners were also held in custody as a bankable commodity for future exchanges, and exchanges were increasingly based on the equivalency of rank. If no one equivalent in rank or importance could readily be found, high-ranking captives were sometimes passed from commander to commander until an exchange was feasible. The quality of food available to prisoners varied widely, as did their treatment, although, on balance, it was still largely barbaric.[17] But the fact is that very few prisoners were taken alive.

Drawing depicting the brutal treatment that prisoners could expect during the Thirty Years War, 1618–1648 (Vincent, Philip. *The Lamentations of Germany*, 1638. Courtesy of David Zeidberg, Director of the Library, Huntington Library, San Marino, CA)

One need look no further than the surrender of the garrison of Hopton Castle in March 1644 to the Royalist troops, who assured the captives that their lives would be spared. As soon as they surrendered, however,

> prisoners were bound together, stripped naked despite the cold and their wounds, and turned over to the common soldiers who presently fell upon them, wounding them grievously. They drove them into a cellar unfinished, wherein was stinking water, the house being on fire over them, when they were every man . . . presently massacred. Most of the victims were clubbed to death.[18]

The Enlightenment changed everything. During the 1700s, Europeans developed a growing sense of pride that they were entering into a period in which the light of reason would free all from the darkness of superstition and ignorance. Fueled by the burst of liberating scientific inventions and the hugely influential publications by such philosophers as John Locke, who wrote that everyone has the right to life, liberty, and the pursuit of property, the value of individuals—even captives and noncombatants—began to improve. It was in this context that America's successful revolution beginning in 1776 further advanced the rights of individuals and the later French Revolution of 1789 championed the concept of the "Rights of Man"—and proved it by killing the king of France.

Rules began to take shape, especially at sea. Dutch trading vessels sailed around the world and dominated commerce through the 16th and 17th centuries. They established elaborate naval traditions and regulations that governed everything from conduct on board to the treatment of friends and enemies. The dominance of the Dutch was replaced by the rise of the British Navy, which held sway over much of the world for the next two centuries. Every seafaring decision was regulated by tradition, the sailor's manual, or captain's fiat. The literary Horatio Hornblower, no less than the real Admiral Horatio Nelson, became the very symbol of Britain's survival and economic success. Combat at sea was well regulated, and the rules accepted by all but "pirates and brigands." When Britain did violate these rules of war, as it did during the Seven Years' War between Britain and France (1756–1763), the offense was minimized. The British classic historian Edward Gibbon, with tongue in cheek, wryly noted that the customary civilities between enemies had temporarily declined. "The resentment of the French at our taking their ships without a declaration had rendered that polite nation somewhat peevish and difficult," Gibbon wrote. "They denied a passage to English travelers."[19] Only an aristocratic Englishman of the 1700s could have pointed out the ill manners of an enemy that had been wronged.

As the illumination of the Enlightenment began to imbue human beings with value, the final remaining obstacle in the upward path of concern for war captives and helpless civilians was the establishment of some sort of international agreement. This was probably the most difficult obstacle of all. All sides had to agree to some level of treatment, but the signing of such an agreement necessitated a modicum of trust between nations in an atmosphere of dark suspicion. Once reassured by international agreement, warring countries entered into a tenuous balance: the well-being of one set of prisoners, or the lack thereof, would swiftly be felt by the prisoners held by the other side. All that remained was to establish the level of treatment to which captives were entitled and to agree to the various aspects of their captivity that could or should be regulated. The final product of so many centuries of concern for the treatment of helpless civilians and war captives was a mosaic of numerous large and small pieces.

Not until 1859 was there another legal milestone in declaring certain wartime acts outside the pale of tolerance. This step came from an unlikely source when Henri Dunant, a Swiss banker on holiday, stumbled across the end of a major battle between the French and the Austrians in Solferino, Italy, in 1859, during Napoleon III's effort to drive the Austrians from Italy. The stunned Dunant was so moved by the thousands of dead and dying scattered across the smoking battlefield that he wrote an account of the savage battle, entitled *A Memory of Solferino*, and proposed the creation of a civilian volunteer relief corps to care for future war wounded. Since its founding, in 1863, that organization has been known as the International Committee of the Red Cross. The energetic Dunant then organized a conference to draft an agreement on the treatment of battlefield casualties, which led to the first Geneva Conference in 1864. Soon, it became almost fashionable for Europe's diplomats to meet at famous spas and watering holes, often in Geneva, Switzerland, or The Hague, Netherlands, where they hammered out rules "civilizing" war.

History indicates that concern for rules of war occur most often during peacetime; when the trumpets blare and the bullets fly, rational thought lags behind. The exceptions, however, often become historic advances.

Such a moment appeared in the midst of America's Civil War when, in 1863, President Abraham Lincoln asked Francis Lieber, professor of history and law at Columbia and a wounded veteran of three major European battles, including Waterloo, to draft instructions for the U.S. armies during war. This took place during the middle of the war, when passions were at their peak and atrocities were commonplace. Lincoln hoped to persuade both the Union Army and the Confederacy to abide by Lieber's Code, promulgated as General Order No. 100, although adherence was spotty at best. According to the new Code, enemy prisoners were recognized as fellow human citizens caught up in the chaos of war, and their captors were required to feed, doctor, and shelter the prisoners. Prisoners were protected against torture or mistreatment inflicted in an effort to obtain military information, and captors were denied the right to execute prisoners who attempted to escape. The Lieber Code became the basis for numerous international agreements for the humane treatment of war prisoners well into the next century.

While many of Lieber's rules were already considered standard policy (e.g., prohibitions against rape and against the murder of children or wounded or unarmed prisoners), his major contribution was to codify both crimes and punishment, beginning, for our interest, with these dicta:

> (70) Unnecessary or revengeful destruction of life is not lawful.
>
> (71) Whoever intentionally inflicts additional wounds on an enemy already wholly disabled, or kills such an enemy, or who orders or encourages soldiers to do so, shall suffer death, if duly convicted, whether he belongs to the Army of the United States, or is an enemy captured after having committed his misdeed.
>
> (72) Money and other valuables on the person of a prisoner, such as watches or jewelry, as well as extra clothing, are regarded by the American Army as the private property of the prisoner, and the appropriation of such valuables or money is considered dishonorable, and is prohibited. . . .
>
> (75) Prisoners of war are subject to confinement or imprisonment such as may be deemed necessary on account of safety, but they are to be subjected to no other intentional suffering or indignity. The confinement and mode of treating a prisoner may be varied during his captivity according to the demands of safety.
>
> (76) Prisoners of war shall be fed upon plain and wholesome food, whenever practicable, and treated with humanity. They may be required to work for the benefit of the captor's government, and paid according to their rank and condition.
>
> (77) A prisoner of war who escapes may be shot, or otherwise killed, in his flight; but neither death nor any other punishment shall be inflicted upon him simply for his attempt to escape, which the law of war does not consider a crime.[20]

The civilized world, at long last, was gaining a handle on the issue of war crimes. In 1874, participants at a meeting in Brussels, Belgium, specifically based their published code on Lieber's, concentrating the most important restrictions in Article 12 ("The laws of war do not allow to belligerents an unlimited power as to the choice of injuring the enemy") and Article 13, which forbid the general category of "arms, projectiles, or substances which may cause unnecessary suffering". The conclusions reached at Brussels in

1874 were included in the Oxford Manual in 1880 and adopted as a model by Oxford's Institute of International Law, which, in turn, established the precedents for the critical Hague Conventions of 1899 and 1907, all of which formed the basis for the Geneva Conventions of 1929 and 1949. Separate regulations concerning naval matters were drawn up in the 1909 Declaration of London, understandably recognizing Britain's right to blockade its enemies and, in the event of future war, expanding the kinds of goods that neutral nations might sell to belligerents.

These humanitarian laws can be divided into two types. The first category, called the *law of Geneva*, protects civilian noncombatants and military personnel who are not involved in the fighting or prisoners of war. The other type, called the *law of The Hague*, largely concerns the rights and protections of those actually doing the fighting and limits the methods either side can use on the battlefield—no explosive (dum-dum) bullets, for example.[21]

Yet, despite these lofty rules established by well-meaning diplomats, little actually changed on the battlefield. Conflicts continued to rage through the late 19th century as changing technology and superheated nationalism combined with perverted Darwinism. Hot spots were erupting around the globe, and with each came atrocities of every kind. During the Franco-Prussian War (1870–1871), for example, 88,306 French and Germans died on the battlefield and of wounds, while an additional 590,000 civilians died from other causes. The Germans, in particular, occasionally faced with French irregulars and guerrillas, responded uniformly unsympathetically and severely—"sometimes inhumane, unreasonable, and unfair."[22] One historian writes that "In October 1870, the Germans took revenge on the French village of Chateaudun . . . the Germans reacted furiously. . . . Prisoners were mutilated, hostages taken to ensure French collaboration, suspected guerrillas shot, and whole towns burned to the ground."[23] The Lieber Code was seldom considered, and the number of noncombatants who died from disease, neglect, or starvation in camps remained startlingly high.

The French, in particular, were so appalled by their own behavior that in 1876 the government commissioned the construction of the Basilique du Sacré-Coeur, with its shining white onion domes, at the top of Montmartre hill in Paris, dedicated to the atonement for France's war crimes in the Franco-Prussian War. Relentlessly advertised as having been funded entirely by the French working class, Sacré-Coeur was completed in 1919 and remains an especially holy, if touristy, presence looking down on the sprawling city of Paris. The victorious Germans, on the other hand, hardly in an atoning mood, declared the foundation of their Empire at the end of the war.

The Anglo-Boer War (1899–1902) was not much more "civilized" than the Franco-Prussian War. The South African war caused a total of 21,932 military deaths, and approximately 46,000 prisoners and civilians were interned in camps where they died of disease and malnutrition. Black Africans who fought on the side of the British or the Boers were usually killed out of hand by the other side. The incomplete records give a death toll of more than 12,000 on one side alone.[24]

The Spanish-American War of 1898 and the Philippine insurgency that followed is another good example of the mistreatment of noncombatants. America's campaign in Cuba and its subsequent need to subdue the prize of the Philippines cost the lives of 4,234 American troops and 16,000 Filipino soldiers. Yet, an astonishing 200,000 additional civilians perished in a brutal and racially charged American victory. One American soldier recalled that " I don't know how many men, women and children the . . . boys did kill. They would not take any prisoners." Americans became specialists in the "water cure," usually administered to extract information. In the words of one observer,

> the "water cure" was a blend of Castilian cruelty and American ingenuity, consisting of forcing four or five gallons of water down the throat of a captive, whose "body becomes an object frightful to contemplate," and then squeezing it out by kneeling on his stomach. The process was repeated until the *amigo* talked or died. Almost invariably he talked.[25]

The Filipino insurrectionists, for their part, committed their own atrocities against the American soldiers, as described in a satiric poem "The Gentle Filipino" by an American trooper.

> With a white flag on his shanty, hanging there to catch your eye;
> And his rifle ready for to plug you bye and bye . . .
> He's as playful as a kitten, and his pastime as a rule
> Is to shoot the flag of truce man, as a sort of April Fool.
> And if he can
> find a tree top and get up there with his gun,
> And pick off all of the wounded, then he knows he's having fun.[26]

The 20th century earned the infamy of being the bloodiest century in the history of humankind—and there is no sign that this legacy is slowing down today. In these years, conflicts seemed to erupt in increasing numbers all over the globe. Nationalism, an irrational motivation for nearly every conflict since the French Revolution, overwhelms logic and defines every individual. Combined with this destructive patriotism are continually improving war technologies, which have become frighteningly widely available and tempting to use. Anyone comforted by the presence of a loyal military and its ability to retain control over weapons of mass destruction needs to read (or re-read) Norman Dixon's *On the Psychology of Military Incompetence* (Basic Books, 1976).

Wars seemed to erupt everywhere. The Greco-Turkish War broke out in 1897, followed by the Herero War in Southwest Africa (1904–1907), the Russo-Japanese War of 1904–1905, the Maji-Maji Revolt in East Africa (1905–1907), and the Balkan Wars (1912), to name but a few. With each war came atrocities, new hatreds, and a public acceptance of the brutal and often senseless outbreak of violence. Tensions were growing, and the public was becoming callously indifferent. Kaiser Wilhelm II routinely delivered bellicose, threatening speeches, and U.S. President Theodore Roosevelt advised his fellow citizens to "Walk softly and carry a big stick—you shall go far." Political assassinations were replacing elections, from the killing of Russia's Czar Alexander II in March 1881 to America's President William McKinley—shot as he shook hands in a receiving line in September 1901.

Violence was especially bloody in America, as class conflict confronted post–Civil War capitalism. Anarchists like Luigi Galleani, Ferdinando Sacco and Bartolomeo Vanzetti, and Emma Goldman—indeed, even McKinley's assassin, Leon F. Czolgosz—advocated striking out at authority individually or exploding high-carnage bombs to induce fear by killing as many hapless people as possible.[27] There was violence at home and abroad.

Yet, in the midst of this growing violence, hopeful diplomats once again gathered at The Hague in 1907, this time to revise the Hague Convention of 1899. Their goal was to revisit the general laws of war with greater precision and to underscore the principle "that the right of belligerents to fight war is not unlimited."[28] While all the signatories understood that it is the right of every state to wage war, if necessary, they agreed that there is also a responsibility to ensure that certain methods are prohibited. It was understood (and this was a first) that persons who commit acts in violation of the Conventions could be prosecuted. There was even a popular suggestion to create a permanent international criminal court "with compulsory jurisdiction that would transcend national boundaries," but this was blocked by immediate opposition, led by the United States, which saw great danger in being called to account for some future unseen action.[29]

This Fourth Hague Convention of 1907 contained no provisions for the imposition of individual criminal responsibility for violations; instead, the Convention specified that the central form of punishment would be the payment of financial restitution by the guilty states, with the amount determined by lengthy negotiations. The agreement accomplished little.

A final contribution to the Hague Conference of 1907 was a paragraph contributed by the Russian representative and legal expert Fedor Fedorovitch Martens. Hereafter called the "Martens Clause," the paragraph states that, in cases not covered by the Hague Convention, the "belligerents remain under the protection . . . of the principles from . . . the laws of nations . . . as established among civilized peoples, from the laws of humanity, and the dictates of public conscience." In other words, the spirit of the rules should cover unseen events during wartime. Lovely sentiments, surely.

The road to World War I during the next decade was littered with conflicts in the Balkans, China, North Africa, the Caribbean, and South America. The rules of war were being sorely tested, but the biggest test was about to arise when the Austrian Archduke Franz Ferdinand was assassinated in the Balkans on June 28, 1914, starting the greatest war in history.

The First World War lasted from 1914 to 1918. Millions perished—an estimated 8,500,000—as Europe divided itself into Allies and the Central Powers. As huge armies rushed at each other in the thousands, they violated nearly every imaginable regulation of the Hague law and the Geneva law, necessitating a new evaluation of the rules at the end of the war. Twentieth-century armies had entered a new world of industrialized warfare dictated by technology, irrational nationalism, and a commitment to total war; in the case of violence against helpless civilians, the war turned the clock back several centuries.

Atrocities against Civilians

In fact, World War One opened with Germany's invasion of Belgium in August 1914, an attack that became known for the atrocities committed by the German Army as it waged a ruthless campaign against civilian targets, murdering 6,000 men, women, and children and burning homes, villages, cultural sites, and the prestigious university library of Louvain, which dated from the 14th century—a stunning act of barbarism. These were not random acts but were ordered from the top. The largest single massacre, on a scale that the German Army would not repeat until 1939, took place in the Belgian village of Tamines on August 22, when 400 men, women, and children were shot, bayoneted, and burned to death—and the war was only beginning.[30]

Toxic Gas

Only nine months after the war began, the Germans introduced an unthinkable new weapon to the battlefield: toxic gas. Whatever the moral implications of the release of chlorine gas against enemy soldiers, it was a remarkable undertaking. The work had to be done at night with a minimum of noise; approximately 330 tons of gas had to be developed and transported with as few leaks, explosions, and resulting casualties as possible. Thousands of cylinders had to be found and filled, and a special unit of 1,600 German soldiers and technicians worked in strict secrecy to accomplish this. The use of the gas began on the evening of April 22, 1915, along the Western Front at the Belgian village of Vijfluege, near Ypres.

> The simultaneous opening of almost 6,000 cylinders which released 150 tons of chlorine along 7,000 meters within about ten minutes was spectacular. The front lines were often very close, at one point only 50 meters apart. The cloud advanced slowly, moving at just over 1 mph. It was white at first, owing to the condensation of the moisture in the surrounding air and, as the volume increased, it turned yellow-green. The chlorine rose quickly to a height of 10–30 meters because of the ground temperature, and while diffusion weakened the effectiveness by thinning out the gas it enhanced the physical and psychological shock. Within minutes the Franco-Algerian soldiers in the front and support lines were engulfed and choking. Those who were not suffocating from spasms broke and ran, but the gas followed. The front collapsed.[31]

Panic ensued, and about 5,000 men, mostly Canadians and French, died. Their headlong retreat was so unexpected that the Germans had not prepared troops to rush into the sudden breach, and the opportunity passed. Many military experts today believe that if the German Army had been prepared to follow up this attack, it might have won the war in the summer of 1915. Instead, the war raged on for three more years.

As the men with goggles and eerie white coats turned the spigots, the world was introduced to a new war crime. The shouts of "poison gas" caused widespread panic as the heavier-than-air gas settled in the trenches and low-lying shell holes where soldiers took shelter. The deadly vapors passed through the enemy trenches and left groups of unfortunate men coughing into bloody handkerchiefs. Gas clouds followed the shifting winds into the farms and pastures for miles behind the lines. Flushed with success, the German military turned its attention to its Eastern Front. It managed (despite wartime shortages) to locate, fill, and transport an astonishing 12,300 cylinders and, between April 22 and August 6, 1915, released 220 tons of chlorine gas along a four-kilometer front. Unfortunately, considering the cost in casualties and the damage to Germany's reputation, the use of the gas did not significantly alter either front. Indeed, so new was this descent into mass murder that German soldiers who were unprepared or too curious perished in their own gas attack: 56 in May against France and Britain and 350 on the Russian front in August.[32] While the Russians never revealed their casualties, we can only assume that they ran into the low thousands during the same period.

The gas came in two kinds: lethal cyanogens, such as mustard gas, phosgene, and chlorine, and dozens of irritants, which caused acute respiratory distress, blindness, and vomiting. Some gases were released from cylinders, but more often the gas was delivered in artillery shells, each with its distinctive color and, to the experienced veterans, incoming sound, as well. The effects of the many hundreds of gas attacks during the war were generally crippling, painful, and usually ultimately fatal. For years after the end of the

First World War, thousands of blind German, British, French, and American former soldiers languished in government hospitals and sanitariums.

Perhaps the most graphic description of a gas attack was written by a British soldier in the trenches, the poet Wilfred Owens. Sarcastically entitled "*Dulce et Decorum Est*" ("It is sweet and right")—the first words of the Latin saying "Dulce et decorum est pro patria mori" ("it is sweet and right to die for your country")—Owens's poem puts the reader in the midst of an attack.

Dulce et Decorum Est

Bent double, like old beggars under sacks,
Knock-kneed, coughing like hags, we cursed through sludge,
Till on the haunting flares we turned our backs
And towards our distant rest began to trudge.
Men marched asleep. Many had lost their boots
But limped on, blood-shod. All went lame; all blind;
Drunk with fatigue; deaf even to the hoots
Of tired, outstripped Five-Nines that dropped behind.

Gas! Gas! Quick, boys!—An ecstasy of fumbling,
Fitting the clumsy helmets just in time;
But someone still was yelling out and stumbling,
And flound'ring like a man in fire or lime . . .
Dim, through the misty panes and thick green light,
As under a green sea, I saw him drowning.
In all my dreams, before my helpless sight,
He plunges at me, guttering, choking, drowning.

If in some smothering dreams you too could pace
Behind the wagon that we flung him in,
And watch the white eyes writhing in his face,
His hanging face, like a devil's sick of sin;
If you could hear, at every jolt, the blood
Come gargling from the froth-corrupted lungs,
Obscene as cancer, bitter as the cud
Of vile, incurable sores on innocent tongues,
My friend, you would not tell with such high zest
To children ardent for some desperate glory,
The old Lie; Dulce et Decorum est
Pro patria mori.

Owens was killed on November 4, 1918, attempting to lead his men across the Sambre Canal at Ors. The news of his death reached his parents on November 11, 1918, the day of the armistice.

We shall never know how many were killed by gas. The British and French (not the United States) used gas, as well. Men died choking in their trenches, and no one took notice or survived to report the numbers. The number of British soldiers killed by gas in the war is estimated at 59,000; France, 63,000; Germany, 40,000; the United States, 15,000—for an estimated total of 177,000 soldiers killed by gas. The number of civilians known to have been killed by gas (French farmers, Belgians on their way to work, Russian peasants, and especially chemical technicians and cylinder loaders) is listed as exactly 5,196.[33]

The use of poison gas by both sides was a war crime by any standard and countermanded every international agreement since 1625. Like the earlier German military campaign against the civilians on Belgium, it would have to be dealt with after the war.

Bombing and Death from the Skies

Not all atrocities were regulated at the end of the war. Unlike such war atrocities as the murder of Belgian civilians and the widespread use of toxic gas in the front lines, some atrocities of the Great War, however outrageous, were deemed acceptable. One, in particular, was simply accepted as a part of war and required no reconsideration, despite the large loss of civilian life it entailed: bombing.

For several years prior to the outbreak of hostilities in 1914, most European nations had been experimenting with dropping explosives from airplanes in hopes of hitting a specific target. Germany had developed a fearsome bombing force of Zeppelin airships by 1914; the French, for their part, soon developed an impressive bombing squadron of 600 rugged French Voisin planes, while the Imperial Russian Air Service created a substantial bomber unit based on Sikorsky's enormous four-engine Ilya Mourometz bombers. Britain already had an effective bomber force at the beginning of the war, built around a plane called the Handley Page.

The key to success, it was believed by all, was to be able to bomb enemy factories and cities, which would erode both enemy morale and fighting capability. The more bombs a plane could carry to the enemy, the better. Governments worked feverishly to equip bombers with larger and larger engines that would allow them to carry more bombs. By 1916, for example, England's Handley Page could carry 16 112-pound bombs; Russia's Ilya Mourometz could carry 1,543 pounds of bombs; the French Voisin bomber could carry 661 pounds; even Italy, which was relatively unprepared for the war, sported an impressive bomber unit, based on trimotor Italian Caproni bombers that carried 1,190 pounds of explosives.

The antagonists bombed one another with a vengeance, despite using different strategies. One Russian squadron, under Major-General M. V. Shidlovski, made more than 400 bombing raids over Germany and the Baltic states. The French conducted sustained bombing campaigns against the Western Front, and the British concentrated on night bombing of German U-boat bases, industrial sites, and railway stations. The Germans placed their hopes of bringing England to its knees on the huge Gotha G.V. bomber and its 1,000-pound payload, the most infamous bomber of World War One.[34] On one occasion, on May 23, 1917, a fleet of 21 Gothas appeared over the British coastal town of Folkestone, killing 95 people; three weeks later, the Gotha fleet appeared again, this time over London, where it dropped bombs every day for the next month. The British public was beginning to panic. The English reported 835 killed and 1,990 wounded.[35]

By all previous rules of war, the indiscriminate killing of helpless civilians—women, children, and the elderly—was a war crime. But, since almost every participating army (particularly the winning side) had developed bomber planes and had intentionally killed civilians in the hope of damaging the enemy's war industry and eroding civilian morale, how could the postwar diplomats condemn the very practice that many believed had contributed to the Allied victory? Instead, the planes became steeds of the skies, and the pilots became the new knights.[36] Enemy pilots who were shot down and survived were often guests at dinner. Bomber pilots took on rules of chivalry as enemies saluted each other in the air and dropped messages and challenges on each other's airfields. The most heroic among them—recognized as "Aces"—received military promotions and public adulation. What happened to the concept of indiscriminate bombing and the killing of civilians as a war crime? A decade before the diplomats met in Geneva in 1929, certain war crimes were being accepted as the new reality of war.

The Worst War Crime of All: Genocide

In 1915, as World War I raged, the Turkish government (which ruled the Ottoman Empire) decided upon the systematic extermination of most of the male Armenian population and forced deportation of the remainder, mostly women, children, and the elderly. All Armenians who survived were driven out of their homes and villages and forced toward the borders of neighboring countries in a series of death marches, with violence and starvation leading to the death of most of the marchers. Until the Holocaust that killed 6 million European Jews during the Second World War, the Armenian genocide was the most massive, brutal, and *unacknowledged* extermination programs in history.[37]

Far from being beneficial to the Turkish cause, the mass murder of the Armenians was a serious drain on the war effort for the Turks as they squandered money, time, and military equipment—and the future good will of the Allied Powers. The treatment of the Armenians by Turkey ominously foreshadowed the treatment of Germany's Jews two decades later. One can only speculate about which of the Germans who served in Turkey during the First World War were instrumental in creating the next genocide in Poland or the Ukraine.

By the time the exhausted and traumatized survivors reached refuge in neighboring countries, as many as three-quarters of the entire Ottoman Armenian population, an estimated 900,000 to 1.2 million people, had been exterminated, although some estimates go as high as 1.5 million Armenians murdered. According to the University of Minnesota's Center for Holocaust and Genocide Studies, there were 2,133,190 Armenians in the Ottoman Empire in 1914 and only about 387,800 by 1922.[38]

In November 1918, the First World War abruptly ended. The largest military mobilization in human history (the Western Powers mobilized 40 million soldiers, the Central Powers close to 20 million) was over. Twenty-one million men were wounded, and 8.5 million soldiers were dead. More than a million Armenian, Greek, and Syrian civilians had been brutally murdered by the Turks under the guise of "deportation," accounting for nearly half of the civilian deaths of the entire war.[39] For four years, the line between civilization and madness had been blurred as war crimes and atrocities became acts of patriotism. The number of prisoners executed, the number of women and children who had been bombed, and the collective devastation caused by penalties, massacres, and the use of civilians as human shields is unfathomable. Small-caliber explosive (dum-dum) bullets had been used; so was the famous German Paris gun, which hurled a shell the size of a Chevrolet 75 miles into the chaos of downtown Paris. With the Great War finally over, it was clear that representatives of the world's nations needed to gather to consider new definitions of war crimes and new regulations to restrain future violators.

Many atrocities were unique and had been possible only because of the appearance of new technologies: machine-gun strafing from airplanes, aerial bombing, poison gas, submarine warfare and deceptive Q-Boats, and torture by electricity, to name but a few. The world community had to come together to discuss these new atrocities and to establish regulations to prohibit future violations of the rules of war. Other atrocities, however, such as the murder of priests and nuns, the destruction of grand libraries and other cultural icons, and the sinking of helpless ships on the high seas, were already considered war crimes and were forbidden by earlier agreements. In such cases, the violators had to be punished—especially if those violators were on the losing side of the war. Last, the war revealed some atrocities that, like aerial bombing, were accepted by all as a requisite part of the new face of war. Despite the fact that, in 1918, U.S. Secretary of War Newton D. Baker said that the

United States would never participate in an air attack "that has as its objective the promiscuous bombing upon industry, commerce, or population in enemy countries,"[40] the German bombing of London, the American and British bombing of Hamburg and Dresden, and, of course, the use by the United States of the atomic bomb over Hiroshima and Nagasaki two decades later would prove otherwise. The killing of civilian populations, a strict violation of every rule of war, was not only pursued but pursued in a way that would kill the greatest possible number of civilians in an effort to collapse support on the home front. Similarly, in 1928,the head of the U.S. submarine service told the Secretary of the Navy that "it is inconceivable that submarines of our service will ever be used against merchant ships as was done during the World War"[41]—a restriction that rapidly fell by the wayside as America entered the next war.

Poison gas was another matter. When the gassed veterans returned home coughing and gasping for breath, the public became outraged anew. In fact, America's anger spread quickly as international representatives answered Washington's call, at the Washington Arms Conference of 1922, for a ban on the use of gas. Two presidents, Woodrow Wilson and Warren G. Harding, and their Secretaries of State, Charles Evans Hughes and Frank Kellogg, spoke out loudly against the use of gas in the future. General John J. Pershing, leader of the American Expeditionary Force during the war, went so far as to state: "It is inconceivable that the United States will initiate the use of gases—and by no means certain that it will use them even in retaliation."[42]

As late as Christmas 1933, President Franklin Roosevelt presented his program for disarmament and world peace, first unveiled the preceding May. It called for nations to scrap offensive weapons, to refuse to open their borders to the armed forces of another power, and to keep the peace. FDR maintained that the people of the world desired peace and disarmament but that their leaders were responsible for stirring up nationalistic feelings and talk of war. War was unnecessary, the President stated, since at least 90 percent of the world's population was "content with the territorial limits of the respective nations."[43] Perhaps an era of peace had arrived.

Notes

1. Leo Tolstoy, *War and Peace*, Book X, ch. 25 (Oxford: Oxford University Press, 1933), pp. 486–487.
2. Quoted in Quincy Wright, *A Study of War* (Chicago: University of Chicago Press, 1965), p. 863.
3. Ernst Jünger, *The Storm of Steel: From the Diary of a German Storm-Troop Officer on the Western Front* (New York: Howard Fertig, 1975), pp. 262–263.
4. Ivor Brown, "Table Talk," *The Observer*, July 6, 1952, p. 5.

5. In the same Book of Deuteronomy, however, amid the thunderous dictums to kill all who represent a different god and those unwilling to convert, is an unexpected restriction: "When you besiege a city for a long time . . . you shall not destroy its trees by wielding an ax against them; if you can eat of them, do not cut them down to use in the siege, for the tree of the field is man's food. Only the trees which you know are not trees for food you may destroy and cut down to build siege works against the city that makes war with you, until it is subdued" (Deuteronomy 20:19–20).

6. Amos S. Hershey, "The History of International Relations during Antiquity and the Middle Ages: International Law Impossible before the Rise of the Modern State System," *American Journal of International Law* 5, no. 4 (1911): 901–933.

7. John Finnes, "The Ethics of War and Peace in the Catholic National Law Tradition," in *The Ethics of War and Peace*, ed. Terry Nardin (Princeton, NJ: Princeton University Press, 1996), pp. 20–24.

8. Letter 138, to Marcellinus, cited in Sydney Dawson Bailey, *Prohibitions and Restraints in War* (London: Royal Institute of International Affairs, Oxford University Press, 1972), p. 8.

9. James Turner Johnson, "Historical Roots and Sources of the Just War Tradition in Western Culture," in *Just War and Jihad*, ed. John Kelsay and James Turner Johnson (Westport, CT: Greenwood Press, 1991), p. 10.

10. Christopher Tyerman, *God's War: A New History of the Crusades* (Cambridge, MA: Harvard University Press, 2006), p. 592.

11. Theodor Meron, *Henry's Wars and Shakespeare's Laws: Perspectives on the Law of War in the Later Middle Ages* (Oxford: Clarendon Press, 1993), pp. 7–8.

12. Christopher T. Allmand, *The Hundred Years War: England and France at War, c. 1300–1450* (Cambridge, MA: Cambridge University Press, 1988), p. 113.

13. Cited in Bailey, *Prohibitions and Restraints in War*, p. 18.

14. Ibid., pp 15–16.

15. Ibid., p. 26.

16. Hugo Grotius, *On the Law of War and Peace: Including the Law of Nature and of Nations*, trans. A.C. Campbell (Washington, DC: M.W. Dunne, 1901).

17. Barbara Donagan, "Prisoners in the English Civil War," *History Today*, 41, no. 3 (March 1991): 28–35.

18. Barbara Donagan, "Atrocity, War Crime, and Treason in the English Civil War," *American Historical Review* 99, no. 4 (October 1994): 1137–1166. The conflict finally ended in 1649 with the monarchy's defeat and the shocking execution of Charles I.

19. Cited in Geoffrey Best, *Humanity in Warfare* (New York: Columbia University Press, 1980), p. 51.

20. Richard Shelly Hartigan, *Lieber's Code and the Law of War* (Chicago: Precedent, 1983), pp. 54–60.

21. David Chuter, *War Crimes: Confronting Atrocity in the Modern World* (Boulder, CO: Lynne Rienner, 2003), p. 59.

22. Best, *Humanity in Warfare*, pp. 195–196.

23. Geoffrey Wawro, *The Franco-Prussian War: The German Conquest of France in 1870–1871* (New York: Cambridge University Press, 2003), p. 254.

24. Thomas Pakenham, *The Boer War* (New York: Random House, 1970), p. 608.

25. Leon Wolff, *Little Brown Brother: How the United States Purchased and Pacified the Philippines* (New York: Oxford University Press, 1991), pp. 252–253.

26. Peter Karsten, *Law, Soldiers, and Combat* (Westport, CT: Greenwood Press, 1978), pp. 60–61.

27. See, for example, the excellent new book by Beverly Gage, *The Day Wall Street Exploded: A Story of America in Its First Age of Terror* (Oxford: Oxford University Press, 2009).

28. *Regulations Respecting the Laws and Customs of War on Land*, annex to the Hague Convention (IV), article 22, in *The Laws of Armed Conflicts: A Collection of Conventions, Resolutions, and Other Documents*, 3rd rev. ed., ed. D. Schindler and J. Toman (Dordrecht: Nijhoff, 1988).

29. Comment, "Security Council Resolution 808: A Step toward a Permanent International Criminal Court for the Prosecution of International Crimes and Human Rights Violations," *Golden Gate University Law Review* 25 (Spring 1995): 443.

30. Jeff Lipkes, *Rehearsals: The German Army in Belgium, August 1914* (Louvain: Leuven University Press, 2007), p. 251.

31. L. F. Haber, *The Poisonous Cloud: Chemical Warfare in the First World War* (Oxford: Clarendon Press, 1986), p. 34.

32. Ibid., p. 37.

33. Ibid., p. 248.

34. U.S. Centennial of Flight Commission, "Bombing During WWI," http://www.centennialofflight.gov/essay/Air_Power/WWI/AP3.htm.

35. Ibid.

36. The Germans, Russians, Americans, and British, all with naval ambitions, refer to aviation in naval terms: groups of planes are called "air fleets," on the "flight deck" are the "captain, co-captain, and first officer," taking on luggage is "stowing cargo" in the "cargo hold," and passengers ride in the "cabin." The pilots and flight attendants are called "the crew." The plane itself is described in nautical terms: "fore and aft," "bulkhead," "starboard and port-side" engines. Airspeed is measured in nautical miles or "knots," airplanes have a "rudder" attached to the vertical stabilizer, and the kitchen is called "the galley."

37. Quoted in G. S. Graber, *Caravans to Oblivion: The Armenian Genocide* (1915; repr., New York: J. Wiley, 1996), pp. 87–88.

38. Laura J. Berberian, "Official United States Documents on the Armenian Genocide: An Annotated Bibliography" (Master's thesis, University of North Carolina at Chapel Hill, 2008), pp. 6–7.

39. See the tables and charts in Harold Elk Staubing, ed., *The Last Magnificent War and Eyewitness Accounts of World War I* (New York: Paragon House, 1989), pp. 402–403.

40. Karsten, *Law, Soldiers, and Combat*, p. 86.

41. Ibid.

42. Quoted in Richard D. McCarthy, *The Ultimate Folly: War by Pestilence, Asphyxiation, and Defoliation* (New York: Knopf, 1969), p. 6.

43. "Text of Roosevelt's Address at Wilson Dinner," *New York Times*, p. 3.

CHAPTER 3

The Worst War Crime of All

Genocide—the murder of a group of people because of their race or religion—is in a category all by itself. All war crimes are horrible, no matter what the scope or motivation, but genocide is different. The intentional bombing of a hospital ship is awful, to be sure, but it doesn't reach the definition of genocide; neither does the poisoning of French water wells by the Prussian military, in 1870, or the arrest and execution of the British nurse Edith Cavell by a German firing squad for her resistance activities in Belgium, in October 1915. All are war crimes, but none can be considered genocide.

For a crime to be declared genocide, it must comprise several elements. It must be an attempt to kill or cause bodily or mental harm to a national, ethnic, racial, or religious (especially if that religious group can be racially defined) minority, with the hope of reducing or exterminating the entire group. In other words, to be considered genocide, crimes have to be committed against groups of people, usually by their government or military power, entirely because of their race or ethnicity—human factors that are difficult to change or camouflage. In fact, their differences from the majority of the population can make them appear threatening and even dangerous: "termites in woodwork," as the Nazis said about their Jewish citizens. Given the advances in technology, genocide can involve the murders of thousands or even hundreds of thousands of helpless people.

Thus, the most basic definition is as follows:

> ***Genocide*: is a form of one-sided mass killing in which a state or other authority intends to destroy a group, as that group and membership in it are defined by the perpetrator.**[1]

But there is more to genocide. History has revealed that the perpetrators fall into three categories: (1) those who actually commit the rapes, tortures, or murders; (2) those who encourage, direct, and command the rapists, torturers, and murderers; and (3) those who are in a position to halt the atrocities and, despite the international laws that forbid them, allow the horrors to continue. In other words, it is not only the killers who are responsible but the leaders who incite them, the Hitlers and Tojos, Stalins and Saddam Husseins, Pol Pots and Mihailovićs. Since World War II, the official definition of genocide includes any conspiracy to incite the public to commit genocide—those who select the victim groups, pass the laws to marginalize them, and finally liquidate them. These acts also constitute genocide.

Genocide in Rwanda

A case in point is Rwanda. Called German East Africa until after the First World War, the country was mandated to Belgium in 1919 by the League of Nations, and in 1962 became independent. The Hutus, with their typically Bantu broad builds and short statures, were the vast majority of the Rwandan population; they were also the crop farmers. Over several centuries they were joined by the Tutsis, tall, thin, angular herdsmen, and the two groups shared languages, customs, and even marriages. . Over time, the tall Tutsis, attractive to their European German and Belgian colonial masters, became the landowners, and the less aristocratic-looking Hutus became the workers. Europe's missionaries followed and soon saw in the Hutus an oppressed group of future converts. The first major eruption came in 1956, when the Hutus rose up against the Tutsis, resulting in more than 100,000 deaths by 1959. The Hutus won and Tutsi survivors retreated to neighboring countries to plan and rearm. Those left in Rwanda were stripped of their land, leading to a cycle of Tutsi resistance, Hutu discrimination, and heightened tension.

In 1990, a Hutu politician named Hasan Ngeze started a publication called *Kangura* that was particularly significant in building hatred. It trumpeted a new Ten Commandments, called "Hutu Ten Commandments," which railed against the Tutsis and reduced the former ruling class to insects and vermin. Commandment number eight was "The Hutu must not have mercy on the Tutsi," which was soon quoted from memory by a large portion of the Hutu population. In 1993, a politically connected Hutu family founded what quickly became the most popular radio station in the small African nation (RTLM or Radio Télévision des Milles Collines—The Thousand Hills Radio Television), which blared a steady mixture of popular music and hatred for the Tutsi minority.[2]

For months before the outbreak of violence in April, psychologist Neil Kressel kept a record of the radio programs on RTLM, which largely consisted of "folk songs, slogans, speeches, and inaccurate news reports demonized the Tutsis and warned against Tutsi plans to retake the land, kill the Hutu, broadcasts depicted Tutsis as snakes, animals, and most often, cockroaches. Government leaders would urge the killers on with slightly more cautious euphemisms, telling them to 'clear the bush,' 'get to work,' or 'clean around their houses.' Peasants understood well these encouragements to slaughter their neighbors."[3]

> RTLM on *April 7 and 8:* "You have to kill the Tutsis, they are cockroaches . . ."
>
> *May 13:* Fight with the weapons you have at your disposal. . . . We must all fight the Tutsis; we must finish with them, exterminate them, sweep them from the whole country. . . . There must be no refuge for them, none at all.
>
> And on *July 2:* we must rise up against this race of bad people. . . . They must be exterminated because there is no other way."[4]

On April 6, 1994, the tension came to a boil when the plane carrying the President/dictator of Rwanda (a Hutu) was shot down, most certainly by extremists from one side or the other. The Hutus, already incensed by newspaper and radio broadcasts, started killing Tutsis. After 100 days, when the bloody fray ended in July, up to 1 million Rwandans—mostly Tutsis and political opponents of the Hutu government—had been hacked to death with machetes by the Hutu population. Throughout the killings of one ethnic group by another, the government's private radio station was far more than an accessory to the acts; it was the instigator. Indeed, the majority of genocides in history—certainly in modern history—have been instigated by governments against elements of their own population. According to the distinguished scholar Irving Horowitz, at Rutgers University, governments have been directly responsible for the deaths of millions, in both civil and international conflicts. One expert suggests that perhaps 15 million people have been killed in 20th-century wars and genocides, most in the past 45 years—and more than three and a half times more people have been killed by their own governments than were killed by opposing states."[5] When the government wasn't the actual murderer, it was the facilitator. "Further, what we are dealing with is not a side-show," concludes Horowitz about future genocides by governments against members of their own populations, "but increasingly the main event, perhaps the only event, given the increasingly high risk of conventional warfare in this post-nuclear environment."[6]

The first act of genocide in the 20th century was perpetrated in 1904, with Germany's bloody suppression of native resistance to its occupation of German South West Africa (Rwanda, Burundi, and Tanzania). In the single year

1904, General Lothar von Trotha's army murdered more than 80 percent of the Herero natives and blocked all escape routes for the survivors except one, which led to the Kalahari Desert. He then placed troops at the water holes in their path and let them die in the desert. According to a native guide attached to the German troops,

> I was present when the Herero were defeated in a battle at Hamakiri in the vicinity of Waterberg. After the battle all men, women and children who fell into the German hands, wounded or otherwise, were mercilessly put to death. Then the Germans set off in pursuit of the rest and all those found by the wayside and in the sandveld were shot down and bayoneted to death. The mass of the Herero men were unarmed and thus unable to offer resistance. They were just trying to get away with their cattle.[7]

According to the official report, "like a half-dead animal [the Herero native] was hunted from water-hole to water-hole until he became a lethargic victim of the nature of his own country. The waterless Omaheke [desert] was to complete the work of the German military: the annihilation of the Herero people."[8] In General Trotha's words: "My intimate knowledge of many central African tribes (Bantu and others) has everywhere convinced me of the necessity that the Negro does not respect treaties but only brute force."[9] Some historians see this brutal extermination of a people as the first step toward the Holocaust.[10]

In 1910, the French "pacified" the Ivory Coast and the French Congo. French Governor Angoulvant believed that the best way to achieve colonization was through force, and he sent out punitive expeditions that confiscated rubber-producing plantations, all weapons, and harvests—and murdered untold thousands of natives. The later Supreme Commander in French Equatorial Africa, General Hilaire, found no problem with his mission, but he lamented the speed demanded by his government to squeeze the colonies. His recollection, however, provides a vivid picture of the French war crimes in Tropical Africa. Hilaire wrote:

> For five or six years, the cruel problem of native labor has led to a disastrous solution, that of intensive depletion—yet again!—of a population already sadly decimated by drastic cuts enforced blindly on its weakest elements, over the 500 kilometres of these homicidal construction sites! . . . . After Bakongo, the Laongo, the Kreche, the Gabonese, the Souma, the Dagba, Baya, Yacoma and others; even the Sara; the ethnic elite of French Equatorial Africa, magnificent and supreme reserves of farmers and soldiers, have been successfully decimated, some of them even exterminated by . . . the "machine"—as, in their language of fear, they call the deadly labor on the railway line.[11]

Conditions appear to have improved over the years, as evidenced by the number of workers in the total labor force who died from starvation and brutality, which dropped from an appalling 42 percent in 1927, to an equally appalling 39 percent in 1928, to a comparatively mild 17 percent in 1929.[12]

Different Types of Genocide

Not all genocides are alike. One difference concerns the distance between perpetrator and victim, best illustrated by comparing the Hutu-Tutsi massacres in Rwanda and the Holocaust against the Jews. In the case of the Holocaust, the Nazis carried out their genocide at distant killing centers in Poland, and the German public did not need to pursue the destination of their disappearing neighbors. Like a bomber who drops a huge explosive on an unseen enemy from 30,000 feet, the mass murder of the Jews, however well known, took place out of the public eye. The organized gassings and shootings were assigned to the SS (the *Schutzstaffel*, the Nazis' ideologically elite force) and special Order Police units. The public did not actively participate, at least until *Kristallnacht* (Crystal Night), November 9 and 10, 1938, although the debate continues about how much the German public knew about the fate of the Jews.

Another difference between genocides concerns planning. The Holocaust against the Jews was planned in detail by the Germans and their Ukrainian and Baltic helpers. Memos, schedules, and the inevitable "lists" litter the path of the Nazi mass murders. So obsessive were the German killers about maintaining proper records that at Auschwitz they tattooed every surviving victim's number on his arm. The Nazis also maintained large, black-covered volumes known as "Death Books," where, in some extermination camps, the names of the victims and their arrival dates were listed in alphabetical order. The German murderers were so intent on keeping proper records that train transports were sometimes loaded and unloaded until the number of people aboard matched the number on the list of those to be deported.

The massacres in Rwanda, however, were unplanned—except, perhaps, by the government. Hutus responded to the ceaseless drone of hatred by turning against their Tutsi neighbors. No bombs were being dropped from 30,000 feet, here. Perhaps as many as 100,000 people killed and tortured one another face to face. Killing a neighbor with a machete is personal. Torturing one's victims and being close enough to the victim to be the one applying the pain is intimate. Hundreds of thousands of people across Rwanda, from priests to farmers, participated in the racial extermination of their minority tribe. Hutu husbands who were married to Tutsis were forced to murder their wives or die. The survivor of one massacre described the horrors he barely escaped:

> On the 7th of April [1994], in the morning, they started burning houses over there and moving towards here. Only a few were killed. The burning pushed us to this place. Our group decided to run to this place. We thought this was God's house, no one would attack us here. On the 7th, 8th, up to the 10th we were fighting them. We were using stones. They had *pangas* (machetes), spears, hammers, grenades. On the 10th, their numbers increased. On the 14th, we were being pushed inside the church. The church was attacked on the 14th and the 15th. . . . Here, there were women, children, and old men. The men had formed defense units outside. Most men died fighting. When our defense was broken through, they came in and killed everyone here. After that, they started hunting for those hiding in the hills. I and others ran to the swamp.

"The genocide [in Rwanda] was characterized by torture and utmost cruelty. . . . They [the killings] ranged from burying people alive . . . to cutting and opening wombs of pregnant mothers. People were quartered, impaled or roasted to death. . . . In some cases, victims had to pay fabulous amounts of money to the killers for a quick death. The brutality . . . was unprecedented."[13]

On June 1, Radio Milles Collines further enraged the Hutu majority by announcing that the enemy Tutsi rebels were "gathering people in a village and killing them with bullets, gathering people in a mosque and killing them with machete, throwing people tied up into the Akagera River, killing a pregnant woman and taking out the fetus, which is ground and given to the family to eat before they are killed."[14] The British philosopher Sir Bertrand Russell described the scene in Rwanda that year as "the most horrible and systematic massacre we have had occasion to witness since the extermination of the Jews by the Nazis."[15]

There is ample evidence to indicate that there were numerous red flags signaling the oncoming massacre. Hoping, perhaps, that it would disappear if ignored, or simply unable to forge a policy, the top three leaders of the United Nations blocked every effort to prevent or calm the approaching storm or to keep its member states properly informed of the spreading massacres. As the massacres began, Belgian requests for additional UN peacekeepers in Rwanda were denied or sidetracked. When it was clear that the situation was out of control, the West panicked, and special units of Italian, American, and French soldiers swept in to rescue the remaining Tutsi. A thoughtful analysis of the opportunities and failures of the United Nations and bystander nations to bring enough pressure to bear on the warring parties to force them to make peace is found in Fred Grünfeld and Anke Huijboom's *The Failure to Prevent Genocide in Rwanda: The Role of Bystanders* (Brill, 2007). The result of the world's indecision and denial was complicity in the deaths of between 10,000 and 50,000 Hutu and between 500,000 and 1 million Tutsi—all in 100 days.[16]

Mahmood Mamdani, an influential Columbia University professor and genocide authority, points out that both the Nazi and the Rwandan massacres were heavily supported by the educated classes, rather than the illiterate masses. A disproportionate number of doctors, nurses, and judges—and even one human rights activist—influenced the direction of the violence in Rwanda. Nazism was also heavily influenced by German science. German doctors legitimized racial purity, diagnosed the Jews as carriers of typhus, and often determined who would live and who would die.[17] The issue of medical experiments on human guinea pigs is a travesty without comparison.

There is yet another type of genocide—what is called cultural genocide, or destroying a group through its forcible assimilation into the mainstream culture. American Indians during the 19th century are a sad example. Native Americans were driven or deceived into leaving their hereditary lands and moved to desolate reservations, where they became wards of the Bureau of Indian Affairs. America's many diverse Indian cultures were not eradicated as much by force as they were by white America's efforts to prohibit the practice of their language and culture. Another case of cultural genocide, or what we call today "ethnic cleansing," was the Great Upheaval: the British roundup of many thousands of French-speaking Catholics who found themselves caught up in a power struggle between the British and the French power struggle in the New World, in 1755. French Acadians who lived in communities in Nova Scotia were shipped to other British colonies, where they tried to survive until the end of the power struggle. In 1763, the broken families and survivors trailed home to Nova Scotia, leaving some thousands of French-speaking refugees in southern Louisiana. Those refugees who stayed behind eventually gave rise to today's Cajuns.[18]

After World War I the angry American nativist movement turned against the use of foreign languages as well as Catholicism in the French-speaking areas of Louisiana. The speaking and teaching of the French language as well as the practice of French culture was forbidden until well after World War II. It was, to most French-speaking Louisianans, a clear effort at cultural genocide.

Relations between tiny Tibet and its vast neighbor, China, have been strained since Tibet declared itself an independent republic in 1911, rebuffing China's (and Britain's) control. In 1949, Mao Zedong proclaimed the founding of the communist People's Republic of China and threatened Tibet with "liberation." The following year, the Chinese Army marched into Tibet, beginning China's heavy-handed pressure on Tibet's religious and cultural traditions. After China's Cultural Revolution began, in mid-May1966, ranks of ideologically crazed Red Guards closed monasteries, smashed Buddhist statues, and forced Buddhist monks to return to nonreligious life. Religious practices were banned, and more than 4,000 monasteries were destroyed. To survive, Tibetan culture and the teaching of the language were hidden underground and remained defiant. Fortunately, the ban on religion was lifted in 1976, and some Buddhist temples have again been in operation since the early 1980s.

In December 1999, the Dalai Lama, Tibet's spiritual leader and the winner of the 1989 Nobel Peace Prize, cast aside his godly circumspection and openly accused the Chinese of cultural genocide. China shrugged off the familiar charge, claiming that Tibet was part of China. Several protests in Tibet in the late 1980s and early 1990s were violently suppressed by the Communist government, and martial law was imposed in 1989. However, the most serious threat came in July 2006, when Beijing opened the Qinghai-Tibet Railway, the world's highest railroad, saying it would help modernize and develop Tibet, while bringing in tourist money. The new train would certainly modernize Tibet, but supporters of Tibet's independence say that the new Chinese railroad is a naked ploy to swamp Tibet with Han Chinese immigrants and to threaten its fragile high-altitude environment. In this conflict, time is probably on China's side. What the Chinese were unable to accomplish by decades of forced change, the world fears it may be able to do by bringing in endless trainloads of Chinese colonists. Given the number of arriving Chinese immigrants and tourists, Tibetan culture may well be facing extinction in the not-so-distant future.

China is also working hard to extinguish the culture of another minority, if not the minority itself—the Turkic-speaking Muslim Uighur people, who have lived for centuries in the northwest province of Xinjiang. Beijing has relied on the old methods: discrimination against Uighurs and an unsuccessful attempt to settle thousands of People's Liberation Army soldiers in the area, followed by the more productive mass immigration program that brought between 1 million and 2 million Han Chinese to Xinjiang Province. For most Uighurs, Xinjiang has become a police state where their culture and language are forbidden. Violence increased when the Chinese government decided, in 2009, to raze the city of Kashgar, the centuries-old center of Uighur civilization. Nearly 50,000 Uighurs were displaced as the ancient cultural city was torn down. Try as they might to calm the Han Chinese around them, offering cigarettes and sweets to their Han Chinese co-workers, the Uighurs, hampered by rumors, language difficulties, and government-sponsored protests, have been subject to beatings and death. A conflict between the two groups of workers at the Early Light Toy Factory in Gungdong Province on June 25, 2009, was described in the Western news this way:

> During a four-hour melee Han and Uighur workers bludgeoned each other with fire extinguishers, paving stones and lengths of steel shorn from bed frames. By dawn, when the police finally intervened, two Uighur men had been killed and 120 people had been wounded, most of

> them Uighur, according to the authorities. 'People were so vicious, they just kept beating the dead bodies,' said one man who witnessed fighting that he says involved more than a thousand workers.

Chen Qihua, deputy director of the Shaoguan Foreign Affairs Office, explained the Early Light Toy Factory dust-up by stating that "The issue between Han and Uighur people is like an issue between husband and wife; we have our quarrels, but in the end, we are like one family."[19] Beijing had nearly lost control of its minority campaign in the Xingjiang and Gungdong provinces.

Similar efforts to obliterate hated or feared minority groups and to force them to blend into the mainstream can be found in nearly every country's history. Social historians believe that the extinguishing of a minority's culture is nearly as bad as the extermination of the people themselves. To many, there is little difference.

Genocide is hardly new. The Bible thunders the destruction of certain racial or ethnic groups. Indeed, there are few better definitions for the crime of physical and cultural genocide that that found in Deuteronomy 7:1–11:

> When the Lord Your God brings you into the land which you go to possess, and has cast out many nations before you, the Hittites and the Girgashites and the Amorites and the Canaanites and the Perizzites and the Hivites and the Jebusites, seven nations greater and mightier than you and . . . you shall conquer them and utterly destroy them. You shall make no covenant with them nor show mercy to them. Nor shall you make marriages with them. You shall not give your daughter to their son, nor take their daughter for your son. . . . But thus shall you deal with them; you shall destroy their altars, and break down their sacred pillars, and cut down their wooden images, and burn their carved images with fire.

In another example, God spoke to King Saul, in 1 Samuel 15:1–3, commanding him to take revenge on the Amalekites for ambushing the Israelites in the wilderness as they fled from Egypt, saying: "Now go and attack Amalek and utterly destroy all that they have, and do not spare them. But kill both man and woman, infant and nursing child, ox and sheep, camel and donkey."

In a final example from Scripture, described in Esther 3:1–11, the evil Haman was promoted to Prime Minister under King Ahasuerus and turned his wrath on the Jews. "And the letters were sent by couriers into all the king's provinces, to destroy, to kill, to annihilate all the Jews, both young and old, little children and women, in one day . . . and to plunder their possessions." Innumerable similar efforts to exterminate particular tribes, ethnic groups, and nations have occurred since the beginning of recorded history.

Yet, this special war crime did not receive a name until 1944, when Raphael Lemkin, a Polish scholar who worked in the U.S. State Department, wrote about the murder of the Jews in his book *Axis Rule in Occupied Europe*.[20] He fashioned the term "genocide" from the Greek word *genos*, meaning race or tribe, and the Latin term for killing, *cide*, and analyzed the crime from every side. The uniqueness of genocide as separate from other types of war crimes suddenly found traction at the famous Nuremberg Trial in 1945, where the term was included in both the opening indictment and the closing argument. Lemkin, seared by the Nazi horrors, continued to work tirelessly to bring the matter before the United Nations. He was successful the following year, in 1946, when the United Nations General Assembly adopted a Resolution affirming that genocide is a "crime under international law." In the preamble to that 1946 Resolution, genocide was declared to be "a denial of the right of existence of entire human groups, as homicide is the denial of the right to live of individual human beings." Two years after that, in 1948, four years after Lemkin first coined the definition, the United Nations Genocide Convention was ratified on December 9, 1948.[21]

Genocide was now officially defined as an act that *intends* (note the narrow construction) to destroy, in whole or in part, a national, ethnic, racial, or religious group (no reference was made to political groups) by (a) killing members of the group, (b) causing serious bodily harm to members of the group, (c) bringing conditions on the group calculated to destroy the group, wholly or in part, (d) imposing measures intended to prevent births within the group, or (e) forcibly transferring children of the group to other groups.

The problems are clear. First of all, how does one measure intent? Second, political groups, often the victims of genocide, were omitted as a category. Third, the categories were vague and riddled with loopholes and challengeable legal problems. Moreover, the Convention failed to identify the greatest source of three-quarters of the world's genocides: the State. Seventy-five percent of the violence committed by states has been directed against peoples within their own borders.[22] Irving Horowitz, mentioned earlier, says simply that genocide is a state crime and, in his view, the product of authoritarian states (or a democracy run amuck).[23] The noted political psychologist Richard Koenigsberg analyzed the issue in his insightful book, *Nations Have the Right to Kill* (2009).

The Armenian Massacre in Turkey and World War I

Living among the Muslim Turks were more than a million industrious Christians: the Armenians, among the most ancient people in the Near East, living in the southern Caucasus for nearly 3,000 years. They were discriminated against by the Turks and in 1896 survived a government-sponsored campaign that killed some 200,000 Armenians. The Great War gave the ruling Young Turk movement another opportunity. Government propaganda portrayed the Armenians as disloyal and in league with Turkey's Russian enemy. In February 1915, the Central Committee of the ruling Committee of Union and Progress Party (CUP) decided, in a closed session, that "if this purge is not general and final, it will inevitably lead to problems. Therefore it is absolutely necessary to eliminate the Armenian people in its entirety, so that there is no further Armenian on this earth and the very concept of Armenia is extinguished. We are now at war. We shall never have a more suitable opportunity than this."[24]

Prior to the meticulously planned genocide, the Young Turks enacted laws that stripped Armenians of their rights to property and their right to bear arms. On April 24, 1915, some 600 Armenian notables, all male, were invited to what turned out to be their executions. Bewildered, they were asked to pose for a group photograph in their suits and were then immediately murdered. The Armenian minority in Turkey was now leaderless. An additional 2,345 Armenian leaders were arrested, briefly jailed, and executed. (To this day, April 24 is still commemorated by Armenians worldwide as "Genocide Memorial Day.") On August 22, 1914, Armenian men between the ages of 18 and 20 and 45 to 60 were conscripted into the Turkish Army, forced into slave labor, and executed by the Turkish military. The Armenian community was now without young men to resist what was about to happen and older men whose respected advice would have directed future military or diplomatic efforts. The next phase was the requisition of all Armenian assets. According to Turkish Finance Minister Hasan Fehmi, not a single Muslim was targeted under this law.[25] On September 13, 1915, the Temporary Law on Expropriation and Confiscation was instituted.

The deportation (read "slaughter") began on May 27, 1915. The estimated 1.3 million Armenians were suddenly without leaders and respected intellectuals and were set upon by the Turks, who drove them in large groups across the country, torturing, raping, and killing as the mood struck them. The Turkish government denied Armenian deportees food, shelter, and water during their arduous journey through the Syrian desert. Hundreds of thousands of Armenians starved to death during the deportations, and those who did not starve were murdered at the whim of Turkish gendarmes, thugs, and Turkish and Kurd bystanders. Driven by war fever and a long history of ethnic hatred, the Turks used the opportunity to also turn on the thousands of Greeks who lived among them.

Henry Morgenthau, the U.S. ambassador to Turkey, was appalled by the sight of hundreds and thousands of broken people, starving and tortured, as they were lashed by Turkish gendarmes and forced into the Syrian desert. A high-ranking Turkish official told him openly that, far from remaining above it all, the leading politicians "constantly ransacked their brains in the effort to devise some new torment. He told me that they even delved into the records of the Spanish Inquisition and other historic institutions of torture and adopted all the suggestions found there."[26] Turkish gendarmes ran ahead of the herds of brutalized people to alert the villages that their victims were on the way, and prison inmates were released to join the horrors. "For a whole month," recalled another eyewitness, "corpses were observed floating down the River Euphrates, nearly every day, often in batches of two to six corpses bound together. The male corpses are in many cases hideously mutilated (sexual organs cut off, and so on), the female corpses are ripped open."[27]

An eyewitness, the Reverend F. H. Leslie, an American missionary in the town of Urfa, wrote to confirm the horrors to the American consul, J. B. Jackson, who was stationed in Aleppo, Syria.

> For six weeks we have witnessed the most terrible cruelties inflicted upon the thousands of Christian exiles who have been passing through our city. All tell the same story and bear the same scars: their men were all killed on the first days march from their cities, after which the women and girls were constantly robbed of their money, bedding, clothing, and beaten, criminally abused and abducted along the way. Their guards forced them to pay even for drinking from the springs along the way and were their worst abusers but also allowed the baser element in every village through which they passed to abduct the girls and women and abuse them.[28]

Viscount James Bryce, the former British ambassador to the United States, received an even more shocking report:

> The leading Armenians of the town and the headmen of the villages were subjected to revolting tortures. Their finger nails and then their toe nails were horribly extracted; their teeth were knocked out, and in some cases their noses were whittled down. . . . The female relatives of the victims who came to their rescue were outraged in public before the very eyes of their mutilated husbands and brothers.
>
> The shortest method for disposing of the women and children concentrated in various camps was to burn them. Fire was set to large wooden sheds in Alidjan, Megtakom, Khaskegh, and other Armenian villages, and these absolutely helpless women and children were roasted to death.[29]

Interestingly, Talaat Pasha, the Turkish leader, freely admitted the government's plan and knowledge of the crimes to Ambassador Morgenthau. During their many conversations on the subject, recorded by Morgenthau, Talaat assured the American diplomat that he "should not get the idea that the deportations had been decided upon hastily; in reality, they were the result of prolonged and careful deliberation."[30]

On one occasion, Talaat told Ambassador Morgenthau:

> I have asked you to come to-day so we can explain our position on the whole Armenian subject. We base our objections to the Armenians on three distinct grounds. In the first place, they have enriched themselves at the expense of the Turks. In second place, they are determined to domineer over us and to establish a separate state. In the third place, they have openly encouraged our enemies.[31]

As is common in the history of genocide, the killers blamed the victims.

Morgenthau responded that massacre was hardly a fair way of treating people who are industrious. To the charge that the Armenians sought political independence, Morgenthau said that the Armenians probably would not contemplate independence if the Turkish government treated all its citizens equally. To the last charge, that the Armenians were sympathetic to Turkey's enemies, such as Russia, Great Britain, and France, Ambassador Morgenthau simply noted that, given the history of discrimination and massacres against the Armenians, it was hardly surprising that they might appeal to foreign nations that might protect them against future assaults.[32] However, Morgenthau lost his temper when Talaat requested a list of all Armenians who had purchased life insurance policies from American companies; the Turkish government intended to collect the payments on all the Armenians it had massacred!

Following his confrontations with Talaat Pasha and other Young Turk leaders, Ambassador Morgenthau telegraphed the U.S. Secretary of State, William Jennings Bryan, calling the Turkish atrocities an attempt at "racial extermination." Secretary Bryan urged Morgenthau to continue to voice the strongest possible protests to the Ottoman government on behalf of the Armenians. The American press, including the *New York Times* and dozens of weekly and monthly journals, reported on the massacres, and the U.S. Senate held contemporary hearings on the subject.

The Turkish government was not on its own as it planned and implemented the Armenian Genocide. Germany was allied with Turkey during World War I, and numerous high-ranking German officers were posted to help lead the Turkish Army and run the railroads. In fact, one of the major instigators of the Armenian genocide was Lt. General Hans Friedrich von Seeckt, Chief of Staff at Ottoman headquarters, who fueled the atrocities from the earliest moment, as did Count Eberhard Wolffskeel von Reichenberg, Chief of Staff of the 8th Army Corps in Urfa, who recommended the total deportation of the Armenian population.[33] General Bronsart von

Schellendorf, also a German, enthusiastically supported the unfolding program of mass deportation of the Armenians in a secret meeting with the Turkish Minister of War Enver Pasha and Interior Minister Talaat. German Admiral Guido von Usedom told Ambassador Morgenthau that "the Armenians were in the way, that they were an obstacle to German success, and that it had, therefore, been necessary to remove them, just like so much useless lumber."[34]

Far from being beneficial to the authorities, the mass murder of the Armenians was a serious drain on the war effort for both the Turks and the Germans; they squandered money, time, and military equipment—and any future good will on the part of the Allied Powers. The treatment of the Armenians by Turkey's German partners ominously foreshadowed the treatment they would inflict on Europe's Jews two decades later.[35]

Twenty-five years later, Adolf Hitler's Germany turned on its Jewish citizens and, with the enthusiastic acquiescence of the German public, allowed its bureaucracy and military to devour millions of hapless victims. The fact that in the midst of World War One the world largely stood by as the genocide of the Armenians took place was not lost on the Nazis. In fact, eight days before the beginning of World War Two, on August 22, 1939, Hitler announced to his generals:

> I have issued the command—and I'll have anybody who utters but one word of criticism executed by a firing squad—that our war aim does not consist in reaching certain lines, but in the physical destruction of the enemy. Accordingly, I have placed my death head formations in readiness—for the present only in the East—with orders to send to death mercilessly and without compassion, men, women, and children of Polish derivation and language. Only thus shall we gain the living space [*Lebensraum*] which we need. Who, after all, speaks today of the annihilation of the Armenians?[36]

Genocide was now a reality of war. There is a clear link between the massacre of the Armenians during the first war and the mass murder of the Jews in the next. Hitler said as much.

In fact, there is a startling connection between genocide and the entire First World War. The Great War was truly the trauma of modern history; that it happened early in the century directed events for the rest of the century, no differently than the misshaping of the branches of a decorative Japanese bonsai tree affects how it grows. The war began with a horrifying clash between nearly equally prepared (or unprepared) armies, led by equally incompetent generals. The battlefields deteriorated into miles of opposing trenches as the war turned into a search for winning weapons and an obsession with ever fiercer artillery bombardments, many lasting days or weeks, and, always, finding more men to charge the enemy. The war became a meaningless rhythm of violence—killing on a mass scale.

Gone were the opportunities for individual heroism, for testing one's mettle, for the glorious death for one's country. Technology, and the damage it could inflict on the enemy forces in the trenches, changed warfare into death on a huge scale. The more destructive the weapon, the better, and success was measured by the number of casualties inflicted. Life became increasingly worthless as thousands of men rushed across the no-man's-land between the sets of trenches to descend into the enemy lines with knives, shovels, and shotguns. Mortars and overhead bursts were designed to kill men as they huddled in their trenches. The massive artillery bombardments churned the ground into mud, in which untold numbers were swallowed up and disappeared.

The survivors came home scarred, often physically but always psychologically, and the two decades between the First and Second World Wars seethed with political, artistic, and religious movements whose dreams and methods evolved from the war. Many of the ideas woven through fascism and socialism and Dadaism and disarmament were conceived around the campfires in the trenches during lulls in the fighting of World War One. More than intellectual ideas, the war produced new cadres and adherents as many former soldiers and home-front civilians came to realize that only in war had they known true comradeship and devotion, sacrifice and meaning.

This dichotomy between the horrors of war and the fascination of living on the edge produces, in the words of historian Omer Bartov, "a world turned upside down, where the boundaries between perpetrator and victim, innocence and guilt, have been shattered, and the immense power of the mobilized bureaucratic state can be used to any end, good or evil, or break out of its controls completely. The Great War was a war of total destruction, frightening and cleansing at the same time, terrifying and yet fascinating and altogether unavoidable."[37] It was the introduction of Industrial Death.

The value of human life had been debated long before World War I, however. In the 1870s and 1880s, a number of spokesmen had drawn on Darwinism to advocate euthanasia, mercy killing, suicide, and the morality of ending lives unworthy of being lived—those of the mentally handicapped, the so-called mongoloids, the disfigured.[38] The Great War only cheapened life and inured society to accept the huge losses of faceless people. The genocide of the Armenians in 1915, unpunished and unacknowledged, made the prospect of future mass murders more plausible than ever before. Indeed, within four years of the war's end, in 1919, the rabble-rousing Adolf Hitler posed these questions in *Mein Kampf*: "Why during the First World War had some men died—sacrificed their lives—while others had not?" And then: "Why did the best die in warfare, while the worst survived?"[39] It was but a short step to define Jews as the "worst to survive." The founder of psychoanalytic sociology, Richard Koenigsberg, notes that Hitler believed that "If a nation's commander-in-chief can send his 'superior' citizen to their deaths, why can he not also send its 'inferior' citizens to their deaths?"[40] Genocide, especially under the cover of a world war, was becoming conceivable and, to the ominous rise of the Third Reich and the Co-Prosperity Sphere, a goal to pursue.

Nazis as Mass Murderers

During World War Two, several genocides were under way simultaneously, and they shouldn't be confused. There was, of course, Hitler's Holocaust against the Jews, the modern world's largest genocide, which caused the massacre of some 6 million Jews.[41] At the same time, there was a second, parallel genocide in which the Nazis murdered an additional 5 million non-Jews (predominantly Poles), as well. Slavs were "subhuman" in the Nazi racial hierarchy, and the German Army was ordered by Hitler to exterminate every expendable Pole, beginning with the Polish leading class, priests, lawyers, teachers, and doctors. The legal scholar Jackson Nyamuya Maogoto notes that "Polish Christians and Catholics were the first victims of Auschwitz."[42]

There was, in fact, a third genocide, the massacre of Russian prisoners of war. The Germans, utterly contemptuous of any regulations against war crimes, murdered POWs by the tens of thousands; they were starved, gassed, bayoneted, and left to the elements to die. Most Russian prisoners were simply shot dead on the spot by their German captors. Even before the first Russian winter descended on the conflict, in 1941, millions of Soviet prisoners were dying in enormous open-air enclosures, subject to the weather and starvation and indiscriminate murder by the German army or force marched or shipped by cattle cars to POW camps, concentration camps, and the factories of Germany. Anyone who faltered along the way was executed without thought. According to Omer Bartov, an expert on the Eastern Front, casualty figures for groups of Russian prisoners never dropped below 30 percent and sometimes rose as high as 95 percent.[43] In point of fact, the Germans killed more Soviet women soldiers than the total of U.S. losses in the war. Like a painting by the medieval artist Hieronymus Bosch, skeletal figures in shredded Russian uniforms hovered around flickering campfires, starved and covered with lice, sometimes feeding on the corpses of the dead and dying. "The total number of prisoners taken by the German armies in the U.S.S.R. was in the region of 5.5 million," writes Peter Calvocoressi and Guy Wint in *Total War*.[44] Of the estimated 5.5 million Russian POWs taken by the Germans, only about 1.8 million survived, though starved and brutalized. Unbelievably, when the remaining Russian prisoners were repatriated back to their homeland, they faced Soviet leader Josef Stalin's dreaded Order No. 270, which declared that all Red Army soldiers who had allowed themselves to be captured alive were "traitors to the Motherland," and most ended their lives in Siberian slave labor camps. One such prisoner, Alexander Solzhenitsyn, wrote the history of his experiences as the Nobel Prize-winning book *The Gulag Archipelago*.

Holocaust of the Jews

The Jewish Holocaust of World War Two was similar to the Armenian genocide during World War One in many respects. Both victim groups adhered to an ancient religion, and both were talented and creative religious minorities with a history of persecution in their respective states. Both groups lived in democratic countries, and the survivors of both groups created new nations: Armenia and Israel. Unlike the genocide in Rwanda, the Nazi extermination of the Jews, Jehovah's Witnesses, homosexuals, and "asocials," as well as the estimated one half million Roma and Sinti Gypsies deported from Romania, Hungary, and Slovakia, took place out of sight of the dominant population. Rwanda was different; people died where they had lived.

If the Nazi mass murders took place in isolated death camps in Poland, anti-Semitism was certainly visible enough. It began as a product of early Christianity as the new religion sought to separate itself from its Jewish roots and took on a damned life of its own. Jews, instead of the Romans, were blamed for the crucifixion of Jesus and were forever tainted by the guilt. They found themselves responsible for every random catastrophe in history, from plagues to unexplainable lunar events. During the Middle Ages, from the 9th to the 16th century, the Jews of Europe lived a particularly precarious existence. Crusades aimed against the Muslims in Jerusalem or heretic Christians in southern France often took a detour to the nearest Jewish community. In addition to sporadic waves of violence, Jews also faced harassment and restrictions of all kinds imposed by governments across Europe. They were crammed into walled ghettos, often required to wear yellow armbands or cone hats, or expelled for political expediency. To celebrate occasional special holidays, local princes might declare that all contracts to repay Jewish moneylenders were null and void.

By the late 1800s, anti-Semitism was nearly mainstream, and political parties routinely espoused anti-Semitic rhetoric. Three strains of thought were about to converge on the Jews. In addition to the centuries of anti-Jewish hatred, which now reached the growing middle class, the parallel development of irrational nationalism arising from the French Revolution in 1789 focused attention on "outsiders," people different from themselves. The third strain was the publication of Darwin's findings, in 1859, which took the world by storm as they dramatized the triumph of the strongest elements in society and the mysticism of eugenics and racial purity.

The eruption of the Great War gave Europe's Jews the opportunity to show their patriotism, regardless of the country they called home. They fought in numbers far higher than their small representation in society warranted, and at home they sacrificed like few others. Germany's defeat in World War I and the hyperinflation of the postwar years nonetheless magnified anti-Jewish passions and made Jews especially vulnerable. A woman named Rachel Straus recalled that "we lived among each other, sat together in the same schoolroom, attended university together, met each other at social events—and were complete strangers."[45] Curiously, Europe's Jews didn't seem to see the danger ahead.[46] The volatile combination exploded when the bottom dropped out of the U.S. economy in 1929. After two more years of political and economic chaos, the German public went to the polls in November 1932 and elected the far right-wing Adolf Hitler to lead the government.

The Nazis, now legally elected to power and supported by a substantial portion of the German public, turned on political opponents and began to single out victim groups, including Gypsies (Roma or Sinti), Jehovah's Witnesses, homosexuals, and "antisocials. Germany's Jewish minority, numbering less than one percent of the nation's population of 62 million, were harassed, marginalized, and forced to sell their business for pennies on the dollar to unscrupulous non-Jews. They were instructed to further identify and humiliate themselves by taking on the middle names of "Israel" and "Sara" and were restricted to certain stores and shopping hours. In addition, they were forced to wear a prominent Star of David. Barred from "German" culture, film, theater, music, art, sports events, most restaurants and cafes, and civic organizations, Germany's approximately 550,000 Jews became terrified pariahs in their own country. Jewish doctors, lawyers, teachers and students, artists and musicians, civil servants and bureaucrats were ignominiously dismissed from the institutions to which they belonged. Lifelong friendships were dissolved.

> Even after a few months of a regime of terror, fidelity and friendship had lost their meaning, and fear and treachery had replaced them. . . . With each day of the Nazi regime, the abyss between us and our fellow citizens grew larger. Friends whom we had loved for years did not know us anymore. They saw that we were different from themselves. Of course we were different, since we were bearing the stigma of Nazi hatred, since we were hunted like deer.[47]

A constant blizzard of laws by the Nazi government reached such lunacy as to forbid Jews to own pets (February 15, 1942).[48] Informers, Gestapo agents, and senseless brutality lurked everywhere, and a thoughtless remark—even a remark overheard—might have dire consequences. Lily Krug described her reaction when an "Aryan" (non-Jewish) neighbor complained to her about the price of butter in front of others: "I hurried away without buying anything. I was frightened. Fear, fear, fear—morning, noon, and night. Fear followed us into our dreams, racking on nerves. How imprudent, how inconsiderate of the woman to speak like that in public."[49]

The economic fate of the Jews continued to deteriorate and further complicated their shattered lives. By November 1938, no more than 20 to 25 percent of all Jewish businesses still remained in Jewish hands; by 1939, dismissals, unemployment, rejections, and marginalization had so impoverished the Jewish communities that more than half (56%)[50] of Germany's Jews were now manual workers who were hated for their poverty and for their reliance on pitiful national assistance payments. Reduced to being considered traitors, foreigners, and a feared bacillus in the body politic, the Jews were at the edge of the precipice. Mass murder was around the corner.

Europe went to war in September 1939, and the massacre of the Jews was conducted under the umbrella of the Second World War. Moreover, the Nazis were willing to murder their own physically and mentally handicapped citizens, even those who were non-Jews. For example, when ministerial superintendent Eugen Stähle, of the Württemberg Grafeneck clinic, where disabled Germans were gassed beginning September 1939, was reproached by the Stuttgart Church Commissioner, Reinhold Sautter, in a private conversation on December 4, 1940, he coolly described the various handicaps of persons "unfit to live" and assured the government official that "The fifth commandment 'thou shalt not kill' is not a commandment from God but merely a Jewish invention."[51]

Once the war began, the Nazis used the opportunity to pursue the near-central obsession of eliminating their racial nemesis, the Jews. That the Germans had long accepted the lunacy that Jews and Communists were interchangeable only made the elimination of the Jews more necessary, they believed, and not a cause for guilt. Four armies of German killers called *Einsatzgruppen*, together with German Order Police and Ukrainian, Belorussian, and Latvian helpers ("Hiwis," short for the German term *Hilfswilligen*),[52] killed Jews in the forests and by the sides of the roads in Poland, Hungary, Russia, and Baltic countries.

> Most of the actions of these mobile killing units more or less followed the same pattern. First they rounded up the Jews in a given area using various ruses to deceive them and relying on local collaborators for denunciations. The Germans ordered large pits dug in some convenient area—a local cemetery, nearby forest, or easily accessible field. Often they forced the prisoners themselves to dig what would be their own graves. At gunpoint they made the victims undress. Then they shot them by groups directly into the graves. In this manner the mobile killing units and their

> accomplices killed around a million people even before construction of killing centers for gassing had begun.[53]

One subunit of *Einsatzgruppen* Army "A" reported that from the invasion of Russia, on June 22, 1941, through November 25, 1941, it had exterminated "1,064 Communists, 56 partisans, 653 mentally ill people, 44 Poles, 28 Russian prisoners of war, 5 Gypsies, 1 Armenian, and 136,421 Jews."[54] There is no indication how they distinguished one group from another.

One SS member was upset, however:

> The victims were shot by the firing squad with carbines, mostly by shots in the back of the head from a distance of one metre on my command. . . . Meanwhile Rottenführer Abraham shot the children with a pistol. There were about five of them. These were children whom I would think were between two and six years. The way Abraham killed the children was brutal. He got hold of some of the children by the hair, lifted them up from the ground, shot them through the back of their heads and threw them into the grave. After a while I just could not watch this any more and I told him to stop. What I meant was he should not lift the children up by the hair, he should kill them in a more decent way.[55]

A staple of German occupation everywhere became a concerted program to incite local anti-Semitic populations to take action against their Jewish minorities. One such example is the infamous story of the small Polish hamlet of Jedwabne, only recently unearthed, where the non-Jewish half of the community clubbed, drowned, gutted, and burned their Jewish neighbors, throwing Jewish infants on pitchforks into burning buildings. This brutal event was only one of many during the war in which the Jews were attacked not by faceless Nazis but by people whose faces and families they knew well.[56]

Germany's Ukrainian, Belorussian, and Latvian helpers (Hiwis) were particularly savage, shooting Jews or "taking them to prison cells already stained with Jewish blood, forced to clean them, and then shot. . . . On one occasion little Nelly Toll watched from the balcony with her cousins as German soldiers beat an old Jewish man. A crowd gathered to laugh and clap."[57] Survivors were rounded up and forced into city ghettos, often living several families to a room, where they were further brutalized and starved by the thousands. Ghettos in Poznan, Lublin, Łodz, Kraków, and Warsaw held tens of thousands of sick and emaciated Jews until the trains took them to their deaths. As the ghettos swelled with Jews from around Europe, the problem of space and the opportunity to commit genocide dawned on the Germans.

The matter was resolved in January 1942 when SS leader Reinhard Heydrich met secretly with representatives of Germany's industry, military, and justice system at the Wannsee Villa in Berlin. In a brief afternoon, they agreed to the unthinkable: the Holocaust. Millions were now condemned at birth to die because of their membership in a religion or ethnic group. With Teutonic precision, the mass murder of the Jews was reaching its ultimate end. Construction bids were solicited, and inmate labor built the camps. There were already some 9,000 concentration camps strewn across Germany and occupied Europe, although they were not necessarily all active at the same time. An inmate could die in any of them, of course, by starvation, disease, or mindless brutality, and many thousands did. However, after the secret decision at the Wannsee Villa in Berlin, a new type of concentration camp was created: extermination camps. Six large installations were constructed in Poland—Auschwitz-Birkenau, Sobibor, Belzec, Majdanek, Chełmno, and Treblinka—whose only mission was to murder the arriving trainloads of victims and burn the bodies.

The West gradually learned about the developing Holocaust early in the war. Through the 1930s, Germany's marginalization of the Jews was known to all, despite Hitler's efforts to sweep violent anti-Semitism under the rug during the Berlin Olympics in 1936. Americans could find the information if interested. In November 1938, for example, photos of burning synagogues in Germany were spread across the front page of the *New York Times*, the flagship of U.S. journalism. On September 14, 1941, the *Times* ran an article headlined "Death Rate Soars in Polish Ghetto" on page 31; other stories about what was going on appeared on June 30, 1942 ("1,000,000 Jews Slain by Nazis, Report Says"), on page 7; on November 25, 1942 ("Himmler Program Kills Polish Jews"), on page 10; on December 4, 1942 ("Two-Thirds of Jews in Poland Slain"), on page 11; on April 21, 1943 ("Warsaw's Ghetto Fights Deportation"), on page 9; on May 15, 1943 ("All Warsaw Jews Held 'Liquidated'"), on page 6; and on October 26, 1943 ("Warsaw Ghetto in Heroic Battle, New Reports on Struggle Reveal"), on page 8. In other words, the information regarding the growing genocide was well known, but readers of America's major newspapers had to read well into the newspapers to find it.

The first eyewitness report arrived as a Western Union telegram at the end of August 1942. Two young men, a German lawyer named Gerhard Riegner, who emigrated to Switzerland, and Jan Karski, a Polish diplomat, learned the horrible details of the Nazi murder program. The information was so startling—that daily trainloads of families were arriving at death centers to be gassed and burned—that the two men decided to reconfirm the unbelievable news. Karski slipped into a ghetto to see conditions firsthand and, dressed as a Ukrainian guard, actually accompanied several death trains. He learned that the reports were indeed accurate. Reigner and Karski wrote the now-famous telegram to Jewish leaders in London and Washington detailing the Nazi program, including the use of prussic acid to gas the Jews and the Gypsies.

To their horror, no one believed them. Wildly frustrated, they spoke to President Franklin Roosevelt, Supreme Court Justices, and community leaders. Their story was considered preposterous, and no action was taken. After they met with the U.S. Supreme Court Justice Felix Frankfurter, the Justice responded that he couldn't believe it. "Not that he thought that Karski was lying," notes Holocaust scholar Doris Bergen, "he could not grasp the enormity of what he had heard."[58] Both Riegner and Karski were haunted by their failure for the rest of their lives.[59]

In July 1942, another German slipped across the border to the safety of Switzerland, where he shared similar information with Swiss authorities. This time the escapee was a well-known German politician and a founder of the German Democratic Party, Ernest Lemmer. He told the Swiss about the gas chambers and about how the Jews were being murdered. All he wanted the Swiss to do was to spread the alarming news. They mistrusted him and did nothing.[60]

If the democracies failed to take the warnings seriously (volumes have been written about what options they had at the time),[61] the victims sensed what awaited them. A survivor recalled that "there were now few optimists among us. We had too many eyewitness reports of the mass killings, both from Jews who had not been mortally wounded and had managed to escape from the execution pits after the Germans had left, and from Gentiles who had watched the killings from a distance."[62] Their greatest fears were confirmed by the occasional sight of Polish farmers on the road to Sobibor shouting, "Jews, you are going to burn!" Another time, Polish peasants gestured to Jews on their way to Treblinka, suggesting that their throats would be cut.[63]

A German guard later described his job at the Treblinka death camp.

> There were always some ill and frail people on the transports. . . . These . . . people were brought to the hospital by a special *Arbeitskommando* and would be taken to the hospital area and stood or laid down at the edge of the grave. When no more ill or wounded were expected it was my job to shoot these people. I did this by shooting them in the neck with a 9-mm pistol. They then collapsed or fell to one side and were carried down into the grave by the two hospital work-Jews. The bodies were sprinkled with chlorinated lime. . . . The number of people I shot after the transport arrived varied. Sometimes it was two or three but sometimes it was as many as twenty or perhaps even more. There were men and women of all ages and there were also children. When I am asked today how many people I killed this way, I can no longer say precisely.[64]

Once the Jews entered the death camp, their lives could usually be measured in minutes. Beaten and forced from their transport trains by SS soldiers and snarling dogs, the Jews were marched to confront a single medical doctor sitting lazily behind a table who, with the wave of his hand, determined who lived and who died. The majority—the young, the old, the infirm, and mothers with children—all died. Bewildered, they were marched toward the four buildings whose chimneys belched a column of thick black smoke and fine, white ash. The few arrivals who were allowed to survive because of their skills or robust health were tattooed and worked until they collapsed and died. Their only crime was that they practiced a particular religion or, in the case of the Gypsies, belonged to a particular ethnic group.

Holocaust scholar Raul Hilberg described the process as a three-stage genocide. First, no Jew was to be overlooked. Status, nationality, and gender didn't matter. The Jews' marginalization and ghettoization were to be relentless and all-encompassing. Second, the complex relationships between Jews and non-Jews were to be severed with the least possible harm to the German economy. Third, "[t]he killings had to be conducted in a manner that would limit psychological repercussions in the ranks of the perpetrators, prevent unrest among the victims, and preclude anxiety or protest in the non-Jewish population."[65]

The only thing that the Jews murdered in the Holocaust shared was their religion. Their extermination was different from mass murder; it reached the level of genocide. Heinrich Himmler, head of the SS and the Gestapo, described the Nazis' goal as he spoke to a group of SS Group Leaders in Posen, Poland, in a notorious private speech on October 4, 1943:

> I shall speak to you here with all the frankness of a serious subject. We shall now discuss it absolutely openly among ourselves, nevertheless we shall never speak of it in public. I mean the evacuation of the Jews, the extermination of the Jewish race. . . . Most of you know what it means to see a hundred corpses lying together, five hundred, or a thousand. To have gone through this and yet—apart from a few exceptions, examples of human weakness—to have remained decent fellows, this is what has made us hard. This is a glorious page in our history that has never been written and shall never be written. . . . We had the moral right, we had the duty to our people, to destroy people which wanted to destroy us.[66]

When the war ended in Europe, on May 8, 1945, millions of Jews (as well as Roma and Sinti) had perished at the hands of the Nazis and their Ukrainian and Baltic helpers. Unknown thousands were tortured and murdered in forests, prison cells, and gas chambers. Jews were beaten to death before cheering crowds and hanged from apartment balconies, their bodies discarded in unknown mass graves throughout Eastern Europe or thrown on burning pyres. So many died at the hands of so many people, in fact, that the exact number of victims is still debated. Gerald Reitlinger (in 1953) said that 4,578,800 Jews had been murdered, Raul Hilberg put the number at

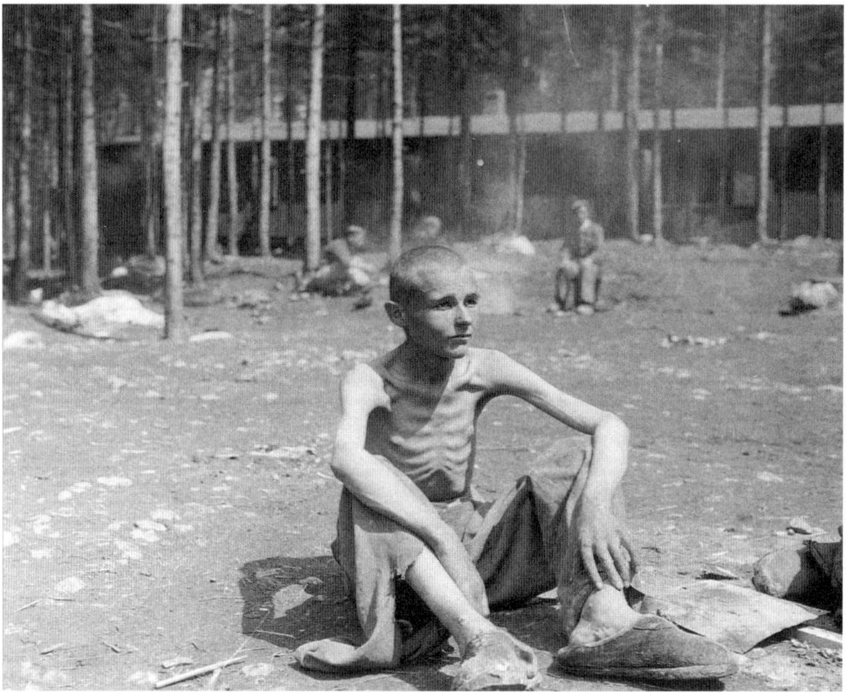

Stunned at the reality of liberation, a single starved survivor sits to await his future, April 23, 1945. (National Archives and Record Administration. U.S. Signal Corps SC-264694, Box 480)

5,109,822 (in 1961), Yisrael Gutman and Robert Rozett at 5,859,622 (1990), and Wolfgang Benz at 6,269,097[67]—the numbers increasing as research improved and the Russian archives became available.[68] Sadly, the numbers may continue to increase as more diaries are unearthed and forgotten mass graves come to light.

Pol Pot and the Khmer Rouge in Cambodia

After the United States had withdrawn its troops from Vietnam and the Cambodian government, plagued by corruption and incompetence, had lost its American military support, both by 1975, the situation in Cambodia was ready for a coup. Taking advantage of the vacuum, a French-educated 50-year-old revolutionary, the son of prosperous farmers, marched his largely teenage guerrillas into the capital city, Phnom Penh, on April 17 and, after nearly five years of fighting the government, effectively seized control of

Cambodia. Once in power, Pol Pot, besotted with Mao's vision of recreating a new society by sweeping aside the old, began a radical experiment to create a communist agrarian utopia inspired in part by his hero's Cultural Revolution, which he had witnessed firsthand during a visit to the People's Republic of China. He renamed the country the Democratic Republic of Kampuchea and, under the pretense of an imminent U.S. bombing attack, ordered the forced evacuation of the major cities at gunpoint. Those who refused to leave were shot, as were hospital patients who were unable to walk. At Phnom Penh, 2 million inhabitants were driven into the countryside; as many as 20,000 died along the way.

With the country under tight control by Pol Pot and the Khmer Rouge Army, the new ruler embarked on his own "Super Leap Forward" to turn Cambodia into a peasant economy in which there would be no class divisions, no money, no books, no schools, and no hospitals. People replaced draft animals, families were separated, and masses of workers were moved to areas of supposed labor shortages. Once they were marched into the countryside, their biographies were repeatedly scoured for signs that they harbored an "enemy virus"—that they opposed the government.

Cambodia's borders were sealed, and the country was closed to outside eyes. Those who objected to any command were executed on the spot, as was anyone who able to read or write, as was so frighteningly portrayed in the film *The Killing Fields*. Anyone who wore eyeglasses was considered a class enemy and was executed. The same thing happened in all the cities and towns, and the whole country was effectively turned into a vast forced-labor camp.

Pol Pot expelled all foreigners, and embassies were closed. Any foreign economic or medical assistance was refused. The use of foreign languages was banned. Newspapers and television stations were shut down, radios and bicycles confiscated, and mail and telephone usage curtailed. Money was forbidden. All businesses were shuttered, religion banned, education halted, health care eliminated, and parental authority revoked. Thus, Cambodia was sealed off from the outside world.[69]

The killings were brutal and random and almost limitless.

> One of the killers, a prison guard named Siv Samon, recounted that on 12 August 1978 a memo arrived from the local security office "to purge away the lives of the people. We had eight people altogether [assigned to the death squad]. We were to kill 250 people of Krosaom Ark . . . they were clubbed on the backside of the head with bamboo pipes and kicked into pits. I myself killed twenty of those people.[70]

A single example of those four terrible years may be seen in the document found in the archives—a page from the "execution log":

> Dated July 23, 1977 . . . the typewritten form lists biographical details on eighteen prisoners executed that day, and almost an afterthought . . . a handwritten note at the bottom from the chief guard adds, "Also killed 160 children today for a total of 178 enemies killed."[71]

"Reactionary religion" was banned in the constitution of January 1976. Ethnic groups were attacked, including the three largest minorities: the Vietnamese, Chinese, and Cham Muslims. Fifty percent of the estimated 425,000 Chinese living in Cambodia in 1975 perished. Khmer Rouge also forced Muslims to eat pork and shot those who hesitated.

Eventually, as in so many revolutions, the Khmer Rouge began to feed on its own. The Communist Party's leaders and rank and file alike followed ordinary people into the maw of the Khmer Rouge killing machine.

Since 1994, the award-winning Cambodian Genocide Program, a project of the Genocide Studies Program at Yale University, has catalogued 158 individual prisons run by Pol Pot's Khmer Rouge regime from 1975 to1979 and has analyzed 309 mass-grave sites with an estimated 19,000 grave pits. The Cambodian genocide, in which approximately 1.7 million people (21% of the country's population) lost their lives, was one of the worst human tragedies of the century.[72] Authoritative estimates suggest that as much as one-third of the population of Cambodia was purged under Pol Pot's regime.[73]

As in every act of genocide, the effects continued long after the killings ended. In the case of Cambodia, there was "a dearth of approximately 570,000 births during the Khmer Rouge years, 1975–1978 . . . caused by famine, family dislocation, the near-complete breakdown of public health and medical systems, and massive losses of women and men (two-thirds male and one-third female) in reproductive ages."[74] Madness abounded.

> "Sometimes I laugh or cry for no reason" says one woman. During DK [The so-called "Democratic Kampuchea," Cambodia's name under Pol Pot's regime] she was sent to Pursat province and suffered the deaths of her parents, husband, four children, and siblings. Villagers have heard that she went "crazy" at some point, weeping and refusing to get up despite threats from DK cadre who also accused her of "laziness" and malingering.[75]

Perhaps the most appalling thing about all this, notes expert Craig Etcheson, is that, 25 years after the end of the Khmer Rouge regime, no senior leader of the Khmer Rouge has ever been brought before a court of law to answer for the heinous crimes that the government committed upon its population.[76] Pol Pot, the communist dictator whose lunacy led his army of teenage killers to murder and torture nearly 2 million people, finally lost control of the Khmer Rouge. In April 1998, Pol Pot, age 73, died of an apparent heart attack following his arrest but before he could be brought to trial by an international tribunal.

Genocide in Bosnia

The Balkans region is mountainous and its inhabitants have long memories of the hundreds of years of ethnic tensions and fighting in the area, fanned by intense religious loyalties to the three dominant religions—Islam, Serbian Orthodoxy, and Catholicism. Passions and hatreds have barely been held in check by their Austro-Hungarian and, later, Communist rulers. Bosnia-Herzegovina is especially vulnerable to change since it is a multi-ethnic state, a confused patchwork of religious and ethnic groups tucked between Croatia (Catholic) on one side and Serbia (Serbian Orthodox Church) on the other, scattered across much of the former Yugoslavia. Roy Gutman, the *Newsday* reporter who broke the story of Serbian ethnic cleansing, described Bosnia-Herzegovina "as a genuine melting pot" characterized by "an atmosphere of secular tolerance" during the 1970s and 1980s, when Yugoslav youth were far more preoccupied with acquiring the trappings of Western European life—color TV, video games, rock concerts, Madonna, and MTV—than with religious strife.[77] Marshal Josip Tito's death, in May 1980, at the age of 92, and the collapse of communism in 1989, changed all the rules. Without a strong hand to contain them, old hatreds erupted, and the Bosnian Serbs (31% of the population) unleashed a genocidal war against the Bosnian Muslims (44%) and the Bosnian Croats (17%).

Two events in the nearby Balkan state of Serbia laid the foundation for what was to follow. Perhaps most important was a Memorandum written in 1986 by the Serbian Academy of Arts and Sciences. The historical road to a "Greater Serbia," which would include Bosnia-Herzegovina, had only been interrupted by the years of communist control. Now that Tito was gone, the Memorandum thundered, it was time to unite all the Serbs in a single national state. As the Memorandum expressed it, "the establishment of the full national integrity of the Serbian people, regardless of which republic or province it inhabits, is its historic and democratic right."[78] Other ethnic groups, especially the Muslim communities, would have to get out of the way, voluntarily or involuntarily.

The secondary contributor to the massacres to follow, as analyzed by Norman Cigar, was the publication in 1982 of a best-selling novel called *Nož* (Knife), by popular author Vuk Drašković. The story is set during World War II, a time of particular sensitivity to East Europeans, who were buffeted between fascism and communism. Drašković portrays the Muslim characters as treacherous, cold-blooded murderers, while the Serbs are pictured as long-suffering patriots, likened to the martyred Jews of Nazi

Germany—marginalized, threatened, and facing extinction. The entire Serbian population throbbed with a call for a Greater Serbia, expanding into Bosnia-Herzegovina to unite with their ethic brothers. The annexation of Bosnia-Herzegovina brought with it nearly 2 million Muslims. It did not take long for the simmering hatred of the Muslims, already present, to break into the open. Newspapers and radio stations picked up the drumbeat—or perhaps, as in Rwanda, orchestrated the drumbeat. Muslims were accused of planning to create an Islamic state at the expense of destroying the Serbs. Muslims, then, were the enemy, and killing them was not only patriotic but an act of self-defense. A Serbian commander later admitted, "I beat up many Muslims and Croatians on vacation in Cavat because of his [Drašković's] *Nož*. Reading that book, I would see red. I would get up and select the biggest fellow on the beach, and smash his teeth."[79]

Rising nationalism and popular books were not sufficient to cause the genocidal horrors that were to follow. Direction came from Belgrade, the capital of Serbia, and the government leader, Slobodan Milošević, head of the Socialist Party of Serbia (SPS). Milošević's fiery speeches, his military muscle, along with the media and the government's financial support, and political machinery, triggered and sustained the subsequent violence. In the vacuum left by retreating communism, he took control of Serbia and proceeded to finance and orchestrate street violence in order to consolidate Serbia's hold over the two autonomous provinces of Vojvodina and Kosovo. Milošević and the new Greater Serbia movement were greatly supported by the Serbian Orthodox Church, which helped organize, finance, and arm some of the most bloodthirsty Serbian thugs of the genocide, many under the control of the warlord Željko Ražnatović ("Arkan").

Even as events unfolded, many Muslims found it difficult to understand what was happening around them. A small percentage formed local militias for protection as well as revenge, but the majority didn't even arm themselves. When groups of Serb thugs burst into Muslim homes and demanded their firearms, families readily handed over the guns to maintain peace. Despite their substantial numbers, the Muslims had few options. Some converted to the Serbian Orthodox Church or "Serbianized" their names for safety, a number emigrated if they could, but the majority of Muslims did what victim groups—Armenians, Rwandan Tutsis, the Jews under the Nazis, the Cambodians—almost always do: hide and hope that sanity, international peacekeepers, or their God will step in to protect them. And, like most other victim groups, the Muslim population of Bosnia-Herzegovina found itself without international help.

The marginalization and ethnic cleansing of the Muslims by the Serbs was every bit as violent as that of the Jews in the years leading to the Holocaust. In November 1991, Serb forces committed one of the most egregious acts when they besieged the Croatian town of Vukovar and murdered more than 200 patients (mostly wounded Croatian soldiers) in the Vukovar hospital and unceremoniously dumped their bodies in a mass grave. By 1992, anti-Muslim posters and news stories were rampant, punctuated by senseless murders committed by roving gangs of Serbian thugs. Soon, televised announcements in towns like Banja Luka set a quota on the number of Muslims allowed to live in the town—1,000 out of 28,000; the rest would have to go. In the town of Bijeljina, local television announced that only 5 percent of the Muslim population could remain. In other cities, like Kozarać, in northwest Bosnia-Herzegovina, houses were color-coded according to the owner's ethnicity and then destroyed systematically. Not unlike the Armenians when assaulted by the Turks in 1915, prominent local Muslim intellectuals were identified, arrested, and marked for extermination. Once Kozarać had fallen under Serb control, Serbian vehicles with loudspeakers roamed the streets, accompanied by tanks, blaring: "Muslims get out! Surrender and everyone will be safe." Despite these assurances, between 2,500 and 3,000 Muslims were killed.[80] Mosques were routinely cordoned off by the authorities and blown up. In the town of Bratunać, a local Muslim cleric was dragged to the soccer stadium, where he was tortured, forced to drink alcohol, eat pork, and make the sign of the cross before being executed to the cheers of the crowd. Those Muslims who escaped were deprived of their livelihood; their lights and utilities were cut off, and they were murdered and raped indiscriminately.

The Serbs also launched an attack on the beautiful and historic Croatian town of Dubrovnik on the Dalmatian coast, a World Heritage site protected by the UN Educational, Scientific, and Cultural Organization (UNESCO).

It is widely accepted that these events, and the thousands of deaths that followed, were planned by Serbian government officials in Belgrade, Serbia, and in Sarajevo, Bosnia-Herzegovina, and were often carried out by the police and Yugoslav Army soldiers under control of General Ratko Mladić, commander of the Bosnian Serb Army, and his minions. Although neither the Croats nor the Muslims are without blame for senseless murders of some on the other side, the U.S. Central Intelligence Agency (CIA) concluded in a classified report that the Serbs carried out 90 percent of war crimes and that they were the only one of the three groups that systematically attempted to "eliminate all traces of other ethnic groups from their territory."[81] According to the United Nations Special Commission of Experts, 6 percent of the remaining atrocities were perpetrated by Croat extremists and 4 percent by Muslim extremists.[82]

As towns and villages fell under the control of the Serb forces or ordinary civilians who decided to turn on their neighbors, the atrocities mounted. Helsinki Watch, which monitors such excesses for the prestigious organization Human Rights Watch, catalogued two complete volumes of random murders, rapes, torture, and the "disappearance" of thousands of non-Serb men of military age. Witnesses were interviewed and medical records were examined to corroborate the witnesses' testimony. As an example,

> Zdravko Brkić (born 1959) suffered from broken facial bones. His tenth and eleventh ribs had been broken. His eyelids had been burned. The doctor believed that the injuries to Brkić's eyelids had been inflicted by cigarette burns. Brkić also suffered from a damaged right kidney and a mild concussion. The medical report stated that the wounds varied in age, i.e., that they were inflicted at different periods during the nine days of detention, thus confirming that the man had been beaten on several occasions.[83]

When the mayor of the Serb-controlled town of Skender Vakuf, Boris Matišić, together with a soldier, Zvonko Volković, went to meet with the commander of the Serbian forces, they were handcuffed together. They reported:

> three men beat us in front of the post office for approximately five minutes . . . one of the men repeatedly punched Volković directly in his kidneys. One police officer held him while another beat him. . . . I was punched in the face several times and a tooth was broken. While we were walking through the hallway, we could hear the screaming from the cells. We presumed that people were being beaten or otherwise tortured. It took us about 30 minutes to walk through the hallway because we were constantly being hit. They would kick us in the testicles and when we would fall to the floor, they would then kick us again. . . . We were released at 5 A.M.[84]

According to Helsinki Watch:

> Yugoslav armed forces have shelled hospitals in Croatia. Hospitals in Osijek, Pakrac, Vinkovci, Vukovar, and Zadar have all been damaged or destroyed by aerial, mortar and artillery attacks. During the course of three days, from September 14–17, Osijek hospital was hit 56 times by mortar shells, 21 times by tank shells, and 17 times by rockets from multiple rocket launchers. The hospital was also hit by bullets from light weaponry. During one attack a 38-year old nurse was killed and two doctors were wounded. Most of the hospital wards, including the intensive care unit, were damaged during the attack.[85]

Then came the appearance of the infamous concentration camps—94 prisons, stadiums, schools, and military barracks whose gaunt inmates, staring vacantly from behind the barbed wire, shocked the civilized world of the mid-1990s. In the heart of "civilized" Europe, Serbian forces set up concentration camps, deported non-Serbs in cattle cars, destroyed towns and villages, organized the systematic rape of Croat and Muslim women, and, despite at least one scholarly book, *The Myth of Ethnic War: Serbia and Croatia in the 1990s*,[86] targeted civilians for ethnic cleansing.

In 1993, mid-way through the war, the Croats entered the war against their former Muslim allies, using many of the same methods as the Serbs—"terror, deportations, concentration camps, indiscriminate bombardments of civilians, massacres, the blocking of humanitarian aid, destruction of religious shrines, and the appropriation of property."[87]

According to the authoritative Helsinki Watch once again:

> Croatian forces maintain more than nine detention centers throughout Croatia, including Bjelovar, Gospić, Zadar, Split, Rijeka, Slavonska Požega, Osijek and several in the municipalities of Karlovac and Zagreb. *Helsinki Watch* has documented cases of torture and mistreatment of prisoners after they have been arrested and detained by the Croatian Army or police. In many cases, abuse of captives also takes place in local police stations. . . . J.K., who was among those arrested in Marino Selo, was beaten during his detention. J.K.'s lower jaw and two ribs were broken and all his teeth were knocked out. When Helsinki Watch spoke to J.K. and his doctor, surgery had been performed on his jaw and metal teeth had been implanted in his mouth.[88]

Estimates of the number of people killed in the Bosnian war between 1992 and 1995 vary widely, ranging anywhere from 25,000 to 300,000. In 2006, an international team of scientists concluded, after three years of research visits to some 300 graveyards and thousands of interviews, that the exact number of people killed is 97,207. "But," says Mirsad Tokaca, head of the investigative post conflict commission, the so-called Bosnian Book of the Dead Project, "the figure could rise by a maximum of another 10,000 due to ongoing research." Moreover, the figure of 97,000 "doesn't include those who died during the war in accidents, starvation or for lack of medication"[89]—the cause of a high, but unknown, number of deaths.

There is no lack of people to blame, however. Slobodan Milošević, the (Serbian) Yugoslav president during the war, and Biljana Plavić, the Bosnian Serb vice president, commanded the government and military and were a driving force in the expansion of a Greater Serbia at the expense of the Muslims and Croats. Both enthusiastically planned and implemented the ethnic cleansing of non-Serbs. Equally culpable is Radovan Karadzić, the political head of the Bosnian Serbs, and the men who led the killers, like Ratko Mladić, the military commander; Radislav Krstić, a high-ranking general; and militia leaders Željko Ražnatović ("Arkan") and Vojislav Šešelj, whose units of murderous thugs were responsible for countless rapes and killings. Under their direction, thousands of Serbs murdered their neighbors, and the Croats and Muslim extremists responded with a vengeance.

The mass murders in the Balkans shook Europeans' conscience to its core. Gruesome photographs jumped out at the world from magazines and newsreels for nearly a decade. This was Europe, after all, not a distant African country like Rwanda or a country in Southeast Asia, like Cambodia. Belgrade was no more than 600 miles from Berlin or 900 miles from Paris. Less than 50 years earlier, fascist Europe had had its own program to exterminate millions of Jews, Poles, Gypsies, and Russian prisoners of war and had fought and lost a devastating war as a result. In spite of that history, the Europeans did little to bring peace to the region. It's true that the United Nations placed an embargo against incoming shipments of weapons. The U.S. ambassador to the UN at the time, Cyrus Vance, negotiated a separation of the warring Serbs and Croats and the insertion of blue-helmeted UN peacekeepers. Thousands, however, continued to perish.

The famous filmmaker Steven Spielberg was quoted in a *Newsweek* article by David Ansen as saying, "[My motivation for making *Schindler's List*] was a combination of things: my interest in the Holocaust and my horror at the symptoms of the Shoah again happening in Bosnia. We were racing over these moments in world history that were exactly what happened in 1943." "I was throwing up my hands," Spielberg remembers saying, " 'My God, it's happening again.' "[90]

Notes

1. Frank Chalk and Kurt Jonassohn, *The History and Sociology of Genocide: Analyses and Case Studies* (New Haven, CT: Yale University Press, 1990), p. 23.
2. Bill Berkeley, "Sounds of Violence: Rwanda's Killer Radio," *New Republic*, August 22, 1994, p. 18–19.
3. Neil J. Kressel, *Mass Hate: The Global Rise of Genocide and Terror*, rev. ed. (New York: Plenum Press, 2002), p. 93.
4. Colette Braeckman, "Incitement to Genocide," in *Crimes of War: What the Public Should Know*, ed. Roy Gutman and David Rieff (New York and London: Norton, 1999), pp. 192–194.
5. R. J. Rummel, "Deadlier Than War," *Institute of Public Affairs Review* 41, no. 2 (August-October, 1987): 24–30, and Rummel, *Death by Government* (New Brunswick, NJ, and London: Transaction, 1994).
6. Irving L. Horowitz, "Science, Modernity and Authorized Terror: Reconsidering the Genocidal State," in *Studies in Comparative Genocide*, ed. Levon Chorbajian and George Shirinian (London and New York: Macmillan and St. Martin's Press, 1999), p. 16.
7. Horst Drechsler, *"Let Us Die Fighting": The Struggle of the Herero and the Nama against German Imperialism (1884–1915)* (London: Zed Press, 1980), p. 157.

8. Mahmood Mamdani, *When Victims Become Killers: Colonialism, Nativism, and the Genocide in Rwanda* (Princeton, NJ: Princeton University Press, 2001), pp. 11–12.

9. Cited in Jan-Bart Gewald, *Herero Heroes: A Socio-Political History of the Herero of Namibia, 1890–1923* (Oxford: James Currey, 1999), p. 173.

10. Benjamin Madley, "From Africa to Auschwitz: How German South West Africa Incubated Ideas and Methods Adopted and Developed by the Nazis in Eastern Europe," *European History Quarterly* 35, no. 3 (2005): 429–464; Jűrgen Zimmerer, "The Birth of the 'Ostland' Out of the Spirit of Colonialism. A Postcolonial Perspective on the Nazi Policy of Conquest and Extermination," *Patterns of Prejudice* 39, no. 2 (2005): 197–219.

11. Jean Suret-Canale, *French Colonialism in Tropical Africa, 1900–1945*, trans. by Till Gottheiner (New York: Pica Press, 1971), p. 202. Quoted in Kurt Jonassohn with Karin Solveig Björnson, *Genocide and Gross Human Rights Violations in Comparative Perspective* (New Brunswick, NJ, and London: Transaction, 1998), p. 243.

12. Jonassohn, *Genocide and Gross Human Rights*, p. 243.

13. Mamdani, *When Victims Become Killers*, pp. 4, 6.

14. Kressel, *Mass Hate*, p. 94.

15. Philip Gourevitch, *We Wish to Inform You That Tomorrow We Will Be killed with Our Families: Stories from Rwanda* (New York: Farrar, Straus and Giroux, 1998), p. 65.

16. Ibid., p. 4; See also Gregory Stanton, "Could the Rwandan Genocide have been prevented?" *Journal of Genocide Research* 6, no. 2(June 2004): 211–228. See, especially, the "Special Issue," *Genocide Studies and Prevention: The 1994 Rwandan Genocide* 2, no. 3 (November 2007).

17. See, for example, Christopher Browning, "Genocide and Public Health: German Doctors and Polish Jews, 1939–1941," in *The Path to Genocide: Essays on Launching the Final Solution* (Cambridge: Cambridge University Press, 1992), pp. 145–168.

18. Bernard Shane, *The Cajuns: Americanization of a People* (Jackson: University Press of Mississippi, 2003).

19. Andrew Jacobs, "Good Will in China Was Fleeting," *International Herald Tribune*, July 16, 2009, p. 2.

20. Raphael Lemkin, *Axis Rule in Occupied Europe; Laws of Occupation, Analysis of Government, Proposals for Redress* (New York: H. Fertig, 1944).

21. John Cooper, *Raphael Lemkin and the Struggle for the Genocide Convention* (Basingstoke, England, and New York: Palgrave Macmillan, 2008).

22. Pierre van den Berghe, *State Violence and Ethnicity* (Niwot: University Press of Colorado, 1990) pp. 1–4.

23. Horowitz, "Science, Modernity and Authorized Terror," pp. 15–30,

24. Quoted in G. S. Graber, *Caravans to Oblivion: The Armenian Genocide* (1915, repr., New York: John Wiley & Sons, 1996), pp. 87–88.

25. Vahakn N. Dadrian and Dadria N. Vahakn, *The History of the Armenian Genocide: Ethnic Conflict from the Balkans to Anatolia to the Caucasus* (Providence, RI: Berghahn Books, 1995), p. 221. See, especially, the "Special Issue on the Armenian Genocide," *Genocide Studies and Prevention* 1, no. 2 (September 2006).

26. Henry Morgenthau, *Ambassador Morgenthau's Story* (Garden City, NY: Doubleday, 1918), p. 307.

27. Ibid., p. 26.

28. Armen Hairapetian, "'Race Problems' and the Armenian Genocide: The State Department File," *Armenian Review* 37, no. 1 (Spring 1984): 111–112. See http://www.armenianreview.org/Thirtysevenvolume.htm#one.

29. *Treatment of Armenians in the Ottoman Empire: Documents Presented to Viscount Grey of Fallodon, Secretary of State for Foreign Affairs*, preface by Viscount Bryce, Account 22 (London: Sir Joseph Causton & Sons, 1916), pp. 85–86.

30. Morgenthau, *Ambassador Morgenthau's Story*, p. 333.

31. Ibid., pp. 336–337.

32. Discussed in Donald E. Miller and Lorna Touryan Miller, *Survivors: An Oral History of the Armenian Genocide* (Berkeley: University of California Press, 1993), pp. 92–93. This is the best book available on the accounts of many who survived.

33. Vahakn N. Dadrian, *German Responsibility in the Armenian Genocide: A Review of the Historical Evidence of German Complicity* (Watertown, MA: Blue Crane, 1996), pp. 263–265.

34. Ibid., p. 256.

35. Laura J. Berberian, "Official United States Documents on the Armenian Genocide: An Annotated Bibliography" (Master's thesis, University of North Carolina at Chapel Hill, 2008), pp. 6–7.

36. Kevork B. Bardakjian, *Hitler and the Armenian Genocide* (Cambridge, MA: Zoryan Institute, 1985). The Nuremberg Tribunal identified this speech as L-3 or Exhibit USA-28. The identical document appeared Louis P. Lochner, *What about Germany?* (New York: Dodd, Mead, 1942), pp. 1–4.

37. Omer Bartov, "Industrial Killing: World War I, the Holocaust, and Representation." http://www.millersville.edu/~holo-con/bartov.html.

38. Richard Weikart, "Darwinism and Death: Devaluing Human Life in Germany 1859–1920," *Journal of the History of Ideas* 63, no. 2 (April 2002): 323–344.

39. Beth A. Griech-Polelle, "Review of Richard Koenigsberg's Lecture: The Logic of Mass Murder: Hitler the Holocaust and War." http://www.ideologiesofwar.com/docs/bgp_rk.htm 3/9/2009. See also Brian E. Crim, "We Ourselves Are the War: Understanding the Relationship between the First World War and the Holocaust." http://www.ideologiesofwar.com/docs/bgp_rk.htm 3/9/2009.

40. Ibid., and Richard A. Koenigsberg, *Hitler's Ideology: A Study in Psychoanalytic Sociology* (New York: Library of Social Science, 1975). See also Koenigsberg, *Nations Have the Right to Kill: Hitler, the Holocaust and War* (New York: Library of Social Science, 2009).

41. See, for example, Raul Hilberg, *The Destruction of the European Jews*, rev. ed., vol. 3 (New York: Holmes and Meier, 1985), p. 1202. On August 22, 1939, a few days before the official start of World War II, Hitler also authorized his commanders to kill "without pity or mercy, all men, women, and children of Polish descent or language. Only in this way can we obtain the living space we need." www.holocaustforgotten.com/poland.htm. Also see Richard C. Lukas, *The Forgotten Holocaust: The Poles under German Occupation, 1939–1944* (New York: Hippocrene Books, 1989).

42. Jackson Nyamuya Maogoto, *War Crimes and Realpolitic: International Justice from World War I to the 21st Century* (Boulder, CO: Lynne Rienner, 2004), p. 84.

43. Omer Bartov, *The Eastern Front: German Troops and the Barbarism of Warfare* (Basingstoke, Hampshire: Macmillan, in association with St. Anthony's College, Oxford, 1985), p. 110.

44. Peter Calvocoressi and Guy Wint, *Total War: The Story of World War II* (New York: Pantheon Books, 1972). See also Hamburg Institute for Social Research, ed., *The German Army and Genocide: Crimes against War Prisoners, Jews, and Other Civilians, 1939–1944* (New York: Hamburg Institute for Social Research, 1999).

45. Cited in Marion A. Kaplan, *Between Dignity and Despair: Jewish Life in Nazi Germany* (New York and Oxford: Oxford University Press, 1998), p, 13.

46. Sidney M. Bolkosky, *The Distorted Image: German Jewish Perceptions of Germans and Germany, 1918–1935* (New York: Elsevier Scientific, 1975).

47. Cited in Kaplan, *Between Dignity and Despair,* p. 41.

48. Boria Sax, *Animals in the Third Reich: Pets, Scapegoats, and the Holocaust* (London and Harrisburg, PA: Continuum International, 2000), p.182.

49. Cited in Kaplan, *Between Dignity and Despair,* p. 21.

50. Ibid., p. 31.

51. Michael Naumann, translation of his speech to the final panel on January 28, 2000, at the International Forum on the Holocaust, "A Conference on Education, Remembrance and Research," Stockholm, January 26–28, 2000. http://www.holocaustforum.gov.se/conference/official_documents/speeches/naumann_eng.htm.

52. Christopher R. Browning, *Ordinary Men: Reserve Police Battalion 101 and the Final Solution in Poland* (New York: HarperCollins, 1992), pp. 52, 80–81, 83–85, 89–91, 93–95, 99, 104, 106, 107–110, 115, 158, 163; see also Dean Martin, *Collaboration in the Holocaust: Crimes of the Local Police in Belorussia and Ukraine, 1941–1944* (New York: St. Martin's Press, 2000).

53. Doris L. Bergen, *War and Genocide: A Concise History of the Holocaust* (Lanham, MD.: Rowman & Littlefield, 2003), p. 150.

54. Hans Buchheim et al., *Anatomie des S.S. Staates,* Vol. II (Olten and Freiburg im Breisgau: DTV [German Paperback Publisher]: 1965), p. 302.

55. Ernest Klee, Willi Dressen, and Volker Riess (eds.), *The Good Old Days: The Holocaust as Seen by Its Perpetrators and Bystanders* (New York: Konecky and Konecky, 1991), p. 197. See also Rudolf Höss, Pery Broad, Johann Paul Kremer, eds., *KZ Auschwitz Seen by the SS.* Foreword by Jerzy Rawicz (Oświęcim, Poland: Auschwitz-Birkenau State Museum, 1998).

56. Jan Gross, *Neighbors: The Destruction of the Jewish Community in Jedwabne, Poland* (Princeton, NJ, and Oxford: Princeton University Press, 2001).

57. Bergen, *War and Genocide,* p.148.

58. Ibid., p. 195.

59. Raul Hilberg, *Perpetrators, Victims, Bystanders* (New York: HarperPerennial, 1993), pp. 220–224.

60. Walter Laqueur, *The Terrible Secret* (Boston and Toronto: Little, Brown, 1980), pp. 211–213.

61. See Michael J. Neufeld and Michael Berenbaum (eds.), *The Bombing of Auschwitz: Should the Allies Have Attempted It?* (New York: St. Martin's Press, 2000).

62. Henry Orenstein, *"I Shall Live": Surviving against All Odds, 1939–1945* (New York: Beaufort, 1987), p. 75.

63. Cited in Hilberg, *Perpetrators, Victims, Bystanders*, p. 216.

64. Klee, Dressen, and Riess, *The Good Old Days*, p. 247.

65. Hilberg, *Perpetrators, Victims, Bystanders*, p. 20.

66. For complete text in both English and German, see http://www.historyplace.com/worldwar2/holocaust/h-posen.htm.

67. Gerald Reitlinger, *The Final Solution* (New York: Beechhurst Press, 1953); Yisrael Gutman and Robert Rozett, "Estimated Jewish Losses in the Holocaust," *Encyclopedia of the Holocaust*, vol. 4 (New York: Macmillan, 1990); Wolfgang Benz, *Dimension des Volkermords: Die Zahl der Jüdischen Opfer des Nationalsocialismus* (Munich: Deutscher Taschenbuch Verlag, 1991).

68. Michael Shermer and Alex Grobman, *Denying History: Who Says the Holocaust Never Happened and Why Do They Say It* (Berkeley: University of California Press, 2000), p. 177.

69. See Unexplained Mysteries of Cambodia Genocide (Pol Pot) 1975–1979, 2,000,000 Deaths, http://theunexplainedmysteries.com/pol-pot.html.

70. Craig Etcheson, *After the Killing Fields: Lessons from the Cambodian Genocide* (Westport, CT: Praeger, 2005), p. 83.

71. Ibid.

72. Ben Kiernan, "The Demography of Genocide in Southeast Asia: The Death Tolls in Cambodia, 1975–79, and East Timor, 1975–80," *Critical Asian Studies* 35, no. 4 (December 2003): pp. 585–597.

73. Ibid., p. 10.

74. Judith Banister and Paige Johnson, "After the Nightmare: The Population of Cambodia," in *Genocide and Democracy in Cambodia: The Khmer Rouge, The United Nations, and the International Community*, ed. Ben Kiernan, Monograph Series 41/Yale Southeast Asia Studies (New Haven: Yale University Law School, 1993), p. 66.

75. Ibid., fn. 26, p. 63.

76. Etcheson, *After the Killing Fields*, p. 10.

77. Neil J. Kressel, *Mass Hate: The Global Rise of Genocide and Terror* (Cambridge, MA: Westview Press, 2002), p. 14; also revised edition, p. 93.

78. Cited in Norman Cigar, *Genocide in Bosnia: The Policy of "Ethnic Cleansing"* (College Station: Texas A&M University Press, 1995), p. 23.

79. Ibid., p. 25.

80. Ibid., p. 56.

81. Roger Cohen, "C.I.A. Report on Bosnia Blames Serbs for 90% of the War Crimes," *New York Times*, March 9, 1995, p. 1A.

82. Florence Hartmann, "Bosnia," in Gutmann and Rieff, *Crimes of War*, p. 56.

83. Helsinki Watch Report, *War Crimes in Bosnia-Herzegovina*, vol. I (New York, Washington, Los Angeles and London: Human Rights Watch World Report, 1992), pp. 103–104.

84. Ibid., p. 93.

85. Ibid., p. 295.

86. V. P. Gagnon, *The Myth of Ethnic War: Serbia and Croatia in the 1990s* (Ithaca, NY, and London: Cornell University Press, 2004).

87. Florence Hartmann, "Bosnia," in Gutmann and Rieff, *Crimes of War*, p. 56.

88. Helsinki Watch Report, *War Crimes in Bosnia-Herzegovina*, p. 319.

89. "Research Shows Estimates of Bosnian War Death Toll Were Inflated," *International Herald Tribune*, June 21, 2007. Also see the prize-winning analysis by Victor Peskin, *International Justice in Rwanda and the Balkans: Virtual Trials and the Struggle for State Cooperation* (Cambridge, UK: Cambridge University Press, 2008), pp. 40–47.

90. David Ansen, "Spielberg's Obsession," *Newsweek*, December 20, 1993, p.112; Susan Spillman, "Spielberg in Black and White: 'Schindler's List' a Work of History," *USA Today*, December 10, 1993, p. 1D.

CHAPTER 4

Punishment, at Last

War crimes, especially genocide, cry out for punishment. What could be more repugnant than crimes committed by armed forces against helpless civilians—against women, children, or wounded prisoners? Yet, most war criminals go unpunished. Churches are burned down by faceless rampaging troops, children are murdered, and women are raped by unknown assailants—and when the wars are over, the culprits too often return to their old lives. Even if the war criminal is caught, the theft or destruction of, say, religious property may bring a mild reprimand; harming innocent civilians historically receives no more than a judicial yawn. War crimes are generally ignored, forgotten, or repressed in the memories of veterans and history, while survivors nurse their hatreds in legend, song, and the potential for revenge.[1]

The points here are twofold. The first is that the mass murder of entire racial or religious minorities is particularly difficult to punish, since a large percentage of the population participated in the murders. Whom do you punish when the majority of the country was complicit? The government? The military, which claimed to be following orders? Bystanders who looked the other way? The bureaucrats who were only shifting forms and papers? Or the public, which claimed to be acting out of nationalism and love of country? The second point is that the failure to punish those responsible for the first acts of genocide in the 20th century (e.g., the 1904 German murders of the Herero tribe in German South West Africa and the Turkish massacre of the Armenians in 1915, as well as the many war crimes attributed to the German Army during World War One), according to international legal authorities M. Cherif Bassiouni and Christopher Blakesley, and "the shortsightedness and xenophobic tendencies of politicians after World War I . . . made the task of establishing Nuremberg and Tokyo more difficult."[2]

The Goals of War Crimes Trials

The arrival of the Second World War brought new legal problems for statesmen. The framers of the Geneva Convention in 1929, which established the rules of war after the horrible experiences and weapons of World War One, built in little power to punish. Indeed, the Geneva Convention was considered by most to be a detailed list of what actions would be considered illegal and thus punishable, rather than a discussion of the punishments themselves. Somehow, the signatories were convinced that issuing such a detailed warning would cause reasonable people to honor the rules. Yet, military technology improved during the 1930s as dictators like Hitler, Mussolini, Stalin, Tojo, and Franco embarked on expansionist wars and the murder of "outsiders." It was becoming clear to the Western Allies that they were witnessing atrocities for which the Geneva Convention left them unprepared. New rules had to be considered.

The first step toward punishing the war criminals of the Second World War came in 1942, when the Allied Powers signed an agreement at London's Palace of St. James to establish the United Nations War Crimes Commission (UNWCC), but the diplomats squabbled for another three years before representatives of 17 Allied nations (most were governments-in-exile) gathered again in London, on August 8, 1945, to make it official. The London Agreement gave rise to three major sets of trials. The first was the International Military Tribunal (IMT), whose many trials would continue until 1949 at Nuremberg. A second set of trials, called the Subsequent Nuremberg Trials, was created by the American Military Governor for Germany; these trials prosecuted a total of 185 Nazi government ministers, industrialists, members of the SS, and judges and medical practitioners. A third set of trials, established by the Moscow Declaration on German Atrocities on November 1, 1943, allowed the U.S. Army to try lower-ranked war criminals and concentration camp guards in its zone of occupation. These trials were conducted at Dachau concentration camp. The U.S. Army began by hunting down war criminals that had victimized Americans, often civilians who had tortured or killed U.S. airmen who had parachuted into enemy hands. (For their part, the British were equally aggressive in punishing German atrocities committed against British personnel while giving short shrift to similar injustices committed against their French and Russian allies.) By December 1947, the U.S. Army had prosecuted 646 accused criminals in 226 trials; 199 of the defendants were sentenced to death, and an additional 93 went to prison for life. Only then did the U.S. Army turn its attention to war criminals whose alleged acts did not involve American victims.[3]

Teams crisscrossed the Allied zones gathering evidence, searching for culprits among the nameless millions of homeless civilians and returning former soldiers, and collecting the names of witnesses by the hundreds every day. The list of suspects reached 150,000.[4] There were also special searches: the Seventh Army was looking for the SS men who had shot and killed 120 American prisoners of war in a field near Malmedy, Belgium, on December 17, 1944. Elsewhere, the Third Army worked out of Dachau, trying concentration camp guards and others. For the next three years, the U.S. Army heard 489 cases against 1,672 accused and passed 297 death sentences.[5]

The Soviet Union, for its part, went its own way. Faced with Germany's brutal treatment of its "subhuman" Slavic enemies, the Russian government assured its citizens that the "fascist beasts" would pay for their crimes. On April 19, 1943, a Decree of the Presidium of the Supreme Soviet prescribed that "German-fascist criminals guilty of grave crimes against Soviet citizens were to be punished with death by hanging, and their accomplices, with hard

People waiting for an hour and a half for the opening of the court in Dachau, Germany, where the trials of the infamous Malmedy defendants are held. On this day, 73 defendants are to be sentenced. July 1946. (SC#249310, World War II Signal Corps Photograph Collection, U.S. Army Military History Institute, Carlisle Barracks, PA)

labor."[6] To underscore Moscow's hard-line position, the official Red Army newspaper, *Krasnaya Zvezda* (The Red Star), announced, on August 4, 1943, that "the first hanging of a German war criminal had been carried out at a village west of Kremenchug after a field court-martial. The gallows was a tree where a village woman had been executed for killing poultry without the permission of the German agricultural authorities."[7] The message to all Russians, soldiers and citizens alike, was clear: permission to kill captive enemy soldiers was granted, even encouraged. In combat, both sides murdered their prisoners with gusto; the Germans killed their Russian prisoners because the Russians were considered subhuman, and the Russians murdered German prisoners because they were, well, German. Long lines of ragged German prisoners of war disappeared into the snow storms of Siberia, and few were ever seen again. With the end of the war, however, the victorious Russians, realizing that they now shared the European continent with another superpower, found it necessary to temper their hatred of the Germans and occasionally to allow themselves to bend to the more lenient prison sentences proposed by the other victors.

The Germans, by the way, established their own "Wehrmacht War Crimes Bureau" (*Wehrmacht-Untersuchungsstelle für Verletzungen des Völkerrechts*), the resurrection of a similar Prussian agency from the First World War, to investigate war crimes committed by or against the German military.[8]

Differing Motives for War Crimes Trials

Three motives were behind the war crimes or genocide trials when they finally did occur after World War II. The first was the wish to exact revenge, to pillory the enemy culprits, to make them pay in terms of plunder, moral or physical enslavement, or to recoup the huge debt run up by the winner. Tempers snapped after witnessing the horrors of World War II, and the need for vengeance was clear. Any war crimes trial becomes a ritual of triumph and retribution against the defeated enemies and the system they represented. Whether it is an American trial of Japanese officers or the Iraqi trial of Saddam Hussein, the desire for vengeance is uppermost. Moreover, the longer the conflict lasted, the more successful the enemy's propaganda, and the greater the casualties suffered, the greater the need for vengeance. That punishment would, it was hoped, also deter other nations from breaking the peace or from committing future crimes against humanity.

War crimes trials are also designed to mold the histories of the conflicts. They become demonstrations of history lessons or vehicles for educating future generations, as was the case with the Nuremberg trials (1945–49), Israel's trial of Adolf Eichmann (1961–62), and Stalin's infamous "show trials" of the 1930s. In such trials, the defendants admit everything and request the harshest punishment for their crimes. The accused are tried, of course, and probably executed, but the motivation behind the trial is to demonstrate the horrors caused by the accused for the history books. As early as the end of World War I, there was a movement to punish German war criminals and to reveal the depths of their depravity (via the so-called Leipzig Trials),[9] but nothing serious was produced by these trials to help mold the public's recollection of the conflict and the issues.

World War II provided the Allies with another opportunity to expose Germany's depravity, although most nations were already convinced. For five years, the Allies, separately and together, conducted numerous trials of the Nazi doctors,[10] concentration camp guards, industrialists from the German companies Krupp and I. G. Farben, government ministers, the military high command, Luftwaffe Field Marshal Erhard Milch, SS officers and police officials, and the Race and Resettlement office of the SS;[11] the British on their own tried the German doctors who had committed medical experiments at the Ravensbrück concentration camp,[12] among others. In the American zone of occupation, the United States prosecuted 1,672 war criminals between 1945 and 1947.[13] The desire for vengeance and punishment may have been ever-present, but the underlying goal was to reveal the evil perpetrated by the Nazis and the Japanese—to write the history of the war. The heroic behavior of Democracy's sons and daughters in uniform must be held in sharp contrast to the detestable acts of the enemy. Despite the ethical issues related to sacrificing justice to education, defenders of the war crime trial as history lesson point out that the failure to expose the vanquished enemy and his ideology to the glare of history can result in the loss of public memory, and this in turn may allow the heinous acts to be repeated.

There is a third motivation for holding a war crimes trial. It sometimes occurs in history that governments find themselves caught on the flypaper of a military misadventure and would very much like to extricate themselves. One diplomatic option is to prosecute as war criminals soldiers who have carried out the very policies that have become an embarrassment to the government.

The major trials after the Second World War that best represent the different motivations for war crimes prosecutions are the Nuremberg trials and the Eichmann trial (educational), the trial of Lieutenant William Calley after the 1968 massacre of Vietnamese civilians at My Lai (the government's effort to distance itself from the policy), and the Tokyo trials of 1946–48 (vengeance).

The Nuremberg Trial (Educational)

The best-known major war crime trial and the source of new law and legal legend, the Nuremberg trial created the template for war crimes trials to follow. The idea of bringing the vanquished leaders to justice was discussed early in the war, but the French, British, Soviet, and American allies couldn't agree on procedures, legal regulations, and the roles of each participant. They also could not agree on what constitutes a conspiracy: two people? One hundred? The entire nation? And aren't all wars acts of aggression? The legal wrangling among the allies continued, but, as the war came to a close and the troops liberated the Nazi concentration camps, the Allies were convinced more than ever that the guilty parties must be brought to justice.

The first issue to be resolved, once it became clear that the Allies would win the war and that the growing revelations of enemy atrocities demanded an accounting, was the site of the future war crimes trial. Locating the trial in a city on either side of the Allied-Soviet dividing line was politically complicated, and Berlin was largely under Soviet control and still volatile. The medieval Bavarian town of Nuremberg was perfect. Located on Germany's "Romantic Road" north of Munich, Nuremberg is rich in German history; the Nuremberg castle dates back to the reign of Fredrich Barbarossa (1122–1190). Nuremberg was the source of Germany's ancient Nordic myths, and Hitler was clever enough to tap into those ancient myths as the man of destiny. Beginning in 1927, the Nazis used the city plaza to deliver speeches and organize torchlight parades, with thousands of chanting pilgrims pledging their obedience and undying loyalty. Nuremberg became the Mount Sinai from which "The Law" was handed down. How could anyone fight such hysteria and the lure of cohesive nationalism? The rallies grew in size and attendance until the mid-1930s, when the annual September rally was the center of the Hitlerian calendar.

Nuremberg took on such an elevated political status to the Nazis that the Allies bombed the city with a special ferocity, sometimes around the clock. It seemed natural at the end of the war to hold the trials of Germany's leaders in the city that best represented them. Ironically, one of the few government buildings to survive the bombing was the Palace of Justice. When the trial began, in November 1945, the city of Nuremberg was in shambles. A correspondent from *Stars and Stripes* recalled that "I could smell the stench of death as I walked through the streets of Nuremberg on my way to the Palace of Justice. Beneath the rubble of the shattered city lay the bodies of 20,000 air raid victims. In that macabre setting the first international trial in history for crimes against humanity and crimes of waging aggressive war was under way."[14] For 11 months, from November 1945 to October 1946, the city of Nuremberg, site of Hitler's yearly rallies and speeches, became the Allied showcase for Nazi horrors.

But it almost didn't happen. A bitter debate erupted in 1944 between those who wanted to see the surviving leaders of the regime executed without debate (the kill-'em-all faction), led by FDR's Secretary of the Treasury, Henry

Morgenthau, Jr., whose "Morgenthau Plan" promoted Germany's return to a nonindustrial nation. Morgenthau was joined by Winston Churchill, who lamented the Allies' post–World War One failure to try Kaiser Wilhelm II, or the random German soldiers and sailors accused of beating prisoners, sinking hospital ships, Allied lifeboats, and murdering French captives. Eventually, in 1921, the so-called Leipzig trial tried a number of German officers for war crimes but its prosecution record was dismal.[15] Churchill was also exasperated by the Allied failure to prosecute the perpetrators of the Armenian massacre after the First World War. Churchill, calling for the firing squads, determined that this time would be different.

Of course, there were also the Soviets, America's wartime allies, whose colossal losses to the invading Germans during World War II (in excess of 10 million)[16] entitled them to influence the final decision. Stalin, surprisingly, was against summary execution, preferring instead to extract political gains from his Western partners[17] as each country argued over the sentences of the 21 defendants (a 22nd defendant, Martin Bormann, was tried in absentia). With the beginning of the actual trial, however, the Soviets reverted to their expected hard-line position, "voting to condemn all defendants on all counts and to sentence every possible defendant to death by hanging."[18]

A surprising number of American politicians didn't want the Germans tried at all. Republican Representatives like John Tabor, Harold Knutson, Francis Case, and William Langer "all believed that American war crimes policies were getting in the way of German reconstruction." Representative Tabor complained that "700,000 of Germany's most active and eligible business leaders were refused an opportunity to work because they were alleged to be Nazis." Allied military leaders stepped forward to defend their German counterparts, such as Admiral Karl Doenitz, who went to prison for directing the German submarine service and who was considered Hitler's heir. An Iowa Supreme Court judge, Henry (Charles) Wennerstrum, made headlines in the conservative *Chicago Tribune* when he claimed that the Germans were being subjected to "victor's justice" and that the German defendants were prevented from getting a full and fair trial, statements that even the Germans called "regrettable."[19] Moreover, conservative American critics of the trials pointed out that some of the German-English translators and court staff were "vindictive Jews." These critics believed that it was time to turn to the real enemy, Stalin's Russia and its minions, and allow the Germans to get back to reconstructing their country.[20] Their mantra was that the communists, after all, were America's true enemy.

On the other side of the debate were those who argued for a transparent, fair, and democratic trial to promote "Americanism." In the forefront were FDR's Secretary of War, Henry Simpson; Justice Robert H. Jackson, who had been persuaded to take a leave of absence from the U.S. Supreme Court to serve as the Nuremberg trial prosecutor; and his brilliant assistant, General Telford Taylor. However, the final arbiter, President Roosevelt, died in April 1945 without settling the issue, leaving the decision to his feisty vice president, Harry S. Truman. As a former Missouri judge himself, Truman had faith in the law and believed that a court made up of reasonable judges would conduct a fair trial and come to the right decision. But, he added, "due to their 'barbaric practices,' we have a stern duty to teach the German people the hard lesson that they must change their ways before they can be received back into the family of peaceful, civilized nations."[21]

Truman's moralizing tone accurately reflected the emotions of the times, but deep down it sounded hollow to everyone. No one's hands were clean at Nuremberg, and the specters of the Katyn Forest massacre, Hiroshima, and Dresden hung over the proceedings in Nuremberg's Palace of Justice. Everyone knew about war crimes committed by all sides, lending a curious sense of hypocrisy that lessened the legitimacy of the process. Helpless

General Telford Taylor speaking before the Nuremberg International Military Tribunal. November 1945. (U.S. Signal Corps SC-265622, Box 483. National Archives and Record Administration)

people had been maltreated and innocent civilians plundered, raped, and murdered by the victors as well as by the vanquished culprits in the dock. That hypocrisy was evident throughout the trial as certain issues were deftly avoided, including the impact of the American strategic air war on the German civilian population,[22] the Hitler-Stalin Pact of 1939, which might embarrass or compromise America's Russian ally. A thoughtful critic of the trial, Montgomery Belgion, said that "if an ordinary decent man from the moon had landed in Nuremberg in 1946 and had been offered the spectacle of the Trial, he would have concluded that irrationality was master. Two parties had committed an act alleged to be a crime, and on the charge of having therefore been criminal one of the two parties was being tried by the other."[23]

Most important, each side maneuvered to place itself in the best historical light as the story of the Nazi system and its horrific acts was shaped for future historians.[24] The history of the conflict is always written by the victorious side, and it is the winner that determines what is a war crime (such as Japan's bombing of Pearl Harbor) and what isn't (the unnecessary Allied firebombing of Dresden three months before the end of World War II). According to the victor's reasoning, the bombing deaths and mutilation of innocent people were considered acceptable when the Allies bombed Hamburg until it was declared a dead city but unacceptable when the Germans bombed Coventry. Similarly, it was ignored when American soldiers liberating the Dachau concentration camp shot captured SS guards out of disgust and rage, but the Nazi murder of dozens of Canadian prisoners at Normandy was declared a war crime, even though both episodes involve the murder of prisoners.

Thus, it was critical that the Allies prove that democracies were better than dictatorships. Further, if America wanted to prove the historic superiority of democracy, it had to conduct the trial of its enemies, however foul, with fairness. To be sure, both vengeance and the shaping of history were of primary importance at Nuremberg, but from the very beginning the key was to maintain fairness. The world was watching to see if this was just going to be another example of "victor's justice," and, given the damage and atrocities committed by Germany, many hoped that it would be.

The chief prosecutor at the Nuremberg trial, U.S. Supreme Court Justice Robert Jackson, said so at his eloquent opening statement. Democracy had triumphed over fascism, and, despite the attractive satisfaction of a punitive show trial for the political, military, and propaganda leaders of Nazi Germany, Justice Jackson pledged to conduct the proceedings according to the highest principles of Western law. Yet he wanted the world to know that it wasn't going to be easy. Stepping up to the lectern in his open morning coat, vest, and striped pants, he encapsulated America's ideal with the words:

Justice Robert Jackson, head of the Nuremberg Trial. (RG 238, Box 2, Series NT. National Archives and Record Administration)

> [T]he wrongs which we seek to condemn and punish have been so calculated, so malignant, and so devastating that civilization cannot tolerate their being ignored because it cannot survive their being repeated. That four great nations, flushed with victory and stung with injury, stay the hand of vengeance and voluntarily submit their captive enemies to the judgment of the law is one of the most significant tributes that power has ever paid to reason.[25]

Confronting the many problems and challenges posed by the first major war crimes trial of the century, the proceedings at Nuremberg stepped into unknown legal territory, creating new law, often as the trial unfolded. An observer at the trial looked over at the characters in the front row and saw "two rows of dazed, defiant, emotionally crippled high-ranking Nazis who slowly absorbed the horrors of their own gross misdeeds" and those committed at their behest or with their knowledge.[26]

Justice Jackson and representatives of Britain, France, and the Soviet Union recognized four categories of crimes: (1) war crimes atrocities, (2) crimes against humanity, (3) crimes against peace or a conspiracy to wage aggressive

Nazi defendants in the Nuremberg war trials stare intently at the chart of party organization introduced on the third day of the trial. Hermann Goering, left, listens to the testimony via earphones. Rudolf Hess, who usually sits between Goering and Ribbentrop, is missing in this photo. He had been complaining previously of severe stomach cramps and was given medical treatment outside the courtroom. Other defendants shown, l. to r., in front row: Field Marshal Wilhelm Keitel, Alfred Rosenberg. Back row: Admiral Karl Doenitz, Admiral Erich Raeder, Baldur von Schirach, Fritz Sauckel, and General Alfred Jodl. November 22, 1945. (SC#215210-S, World War II Signal Corps Photograph Collection, U. S. Army Military History Institute, Carlisle Barracks, PA)

war, and (4) membership in a criminal organization. These four categories constitute the Nuremberg Charter and became the foundation of war crimes trials in the future. The Nuremberg Principles, endorsed by the United Nations General Assembly on December 14, 1946, went on to become the United Nations Declaration of the Rights and Duties of Man.

It now became a prosecutable crime to have committed any of the following:

1. ***War crimes* (atrocities).** This category was the simplest for all parties to agree upon. War crimes, after all, had been discussed and defined for generations—even centuries—and punishments evaluated. The issue of what constituted a war crime

had been examined in medieval descriptions of knightly behavior and as recently as the Geneva Accords of 1929. Here, the prosecution faced a dilemma: among the Allies were nations that had turned against portions of their own populations as the Turks had in committing genocide against Turkish Armenians in 1915, thus violating the law; at the same time, international law defined the killing or torturing of enemy civilians or helpless combatants as a crime. It seems that "states didn't mind their citizens dying, they just didn't want anyone else killing them."[27]

2. ***Crimes against humanity.*** Before the Nuremberg trial, individuals had no protection from their own governments. Dictators could treat citizens as they liked—they could torment, evacuate, enslave, and even murder them when it suited them. Victims could be made to look evil or dangerous, since the government controlled the bureaucracy and propaganda and made the laws that everyone had to observe. Inquisitive outsiders were told that a sovereign country has the right to treat its citizens as it likes. In spite of this, Tibetans and the many thousands of minority Uighur Turkic-speaking Muslims living under siege in China's northwest Xinjiang are treated according to Beijing's decisions. Similarly, the victims living in Darfur are Sudanese citizens. The reclusive dictator of North Korea has reduced his starved citizens to eating tree bark. Despots traditionally have little concern for their subjects, who, in turn, have no one to protect them if the government turns on them.

   With the establishment of the legal precedent forbidding crimes against humanity, the average citizen has had at least theoretical protection. Yet, in the 50 years after Nuremberg, there wasn't a single prosecution of a war criminal for a crime against humanity. "In fact," notes one expert angrily, "not a single torturer or murder was put in prison by an international court until 1997, when a Bosnian Serb pub owner named Dŭsko Tadić was tried by the International Criminal Tribunal for Yugoslavia (ICTY)."[28] Despots the world over were, however, put on notice: they might consider their citizens valueless, but any serious action against them could end in a prosecution by the government.

3. ***Crimes against peace and conspiracy to wage aggressive war.*** This was probably the most contentious of the new legal categories created at Nuremberg, but the easiest one to prove. The charge of crimes against peace was promoted primarily by Britain, while the conspiracy charge was prosecuted primarily by the United States. The tribunal argued that Germany, after all, was a party to the 1928 Kellogg-Briand Pact, making it one of a total of 63 states that had solemnly agreed to "condemn war for the solution of international controversies, and to renounce it as an instrument of national policy in their relations with each other." Germany had promised not to resort to war to settle problems, but, on September 1, 1939, it had broken its promise by invading Poland. Granted, it's a rather thin argument, especially since, on September 17, 1939, the Russians attacked the other half of Poland, and France declared war on Germany, Britain declared war on Germany, Italy on Ethiopia, and so on. But the solution was the tribunal's conclusion that there are two types of aggressive war: legal belligerency and illegal belligerency. If the war is defensive, there is clear justification; but if the belligerency violates a treaty signed by the accused, the argument is that there cannot be a lawful justification.[29] By this definition, America's invasion of Iraq constitutes a war crime.

Criminal Organization Membership

Killer organizations like the SS, the *Sicherheitsdienst* (SD), (the Nazi Security Service), the Gestapo, and the *Einsatzgruppen* armies that followed the invading German armies into Poland and Russia to murder Jews and communists, committed hundreds of thousands of inhuman acts. Each organization maintained its own prisons, followed its own rules, and was answerable to separate hierarchies from the German Army. There can be no debate about the justifiability of considering membership in such organizations a war crime, particularly considering their missions and their merciless acts of torture and murder. By the end of the war, most people, including many thoughtful Germans, agreed. According to this legal logic, a French resistance fighter could shoot a German SS officer sipping coffee in a Paris bistro so long as the officer didn't change the rules by surrendering first.

How could the victors punish the entire population? They couldn't. Instead, they conveniently portrayed everything as having been directed by a limited number of criminal organizations. With the Führer dead, the guilt for the war and its atrocities settled largely on his political henchmen and on medical opportunists, identifiably brutal concentration camp guards, industrial giants, and some compliant military leaders. According to this logic, the German people were portrayed, at worst, as only marginally complicit in the crimes of the Nazis, and the German Wehrmacht convinced itself that it had always acted honorably for their country, a whitewash that books like Daniel Goldhagen's *Hitler's Willing Executioners* have revealed to be untrue. In reality, German soldiers, from generals to enlisted men, were often called upon to participate in the murder of Jews or to look away as others committed horrendous acts.[30]

Never mind that none of this could have occurred without the faithful cooperation of Germany's citizens.[31] Perhaps the tribunal actually believed that the German public had followed the Nazis out of blind obedience or had simply been unaware of the rabid racial programs of their government, but, more than likely, Allied policymakers foresaw the need for a "forgiven" Germany as a buffer against an increasingly menacing Soviet Union. Legal purists may be comforted to learn, however, that most of Nazi Germany's war criminals belonged to such killer organizations, including physicians and judges, who were usually members of the SS.[32]

In recent years, the use of the "criminal organization" precedent by the United States has not worked well. For example, after the fall of Baghdad, Saddam Hussein's Arab Ba'athist Socialist Party was declared to be a "criminal organization." The party was disbanded and its thousands of members forbidden to participate in the new government, It was quickly realized that the Ba'ath Party members were the only ones who had the experience to run the country—they were the doctors and managers and scientists. America's occupation policy suffered greatly as a result.

Nuremberg as Education

If the goal of the trial was ever in doubt, it was clarified by Robert G. Storey, executive trial counsel at Nuremberg, who stated that the mission of the trial was to "make a record of the Hitler regime which would withstand the test of history."[33]

However, there are problems in putting war criminals on trial with a view to educating the population. Can one teach history and pursue justice at the same time? Is there not a temptation to ignore or minimize facts that run counter to the lessons being projected? Would an "inconvenient fact" about a helpful SS prison camp guard who treated his prisoners with care and humanity (however rare such an occurrence might be) receive equal consideration as an inhumane act during deliberations? What about Jewish concentration camp inmates who informed on each other? Or American prisoners of war in German hands who sometimes pointed out the Jewish American soldiers among them? (These Jewish POWs were then separated and transported to concentration camps, such as the dreaded Berga camp in eastern Germany, where some 350 Jewish American soldiers were brutalized, sometimes to death.)[34] Such anomalies are often omitted from trial procedures in order to preserve the theme of the history lesson. There is no way of knowing how often justice was overshadowed by the need to package a history lesson.

Critics point to other problems with the Allied war crimes trials. From the beginning, "the United States, more than any other country, was the prime mover in the creation of the International Military Tribunal and carried out its responsibilities . . . to a greater degree than any other power."[35] One problem with America's leadership was, frankly, that the process was skewed to please the Americans, and that led to the trial's reliance on awkward, imported legalese. In fact, the very structure of the American court system, which is adversarial in nature, differed from that of its European counterparts. In American jurisprudence, for instance, the judge is to remain neutral, and witnesses are allowed to be cross-examined. Not so in European courts, where the judges take an active role. Another bewildering obstacle was the American insistence on introducing the legal principle of "discovery," which protects the defendant's right to see all the evidence in the prosecutor's hands; everyone has to show everybody everything—no more "Perry Mason moments" when the sudden appearance of an unknown letter unmasks the killer in the dock. The principle of discovery, the sharing of information between the prosecution and the defense, was still such a new concept in 1945 that it

American editors visit Buchenwald to look at the bodies of the people who died of starvation at the camp. l. to r: William I. Nichols, This Week magazine; Ben McKelvay, Washington Star; Julius Ochs Adler, New York Times; Norman Chandler, Los Angeles Times; A. C. Carter, Fort Worth Star-Telegram; John Randolph Hearst, Hearst Publications. Weimar, Germany, April 25, 1945. (SC#203907-S, World War II Signal Corps Photograph Collection, U.S. Army Military History Institute, Carlisle Barracks, PA)

was not yet accepted in most American courts, although it has since become a required part of American jurisprudence. The Russians were simply baffled by the whole process, from the assumed innocence of the accused and the many legal privileges accorded the witnesses to the principle of the judges' neutrality.

There were other problems, although not necessarily due to America's involvement. No one even pretended that all the perpetrators or witnesses could be found in the chaos of postwar Europe. Who knew how many people had been killed, had escaped to different countries, had changed their names, or were simply hiding? Languages were another huge problem. The documents might be written in German or Russian or Latvian or Estonian; the court staff might speak only English; and the witnesses might be Hungarian or Romanian or speak only Yiddish.

Another major issue concerned the internationally recognized principle of ex post facto (Latin for "after the fact"), which prohibits punishment for acts that were not illegal at the time they were committed.[36] Most democracies have such a law built into their constitutions (America's constitution contains such an admonition in Article 1) to prevent future government leaders from abusing power by punishing opponents for actions that were legal under previous governments. In other words, if a person belonged to an organization that was once perfectly legal, that membership cannot be made illegal by later legislation. Could that principle have been applied to the Nazi leadership in 1945 Nuremberg? Is it possible that the Germans who participated in the Nazi atrocities were being tried for actions that weren't crimes when they were committed? The answer is a resounding "no." For centuries, churches, diplomats, lawyers, soldiers, and philosophers have shaped and evaluated the definition of war crimes; these rules were understood by all.

Adolf Eichmann Trial (Educational)

When David Ben-Gurion, premier and founder of Israel, strode before the Knesset (the Israeli parliament) on May 24, 1960, and announced that Israel had located and captured Adolf Eichmann and that he was being held in Israel for trial, the world gasped. Eichmann had been a key figure in the Holocaust, fourth in importance only to Heinrich Himmler, Reinhard Heydrich, and Hitler himself. Eichmann was the faceless bureaucrat who made the Holocaust go smoothly. For the six months after his arrest, the world was fascinated to learn how the Israeli secret service had tracked the former Nazi to his new life as a simple worker in a suburb of Buenos Aires, Argentina, abducted him as he walked home from the bus stop, and smuggled him back to Israel aboard an official flight. As the trial opened, on April 10, 1961, the atmosphere in Israel was charged. The monster was in a glass booth, and the world was going to hear what had been done to the Jewish people.

From the beginning of the trial—indeed, from the very first sentence of the Israeli attorney general's 15-page passionate opening remarks—everyone knew that the goals were going to be vengeance and education. The call for vengeance was clear:

> When I stand before you here, Judges of Israel," began Gideon Hausner, ". . . I am not standing alone. With me are six million accusers. But they cannot rise to their feet and point an accusing finger at him . . . for their ashes are piled up on the hills of Auschwitz and the fields of Treblinka, and are strewn in the forests of Poland. . . . Their blood cries out, but their voice is not heard. I will be their spokesman and in their name I will unfold the awesome indictment.

But, the call for education was equally clear:

> Men still ask themselves: how could it have happened? The judges at the Nuremberg trials also asked themselves this question, examined its various aspects, and arrived at interesting formulations; yet it would be difficult to claim that a full or satisfactory answer was given. . . . But we shall nevertheless endeavor . . . to explain to the world . . . what is perhaps altogether inexplicable by the standards of ordinary reason.[37]

Fifteen charges were brought against Eichmann, available in detail in the English translation of the trial proceedings[38]—all of which were formulated according to the example of the Nuremberg trial.[39] The first eight pertained to crimes against the Jews, and the next four accused Eichmann of crimes against non-Jewish groups such as Polish Catholics, Gypsies, and Russian POWs. The last three charges accused him of membership in criminal organizations. As had Justice Jackson at Nuremberg, Israel went to great lengths to maintain an aura of fairness, going so far as to pay a top German lawyer, Robert Servatius, to defend Eichmann. The slightly built, balding Eichmann, so average that author Hannah Arendt titled her analysis of the trial *The Banality of Evil,* denied all 15 charges. The world listened as a horrible parade of broken witnesses told their stories of murder, torture, shootings, and death marches and pointed directly at the little man in the glass booth. Eichmann took notes and seldom reacted, except, astonishingly, to courteously fill in any missing pieces of their stories. For the first time, the interested public learned that the genocide of the Jews was a government racial program conducted separately from the war. The army answered to one chain of command, while the mass murderers answered to quite another hierarchy.

Viewers of the trial watched as each defense argument was refuted, as they had been at Nuremberg: "I didn't know about these war crimes"; "I was only following orders"; "I wasn't personally involved"; "I actually showed the Jews kindness, since gas is more humane than sadistic torture." By the end of his testimony, Eichmann admitted his "moral guilt" in the slaying of European Jewry and conceded that the mass murder of the Jews was a "hideous crime," but, after all, what could he do?

Testimony and summations were completed in August, and the five-month trial recessed. On December 10, 1961, the judges found Eichmann guilty and sentenced him to hang. His appeal was unanimously rejected, as was his personal appeal to the President of Israel, Itzhak Ben-Zvi. Adolf Eichmann was hanged on May 30, 1962, with Hitler's name on his lips, and his ashes were scattered over the Mediterranean to ensure that his burial place couldn't be a memorial to the lunatic fringe. The trial had been a national catharsis for Jews and, to an understandably lesser degree, non-Jews, as well. Before 1962, the study of the Holocaust was nearly unknown, and then, it was seen only as part of the history of the war. In fact, the word "Holocaust" came into general parlance only after the Eichmann trial.

But what of the goals of the trial? Eichmann was certainly punished, but was the world better educated about the calamity suffered by Europe's Jews and the dangers of anti-Semitism to the future peace of the world? How influential was the history lesson? The Israeli population, many of whom were Holocaust survivors, had followed the trial closely. For thousands, the revelations of the trial were an affirmation of their suffering; for others, they offered an explanation for the fate of lost friends and relatives.

But the United States was different. America was far less concerned about the plight of Europe's Jews than people are today willing to admit. During the 1930s and the 1940s, Jews were blamed for the usual crises: the economic depression, communism, parasitism, and anti-Christianity, and hundreds of thousands of Americans rushed to support an almost endless array of right-wing anti-Semitic movements in America. More than 15,000 people joined William Pelley's Fascist Silver Shirts; about 100,000 read Reverend Gerald B. Winrod's *Christian Defender* magazine, which warned of a Jewish-Communist conspiracy to dominate the world. Perhaps the most notorious anti-Semite of the 1930s and 1940s was Father Charles E. Coughlin, an admirer of Adolf Hitler. Many thousands supported his anti-Semitic Union for Social Justice, and unknown millions listened to his weekly radio broadcasts, which nicknamed Roosevelt's New Deal the "Jew Deal." The rabidly anti-Semitic Henry Ford published a nasty newspaper called the *Dearborn Independent*, which reached upwards of 700,000 American readers; he also wrote a book entitled *The International Jew* and sponsored endless reprintings of the notorious Russian forgery *The Protocols of the Elders of Zion*, which describes a Jewish plot for world conquest.[40] The beginning of the war, in 1941, however, brought the end of several long-running anti-Semitic movements, such as Gerald L. K. Smith's Committee of One Million, which rode the wave of hatred until Smith's unsuccessful race to represent Michigan in the U.S. Senate in 1942.[41] Predictably, Smith blamed his eclipse on the Jews.[42] Support for Father Coughlin also fell sharply when the country entered World War II, and, threatened with excommunication by the Church, he abandoned his radio crusade.

News of the Eichmann trial did not seem to influence most Americans polled, and, as expected, their knowledge of the event depended largely on their level of anti-Semitism. Those who were suspicious of or didn't care for Jews were less aware of the trial or its importance. Only 84 percent said they had even heard of the Eichmann trial, unlike the population of Israel, to whom the trial was personal and immediate. (One wonders how 16 percent of Americans surveyed could have missed the event.) Even those Americans who were aware of the trial didn't always understand: only about a third of the 84 percent who knew of the trial replied correctly that Eichmann had been captured in Argentina, 50 percent knew that he had been arrested by Israel, 59 percent correctly identified him as a Nazi (9 percent thought he was a Jew!), and 33 percent correctly identified the official estimate of the number of Jews killed by the Nazis as six million.[43] A shocking 30 percent said that the Holocaust was *partly* the fault of the Jews themselves. Two percent actually concluded that it was *entirely* their fault. Together, 32 percent (or one-third of those surveyed) believed that the Jews were in some measure responsible for their own genocide.[44] These numbers are particularly disappointing when one considers the many avenues of information available to Americans: news updates in magazines, newsreels, newspapers, word of mouth—and television, in time for the 1961 Eichmann trial.

Can one say that the Eichmann trial and the earlier Nuremberg trial were successful as educational tools? Probably not in the short run. Following the Eichmann trial, the polls indicated that fewer than half of those Americans questioned understood the major facts in the case. There were no surprises: surveys confirmed that awareness of the trials increased with the levels of education, just as anti-Semitism decreased with more schooling. Social scientists were not impressed. The surveys immediately following the Nuremberg trial were equally disappointing. An Allied survey of 2,000 Germans in 1950 indicated that only 38 percent thought the trial had been fair.[45] Four years later, however, that percentage had jumped to 78.[46]

On the positive side, the same surveys indicated an increase in American sympathy for Israel and for Jewish people. Overt anti-Semitism was still present through the 1950s but was declining rapidly. In 1947, a film exposing anti-Semitism won three Academy Awards, including Best Picture, and was nominated for five other Oscars. The film, *Gentlemen's Agreement*, starring Gregory Peck, was about a journalist who went underground in New York to experience discrimination against Jews at first hand. Surprisingly, another film nominated for the Academy Award for Best Picture in the same year, 1947, was *Crossfire*, starring Robert Mitchum, about the murder of a Jewish U.S. soldier and the reality of widespread anti-Semitism in the American military. While it is true that Americans were being made to confront their prejudice against Jews, anti-Semitism continued to exist, and even grow, before sharply dropping in the 1950s.

Gordon Allport, in his book *The Nature of Prejudice*, concluded that, in 1944, "5 to 10 percent [of Americans were] violently anti-Semitic, while perhaps 45 percent [were] mildly bigoted in the same direction." Additional polls indicated that, although some Americans sympathized with the victims in Europe, a startling 70 percent would have supported a campaign against Jews in the United States (or would have stood by without protesting); in June 1944, a full 57 percent of Americans polled expected such a campaign against the Jews.[47] In a 1938 poll, for example, 41 percent of the public had agreed that Jews had too much power in the United States; this figure rose during World War II, reaching a peak of 58 percent in 1945.[48] Then, suddenly, anti-Semitism began to decline. The percentage of respondents holding discriminatory attitudes toward Jews dropped to 30 percent by 1950; by 1962, the percentage of such people in one discrimination index had dropped to 17 percent.[49]

If the general public was only mildly influenced by the Eichmann trial, it was a cornucopia for the academic world as historians, psychologists, philosophers, and economists rushed forward to answer the questions posed by both the Eichmann proceedings and the Nuremberg trial: how did this happen? Books on every facet of the Holocaust appeared in print, and studies sprang up in many universities. Today, *The Diary of Anne Frank* is included in the curriculum of most American high schools. Many German high school students and army recruits today make a class pilgrimage to the numerous concentration camp memorials around Germany, such as Dachau, on the outskirts of Munich; Buchenwald, outside of Weimar; Bergen-Belsen near Hanover; or Sachsenhausen, near Berlin. The educational value of the two trials, then, took place over the long haul.

My Lai Trial (Government's Need to Create Distance)

The second motivation for war crimes trials, although rarely seen, is a government's effort to distance itself from the crimes it may have created or authorized. A good example is the case against Lieutenant William L. Calley for his crimes in Vietnam.

In 1968, Lt. Calley led his men in the senseless murder of between 347 and 504 Vietnamese civilians in the hamlet of My Lai 4, Quang Ngai Province. The sensational 1970 trial revealed that Calley's superior officers had authorized his actions. For example, Colonel Oran K. Henderson had urged his officers to "go in there aggressively, close with the enemy and wipe them out for good."[50] Further down the chain of command, Lieutenant Colonel Frank A. Barker ordered the 1st Battalion commanders to burn the houses, kill the livestock, destroy foodstuffs, and perhaps to close the wells.[51] At the Charlie Company briefing on the eve of the attack, Captain Ernest Medina informed his men that nearly all the civilian residents of the village of Son Mỹ would have left for the market by 7:00 and that any who remained could only be considered members of the National Liberation Front (NLF), the South Vietnamese rebel army, an arm of the regular North Vietnamese Army, America's enemy. At the very least, anyone left in the hamlet after the "true capitalists" had left for the market or were going about their rightful daily responsibilities, were NLF sympathizers. And so the massacres began.

According to the trial transcript, Calley recounted:

> I was ordered to go in there and destroy the enemy. That was my job on that day. That was the mission I was given. I did not sit down and think in terms of men, women, and children. They were all classified the same, and that was the classification that we dealt with, just as enemy soldiers.

The BBC News described the scene this way:

> Soldiers went berserk, gunning down unarmed men, women, children and babies. Families which huddled together for safety in huts or bunkers were shown no mercy. Those who emerged with hands held high were murdered. . . . Elsewhere in the village, other atrocities were in progress. Women were gang raped; Vietnamese who had bowed to greet the Americans were beaten with fists and tortured, clubbed with rifle butts and stabbed with bayonets. Some victims were mutilated with the signature "C Company" carved into the chest. By late morning word had got back to higher authorities and a cease-fire was ordered. My Lai was in a state of carnage. Bodies were strewn through the village.[52]

Members of Calley's unit recall that "[On one occasion, someone] fired at it [the baby] with a .45. He missed. We all laughed. He got up three or four feet closer and missed again. We laughed. Then he got up right on top and plugged him."[53]

After a four-month-long trial in the charged atmosphere of Nixonian America, Calley was convicted and initially sentenced to life imprisonment. Two days later, President Richard Nixon, in the face of a decision as controversial as the war that spawned the massacre, freed Calley pending a review of the case, since he could be viewed as having followed orders (if one doesn't consider the torture and rapes). Eventually, Calley served four and a half months in the brig at Fort Benning, Georgia.

A government investigation of the massacre raised doubts about the actual number of Vietnamese civilians killed by the defendants, pointing out that the families living in the cluster of hamlets had been repeatedly warned that they were in a battle zone. The government investigation asked, "who can judge the cumulative effects of the horrors, fears, and frustrations which the men of 'C' Company had been forced to endure just prior to their action at My Lai on March 16, of that year?"[54] The congressional investigation closed on this conclusion:

> What obviously happened at My Lai was wrong. It was contrary to the Geneva Conventions, the Rules of Engagement, and the MACV Direc-

> tives. In fact, it was so wrong and so foreign to the normal character and actions of our military forces as to immediately raise a question as to the legal sanity at the time of those men involved.[55]

The Tokyo Trials (Vengeance)

Every trial, whatever its other goals, intends to punish the accused. The public has to be convinced that the sacrifices it was called upon to make on the Home Front—rationing, managed news, endless appeals to patriotism, separation from loved ones, not to mention the real possibility of injury or death—had been worthwhile. The enemy leaders, and perhaps identifiable evil individuals, are to be pointed out for what they were and suitably punished. Indeed, until relatively recently, the public demanded to witness those executions, crowding around open gallows and beheadings; today's audiences have to settle for justice in the movies or daytime courtroom television shows. Justice is entertainment. The public's argument is that since the verdict is pronounced in the public's name, its deliverance belongs to all. Of the dozen war crimes trials that followed World War II, in only one particular group of war crimes trials, those against the Japanese, was the issue of fairness ignored.

The idea of fairness was not easily applied to the Japanese in World War II: the war against the Japanese was savage, racial, and personal. From the surprise Japanese attack on Pearl Harbor, in 1941, through the battles across the South Pacific—the Philippines, the Bataan Death March, Guadalcanal, Coral Sea, Guam, and Tarawa—Americans were shaken and enraged at the mounting casualties and the reports of starved and beheaded American POWs. Japanese Americans living on the West Coast—120,000 innocent people—were rounded up and shipped to War Relocation Camps. By May 22, 1944, a shocking full-page photo appeared in *Life* magazine, the flagship of photojournalism, of a pretty woman staring dreamily at the gift of a "Jap skull" sent to her by her Navy boyfriend; the picture produced no public protest. The war in the Pacific was quite unlike that being waged against the Germans in Europe. This war was racial and pitiless. After nearly five years of a savage conflict, where the most heinous atrocities had become commonplace, vengeance was uppermost in the public mind.

A good example of the differences between the Japanese and the German trials concerns the issue of "obeying orders." The German military men charged at the Nuremberg trial claimed that they were innocent because they had committed their war crimes as the result of orders from their superiors. They had been commanded from higher up, and, unfortunately, Hitler and Goebbels and many others had committed suicide, taking responsibility with them. There was no such thing as an illegal order, they argued. An order was an order. But, American jurisprudence had long placed responsibility for the commission of atrocities on the soldiers who committed them, rather than going to the top of the chain to find the one who had given the order. Hence the trial of Lt. William Calley.

While the principle of blaming the individual was novel in international law, it was commonplace in American law, sometimes even when there was a clear link to a senior officer. For instance, after the American Civil War, the Confederate commandant of the Andersonville, Georgia, prisoner-of-war camp, Henry Wirz, was tried for the inhumane deaths of some 14,000 Union prisoners under his control. Wirz denied individual responsibility by displaying the order of his superiors and argued that he was only following orders. The infamous Confederate prison commandant was nonetheless found guilty and hanged,[56] perhaps as much due to inflamed public outrage as to legal principle. Nonetheless, American law had a strong tradition of considering individual soldiers responsible for their actions, denying them the ability to pass the responsibility to their senior officers. A cynic might say that the principle was molded by the very authorities who gave the orders and who expected the killers under their command to fend for themselves if caught.

Thus, according to the so-called Nuremberg Principles, no defendant could avoid prosecution by claiming that he had acted on the orders of his superior. The tribunal determined that there are differences between a legal order and an illegal order—some orders are blatantly illegal and need not be obeyed. Justice Jackson solemnly reminded the courtroom that every German soldier's pay book, his *Soldbuch*, contained a commandment that no soldier should obey an illegal order—and slowly quoted it word by word to the courtroom.[57] In the words of Brigadier General Telford Taylor, a luminary on Justice Jackson's prosecution team: "Who could ever argue to a court that 'I didn't know the order to gas a thousand Jews was illegal'?" Taylor declared, in his book *The Anatomy of the Nuremberg Trials*, that, while such orders could be considered a mitigating factor at sentencing, any soldier knew when he received an illegal order (a curious contradiction since orders from a superior are irrelevant with respect to guilt or innocence but are relevant with respect to appropriate punishment). In more contemporary terms, Judge Norbert Ehrenfreund, a renowned trial judge of the Superior Court in California for 30 years, posed this question at a conference titled "The Legacy of Nuremberg" in San Diego in August 2004: "Would our treatment of the prisoners at Abu Ghraib—which, while not as lethal as Saddam's henchmen's actions, although perhaps even more humiliating and devastating to Muslims—be war crimes for which Donald Rumsfeld or our generals would be tried?" Ehrenfreund concluded, "I would think so."[58]

Two cases in point occurred near the end of the war in Europe. In early April 1945, in the small Rhineland city of Duren, 20 miles east of Aachen, a 1st Army military commission convicted a German officer, Captain Curt Bruns, of having murdered two American prisoners of war during the Battle of the Bulge.[59] Punishment was swift and direct, although no superior officers were charged. Another case tried by the U.S. occupation authorities concerned an American pilot who had bailed out over the village of Preist in the Rhineland in mid-August 1944. A rural policeman went to take him into custody but was prevented by the arrival of a local Nazi official named Peter Back. The policeman stood by while the Nazi shot the American and encouraged a growing crowd of civilians to beat the dying pilot to death in retaliation for a recent air raid on a nearby town. Two sympathetic German soldiers and the policeman were pushed aside. Retribution came a year later, on June 1, 1945, when an American military commission finally located and tried the policeman, the two citizens, and the Nazi official. The Nazi and the two citizens received death sentences, while the policeman was sentenced to life imprisonment. According to the record, "by the end of summer 1945, war crimes investigating teams collected evidence in 800 such cases; the great majority charged to civilians or the police, very few to soldiers, and none to commanding officers."[60]

The law was not evenly applied, however, particularly when it concerned the defeated Japanese. The first trial against the Japanese convened a month after the end of the war, while hatred of the Japanese was still white-hot. Atrocities committed by average Japanese soldiers against enemy prisoners were legendary, and most Americans at the time considered the two atomic bombs dropped on Japan to be not only militarily necessary but morally justified. R. J. Rummel, professor emeritus of political science at the University of Hawaii, estimates that, between 1937 and 1945, the Japanese military murdered more than 6 million Chinese, Indonesian, Filipino, Korean, American, Dutch, and British prisoners. In a single six-week period beginning in December 1937, Japan's notorious Rape of Nanking, then China's capital city, resulted in the genocide of some 300,000 Chinese civilians by Japanese soldiers.[61] Astonishingly, only a single high-ranking Japanese officer, Lieutenant General Hisao Tani, was prosecuted for the Nanking massacre.[62] He was found guilty on February 6, 1947, and executed by firing squad the following month. The point is that none of the actual killers were prosecuted; responsibility was shifted to the superior officers who presumably had issued the orders, completely contradicting the Nuremberg Principles, that German soldiers and political leaders could not shift the blame to senior officers.

Moreover, it was not always necessary to prove guilt. A major figure, General Yamashita, the so-called Tiger of Malaya and Beast of Bataan, was arrested and charged with responsibility for the war crimes committed by the soldiers under his command in the Philippines. There is no question that thousands of Filipino civilians and Allied prisoners of war suffered grievously at the hands of the Japanese, as men, women, and children were indiscriminately bayoneted, raped, tortured, mutilated, cannibalized, and even skinned alive. The record is replete with horrifying examples. The following occurred at Canangay, in the Philippines:

> A young woman, about twenty years of age, was caught hiding in the grass. The officer in command of the Japanese patrol which discovered her tore off all of her clothes whilst two soldiers held her. She was then taken to a small shelter without walls where the officer with his sabre cut off her breasts and cut open her womb. Soldiers held her while the officer did this. At first the girl screamed but finally lay silent and still . . . the Japanese then set fire to the shelter.
>
> Another eye-witness described how in Manila his house boy was tied to a pillar. While still alive the Japanese cut off his genitals and thrust his severed penis into his mouth.[63]

As it turned out, Yamashita was not in direct charge of these criminals, although he doubtless was in command of numerous other units, but he was hanged nonetheless. In fact, the evidence indicated that he tried, however modestly, to prevent atrocities. None of that mattered. Despite the lack of evidence, General Douglas MacArthur and his tribunal were determined to find the Japanese general guilty from the start. Interestingly, the International News Service took a straw vote of 12 fellow newsmen who had covered the trial to ascertain how many would vote guilty on the basis of the evidence. The vote was 12–0 **against** conviction. The decision to blame the senior officials for the atrocities committed by criminals or criminal groups applied *only* to the Japanese; the principle of command responsibility was not used against German war criminals at Nuremberg, or against U.S. officers during the Vietnam War. "Yamashita was not convicted merely because he was a commander," says noted legal author Ann Marie Prévost. "He was convicted because he was a *Japanese* commander."[64]

There appears to be no end to the inhumanity inflicted by the Japanese for which only the highest-ranking officers, if anyone, were punished. Among the countless war crimes is that described in this eyewitness account of brutality inflicted on a Dutch officer and a Dutch policeman in Balikpapan in Borneo:

> I saw a [Dutch] district officer and a police inspector, both in uniform, in conversation with a Japanese Army officer. . . . Suddenly the [Japanese] officer drew his sword and hacked off both the Dutchman's arms just above the elbows, and then both his legs above the knees. The trunk of his body was then tied to a coconut tree and bayoneted until life was extinct. The Japanese officer then turned his attention to the Dutch

> policeman, who had his arms and legs hewed off in like manner. The policeman struggled on to the stumps of his legs and managed to shout "God save the Queen," he then fell dead, a bayonet through his heart.[65]

In this case, no Japanese officer or soldier of any rank was brought to trial or punished.

However poorly handled, the Tokyo trials pressed on for the next 30 months, until 1948. The judges were decidedly second-rate when measured against the high quality of the participants in the parallel trial in Nuremberg and were led by the "American chief counsel Joseph B. Kennan, whose in-court drunkenness and general incompetency cast a pall on the entire prosecution."[66] Unlike Nuremberg, where 3 of the 22 defendants were acquitted, Tokyo acquitted no one.

To date, the Japanese refuse to acknowledge their crimes in Nanking or anywhere in Asia during the war; these atrocities simply "never happened," said Japan's justice minister.[67] In 1994, nearly 50 years after the end of the war, a top Japanese government official was forced to resign for making an embarrassing admission about the war. The ministry of education in Tokyo regularly orders teachers and textbook writers to downplay Japan's war crimes. Japan's Justice Minister summed up his nation's culpability:

> Japan's war in Asia had not been aggressive. Calling that war "a war of aggression" is incorrect. If you say it was done with the intention to invade, that's wrong. We were seriously thinking about the liberation of colonies and the [Greater East Asian] Co-Prosperity Sphere.[68]

In May 2009, the 64th annual reunion of survivors of Corregidor and the Bataan Death March was unexpectedly interrupted by the appearance of Japan's ambassador to the United States, Ichiro Fujisaki, who rose to

> extend a heartfelt apology for our country having caused tremendous damage to many people, including prisoners of war; who have undergone tragic experiences in the Bataan Peninsula . . . . and other places. . . . I would like to express my condolences to all those who have lost their lives in the war, and after the war, and their family members.[69]

At the end of his six-minute speech, Fujisaki got a standing ovation from half of the 400 stunned attendees; the remainder refused to accept what they called an insincere apology six decades too late. Fujisaki mingled with the survivors, shaking hands and pausing for photos.

The Tokyo trials after the war were not as benevolent; the Nuremberg Principles were swept aside, and most of those indicted were executed. Moreover, the Americans weren't the only Allied power to apply a different legal standard to the Japanese than to the Germans. In December 1949, the Russians tried 12 former high-ranking Japanese officers in Khabarovsk, Russia, in the Russian Far East, and charged them with extensive murderous biological experiments. As usual, the men brought to trial were not the thousands of members of the notorious Detachment 731 (the Ishii Detachment) or Detachment 100, for inflicting the most terrible experiments on an estimated 3,000 defenseless victims and prisoners (including American POWs) but the commanding general of the Japanese Army in China, General Yamada Otozoo, and 11 other senior officers.

From August 1939 until Japan's surrender in 1945, these "medical units" produced lethal bacterial weapons such as plague, anthrax, and cholera on a mass scale and tested them on living captives, often dissecting the "patients" to see the progress of the experiment while guards held them down.

Japanese atrocities in the Philippines. Through study of bones and teeth, U.S. officers and medical corpsmen are attempting to identify the more than 100 American POWs captured at Bataan and Corregidor and burned alive by the Japanese at a POW camp. One search began at this former air raid shelter in Puerto Princesa, Palawan, Philippine Islands, where charred remains were found. (SC#211410-S, World War II Signal Corps Photograph Collection, U.S. Army Military History Institute, Carlisle Barracks, PA)

An eyewitness recalled that the Japanese brought out an unwounded POW, in perfect health, and used him to display the workings of the human heart.

> The prisoner was tied to a tree outside the . . . office. A Japanese doctor and four Japanese medical students stood round him. The first removed his finger nails and then cut open his chest and removed his heart with which the doctor then proceeded to give a practical demonstration.[70]

These Japanese "medical units" also maintained high-pressure chambers where they filmed the death agonies of their victims, conducting experiments that would have impressed the Nazi doctors at Dachau and Auschwitz. None of the participants were charged.

The Russian trial of the 12 Japanese officers in 1949 was reminiscent of the Stalinist show trials of the 1930s and 1940s. All those charged were found guilty and sentenced to periods in the slave labor system (from which few returned). Like the classic Soviet show trials, the guilty parties confessed their

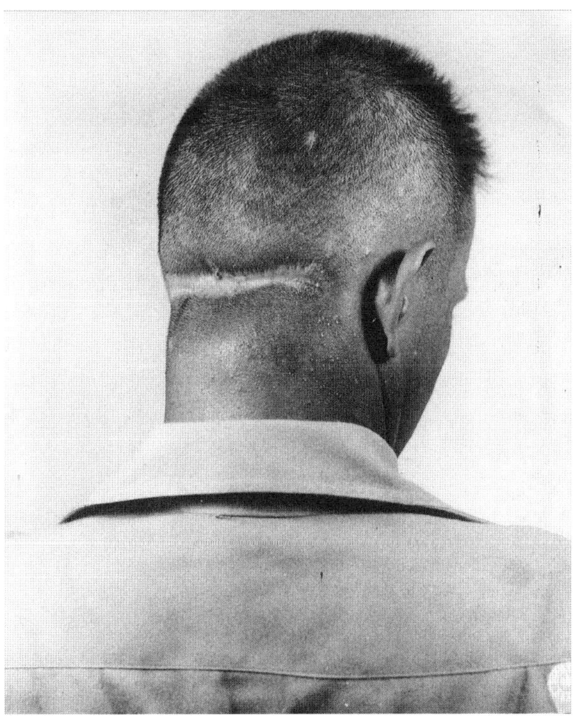

A Filipino survivor of Japanese beheading: Pablo Martinez, Luzon, P.I. August 2, 1945. (National Archives and Record Administration, Box 484, U.S. Signal Corps SC-265975)

political sins and begged forgiveness. One Japanese member of Detachment 100, Mitomo Kazou, closed his testimony by saying:

> At the time I was serving in Detachment 100 I did not realize the full depth of my wicked deeds and crimes, but having lived in the Soviet Union for four years, and also, and particularly, having been in this Court for the past few days, I deeply feel the whole weight of the crimes I committed.
>
> Here, for the first time, I learned the truth about the Soviet Union. I learned to know the Soviet people, I saw that they are humane and noble.
>
> I fully realize my responsibility. I repent of having participated in the crimes.[71]

None of the many thousands of other Japanese soldiers were tried or punished. Indeed, the majority of contemporary Japanese society refuses to accept any responsibility for the war crimes committed during the war. At the Tokyo trials, the responsibility of command, rejected at Nuremberg, was the operating legal principle against the Japanese, both military officers and diplomats, as well.[72]

Passions were more measured in Europe than in the Far East. In postwar Europe, the atmosphere was slightly less poisonous; ideology, rather than race, triumphed.

Trial Results

The outcomes of these many trials at Nuremberg, Dachau, and Tokyo are less important to this study than the legal precedents they produced and the changes they brought to future war crimes trials. Media coverage reflected the public's lack of interest: "What had been billed as an exciting trial did indeed become a bore," read one comment. "Interest waned. Most of the big-name journalists such as Walter Cronkite, Rebecca West, Edward R. Murrow, Howard K. Smith, William L. Shirer, Drew Middleton, Eric Sevareid and others had either returned to the States or to more interesting assignments in Europe," said another.[73] Despite the drama of the 1961 Academy-Award-winning movie *Judgment at Nuremberg,* the real activity, equally exciting, took place behind closed doors as representatives of the United States, Britain, France, and Russia haggled over politics and the sentences.[74]

Legacy of the Nuremberg Trial

The legacy of the Nuremberg Trial is huge, although not entirely positive.

1. First and foremost, the trial was the first such effort to arrest the perpetrators and force them to confront their war crimes. The victorious nations were going to

try the prominent political and military leaders of the enemy on the basis of laws drafted by themselves and before judges representing only the victor states. The rest of the world waited to see how nations that espoused democracy would treat the accused war criminals. They were on exhibit for all to see. Survivors and other witnesses could come forward to tell their stories and accuse the guilty. Punishment for some was assured.

2. A second important legacy of the Nuremberg trial is that it provided a record of the events. Call it education or history, but it is critical that nations confirm the motives and details of the crime and the war, punish the guilty, praise the heroes, and, one hopes, prevent a reoccurrence of the war crimes judged. As an indication of the importance attached to such trials, they nearly always open with a speech looking to the future and reflecting the spirit of the victims. War crimes trials claim to speak on behalf of Every Person, the Righteous, the Victors. Justice Robert Jackson told the defendants at Nuremberg that "the real complaining party at your bar is Civilization."[75] At the opening of the Eichmann trial, the prosecutor, Gideon Hausner, outlined the horrors of the Holocaust and closed by assuring both victims and survivors that he was speaking in their names. The trial transcript is entitled "The 6,000,000." A war crimes trial, regardless of the nations or

General Anton Dostler is tied to a stake before being executed by a firing squad at Averea, Italy. The General was convicted and sentenced to death by an American military tribunal. December 1, 1945. (SC#217267-S, World War II Signal Corps Photograph Collection, U.S. Army Military History Institute, Carlisle Barracks, PA)

groups involved, becomes a mass purification ritual. The enemy criminals must be confronted and shown to be evil. This may even be necessary as the first step in reconciliation and reconstruction following a war.

3. The fact that the Nuremberg trial was demonstrably fair calmed America's friends and enemies alike and reflected well on America's values. The trials were public, witnesses spoke out against the accused, transcripts were available, newspapers reported on the proceedings, and the sentences were fair—almost lenient when one considers that the new German government freed many before their prison sentences had been fully served. Germany, in particular, breathed a sigh of relief when it became clear that only those whose participation in war crimes could be proven would be brought to trial and that the general public was to be "de-Nazified" and absolved. Europeans were being lured by the competing ideologies of capitalism and socialism as the Cold War heated up, and the decorum and general legality of the Nuremberg trials helped many make up their minds.
4. Historian Bradley Smith points out a legacy that is seldom considered: that the Nuremberg trial acted to dampen the possibility of postwar violence. The atmosphere in Europe at the end of the war was explosive, and it is remarkable that there wasn't a bloodbath by the French or Russians against the hated Germans,

A Russian slave laborer, among prisoners liberated by the 3rd Armored Division of the U.S. First Army, points an accusing finger at the former Nazi guard who brutally beat prisoners. April 24, 1945. (SC#203466-S, World War II Signal Corps Photograph Collection, U.S. Army Military History Institute, Carlisle Barracks, PA)

especially if they feared that the Germans might go scot-free. Further, the Nazi SS units were still meeting in secret with hopes of reestablishing control over Germany. The Germans themselves, despite their complete national collapse, might have somehow mustered enough strength for a suicidal spasm if they had suspected that the Allies would punish the country collectively; the defeated enemy's back was to the wall, so to speak, because it had surrendered "unconditionally" and had no reason to expect passable treatment.

As improbable as it may seem today, violence was close at hand. By the war's end, many Germans had convinced themselves that they were simply good German citizens who had been misled by a criminal government; punishment of the entire society might have created a Germany like the defeated Germany after World War One: despondent and searching for a leader. As happened in the political vacuum in Germany at the end of the First World War, minor uprisings erupted in large cities across Germany after the conclusion of World War Two. In fact, in March 1946, 1,100 Nazis—members of the so-called SS Werewolves—were arrested in simultaneous raids in 200 towns in the American and British Zones of Germany and Austria. Called "Operation Nursery," the mass arrests of the rabidly Nazi Hitler Youth culminated a 10-month investigation by the Allied authorities aimed at crushing a mass revolution by an army of young Nazis that hoped to reestablish dictatorship and return the Third Reich to power.

At the very least, the proximity of so many armies in the limited space of devastated Europe, each bristling with weapons, wild-eyed with dreams of vengeance, and influenced by propaganda, made the prospect of a shoving match a dangerous possibility. The swift decision to establish a democratic trial of only those deemed responsible for the atrocities, in Smith's opinion, lessened any threat of a bloodbath.[76]

5. The exposure of the medical experiments inflicted on human beings was so appalling that the judges who tried the Nazi doctors in one of the Supplemental Nuremberg Trials went beyond punishing the doctors; they created a new code of medical ethics. Still called the Nuremberg Code, it imposes on those who practice medicine in the United States certain requirements: patients must consent to any procedure, that any novel experiment be tried first on animals, and that the experiment be conducted by qualified experts. Since this new medical code did not carry the force of law, the U.S. government stepped in in 1962 when the Food and Drug Administration (FDA) established the current code of patient's rights. Today's requirement that every patient sign a consent form before treatment is a direct result of the Nuremberg trials in 1947.
6. Among the most important precedents and a mainstay of war crime law are the Nuremberg Principles, which hold culprits accountable for their actions rather than passing responsibility to their senior officers. It is certainly true that in some cases, such as the trials of the Japanese in Tokyo, wartime hatred and an incompetent legal process rejected Justice Jackson's emphasis on fairness in favor of General Douglas McArthur's need for vengeance. But, overall, the soldiers or civilians who commit war crimes can no longer as easily shift responsibility to a higher-up. Even in cases where there is a clear link between the soldier and his superior officers, such as in the case William Calley at My Lai or the nine low-level American

guards at Abu Ghraib prison who were convicted of tormenting and humiliating their prisoners, the blame is rarely shifted to senior officers.

In Iraq, for example, American soldiers, rather than their commanding officers, are brought before courts-martial for atrocities committed against Iraqi civilians. In the case of the Abu Ghraib scandal, the culprits who committed the illegal acts, including Army Private First Class Lynndie England, received jail time, justifiably, but the officers in charge of the prison wing, Army Lieutenant Steven L. Jordan and Colonel Thomas M. Pappas—rightly or wrongly—each received a Letter of Reprimand.[77] So did General Janis Karpinski, the newly arrived commander of America's 17 prisons in Iraq, who was also demoted and relieved of command. Karpinski became the public face of the scandal. Any charges against Lieutenant General Ricardo Sanchez, then the top U.S commander in Iraq; his deputy, Major General Walter Wojdakowski; Major General Barbara G. Fast, Sanchez's top intelligence officer; and Colonel Marc Warren, Sanchez's top military lawyer (all of whom may have been well aware of the treatment of detainees) were found to be "unsubstantiated."[78] In 2005, one of the defendants, Corporal Charles Graner, was court-martialed at Fort Hood, Texas, and his attorney argued that he was only following orders, the same defense that the Nazis used at Nuremberg. The tribunal denied Garner's argument, citing the Nuremberg precedent.[79] One hopes that potential killers will pause if they know that they may be faced with personal consequences.

7. Yet another legacy, this one social rather than legal, concerns anti-Semitism, hatred of the Jews. One would imagine that anti-Semitism in America would have declined immediately in the face of the liberation of Nazi concentration camps and their hollow-eyed camp survivors, but it did not happen that way. After the initial shock, Americans came to see the liberated concentration camp victims as a potential blight of "untrustworthy" immigrants,[80] and Jewish soldiers in the U.S. Army continued to be viewed with suspicion. The combination of a long American tradition of anti-Semitism, America's grudging admiration for the tenacity and the spit-and-polish of the German Army, and the smoldering Cold War against communism actually caused anti-Semitism to increase dramatically.

But it didn't last long. As the indices cited earlier indicated, anti-Semitism gradually began to evaporate throughout the late 1940s and 1950s, although it was a sporadic at best. The reasons range from a growing awareness of civil rights, strong law enforcement against hate crimes, increased intermarriage, and the work of public advocacy groups to the revelations of the Nuremberg Trials and the later tumultuous Eichmann trial in Israel, in 1961.[81] Anti-Semitism seemed to lose its appeal, and, according to a noted legal jurist, Ellen Ash Peters, the former Chief Justice of the Connecticut Supreme Court, the decline of anti-Semitism in America after the war is a direct legacy of Nuremberg.

> Nuremberg produced a graphic record of the horrors of the systematic torture and genocide undertaken by that regime. Widespread dissemination

> of that appalling record increased American sensitivity to racial injustice. . . . Pictures of southern sheriffs attacking peaceful civil rights protestors bear an undeniable resemblance to pictures of SS troopers attacking Jews. Whatever Justice Jackson took from his experience at Nuremberg, the force of these analogies, even if unspoken, became a factor in awakening the judiciary in the 1960s. . . . I am persuaded that the legacy of Nuremberg contributed to the heightening of judicial concern . . . for the protection against intentional segregation and against abuses.[82]

At least one expert disagrees, however. Bradley F. Smith, the noted historian of the Nuremberg Trial mentioned earlier, wonders "whether the whole Nuremberg enterprise was so flawed that it produced no positive results at all. . . . Large portions of the American trial plan appear to be mistakes piled on folly. The actions of the negotiators and the prosecutors are also replete with blindness, miscalculation, and a suicidal passion for complexity."[83] Was it possible for the Allies to be objective so soon after the war? Could true justice be expected in the midst of the ruined city that had come to represent the Reich itself? The fact that great swatches of Germany had been mercilessly bombed by the Allies seemed to "level the playing field," in that all parties were guilty of some crimes against humanity, and everyone knew it.

Two other legal experts, Michael Scharf and William Schabas, reduced the criticism of the Nuremberg to the following three points:

1. Nuremberg was the victor's tribunal, before which only the vanquished were called to account.
2. Defendants were prosecuted and punished for crimes that had never before been defined in international law.
3. The Nuremberg Trial functioned on the basis of limited procedural rules that inadequately protected the rights of the accused.[84]

The overwhelming opinion of the trial in the legal profession is positive, however, and most give the credit to Justice Robert Jackson and Telford Taylor. Some experts go further. Norbert Ehrenfreund, he renowned judge of the California Superior Court, who was in his younger days the *Stars and Stripes* journalist present in the original Nuremberg courtroom, ranks the principles established at Nuremberg with the Magna Carta, the Constitution and the Bill of Rights, and the Geneva Conventions. "Jackson's decision to have a fair trial at Nuremberg . . . was a splendid victory for Robert Jackson, an even greater victory for humanity."[85] Even the Germans agreed:

> "It is obvious," said the German legal profession in August 1947, "the trial and judgment of such proceedings require of the Tribunal the utmost impartiality, loyalty, and sense of justice. The Nuremberg Tribunal has

> met these requirements with consideration and dignity. Nobody dares to doubt that it was guided by the search for truth and justice from the first to the last day of this tremendous trial. According to world opinion, this endeavor has found its humanly possible realization in the Judgment."[86]

Remember, this comes from the Germans.

Judge Ehrenfreund traces the path from precedents established by the Nuremberg trial directly to the 1948 United Nations Convention on the Prevention of the Crime of Genocide. That, in turn, led to the creation of the new Geneva Convention, in 1949, relative to the treatment of prisoners of war, and the protection of civilians in time of war, which was signed by 58 nations. It was this very agreement, Judge Ehrenfreund points out, that was used by the U.S. Supreme Court to strike down President George W. Bush's plan to deny open trials to the detainees at Guantanamo.[87]

Judge Ehrenfreund holds Robert Jackson in the highest esteem, maintaining that he is a hero and that the achievements at Nuremberg had a fundamental influence on American and, in some cases, worldwide jurisprudence.

> More than anyone else Jackson made the trial happen and established its reputation as remarkably fair and effective, despite the charged circumstances under which it was held. . . . On his return from Nuremberg, Jackson should have been honored with national acclaim. Instead, he resumed his seat on the Supreme Court without fanfare.

He spent his few remaining years on the bench speaking out against religious and racial discrimination, regularly citing his exposure to Nazi crimes at Nuremberg. Justice Jackson died only a few years later, in 1954, and one of his last acts was to confirm the landmark decision *Brown v. Board of Education*, which ended segregation in American public schools. The fairness and sensitivity toward the victims that he honed in Nuremberg were brought home to help revolutionize America.

This is all well and good, but the reality is that, since the end of World War II, there have been a jaw-dropping number of conflicts, uprisings, insurrections, and ethnic cleansings, but rarely have military leaders or political despots been held accountable: China's Cultural Revolution; Cambodia's killing fields; massacres in Darfur; Argentina's "dirty war"; mass murder in East Timor, Sri Lanka, and Rwanda; civil wars in Biafra, Greece, and Indochina; ethnic cleansing in Yugoslavia; Russia's invasion of Hungary, Czechoslovakia, Chechnya, Afghanistan, and Georgia; Iraq's bloody war with Iran; Israel's invasion of Lebanon, and Gaza; the gassing of the Kurds by Saddam Hussein; and, it must be said, America's invasion of Korea, Vietnam, Panama, and Iraq—to name only some. Governments have murdered millions of their own citizens, and the Nuremberg principles have been ignored for decades. Interestingly, one of the few applications of the Nuremberg precedents took place at Saddam Hussein's trial, in 2003, when the Iraqi Special Tribunal indicted Saddam for crimes against humanity, war crimes, and serious violations of the rules of war.

Nearly half a century after Nuremberg, in 1994, the International Court in The Hague, heir to Nuremberg's International Military Tribunal, confronted its first case—the genocide in Bosnia by the Serbs. The rules were about to be tested.

Notes

1. "Survivors are frequently told that time will heal the wounds of torture. But as Jean Améry, an Austrian philosopher tortured by the Gestapo, said, 'Anyone who has been tortured remains tortured. Anyone who has suffered torture never again will be at ease in the world, the abomination of the annihilation is never extinguished. Faith in humanity, already cracked with the first slap in the face, then demolished by torture, is never acquired again.' (Primo Levi, *The Drowned and the Saved* (New York: Vintage International, 1988, p. 25). Torture for Améry was an interminable death. He took his life in 1978." Sister Dianna Ortiz, OSU, "Government-Sanctioned Torture and International Law: A Survivor's Perspective," in *Fear of Persecution: Global Human Rights, International Law, and Human Well-Being*, ed. James Daniel White and Anthony J. Marsella (Lanham, MD: Lexington Books, 2007), p. 179.

2. M. Cherif Bassiouni and Christopher L. Blakesley, "The Need for an International Criminal Court in the New International World Order," *Vanderbilt Journal of Transnational Law* 5 (1992): 154.

3. Lisa Yavnai, "U.S. Army War Crimes Trials in Germany, 1945–1947," in *Atrocities on Trial: Historical Perspectives on the Politics of Prosecuting War Crimes*, ed. Patricia Heberer and Jürgen Matthäus (Lincoln and London: University of Nebraska Press, 2008), p. 49.

4. Earl F. Ziemke, *The U.S. Army in the Occupation of Germany, 1944–1946*, Army Historical Series (Washington, DC: Center of Military History, U.S. Army, 1975), p. 392.

5. Ibid.

6. *Ugolovnoye pravo, abshchaya chas*, 4th ed. (Moscow, 1948), p. 159, cited in George Ginsburgs, "Laws of War and War Crimes on the Russian Front during World War II: The Soviet View," *Soviet Studies* 11, no. 3 (January 1960): 263.

7. "Russians Hang German," *New York Times*, December 5, 1943, p. 24.

8. Alfred M. de Zayas, with Walter Rabus, *The Wehrmacht War Crimes Bureau, 1939–1945* (Lincoln: University of Nebraska Press, 1989). See also David Raub Snyder, *Sex Crimes under the Wehrmacht* (Lincoln: University of Nebraska Press, 2007).

9. Jürgen Matthäus, "The Lessons of Leipzig: Punishing German War Criminals after the First World War," in *Atrocities on Trial: Historical Perspectives on the Politics of Prosecuting War Crimes*, ed. Patricia Heberer and Jürgen Matthäus (Lincoln and London: University of Nebraska Press, 2008), pp. 3–23; see also James F. Willis, *Prologue to Nuremberg: The Politics and Diplomacy of Punishing War Criminals of the First World War* (Westport, CT: Greenwood Press, 1982).

10. Michael R. Marrus, "The Nuremberg Doctors' Trial and the Limitations of Context," in *Atrocities on Trial*, pp. 103–122.

11. Norbert Ehrenfreund, *The Nuremberg Legacy: How the Nazi War Crimes Trials Changed the Course of History* (New York: Palgrave Macmillan, 2007), pp. 93–106.

12. Ulf Schmidt, "The Scars of Ravensbrück: Medical Experiments and British War Crimes Policy, 1945–1950,", *Atrocities on Trial*, pp. 123–157.

13. Lisa Yavnai, "U.S. Army War Crimes Trials in Germany, 1945–1947," *Atrocities on Trial*, p. 49.

14. Ehrenfreund, *The Nuremberg Legacy*, p. xiii.

15. Telford Taylor, The *Anatomy of the Nuremberg Trials* (New York: Knopf, 1993), pp. 16–17.

16. David T. Zabeck, ed., *World War II in Europe: An Encyclopedia* (New York: Garland, 1999), p. 33.

17. George Ginsburgs, "Laws of War and War Crimes on the Russian Front during World War II: The Soviet View," *Soviet Studies* 11, no. 3 (January 1960): 254.

18. Bradley F. Smith, *Reaching Judgment at Nuremberg: The Untold Story of How the Nazi War Criminals Were Judged* (New York: Basic Books, 1977), p. 7.

19. Wilbourn E. Benton and Georg Grimm, eds., *Nuremberg: German Views of the War Trials* (Dallas, TX: Southern Methodist University Press, 1955), p. 183.

20. Peter Maguire, *Law and War: An American Story* (New York: Columbia University Press, 2000), pp. 170–173.

21. Smith, *Reaching Judgment at Nuremberg*, p. 47.

22. See Olaf Groehler, "The Strategic Air War and Its Impact on the German Civilian Population," in *The Conduct of the Air War in the Second World War: An International Comparison*, ed. Horst Boog (New York and Oxford: Berg, 1992), pp. 279–297.

23. Montgomery Belgion, *Victors' Justice* (Hinsdale, IL: Regnery, 1949), p. 23.

24. See Wilbourn E. Benton and Georg Grimm, eds., *Nuremberg: German Views of the War Trials* (Dallas: Southern Methodist University Press, 1955).

25. Secretariat of the International Military Tribunal, *Proceedings: Trial of the Major War Criminals before the International Military Tribunal, Nuremberg*, vol. 2 (Originally published by the Allied Control Authority for Germany, Nuremberg, Germany, 1947. (Buffalo, NY: William S. Hein, 1995), pp. 98–155.

26. Gerry Simpson, *Law, War and Crime: War Crimes Trials and the Reinvention of International Law* (Cambridge: Polity Press, 2007), p. 54.

27. Malcolm Bull, "States Don't Really Mind Their Citizens Dying (Provided They Don't All do it at Once): They Just Don't like Anyone else to Kill Them," *London Review of Books* 26, no. 24 (December 16, 2004)

28. Ehrenfreund, *The Nuremberg Legacy*, p. 125.

29. A. S. Comyns-Carr, K.C., "The Tokyo War Crimes Trial," *Far Eastern Survey* 18, no. 10 (May 18, 1949): 109–114.

30. Christian Reuther and Johannes Bacher, *Vernichtungskrieg: Verbrechen der Wehrmacht 1941 bis 1944. Katalog zur Ausstellung* (Hamburg: Hamburger Verlag, 1996).

31. Simpson, *Law, War and Crime*, pp. 90–91.

32. Lord Russell of Liverpool, C.B.E., M.C. [Edward Frederick Langley Russell], *The Scourge of the Swastika: A Short History of Nazi War Crimes* (London: Greenhill Books, 1954; Mechanicsburg, PA: Stackpole Books, 2002).

33. R. Minear, *Victor's Justice: The Tokyo War Crimes Trial* (Princeton, NJ: Princeton University Press, 1971), p. 126.

34. See Roger Cohen, *Soldiers and Slaves: American POWs Trapped by the Nazis' Final Gamble* (New York: Knopf, 2005); Flint Whitlock, *Given Up for Dead: American G.I.s in the Nazi Concentration Camp of Berga* (Cambridge, MA: Westview Press, 2005); and Mitchell Bard, *Forgotten Victims: The Abandonment of Americans in Hitler's Camps* (Boulder, CO: Westview Press, 1994). Also see Roger Cohen, "A Filmmaker Remembers G.I.s Consumed by Holocaust's Terror," *New York Times*, April 17, 2001, p. E1.

35. Franz Neumann, "The War Crimes Trials," *World Politics* 2, no. 1 (October 1949): 144.

36. See, for example, Jesse Hobbs, "Ex Post Facto Explanations," *Journal of Philosophy* 90, no. 3 (March 1993): 117–136.

37. Shabtai Rosenne, ed., *6,000,000 Accusers: Israel's Case against Eichmann* (Jerusalem: Jerusalem Post, 1961), pp. 29, 32.

38. Ibid., pp. 11–26.

39. For an excellent, detailed evaluation of the many Nuremberg precedents applied to the Eichmann trial, see Peter Papadatos, *The Eichmann Trial* (New York: Praeger, 1964).

40. Anti-Jewish hatred in the United States was so common that *Time* discussed the work of a James True, inventor of a truncheon he named "The Kike Killer," and his recently granted U.S. patent. Although True is identified as a "Jew baiter" and is described "as dangerous as Nazi Germany's Jew-baiting Julius Streicher," the article goes on to calmly describe his wife's smaller "Kike Killer, ladies size," and notes that "Mr. True" said that the "Jews pay Negroes to rape white girls. . . . Franklin Roosevelt is really named Rosenfeld and Jew Rosenfeld is insane; and the Jews have been plotting the destruction of Christian civilization for 500 years." *Time*'s article about "Mr. True," as he was so courteously addressed, closes with his call to shoot Jews. Said *Time*, one hopes with deep sarcasm: "For all who care to join his September Jew shoot, True 'promises he can obtain revolvers' from a Washington hardware firm at wholesale prices." *Time*, August 24, 1936, p. 41.

41. Isabel B. Price, "Gerald L.K. Smith and Anti-Semitism" (Master's thesis, University of New Mexico, 1965); see also Albert Lee, *Henry Ford and the Jews* (New York: Stein and Day, 1980).

42. Glen Jeansonne, "Combating Anti-Semitism: The Case of Gerald L.K. Smith," in *Anti-Semitism in American History*, ed. David A. Gerber (Urbana and Chicago: University of Illinois Press, 1986), pp. 152–166.

43. Harold E. Quinley and Charles Y. Glock, *Anti-Semitism in America* (New York: Free Press, 1979), pp. 114–115.

44. Ibid., p. 125.

45. Anna J. Merritt and Richard L. Merritt, eds., *Public Opinion in Semisoverign Germany: The HICOG Surveys, 1949–1955* (Urbana: University of Illinois Press, 1980), p. 101.

46. Donald Bloxham, "Milestones and Mythologies: The Impact of Nuremberg," in *Atrocities on Trial*, pp. 263–282.

47. Robert Michael, *A Concise History of American Antisemitism* (Lanham, MD: Rowman and Littlefield, 2005), pp. 147–148.

48. Charles Herbert Stember et. al., *Jews in the Mind of America* (New York: Basic Books, 1966).

49. Quinley and Glock, *Anti-Semitism in America*, pp. 12–14; and Spencer Blakeslee, *The Death of American Antisemitism* (Westport, CT: Praeger, 2000), p. 44.

50. "My Lai: A Question of Orders," *Time*, January 25, 1971, p. 24.

51. Department of the Army, *Report of the Department of the Army Review of the Preliminary Investigations into the My Lai Incident* (hereafter The General William R. Peers Report), Vols. 1–3 (1970). Available at http://www.law.umkc.edu/faculty/projects/ftrials/mylai/MYL_Peers.htm, as well as at http://www.loc.gov/rr/frd/Military_Law/Peers_inquiry.html. See an analysis of the Peers Report, by William Eckhardt, at http://www.law.umkc.edu/faculty/projects/ftrials/mylai/ecktragedy.html.

52. "Murder in the Name of War—My Lai," BBC, July 20, 1998.

53. The Peers Report, "The Omissions and Commissions of Cpt. Ernest L. Medina."Available at http://www.law.umkc.edu/faculty/projects/ftrials/mylai/MYL_Peers.htm.

54. U.S. House of Representatives, Report of the Armed Services Investigating Subcommittee of the Committee on Armed Services, "Investigation of the My Lai Incident," 91st Cong., 2nd sess. (Washington, July 15, 1970), p. 53. Available at http://www.loc.gov/rr/frd/Military_Law/pdf/MyLaiReport.pdf.

55. Ibid.

56. Telford Taylor, *Nuremberg and Vietnam: An American Tragedy* (Chicago: Quadrangle Books, 1970), pp. 45–46.

57. Article 47, German Military Code, quoted by Jackson at the International Military Tribunal, November 21, 1945, cited in Ann Tusa and John Tusa, *The Nuremberg Trial* (London: BBC Books, 1995), pp. 87–88.

58. See http://www.wbsi.org/ilfdigest/msdocs/TheLegacyofNuremberg.doc.

59. Ziemke, *The U.S. Army in the Occupation of Germany, 1944–1946*, p. 391.

60. Ibid.

61. Rudolph J. Rummel, *Death By Government* (1994; repr., New Brunswick, NJ: Transaction Publisher, 2002), pp. 120–121, 145, 151.

Iris Chang, *Rape of Nanking: The Forgotten Holocaust of World War II* (New York: Basic Books, 1997). For a Japanese response, in both English and Japanese, see Mosaki Tanaka, *What Really Happened in Nanking: The Refutation of a Common Myth* (Tokyo: Sekai Shuppan, 1987), or Takemoto Tadao and Ohara Yasuo, *The Alleged "Nanking Massacre": Japan's Rebuttal to China's Forged Claims* (English and Japanese) (Tokyo: Meisei-sha, 2000).

62. Other high-ranking Japanese officials had earlier committed suicide (e.g., Isamu Cho), had been granted immunity by MacArthur as members of the imperial family (e.g., Prince Asaka), or were protected by personal order of Nationalist leader Chiang Kai-shek as future advisers (e.g., General Yasuji Okamura). See Akira Fujiwara and Bob Wakabayashi, *The Nanking Atrocity 1937–1938: Complicating the Picture*

(New York: Berghan Books, 2007), and Philip R. Piccigallo, *The Japanese on Trial: Allied War Crimes Operations in the East, 1945–1951* (Austin: University of Texas Press, 1980), pp. 33, 73.

63. Lord Russell of Liverpool, C.B.E., M.C. [Edward Frederick Langley Russell], *The Knights of Bushido: A Short History of Japanese War Crimes* (London: Greenhill, 1958; Mechanicsburg, PA: Stackpole Books, 2002), p. 234.

64. Ann Marie Prévost, "Race and War Crimes: The 1945 War Crimes Trial of General Tomoyuki Yamashita," *Human Rights Quarterly* 14, no. 3 (August 1992): p. 305.

65. Liverpool, *The Knights of Bushido*, p. 234

66. Fred L. Borch, Review of Yuma Totani, *The Tokyo War Crimes Trials: The Pursuit of Justice in the Wake of World War II*, in *Journal of Military History* 73, no. 1 (January 2009): pp. 323-325.

67. Sebastian Moffett, "Japan Justice Minister Denies Nanking Massacre," Reuters, May 4, 1994. Also James Sterngold, "Japan Official Forced to Quit over Remark," *New York Times*, August 15, 1994, p. A5. Available at http://www.nytimes.com/1994/08/15/world/japan-official-forced-to-quit-over-remark.html?scp=1&sq=Sterngold&st=nyt; "Okinawa Slams History Text Rewrite," *Japan Times Online*, June 23, 2007.

68. Moffett, "Japan Justice Minister Denies Nanking Massacre."

69. Guillermo Contreras, "Bataan Death March Survivors Hear Apology," *San Antonio Express-News*, May 31, 2009, p. 1.

70. Liverpool, *The Knights of Bushido*, p. 233.

71. *Material on the Trial of Former Servicemen of the Japanese Army Charged with Manufacturing and Employing Bacteriological Weapons* (Moscow: Foreign Languages Publishing House, 1950), p. 520.

72. For example, Japan's energetic ambassador to Nazi Germany, Hiroshi Oshima, was charged with war crimes after World War II. See Oshima records, RG 100S, located at U.S. Army Heritage Education Center, Carlisle, Pennsylvania.

73. In 2001, Judge Ehrenfreund received the American Bar Association's prestigious Award of Judicial Excellence, an award given annually to honor the trial judge of the year.

74. Smith, *Reaching Judgment at Nuremberg*.

75. For Justice Jackson's opening remarks, see http://www.law. umkc.edu/faculty/projects/ftrials/Nuremberg/Jackson.html#The%20Lawless%20Road%20to%20Power.

76. Smith, *Reaching Judgment at Nuremberg*, p. 303.

77. Associated Press, "Soldiers Convicted in the Abu Ghraib Case," September 28, 2005; Josh White, "Reprimand Is Sentence for Officer at Abu Ghraib," *Washington Post*, August 30, 2007, p. A03.

78. Josh White, "General Demoted, but Cleared in Abuse Probe," *Washington Post*, May 6, 2005, A08; Libby Copeland, "Prison Revolt," *Washington Post*, May 10, 2004, p. C01.

79. Scott Horton, "A Nuremberg Lesson," *Los Angeles Times*, January 20, 2005, B13; also Horton, "An Idea Whose Time Has Come—and Gone?" *The Economist*, July 25, 2009, pp. 58–59.

80. Joseph W. Bendersky, *The "Jewish Treat": Anti-Semitic Politics of the U.S. Army* (New York: Basic Books, 2000), pp. 242, 296, 350.

81. Blakeslee, *Death of American Antisemitism*, pp. 208–210.

82. John Hagan and Scott Greer, "Making War Criminal," *Criminology* 40, no. 2 (2002): 231, cited in Ehrenfreund, *The Nuremberg Legacy*, p. 137.

83. Smith, *Reaching Judgment at Nuremberg*, p. 301.

84. Michael P. Scharf and William A. Schabas, *Slobodan Milošević on Trial: A Companion* (New York and London: Continuum, 2002), p. 43.

85. Ehrenfreund, *The Nuremberg Legacy*, p. 218.

86. Ra. Th. Klefisch, "Thoughts about Purport and Effect of the Nuremberg Judgment," in *Nuremberg: German Views of the War Trials*, ed. Wilbourn E. Benton and Georg Grimm (Dallas, TX: Southern Methodist University Press, 1955), p. 201.

87. Ehrenfreund, *The Nuremberg Legacy*, p. 124.

CHAPTER 5

The Rules Are Changing

Interestingly, it was the fall of the Berlin Wall and the subsequent collapse of Soviet communism that caused a renewed interest in some sort of world court or international tribunal. It had been a long time since the Nuremberg Principles was codified in international law, in December 1946, and the United Nations ratified the Genocide Convention, in 1948. Either Nuremberg or the Geneva negotiations would have been an excellent opportunity for the establishment of an international court. The Cold War, however, was well under way, and the creation of such a court would have faced the reality of reigning over a world divided between communism and capitalism. What if the culprit or the witnesses or the crime scene itself were located behind the Iron Curtain? How could the West punish war crimes committed in Poland or Hungary or, for that matter, in one of the Baltic republics of Estonia, Latvia, and Lithuania? How could the communist East be held to testimony regulated by religious oath? And without including the communist Soviet-Chinese bloc, how could the organization be considered a "world" court or an "international" tribunal? Besides, the moral outrage of the postwar years had passed.

Legal authorities M. Cherif Bassiouni and Christopher Blakesley conclude that "the shortsightedness and xenophobic tendencies of politicians after World War I. . . . made the task of establishing Nuremberg and Tokyo more difficult."[1] The Cold War made the search for justice more difficult still. War crimes were still being committed, and no one was being punished.

There hadn't been an internationally supported tribunal since Nuremberg in 1946. Interested parties led themselves to believe that the UN Genocide Convention, passed in 1948, was sufficient to punish war criminals since its Article VI provided that persons charged with genocide "shall be tried by a competent tribunal . . . or by such international penal tribunal as may have jurisdiction." "Nonsense," points out political writer Ronnie Dugger. The UN Convention against Genocide was simple "piety," and its mandate "to prevent or to stop mass murders was totally ineffective."[2] He was correct.

Yugoslavia and the International Criminal Tribunal

The first opportunity to face the issue whether and how to punish war criminals occurred four decades later, in 1989, when the Soviet satellites of Eastern European nations began to fall apart. Hungary opened its border with Austria, and nearby populations followed suit. Poland held its collective breath as it watched the new Polish Pope, John Paul II, lecture the Soviet puppet dictator in Warsaw. Poles marched on the streets of many cities carrying signs in support of *Solidarity*, the workers' union that launched a social movement. East Germans also poured into the streets, and, completely confused, the East German government threw up its hands and voted itself out of existence. The government ceased to exist. The Berlin Wall was attacked by the populations of both sides, bringing an effective end to the separation of East and West Berlin. The Soviet Union collapsed two years later. A world court was now possible (although some countries that had previously supported such a court now became reluctant to participate as national leaders began to wonder if they might someday be called before the bench).

Discussions continued through five contentious conferences sponsored by the United Nations and supported by every major legal and humanitarian organization, without the creation of a world court. Sometimes, however, a genocidal eruption is so violent and so public that a special tribunal must be created. Such an occasion occurred in the former Yugoslavia.

The murders in Yugoslavia started as early as 1991, as the nation dissolved during the collapse of the communist world. The ethnic groups within the country (which was 44% Bosnian [Muslim], 31% Serbian [Orthodox], and 17% Croatian [Catholic]), traditional enemies all, suddenly faced a violent Serbian movement in their midst that sought to create an "ethnically pure" Greater Serbia. The movement was led by Slobodan Milošević, head of the Socialist Party of Serbia (SPS), whose fiery speeches, control of the media, and sustained violence expanded Serbia's control over the two autonomous provinces of Vojvodina and Kosovo. Milošević and the new Greater Serbia movement were supported by the Serbian Orthodox Church, which helped organize, finance, and arm some of the most bloodthirsty Serbian thugs of the genocide, many under the control of the warlord Željko Ražnatović (known as "Arkan").

The world watched it all. The news was filled with horror stories of Serbian and Bosnian Serb roundups of non-Serbs in Bosnia, later found in mass graves or as gaunt survivors peering at the news cameras through barbed-wire fences. Individual nations did little for nearly two years. The UN, however, intervened in 1991, assigning U.S. diplomat Cyrus Vance to serve as an envoy and, in December, inserting UN peacekeepers, known as UNPROFOR (an acronym for "United Nations Protection Force," headquartered in Zagreb, Croatia, and made up of 38,000 troops, 2,100 local staff, 680 military observers, and 1,800 international civilian staff members).

The UN acted quickly, although largely ineffectively, after atrocities became widely known. In December 1991, the UN Security Council hoped to dry up the flow of weapons pouring into the Balkans by establishing an arms embargo. It hardly made a dent in Serbia's violent program of ethnic cleansing. In January 1992, the UN envoy Cyrus Vance managed to negotiate a ceasefire between the Serbs and the Croats, getting both parties to agree to the UN force of peacekeepers, UNPROFOR, to oversee the withdrawal of Serb forces from Croatian territory.

The Serbian attacks and purges escalated throughout the mid-1990s in other parts of the former Yugoslavia. Serbian militias violated internationally protected cities like Srebrenica, Bosnia, where, in 1995, policemen and paramilitary thugs, sometimes wearing ski masks, murdered nearly 8,000 Bosnian Muslim men and boys. Then came the attack on Kosovo, formerly a part of Serbia, where, in 1999, Serbians killed several thousand Kosovar Albanians. The term "ethnic cleansing" was coined to describe these horrific actions by the Serbs.

As the Serbian war continued to escalate, the United Nations acted again. UN Resolutions 808 and 827, ratified in 1993, created an ad hoc International Criminal Tribunal for Yugoslavia (ICT[Y]). It was hoped that this move would frighten the warring parties into more peaceful behavior, even though it took another two years just to name a prosecutor.

This was a unique moment in modern jurisprudence. For the first time since the Nuremberg trial, in 1946, and despite decades of obstacles, an international tribunal had been created with the express purpose of prosecuting crimes of genocide and other war crimes, although only those committed during the breakup of Yugoslavia. The ICT(Y) and the later International Criminal Tribunal for Rwanda (ICT[R]) were the first truly international criminal courts. Both were established by the United Nations Council and funded by the regular UN budget under the control of the General Assembly. More than that, for the first time in modern history, both the ICT(Y) and the ICT(R) could indict the sitting leader of a country for war crimes committed under his direction. (Hitler committed suicide, of course, and was never brought to justice.)

The new court contained improvements over the Nuremberg trial: rather than answering to only 4 judges, representing the 4 victorious allies in 1946, the ad hoc ICT(Y) had 11 judges, from Asia, Europe, Africa, North America, Latin America, and Australia. It would thus be a truly international panel, and there would be no whispers of "victor's justice." Moreover, unlike the Nuremberg trial, the proceedings were removed from the ruins of the former Yugoslavia and moved to The Hague, Netherlands, an historically neutral site, where a new courtroom was built, complete with facilities for sophisticated simultaneous translations and bulletproof glass partitions.

There were other differences between Nuremberg and the UN tribunals half a century later. Nuremberg was supported, to varying degrees, by the victorious countries of World War II. Not so with the ICT(Y) and the ICT(R), which relied on the support of cooperative governments and individuals who often feared reprisals. The prosecution at Nuremberg had sweeping military police powers at its disposal and an occupation Allied army; accused defendants and witnesses could hardly escape the postwar net. The Allies were also fortunate that the Germans almost obsessively maintained records of their atrocities. The later tribunals are a different matter. Justice Theodor Meron, president of the ICT(Y), lamented that "governments do not always cooperate, and when they do are often willing to share information only if its sources are kept confidential, a demand clearly in tension with the defendant's right to challenge the evidence against him."[3]

Once a prosecutor was finally appointed, the court's schedule moved quickly; nearly 100 people were indicted, of whom more than 50 were actually held in jail in The Hague. The majority of the rest are living openly in Serbia and other places, protected by loyal followers.

In May 1999, nearly a decade after the Serbian war began, Slobodan Milošević, despite his position as president of Yugoslavia and his fanciful posture as a world peacemaker, was indicted as a war criminal. Ironically, it was the United States that had propelled him to the level of senior statesman when it invited him to Dayton, Ohio, in November 1995, to meet with negotiators and the presidents of Croatia and Bosnia to work out a plan for peace: the Dayton Agreement. Everyone knew that he was the mass murderer responsible for ethnic cleansing in Bosnia, but, bluntly put, most Americans were not particularly concerned with what was happening there. Where was Serbia located, anyway? And shouldn't Europe be taking care of its own backyard? Where was the emerging European Union? Even after Milošević returned to Serbia following the Agreement, and after a brief period of world statesmanship, he went back to his original plan of ethnic cleansing. In 1998, the Serbian Army, under Milošević's command, drove 700,000 people out of Kosovo, many of whom were never seen alive again. Finally, the ICT(Y) reached out in 1999 and indicted him for war crimes. Milošević became the star defendant, overshadowing the rest of the collection of sadists and monsters, including the 40-year-old Bosnian Serb pub owner Dŭsko Tadić, charged with such atrocities as forcing a prisoner at knife point to bite off the testicles of another. Even against such horrifying standards, it was clear that Milošević, who had ordered that Serbia be "cleansed" of Bosnian Muslims, Bosnian Croats, and Kosovar Albanians, was driving the mass murder across the region. Consequently, the original charge of war crimes was upgraded to include genocide. All eyes turned to the Nuremberg precedents and the legal definition of genocide that had been outlined in 1948 in the UN Convention on the Prevention and Punishment of the Crime of Genocide. It was now included as Article 4 of the ICT(Y) statute—under which Milošević was clearly guilty.

The ICT(Y) moved ahead, despite the number of witnesses to be assembled, the unknown number of hidden mass graves, the legal difficulties of linking some of the leaders directly to the atrocities, the various languages involved, the poor health of at least one major defendant (Milošević), and a nearly impenetrable shield of protection by thousands of devoted followers.

The trial against him finally began in February 2002 with the defiant and hostile Milošević rejecting the court's authority. When that failed, the Serb leader refused to accept his court-appointed lawyers and elected to represent himself. The trial limped along for months as a list of some 1,200 witnesses was assembled, including the former Soviet Premier Nikolai Ryzhkov and Ramsey Clark, the former U.S. Attorney General. On occasion, claims of Milošević's failing health halted proceedings for as much as six months at a time. The trial ended suddenly on March 11, 2006, when Milošević was found dead in his cell. For a brief time, poisoning was suspected, a rumor fanned by his widow, Mirjana Markovic, who proclaimed his innocence in Belgrade's *Vecernje Novosti* newspaper. Then followed new rumors that he had died by suicide, conceivable since both of his parents had killed themselves. However, an official autopsy confirmed that he had died of a heart attack.[4] Victims felt cheated that a mass murderer had died in such an ordinary way, but they took solace in the fact that the brutality of the conflict and their sacrifices were now part of the historical record—at least so it seemed until February 2007.

It didn't seem possible that any decision but "guilty" could be reached, but a stunned world learned otherwise. The newly created United Nations International Criminal Court, established in 2002, conceded in 2007 that the 1995 massacre of nearly 8,000 Bosnian Muslim men in Srebrenica constituted genocide but concluded that Serbia was not responsible for the crime.[5] The responses varied. Most Serbians were grudgingly satisfied that they had not been blamed; the court was pleased that it had properly defined genocide, and the Bosnian Muslims seethed. Case closed. Meanwhile, an indicted war criminal, Serb general Ratko Mladić, among many others, is still at large, protected by prominent people in Serbia.

On July 22, 2009, according to a barely visible article buried on page 4 of *USA Today*, the UN High Court in The Hague announced the conviction of two Bosnian Serb cousins, Milan Lukić and Sredoje Lukić, for a killing spree in 1992 in the eastern Bosnian town of Visegrad. Among their crimes, the Lukić boys herded 119 Muslims into two buildings, the victims ranging from 2 days old to 75 years old, and burned both buildings to the ground, shooting all who tried to escape. Sredoje Lukićc was sentenced to 30 years, and his cousin Milan, the convicted ringleader, received life imprisonment.[6]

The International Criminal Tribunal (Rwanda)

In April 1994, while the Milošević trial was limping along, a new genocide erupted in Rwanda as half the country's population, the dominant shorter, broader Hutus, turned against the minority Tutsis, who were taller and thinner, killing an estimated 800,000 in just 100 days, in plain view of an unmoved world, until they ran out of strength. As governments dithered and the UN debated whether the Rwandan massacres fit the definition of true genocide since Rwanda was not at war (and the massacres occurred within the nation's borders), many of those responsible escaped to Zaire, where the killers were mistakenly seen by relief agencies as victims. Many who had only the day before killed Tutsis were now being welcomed into UN and Red Cross camps as refugees. Once in the camps, they ran the camps with the same terror they had employed in Rwanda, but right under the UN's nose.[7]

The UN Security Council finally acted by passing Resolution 955 in November 1994, which established another ad hoc UN International Criminal Tribunal (ICT[R]). This one went to work in Arusha, Tanzania, in 1997. Like the ICT(Y), the Rwanda trial made additional modifications to the Nuremberg precedents. If the Yugoslavian tribunal made it acceptable to indict a sitting leader, the Rwandan court made it legal to adjudicate genocides within a nation's borders and during peacetime, if applicable. But, the Rwanda tribunal faced the prospect of punishing tens of thousands of unknown killers, so it turned once again to the arrest and trial of the nation's leaders—to be tried as individuals, rather than as leaders. This modification of the original Nuremberg Principles was now firmly fixed in international law.[8]

Eventually, a smattering of high-ranking culprits were indicted and convicted: the former Rwandan prime minister Jean Kambanda was sentenced to life imprisonment in 1998 (thereby establishing the UN courts' authority to arrest Milošević the following year), followed by the former government official Mika Muhimana; a retired army officer, Lieutenant Colonel Aloys Simba; Joseph Nzabrinda, a businessman; and even a Roman Catholic priest. As of December 2009 the ICT(R) had indicted a total of 80 people, including paramilitary leaders, radio broadcasters, leaders of the Hutu government, even nuns and priests; 31 cases had been completed, 26 more were still in progress, 8 were acquitted, 9 were on appeal, 7 were released after completing their sentences, and 2 were still awaiting trial.[9]

It was clear to all that many thousands of killers were involved, most of whom would never face justice. As a result, Rwanda has undertaken one of the world's boldest experiments in postwar reconciliation: "Gacaca," which means "justice on the grass." Patterned on the South African "Truth and Reconciliation" commission, the government has brought prisoners back to the scene of the massacre to stand before a gathering of survivors. There the prisoners confess all, to the satisfaction of the citizen-judges and the survivors, in effect begging forgiveness of the people they harmed. Local citizen-judges weigh survivor accounts of the massacres against the testimony of perpetrators. Once the truth of the particular event has been agreed upon by both perpetrators and victims and the culprit has purged his conscience to the satisfaction of the survivors, the prisoner is supposedly accepted back into the community to live, as best as he is able, living side-by-side in the same neighborhoods as the relatives of the people they killed.[10]

This wrenching emotional process was recorded at the village level by award-winning documentary filmmaker Anne Aghion in a trilogy that begins with *Gacaca: Living Together Again in Rwanda* (2002). The film, which ventures into rural Rwanda to follow the first steps of the truth and reconciliation process, was awarded the 2003 UNESCO Fellini Award. Two years later, Aghion released the second documentary, this one examining the impact of the return of a prisoner to his community before his trial; the film, titled *In Rwanda We Say . . . The Family That Does Not Speak Dies*, won an Emmy Award in 2005. In 2008, the third film of the trilogy, *The Notebooks of Memory*, which focuses exclusively on the trials in which local citizen-judges weigh survivor accounts against the testimony of perpetrators, was released. Kenneth Turan, in the *Los Angeles Times*, called it "quietly devastating." Most recently, in 2009, Aghion produced a feature-length documentary titled *My Neighbor My Killer*, which played to sold-out screenings at the Cannes Film Festival in 2009 and won the U.S. Sterling Competition and the Nestor Amendros Prize for Courage in Filmmaking, awarded by the Human Rights Watch International Film Festival. The results of the reconciliation experiment following the Rwanda genocide of 1994 are available for all to witness,[11] although the success of the program is still under debate.[12]

Cambodia

Cambodia, which experienced the most horrific atrocities since the Holocaust, is still awaiting justice.[13] More than 2 million men, women, and children were murdered, and an additional million died of starvation, disease, and madness. The despotic leader of the Khmer Rouge government, Pol Pot, died a natural death in 1998. His henchmen, all guilty, simply melted back into Cambodian society. The United Nations tried valiantly to convince the new prime minister, Hun Sen, to bring the well-known killers to trial, but to no avail. Hun Sen had himself been a leading member of the Khmer Rouge. In 2005, an international tribunal, called the Extraordinary Chambers in the Courts of Cambodia (ECCC), was sworn in, with 17 Cambodian judges and an additional 13 judges from other countries. The trials were scheduled for 2007 but were postponed indefinitely.[14] In the meantime, the culprits, now in their 70s and 80s, were passing from the scene.

Finally, in March 2009, one of the surviving leaders of the Khmer Rouge, 66-year-old Kaing Guek Leu, a former math teacher better known as "Comrade Duch" (pronounced "Doik"), faced a UN-backed tribunal. Standing in a 500-seat auditorium filled with Khmer Rouge survivors and other members of the public, a 45-page indictment was read that accused him of murdering 16,000 men, women, and children in his care. "Duch" admitted that, under his watch as commander of the Tuol Sleng (S-21) Interrogation Center, "prisoners were beaten, electrocuted, smothered with plastic bags or had water poured into their noses; children were taken from their parents and dropped from third floor windows to their deaths, and some prisoners were bled to death." Vowing to cooperate fully with the UN-backed tribunal, "Duch" expressed his "deep regret and heartfelt sorrow," even demanding, at one point, that he be given amnesty and released.[15] His trial lasted from February 2009, when Duch was arrested masquerading as a Christian field hand, until November when punishment was determined. Since Cambodia has no capital punishment, life imprisonment is the most severe penalty that can be imposed. He was given 40 years in prison.

The Cambodian Genocide Program at Yale University, established in 1994 by the U.S. Congress, continues to systematically catalogue the crimes of the Khmer Rouge.

Armenia

Justice for the victims of the Armenian genocide in 1915 will likely never come. The Turkish government "solved" the issue by maintaining that it never happened, despite the fact that there were thousands of survivors and eyewitnesses as prominent as the American ambassador, Henry Morgenthau. To this day, the Armenian massacre is unmentionable in Turkey. Although there are shelves of books on the history of the genocide and volumes of recollections in libraries around the world,[16] the Turkish archives are closed to researchers on the subject,[17] and journalists and scholars are intimidated by government repression. Violators are subject to immediate legal prosecution under the notorious Law 301, which forbids the defaming of Turkey. No one is too important to face the Turkish government's culture of genocide denial, as the world saw on September 2, 2005, when Orhan Pamuk, a Turk and the winner of the Nobel Prize for Literature, was indicted for "publicly denigrating Turkish identity" following a single reference to the Armenian genocide in a February 6, 2005, interview in the Swiss newspaper *Tages Anzeiger*.[18] That same year, 2005, Hrant Dink, the editor-in-chief of the bilingual Turkish and Armenian weekly newspaper *Agos*, was also indicted for "insulting Turkish identity" after he wrote an article on the Armenian genocide. Perhaps because of his popularity as a writer, Dink received only a six-month suspended sentence, but he continued to be a target for angry Turkish nationalists. Dink was shot to death by an unknown assailant on January 19, 2007, in front of his newspaper office building.[19]

The issue is still unresolved and, like an unchecked infection, is becoming costly to Turkey. Two French presidents, Jacques Chirac and his successor, Nicolas Sarkozy, have stated separately that Turkey will have to recognize the Armenian massacres as state-directed genocide before it is allowed to join the European Union.[20] Six weeks after Chirac's statement, in 2006, Turkey responded by suspending military relations with France.[21]

The International Criminal Court

Despite the two ad hoc trials for war crimes in Yugoslavia and Rwanda, the world seemed to ignore the nearly one dozen conflicts and civil wars raging in 1998, as well as the war criminals who walked away unscathed. That year, 1998, the UN Human Rights Commissioner, Mary Robinson, admitted as much, when she said:

> Count up the results of fifty years of human rights mechanisms, thirty years of multibillion dollar development programs and endless high-level rhetoric and the general impact is quite underwhelming . . . this is a failure of implementation on a scale that shames us all.[22]

That summer of 1998, the United Nations finally passed what was called the Rome Statute, which became the foundation of the new International Criminal Court (ICC). (Despite America's rhetoric, Washington, Moscow, and Beijing have consistently voted against participating. Because of these obstacles, the Rome Statute was not ratified until April 2002.) Finally, in July 2002, the ICC was officially formalized, almost 60 years after the Nuremberg and Tokyo trials ended and 54 years after the UN's Genocide Convention was adopted. Adopting the sentiments of Nuremberg's Justice Robert Jackson, the Court considers every defendant, however heinous the accusations against him, to be innocent. The ICC declared that "if a nation-state cannot or will not provide a fair trial for those charged as a defendant, then ICC jurisdiction enables the independent prosecutor to initiate action in The Hague."[23] Chief UN legal counsel Hans Correll predicted that "A page in the history of humankind is being turned."[24]

General Augusto Pinochet

In the midst of these negotiations, justice against a South American dictator and mass murderer established yet another advance in the acceptance of international law dealing with war crimes and crimes against humanity. General Augusto Pinochet was the dictator of Chile after he seized power from the legally elected government of President Salvador Allende in a bloody coup on September 11, 1973. Allende, a Marxist, was not popular with the U.S. government, and it is probable that the CIA participated in the coup, even though Allende had been elected by the Chilean people.

Once Pinochet took power, and with the army behind him, he rounded up and murdered thousands of suspected Allende supporters, crowding them into Santiago's main soccer stadium to be tortured and shot. People continued to "disappear" long after Allende's name was a mere memory. For 17 years, Pinochet was the worst violator of human rights violations to be found in South America. Bowing to advancing age, Pinochet stepped down as president of Chile in 1989 but retained control of the army. At his demand, the Chilean government bestowed on him the title of senator for life. At the same time, he was granted lifelong immunity from criminal prosecution. Now came the legal twist.

Assuming that his blanket of immunity protected him worldwide, Pinochet planned a medical visit to London, where he was unexpectedly arrested pursuant to a warrant for human rights violations issued by Spain. The question of whether one could be arrested and charged with crimes against humanity that occurred place in a different country and not during wartime exploded before the British Parliament's House of Lords. After a bitter debate, Pinochet was found to have violated the Nuremberg rulings and was ordered to be transported to Spain for trial and punishment. This momentous British decision, in the words of the leading authority on Nuremberg, Judge Norbert Ehrenfreund, "was based on three points: (1) the Nuremberg Principle that no one is above the law; (2) genocidal crimes do not require a state of war in order to be prosecuted; and (3) Spain had jurisdiction to prosecute Pinochet even though his crimes occurred across the sea in Chile."[25]

Pinochet never made it to Spain. Because of his failing health, he was allowed to return to Chile, where he was stripped of his honors and legal protection. Like Milošević, Pinochet died of heart failure, on December 10,

2006; he was 91. Human rights supporters around the world, while rejoicing over his death, lamented that someone so evil could have escaped justice and died such an ordinary death.

The U.S. Position

In the meantime, the United States was carrying on an interesting diplomatic dance. After decades of support for war crimes trials, whether in Nuremberg or Tokyo or Dachau, and of championing the ad hoc tribunals for Rwanda and Yugoslavia, the United States remained uncomfortable at the prospect of using the Nuremberg Principles to indict a leader of one country (e.g., Pinochet), in another country (Britain), at the behest of still another country (Spain).[26] The Rome Statute, which created the International Criminal Court (ICC), contained several flaws that Washington considered serious. First, the Court lacked what the United States believed were prudent safeguards against political manipulation; in other words, the Court was answerable to the UN Security Council, which, as the United States knew well, is a highly political body. Another flaw was that, despite its ties to the Security Council, the Court possessed sweeping authority—too much, its opponents said. The final problem was that the Rome Statute that established the Court had broken with international legal precedent and claimed jurisdiction over nationals and military personnel from states that were not party to the treaty; it could reach out and charge any national leader with war crimes.[27] The existence of a court with such powers would clearly influence future policies and foreign affairs. To snub another state in the process of foreign affairs might easily lead to legal consequences.

Moreover, the United States was not sure how it felt about who should be held responsible for war crimes: the commander or the actual perpetrator of the atrocity. As far back as the Civil War, U.S. jurisprudence rejected the principle of "command responsibility." That changed with the Nuremberg and Tokyo trials, where it was often easier to scoop up the higher ranked leadership if the actual criminals were not available. U.S. leadership also flipped several times on the issue of whether it was legal to hold a country responsible for starting an aggressive war. At Nuremberg and Tokyo, the United States argued that the Germans and the Japanese were guilty of "crimes against peace" and of initiating an aggressive war. But, 60 years later, Justice Theodor Meron, president of the International Criminal Tribunal for Yugoslavia, argued bitterly against the "crime against peace" clause in the ICC.[28]

Both the Clinton and the George W. Bush administrations considered the Court a possible threat to American soldiers or government officials. If Slobodan Milošević, the sitting president of Serbia, and Augusto Pinochet, despite lifelong immunity granted by his admittedly puppet government, could be indicted, why not an American president? As a result, both administrations rejected membership in the International Criminal Court. President Clinton eventually yielded to constituent pressure and reluctantly signed the ICC treaty, although he waited until the very last possible day, December 31, 2000. President George W. Bush, in May 2002, "unsigned" the Rome Statute, concerned that the ICC would be an unchecked power able to prosecute U.S. soldiers and their superiors, especially in light of Washington's invasion of Afghanistan and the planned incursion into Iraq as well,. The logic was that the United States would bring its own soldiers and leaders to justice, rather than turning them over to the possibly politically tainted hands of others. Indeed, on occasion, the U.S. military has moved quickly to court-martial flagrant violators among the American forces in Iraq, those accused of the murder or rape of Iraqi nationals, to prevent the ICC from becoming the favored arena of justice.

Michael Posner, executive director of the Lawyers Committee for Human Rights, said in an interview that "no American president in 200 years has unsigned a treaty, as far as we can find." "It would also send a signal to other governments around the world that treaties they signed are unsignable."[29]

Critics howled that Bush's withdrawal from support of a world court, especially in the face of the Court's ratification by every other Western democracy, eroded America's moral standing among friends and foes alike. After all, America endlessly trumpets the call for democracy and fair play. Treaties and trade agreements with Washington routinely contain rhetoric about human rights, and foreign nations that do not comply are threatened with inclusion on lists of countries in disfavor. America has gone so far in defense of human rights that President Jimmy Carter canceled America's participation in the 1980 Moscow Olympics to protest the Soviet invasion of Afghanistan. Now, Washington's refusal to support the ICC implied that "the city on the hill" did not live up to its own propaganda. Critics of America's open defiance of the ICC also claimed that it weakened the legal clout of the Court.

On the other side of the issue, supporters of the Bush administration's decision point out that withdrawing from the ICC might not be sufficient. Anti-Americans or zealous advocates of the ICC might well use the Security Council against the United States, particularly U.S. citizens and military personnel, even after the United States had withdrawn from the Rome Statute. The Bush administration demanded immunity for all American leaders and all American nationals. This resulted in the passage of UN Resolution 1422, which extends a year's immunity, renewable each year, to American soldiers and leaders. As a means of further protecting American military personnel and their political leaders, in 2002 Congress passed the American Service Members' Protection Act (ASPA), which restricts U.S. participation in peacekeeping operations and prohibits direct or indirect transfer of military assistance or information or American personnel to the ICC. To further separate American policy from the influence of a world court, Congress passed the Nethercutt Amendment, in 2004, which prohibits sending U.S. assistance to any ICC party that has not entered into a separate agreement with the United States that it will not surrender American citizens to the ICC. In other words, a country that doesn't agree to protect American citizens from international courts will not receive any military or financial support from the United States. Law professor and author Marjorie Cohn points out the Bush administration's not-so-hidden cudgel: "And if a country refuses to enter into such an agreement, the U.S. will often withdraw military assistance . . . it has done so with respect to a staggering 35 countries."

What is the overall evaluation of America's failure to support a world court against war crimes? Professor Cohn summarizes: "As with the U.N. and other peacekeepers, the U.S. has put lives in danger by insisting on opposing the ICC treaty in every way possible."[30] Ninety-nine countries have entered into bilateral agreements with the United States to protect American citizens from trial by the International Criminal Court. Meanwhile, the ICC's jurisdiction is recognized by 108 countries, though not by the United States, Russia, and China.

The United States entered the new millennium following a course that relied on the Nuremberg precedents when applicable but that kept the country out of the grasp of unpredictable foreign legal entities. America's traditional reputation as a defender of the world's underdog—and supporter of international law—was growing tarnished as governments struggled to retain America's foreign aid funds by promising to protect U.S. citizens, soldiers, and political leaders from the reach of international law. Looking back to those moments prior to the terrorist attack on September 11, 2001, one sees a self-satisfied America, internationally arrogant, self-absorbed, and secure in its hegemonic world dominance. Its new president, George W. Bush, with a questionably obtained mandate, bragged before a news camera on the golf course that his new job required no work. However, the world was about to change, and allies and international events would undergo a stressful and arguably illegal redirection.

9/11 Attacks against America

At 8:45 in the morning, a hijacked passenger jet, American Airlines Flight 11 out of Boston, circled the New York skyline, and plowed into the north tower of the World Trade Center, setting it on fire. As New Yorkers watched, transfixed, a second hijacked airliner, United Airlines Flight 175, appeared in the sky and crashed into the south tower, which also exploded into flames. More than 200 people jumped to their deaths from the burning towers. By

9:40 A.M., every airport, bridge, and tunnel in New York and New Jersey had been closed by the authorities. Suddenly, a third hijacked passenger plane, American Airlines Flight 77, crashed into the Pentagon building in Arlington, Virginia. The United Nations and all federal buildings and agencies were evacuated. Secret service agents armed with automatic rifles poured into Lafayette Park, across from the White House, to protect the government. Although this was unknown at the time, a fourth hijacked plane en route to Washington, United Airlines Flight 93, had been wrenched from the hijackers' control by courageous passengers but had crashed in rural Pennsylvania. By noon on September 11, 2001, America found itself at war against an unknown enemy. A total of 2,974 victims and 19 Arab hijackers died in the attacks, more than died at Pearl Harbor or on D-Day.

The nation and the government were understandably stunned as each looked to the other for direction. Not knowing if additional attacks were to come, the public enveloped itself in nationalistic excess, and the government hid in safety. President George W. Bush ventured out onto the New York rubble to urge Americans to defy its antimaterialistic enemies by shopping at local stores. The Bush administration used its unexpected new "war powers" to reorganize government bureaus into such new security agencies as the Department of Homeland Security, to restrict domestic rights by passage of the Patriot Act, and to direct American military wrath toward enemies, real and imagined, domestic and foreign.

Ingredients for War Crimes in the Making

The government was wholly unprepared for the attack of September 11, 2001, despite the many warnings and intercepted transmissions that preceded it. An independent, bipartisan congressional commission known as the 9/11 Commission or the Kean/Hamilton Commission finally convened on November 26, 2002 (441 days after the attack!) to dissect the events that had led to it. The Final Report of the National Commission on Terrorist Attacks upon the United States was issued on July 22, 2004, without being able to obtain pertinent records from an increasingly secretive Executive Branch. The official 9/11 Commission found that a combination of incompetence; bureaucratic infighting among the CIA, the Federal Aviation Administration (FAA), and the FBI; ignorance of the Middle Eastern groups involved; and plain hubris had enabled a dedicated suicidal enemy to succeed. Outstanding books with a longer perspective, such as Jane Mayer's *Dark Side* (2008, 2009), and Amy B. Zegart's *Spying Blind: The CIA, the FBI, and the Origins of 9/11* (2007), to name two, are readily available to the interested reader.

The point is that the government was caught unaware by the attack and it's response was impulsive and poorly thought out. President Bush had virtually no experience in foreign affairs and was heavily influenced by Vice President Dick Cheney, who viewed the world as dangerous, hostile, and in need of American dominance. In general, America and, frankly, the West barely understood the motives, ideology, tactics, or languages of the new enemy.[31] In this chaotic atmosphere, mistakes began to mount up quickly.

A Shortage of Arabic Translators

The U.S. military, in particular, was wholly unprepared for a war in Afghanistan and, later, in Iraq. Weapons, tactics, equipment, and leadership had not changed significantly since America's humbling withdrawal from its 12-year debacle in Vietnam almost 30 years earlier. If America was not prepared for a new conflict, it certainly was not ready for entrance into the Middle East. Only a handful of government officials or agencies were experts on Afghanistan, its multilayered ethnic and religious problems, or its languages. Indeed, the U.S. Army went to war against Obama Bin Laden's al-Qaeda (The Source) with only a handful of Arabic speakers, and many of those were gay people who were later dismissed from the military for violating its "Don't Ask—Don't Tell" policy, which requires that military personnel keep their sexual preference secret.

The situation only deteriorated once the United States invaded Iraq in 2003. As of the beginning of 2009, a total of 54 American soldiers and officers, male and female, who were serving as Arab translators had been dismissed, some for their sexuality and others for their questionable loyalty to America. This hampered efforts to translate radio transmissions and to interview Iraqi citizens who might possess useful information. American and coalition soldiers were sent into battle or encouraged to befriend deeply suspicious religious Sunni and Shia zealots without Arabic translators and knowing only a few phrases and hand gestures. How can an occupying force reach hearts and minds if its personnel can't speak the local language? Both the American soldiers and the Iraqi citizens, whether potential friends or foes, grew increasingly frustrated. Nor did the situation improve as the war in Iraq progressed. In 2006, another nonpartisan congressional commission, this one called the Lee Hamilton-James Baker Commission (the so-called Iraq Study Group) reported that the U.S. Embassy in Baghdad had only six fluent Arabic speakers on its staff—a fact that went largely unnoticed.

The failure to provide and maintain a sufficient number of Arabic translators as the nation launched into a war in Afghanistan, with another war in Iraq looming on the horizon, was only one factor contributing to an atmosphere in which war crimes would occur. The very definition of the enemy and the rules on treatment of enemy prisoners were open to new interpretation.

The Military's Changing Role

The U.S. Army was conflicted from the beginning of the Iraqi war. The military began as an invading force, trained to plow through the ranks of Saddam Hussein's elite Republican Guards to deliver "shock and awe" in the "mother of all battles." The combat army soon became an occupation army, embroiled in urban warfare against insurgents. Throughout history, combat armies, trained to fight, have not made good occupation troops. For one thing, their mission is unclear. Part of the military leadership in Iraq saw its mission as befriending the inhabitants, walking among them to provide security and safety, and, perhaps, leading them to appreciate democracy. Others in the military relied instinctively on their training as soldiers to fight and kill the enemy, of whom there seemed to be no shortage.

But who was the enemy? The face of warfare—indeed, its very nature, tactics, weapons, training, goals, and rules of engagement—was now different. Gone were set-piece battles, flags and buglers, and the ethical treatment of POWs. Western armies still had not grasped the profound change in warfare, as evident by the 2006 Israeli conflict against Hezbollah fighters in southern Lebanon and the more recent Israeli invasion of Gaza. The vaunted Israeli military, Western in orientation and materiel, found itself fighting an urban guerrilla war for which it was unprepared.

This, then, brings us to a central question: do warring soldiers need to wear identifiable uniforms, like members of opposing football teams? What about people who are not in the army but who pick up rifles and shoot from rooftops or fire rockets at foreign invaders? Are they considered soldiers who deserve protection if captured, or are they civilians? In years past, enemy soldiers captured in civilian clothes were considered partisans, irregulars, or just plain spies, and most were promptly shot. It was one's uniform or identification dog tags that proved one's status as a soldier and thus as someone deserving of protection. Or is simply carrying a weapon enough to signify that one is an enemy? Some captives, in fact, may not have been local fighters, at all; many prisoners were new recruits or hardened fighters from nearby countries who had come to fight a religious war. Regardless of their origin, enemy captives relied on the deadly weapons of guerrillas: road bombs triggered by remote cell phones, unseen booby traps, women and children couriers, and hit-and-run tactics. The enemy looked like everyone else; in fact, they were like everyone else. The question quickly arose: if enemy fighters don't look like soldiers, must they be treated according to the Geneva Convention of 1929 or its upgrade in 1949?

Clearly, the world was facing a new kind of war. Article 4 of the 1949 Geneva Convention determined that only lawful combatants, soldiers wearing distinctive uniforms and who answer to a recognized hierarchy, are eligible for POW protection—a stipulation that the floating membership of al-Qaeda, the Taliban, Hezbollah, or any of the burgeoning number of terrorist splinter groups do not meet. Despite the fact that terrorists often describe themselves as "soldiers" and "soldiers of God," they do not wear uniforms or represent an identified enemy. Even the International Red Cross, guardian of the wounded and war prisoners, found that captive "terrorists" fail to meet its four guidelines for determining official POW status: (1) they must have been commanded by a person responsible for his subordinates; (2) they must have a fixed distinctive symbol recognizable at a distance; (3) they must carry weapons openly; and (4) they must conduct their operations in accordance with the laws of war. The only thing these "soldiers of God" seem to have in common is an abhorrence of the "immorality" of Western customs and a willingness to hijack and reshape Islam to justify their actions.

The End of Legal Protection for Prisoners

On September 25, 2001, two weeks after the attacks of 9/11, Deputy Assistant Attorney General John Yoo and a fellow member of the Office of Legal Counsel, Robert Delahunty, itemized the many reasons that President Bush could assume broad executive powers in the war on terror. The last footnote of the Yoo-Delahunty Memo, chilling in its sinister potential, declared: "In the exercise of his plenary power to use military force, the President's decisions are for him alone and are unreviewable."[32]

On January 9, 2002, John Yoo wrote another detailed and secret memo explaining why the administration's violation of international standards of care for POWs would not constitute a crime. The Geneva Conventions of 1929 and 1949 were redefined by the administration to place Iraq and Afghanistan outside the jurisdiction of the Geneva regulations. The memo flatly asserts over and over that "As a constitutional matter, the President has the power to consider performance of some or all of the obligations of the United States under the Conventions suspended." Thus, the Bush administration suspended the Geneva Conventions—just like that.

The next step in the government's efforts to place prisoners outside the historical pale of protection came on January 19, 2002, when Secretary of Defense Donald Rumsfeld ordered the Chairman of the Joint Chiefs of Staff to inform combat commanders that "al Qaeda and Taliban individuals are not entitled to prisoner of war status for purposes of the Geneva Convention of 1949." Commanders were thus given permission to depart from the provisions of the Geneva Conventions wherever they deemed it appropriate.

The government's immunity was further endorsed by Alberto Gonzales, then counsel to the president, and William Haynes, counsel to the Department of Defense, who both concurred with the Office of Legal Counsel in assuring the administration that "We conclude that customary international law does not bind the President or the U.S. Armed Forces in their decisions concerning the detention conditions of al Qaeda and Taliban prisoners." Not only were there no restrictions on the president's actions, but, according to Assistant Attorney General Jay S. Bybee, in his Memo of January 22, 2002, anything that prevented the president from acting as he pleased was actually unconstitutional. According to Bybee, "Any effort to apply Section 2340A (restricting torture or cruel treatment) in a manner that interferes with the president's direction of such core war matters as the detention and interrogation of enemy combatants thus would be unconstitutional."[33] Thus, the president could do as he pleased with enemy prisoners, and anyone who tried to stop him was acting against the Constitution! In other words, the administration argued, it might actually be considered illegal for any misguided humanitarian to interfere with torture! A three-page guide to the web of memos was published by the *New York Time*[34]—memos that circulated among President Bush, John C. Yoo, Alberto R. Gonzales, William H. Taft IV, Jay S. Bybee, Donald Rumsfeld, General James T. Hill, and Brigadier General Janis Karpinski, among others, by which they provided legal cover for torture and war crimes.

President Bush's official declaration on the matter, on February 7, 2002, set aside the protections of the Geneva Convention of 1929 and the centuries of painstakingly argued definitions of the requirements and guarantees offered to prisoners and civilians in enemy hands.

> Based on the facts supplied by the Department of Defense and the recommendation of the Department of Justice, I determine that the Taliban detainees are unlawful combatants and, therefore, do not qualify as prisoners of war under Article 4 of Geneva. . . . Al-Qaeda detainees also do not qualify as prisoners of war.[35]

Prisoners were no longer protected by the Geneva Convention of 1929.

Now that enemy prisoners were not protected by the Geneva Conventions, any treatment was possible. Once in U.S. custody, the president's lawyers claimed, detainees could be held incommunicado from their families and the Red Cross and tormented with unending abuse, so long as their treatment did not meet the president's lawyers' own definition of torture, for the duration of an open-ended conflict against "terror." Suspects could and would be held for months or years without charge. Torture was tolerated, even encouraged, if the detainee appeared to know important information. Astonishingly, America declared torture to be legal in 2002. A nation that had declared war on poverty and historically supported the underdog in nearly every conflict now became the first nation in the world to officially authorize violations of the Nuremberg Principles and the Geneva Conventions.

Lashed by Vice President Dick Cheney, the so-called neoconservatives, and Cold War holdovers from decades past, and wreathed in legal security, the Bush administration quickly expanded its cavalier tolerance of torture in the new "war on terror." Secretary of Defense Donald Rumsfeld authorized the use of dogs, as well as forced nudity and sexual humiliation specifically selected to embarrass Arabs and Muslims, to intimidate prisoners,. Beating prisoners was no longer considered torture. The use of hooding became standard, and interrogations occasionally involved rape and electric shocks. In one memo, Assistant Attorney General Bybee actually suggested that kicking an inmate in the stomach with military boots while the prisoner is in a kneeling position does not by itself rise to the level of torture.[36] One can only wonder what might be considered torture.

The Bush administration had an important point here. As any soldier knows, intelligence is perishable. The alleged justification for torture was that it helped elicit information from terrorists as quickly as possible. They had proved their enemy status, having been captured in battle, after all, fighting for what was seen as an unfathomable cause, for a religion little understood in the West, and were perhaps in possession of knowledge about pending craven attacks on America. In short, because an unimaginable number of lives may have hung in the balance (not an idle concern in the months after 9/11), legal niceties were weighed against the potential threat. The use of force superseded negotiation. In fact, the government suggested that torture might even be considered "self-defense" on the grounds that "the threat of an impending terrorist attack threatens the lives of hundreds if not thousands of American citizens." However, the use of torture seldom resulted in "actionable" intelligence, and when asked how he felt about the value of torture, General John Vessey, a battle-hardened veteran and chairman of the Joint Chiefs of Staff, said, "No information that we could obtain through cruel, inhumane or torture could in any way counterbalance the damage that's done to the image of the United States of America by doing it."[37] Studies and personal recollections indicate that information retrieved under duress is notoriously unreliable.

Capture

Because enemy soldiers were often ordinary citizens living in their homes with their families, their capture was generally unorthodox. An American soldier of the 3rd Brigade, 2nd Infantry Division, recalls that after a ritual of drinking coffee and listening to a blaring CD rendition of Barry Sadler's "Ballad of the Green Berets" to get "pumped up," Army Specialist Colby Buzzell's squad went out into the Iraqi night to find "evil-doers."

> We arrived at the target individual's neighborhood. . . . We crept silently through the dark shadows in these really narrow mazed alleys for almost half an hour before we finally located the target house. . . . These people never knew what hit them. We busted in when they were sleeping. Scared the living shit out of them. Half a dozen little kids, a woman in traditional black Arabic clothing, and the target individual, all sleeping on the ground in the outdoor part of the house. The kids were screaming in fear and crying and so was the lady. . . . We separated the target individual in another room, tied his hands with a plastic zip tie, and put a blindfold on him. . . . They put the vapor sniffer up to the target individual's hands. . . . and the test results showed that he come up positive for several types of explosives. So we had our guy.[38]

In this case, a compromised enemy soldier may have been captured, however heavy-handed the method of seizure. But, since there is little visible difference between an Iraqi insurgent and an ordinary civilian, the chances of bursting into the wrong home and apprehending or humiliating an innocent party are high. Mark Danner, a noted author on human rights, recalled hearing bitter complaints in Baghdad and Fallujah as he investigated the treatment of Iraqi prisoners, "not only about the brutality of the tactics but about the obvious randomness of the arrests." This was confirmed by two-star U.S. Major General George R. Fay, in his investigation of the excesses at Abu Ghraib: SCT Jose Garcia, assigned to the Abu Ghraib Detainee Assessment Board, estimated that "85 to 90 percent of the detainees were of no intelligence value."[39] Eighty-five to ninety percent of the arrested detainees were valueless!

A young Iraqi man explained to Danner what American planners and soldiers were doing wrong in Iraq.

> For Fallujans [or any Iraqi, one assumes] it is a *shame* to have foreigners break down their doors. It is a *shame* for them to have foreigners stop and search their women. It is a *shame* for the foreigners to put a bag over their heads, to make a man lie on the ground with your shoe on his neck. This is a great *shame*, you understand? It is a *great shame* for the whole tribe.
>
> It is the *duty* of that man, and of that tribe, to get revenge on this soldier—to kill that man. Their duty is to attack them, to *wash the shame*. The shame is a *stain*, a dirty thing; they have to wash it. No sleep—we cannot sleep until we have revenge. They have to kill soldiers. . . . The Americans *provoke* the people. They don't *respect* the people.[40]

Torture

Then came the interrogations. The International Committee of the Red Cross documented approximately 50 random allegations of ill treatment, including:

> hooding; tight handcuffing; use of stress positions (kneeling, squatting, standing with arms raised over the head) for three or four hours; taking aim at individuals with rifles, striking them with rifle butts, slaps, punches, prolonged exposure to the sun, and isolation in dark cells.
>
> ICRC delegates witnessed marks on the bodies of several persons deprived of their liberty consistent with their allegations. In one illustrative case, a person deprived of his liberty arrested at home by the CF [Coalition Forces] on suspicion of involvement in an attack against the CF, was allegedly beaten during interrogation. . . .
>
> He alleged that he had been hooded and cuffed with flexi-cuffs, threatened to be tortured and killed, urinated on, kicked in the head, lower back and groin, force-fed a baseball which was tied into the mouth using a scarf and deprived of sleep for four consecutive days. Interrogators would allegedly take turns ill-treating him. When he said he would complain to the ICRC he was allegedly beaten more. An ICRC medical examination revealed haematoma in the lower back, blood in urine, sensory loss in the right hand due to tight handcuffing with flexi-cuffs, and a broken rib.[41]

In 2005, the American Civil Liberties Union managed to obtain the actual U.S. military autopsies of 44 Iraqi captives who were "interrogated to death" by American forces. This is one example:

> Final Autopsy Report: DOD 003164, (Detainee) Died as a result of asphyxia (lack of oxygen to the brain) due to strangulation as evidenced by the recently fractured hyoid bone in the neck and soft tissue hemorrhage extending downward to the level of the right thyroid cartilage. Autopsy revealed bone fractures, rib fractures, contusions in mid abdomen, back and buttocks extending to the left flank, abrasions, lateral buttocks. Contusions, back of legs and knees; abrasions on knees, left fingers and encircling to left wrist. Lacerations and superficial cuts, right 4th and 5th fingers. Also, blunt force injuries, predominantly recent contusions (bruises) on the torso and lower extremities. Abrasions on left wrist are consistent with use of restraints. No evidence of defense injuries or natural disease.[42]

The other 43 autopsies are frighteningly similar.

In 2008, a scathing exposé by a German author, Egmont R. Koch, titled *Die CIA-Lüge: Folter im Namen der Demokratie* [*The CIA Lies: Torture in the Name of Democracy*] (Berlin: AufbauVerlagsgruppe, 2008), caused a public stir in Europe. The study compared in detail the interrogation techniques used by American jailers on captured Arab insurgents and the techniques developed by the Nazi Gestapo. Scattered throughout the book are comparison photos and drawings. America was unmoved by the comparison.

It gets worse. When circumstances or public scrutiny made it impossible to treat Iraqi captives in a heavy-handed manner, American interrogators sometimes turned to a process called "extraordinary rendition."[43] It was a simple solution to a thorny legal problem that came up when it was necessary to increase the pressure on uncooperative captives. Stubborn prisoners who were suspected of withholding important and dated information were secretly flown to foreign countries where there is no reluctance to torture. In short, if American personnel believed that a prisoner was withholding information that could save lives, the prisoner was secretly flown to Egypt, Jordan, Yemen, Morocco, Pakistan, or Uzbekistan ("where partial boiling of a hand or arm is quite common").[44]

Captives who were determined to have special intelligence value were shipped to the secure American base at Guantánamo Bay, Cuba, for further interrogation. Many disappeared into the Guantánamo maw for years. According to Amnesty International, of the nearly 500 detainees captured in terrorist sweeps in Iraq and Afghanistan, Guantánamo held 85 Yemenis, 5 Bahrainis, 13 Kuwaitis, 6 prisoners from Bosnia-Herzegovina, one each from Sudan, Saudi Arabia, Chad, Mauritania, and prisoners with both Turkish and German citizenship. Interrogations were carried out behind closed doors, using techniques that are only now coming to light.

The U.S. government's initial rules for interrogation as laid out in the U.S. Army's Field Manual, pages 34–52 [*Intelligence Interrogation*, HQ, U.S. Army, Washington, D.C. September 28, 1992] were quickly seen as inadequate in the face of the new challenges of asymmetrical warfare. A member of the Guantánamo Interrogation team, Lieutnant Colonel Jerald Phifer, almost immediately sent a report to that effect to no-nonsense Major General Michael Dunlavey, in charge of the interrogation program at Guantánamo. In it he proposed toughening up interrogation techniques and suggested the following:

> **The category I techniques** fall within manipulation and the pure and simple intimidation.
>
> During the initial interrogation phase the detainee is installed on a chair in a relatively comfortable environment. There is no trace of hostility in the way one addresses him in order to win his confidence. Cookies or cigarettes can serve as reward if he answers the questions. If the detainee is not cooperative enough the pressure can be increased by elevating the voice or by yelling (but not directly in his ear or at such a level that it could cause an intolerable pain or hearing problems) or also by using tricks.
>
> The interrogator can also make believe he is a citizen from a foreign country or a specialist of a country reputed for the cruel treatments inflicted on its prisoners. [countries such as Morocco, Egypt, Jordan are often named.]

> **The implementation of the category II techniques** require the authorization of the director of the Joint Interrogation Group (JIG). They allow the isolation of the detainee for a period up to thirty days. Above that period the authorization of the detention base commander is necessary. It is recommended to sometimes deck the detainee with a hood while transferring him to the venue where the interrogations take place and during the interrogations. The hood mustn't hinder breathing. The interrogations which can last up to 20 hours can take place in unusual places.
>
> There is a gradation of punishment if the detainee doesn't cooperate or resists. The detainees can have light and sensorial functions privation, comfort items can be confiscated, the Koran included. Furthermore detainees can be totally stripped, their hair and beard cut. The interrogator is allowed to use all the tricks in order to get the detainee to talk, notably in exploiting his individual phobias—for example the fear of dogs (considered as impure animals by Muslims)—in order to accentuate the stress or to put them in humiliating or uncomfortable positions for four hours maximum.
>
> **Category III techniques** can only be implemented upon request of the Joint Interrogation Group director to the camp commander who has to give his approval and immediately inform his US Southern Command hierarchy. These are aimed at the least cooperative detainees and can only be carried out by specially trained soldiers. They recommend the use of "moderate physical contacts" which don't lead to any injuries, such as fight, finger-pressure on the breast or a light thump, or also exposure to cold or cold water (with an appropriate medical follow-up). One also makes the detainee believe that he is going to undergo great suffering; that his execution, or one of his family member's, is imminent. Finally the interrogators can also use "a wet towel and streaming water to give a false suffocation sensation." [The water-boarding technique largely used in the secret CIA camps abroad.][45]

General Dunlavey turned to the Secretary of Defence and on April 16, 2003, Donald Rumsfeld approved a new list of "counter-resistance techniques used to facilitate the interrogation of Guantánamo detainees."

He approved a major reinforcement of fear towards detainees, the deprivation of food and water, environmental manipulations (for example, temperature-adjustment or introduction of an unpleasant smell in the interrogation-room), the inversion of sleeping-cycles (inversion of day and night, without sleep-deprivation), isolation, for periods that can go up to 30 days and even more, and the persuasion of the detainees that the interrogators come from another country than the United States.

More coercive measures (slaps, nakedness, use of dogs) were not part of the list, but they are authorized individually. The final phrase of the document states that nothing in this report limits in any way the authority of the American Forces regarding the maintenance of law and order and the discipline among the detainees.

Interrogation techniques now officially rested on fear and humiliation. The interrogators and their military police auxiliaries were allowed to create a climate in which the prisoners are led to believe that everything is allowed to their jailers and that they have come to the end of the road. The degrading acts follow the same logic. The aim is to show that everything is possible, and that there should be no expectation of safety or an early conclusion The detainee, unlike a soldier in uniform, will not be granted the rights afforded to POWs. If these manipulative techniques avoid torture itself, they fall within the same coercive logic. It's a rational system: to obtain information one has to break the subject, to weaken him by plunging him into anxiety, into the loss of all bearings.

This is not to imply that many of the captured insurgents were not dangerous people who would have given their lives to kill American or coalition soldiers. Clearly, these captives needed to be isolated. Moreover, if the captives were suspected of concealing important intelligence, speed was of the essence. Still, there appeared to be no legal restrictions on the treatment meted out to detainees or on the practice of outsourcing serious torture to less sensitive allies. Frustrated soldiers, unable to communicate in Arabic and confused by the changing rules of engagement—which sometimes required that they wait to be attacked and at other times allowed them to shoot if they believed that the enemy *intended* to shoot—were losing sight of the rules of war. Increasing their stress and frustration, American soldiers were recycled for two and even three tours of 15 months each, as their families at home languished or thrived without them. The Army was beginning to notice and hired "180 new mental-health workers to treat troops at home bases, but they did not announce plans to beef up the contingent of counselors treating troops deployed in Iraq. Despite the rising suicide numbers in Iraq, the ratio of mental-health counselors to soldiers in the war zone has dropped—from one provider for every 387 troops in 2004, to one for every 734 last year (2007)."[46] American and coalition policy regarding war crimes teetered on the brink of chaos.

One particularly heinous war atrocity occurred in Mahmudiyah, south of Baghdad, on March 12, 2006, when Private First Class Steven D. Green, age 21, and other members of his platoon noticed a young Iraqi girl near the traffic checkpoint they staffed. The soldiers carefully worked out an elaborate plan to rape and murder the girl by storming her family compound while wearing dark clothing. Drunk and crazed, they later burst into the compound. Using a local AK-47, Private Green took the family into another room, where he killed the mother, the father, and a seven-year-old boy. They gang-raped the teen-age girl they had originally followed, killed her, and set the bodies on fire. They could not later claim that they did not know what they were doing, since they carefully burned their bloody clothes and threw the AK-47 into a canal. They went back to their routine duties. The story quickly came to light after they whispered about their exploits to others; their actions were confirmed by local witnesses, and local Iraqi relatives and friends of the victims demanded justice. Ordinarily, it would have been a straightforward case, with Green and his mates paying the ultimate price.

But, by the time the Army finished investigating the crime, Green had been discharged from the military. Not only was the case was becoming a national scandal in Iraq; it was the fifth case in recent weeks in which U.S. troops had been accused of killing civilians in Iraq.[47] Consequently, the military pursued him into civilian life and hauled him back to Fort Campbell, Kentucky, base of his former unit, the 101st Airborne Division, where he was tried in a civilian court. Two other soldiers convicted in the attack testified against him.

"While there's no excuse for what Steven Green did," his defense attorney acknowledged in closing, "there is an explanation . . . three months earlier, enemy attacks over 12 days killed two command sergeants, a lieutenant and a specialist in his unit . . . lack of military leadership and the Army's failure to recognize that Pfc. Green could act on homicidal thoughts of killing Iraqi civilians that he expressed after several fellow soldiers had been killed. . . . The United States failed Steven Green." He ended his remarks by thundering, "America does not kill its broken warriors! Spare this boy. For God's sake, spare him."[48] At least one juror agreed, and Steven Green was sentenced to life imprisonment rather than death. At the sentencing, distraught Iraqi family members shrieked and lunged at Green as he was led out of the courtroom. Retired Major General Batiste, who commanded Green's unit in Iraq, said that "the people of Iraq respect the U.S. military and will keep that in perspective. They'll appreciate the way we investigate and hold people responsible."[49]

The Steven Green case is certainly not the only American atrocity committed in Afghanistan or Iraq or, depending on the level of criminality, in other places (including the widespread violations of domestic privacy restrictions in the United States), but it stands out as one of the worst examples. It reflects the serious slippage that has occurred since the turn of the 21st century, particularly since 9/11. Until then, the Geneva Conventions of 1929 and 1949, the Nuremberg Principles, and the 1948 United Nations Convention on Genocide had combined to establish the framework for an international body of law. Still, numerous conflicts and civil wars continued to rage unpunished across Eastern Europe and Africa through the 1990s. No one responded. The end of the Cold War in 1989 and the eruption of the genocides in Rwanda and Yugoslavia finally galvanized the United Nations into action, resulting in the UN ad hoc trials and the later arrest of Chilean dictator Augusto Pinochet. Each trial further refined the protection against war crimes afforded by international law. Finally, in 2002, the UN International Criminal Court was established (without the support of America, Russia, or China) and ratified by 108 nations.

It was the attack on September 11, 2001, that changed everything. The U.S. government centralized power and eventually embarked on two wars that were plagued by the country's lack of preparedness. The new enemy was fanatically religious and suicidal—and inscrutable to the West. While the military fought bravely, it was faced with contradictions about tactics and rules of engagement, and above all, questions about just who was an enemy soldier and what legal protection he was guaranteed.

The decision by the United States to tolerate brutal interrogation, humiliation, and open-ended imprisonment without access to visitors or legal counsel has meant the end to any semblance of legal protection and means that members of the U.S. military have lost the safety of reciprocity. One can expect Americans captured by insurgents to receive treatment like that accorded to their comrades captured by the United States. Indeed, it was not long before the first American captive was executed by the Taliban; his name was U.S. Navy SEAL Neil Roberts, and he was killed on March 4, 2002 in Afghanistan. Since then, American prisoners in Iraq or Afghanistan have been routinely mistreated, starved, tortured, or executed. The basic idea of reciprocity is gone. The justification is clear: if you don't protect the captives in your hands, we won't, either. The treatment of war prisoners is now an issue of expediency—whatever is required to extract critical information, immobilize enemy fighters, or break the nationalist spirit or religious devotion of opponents is acceptable.

A momentary bright light recently appeared in the General Assembly of the United Nations. After years of unproductive committee meetings and earnest but unenforceable speeches, the concept of a nation's responsibility to protect its citizens was unexpectedly approved by the General Assembly in 2005. Known by the initials "R2P" for "Responsibility to Protect," its approval marks the farthest-reaching expression of international cooperation regarding war crimes on the books. R2P's underlying principle "is that governments have the responsibility to protect human beings against genocide, ethnic cleansing, war crimes, and crimes against humanity. . . . This concept referred mainly to the responsibility of states for their own people . . . when states could not or would not protect their own citizens or were actively harming them, others might step in."[50] It was too good to last, and in 2009 a number of states, fearing possible interference by foreign powers, are attempting to roll back the R2P principle on the grounds that it has been misused.

Perhaps the brutal treatment of captives may be necessary in the face of the new type of warfare, and the cycle of torture it creates acceptable, but it signals a sad return to earlier and more barbaric times. Progress on this thorny legal question, which concerns us all, appears to be stumbling.

The organization Genocide Watch is charged with the mission to track every potential genocide, grading the volatility of each situation. In December 2009, Genocide Watch posted its annual list of possible—even probable—genocides: 31 nations were listed. Some are considered failed states overrun by lawlessness. Others, like Nigeria, Equatorial Guinea, Sierra Leone, Chechnya, and Georgia, are home to minority groups whose safety is threatened. Overall, war crimes are brewing in nations like Burma/Myanmar, the Democratic Republic of Congo, Somalia, Chad, Uganda, Sri Lanka, Colombia, North Korea, Afghanistan, Iraq, Burundi, Uzbekistan, Kenya, and 18 others.[51]

It is tragic how little we have learned.

Notes

1. M. Cherif Bassiouni and Christopher L. Blakesley, "The Need for an International Criminal Court in the New International World Order," *Vanderbilt Journal of Transnational Law* 5 (1992): 154.
2. Ronnie Dugger, "To Prevent or to Stop Mass Murder," in *Genocide, War, and Human Survival*, ed. Charles B. Strozier and Michael Flynn (Lanham, MD: Rowman and Littlefield, 1996), p. 59.
3. Theodor Meron, "Reflections on the Prosecution of War Crimes by International Tribunals," *American Journal of International Law* 100, no. 3 (July 2006): 561.
4. Judge Kevin Parker, Vice President, to Judge H. E. Fausto Pocar, President, "Report to the President, Death of Slobodan Milošević," May 2006, www.un.org/icty/milosevic/parkerreport.pdf.
5. Peter Cave, "Serbia Not Responsible for Bosnia Genocide: UN," Australian Broadcasting Corporation, February 27, 2007, http://www.abc.net.au/lateline/content/2007/s1858837.htm. See also the excellent essay by William A. Schabas, "Whither Genocide? The International Court of Justice finally pronounces," *Journal of Genocide Research*, 9, no. 2 (June 2007): 183–192.
6. Associated Press, "Cousins Convicted of War Crimes in Bosnia," *The New York Times*, July 21, 2009, p. A7.
7. Philip Gourevitch, *We Wish to Inform You That Tomorrow We Will be Killed with Our Families* (New York: Farrar, Straus and Giroux, 1998).
8. Nigel Eltringham, " 'We Are Not a Truth Commission': Fragmented Narratives and Historical Record at the International Criminal Tribunal for Rwanda," *Journal of Genocide Research* 11, no. 1 (March 2009): 55–79; Kasaija Phillip Apuuli, "Procedural Due Process and the Prosecution of Genocide Suspects in Rwanda," *Journal of Genocide Research* 11, no. 1 (March 2009): 11–30.

9. See U.N. International Criminal Tribunal for Rwanda, http://www.ictr.org/default.htm.

10. Aaron Karnell, "Justice on the Grass: Three Rwandan Journalists, Their Trial for War Crimes, and a Nation's Quest for Redemption," *Journal of Genocide Research* 8, no. 1 (March 2006): 89–91; Christian A. DesRoches, "Accounting for Horror: Post-Genocide Debates in Rwanda," *Journal of Genocide Research* 8, no. 1 (March 2006): 91–94.

11. See, Anne Aghion, My *Neighbor* My *Killer,* video trilogy, 2009, http://www.myneighbormykiller.com/.

12. Eugenia Zorbas, "What Does Reconciliation after Genocide Mean? Public Transcript and Hidden Transcripts in Post-Genocide Rwanda," *Journal of Genocide Research* 11, no. 1 (March 2009): 127–147.

13. George Chigas, "The Politics of Defining Justice after the Cambodian Genocide," *Journal of Genocide Research* 2, no. 2 (June 2000): 245–265.

14. Jörg Menzel, "Justice Delayed or Too Late for Justice? The Khmer Rouge Tribunal and the Cambodian 'Genocide' 1975–79," *Journal of Genocide Research* 9, no. 2 (June 2007): 215–233.

15. Grant Peck, "Ex-Prison Chief Regrets Killing 16,000," Associated Press, March 31, 2009; also Brendan Brady and Keo Kounila, "Khmer Rouge Prison Chief Takes Blame for Killings," *Los Angeles Times*, April 1, 2009, p. A28.

16. See, for example, the *Armenian Genocide Resource Guide* (Washington, DC: Armenian Assembly of America, 2001, 1988); Donald E. Miller and Lorna Touryan Miller, *Survivors: An Oral History of the Armenian Genocide* (Berkeley: University of California Press, 1993); and Vrej Nerses Nersessian, *Armenia,* World Biographical Series, Vol. 163 (Oxford and Santa Barbara, CA: Clio Press, 1993), pp. 60–86.

17. Taner Akçam, "The Anatomy of a Crime: The Turkish Historical Society's Manipulation of Archival Documents," *Journal of Genocide Research* 7, no. 2 (June 2005): 60–86; 255–277.

18. Pamuk said: "Thirty thousand Kurds and a million Armenians were killed in these lands and nobody but me dares to talk about it." *Das Magazin*, February 6, 2005, weekend supplement to *Tages Anzeiger* (Zürich), February 6, 2005. See http://www.pen.org/viewmedia.php/prmMID/369/prmID/1331. See also Letter to the Editor, *New York Review of Books*, December 15, 2005.

19. "Turkish-Armenian writer shot dead," BBC News, January 19, 2007. See http://news.bbc.co.uk/2/hi/europe/6279241.stm.

20. Agence France-Presse, "Chirac Urges Turks to Recognize Genocide," *New York Times*, October 1, 2006, p. A6.

21. Associated Press, "Turkey Freezes Military Ties with France," *New York Times*, November 16, 2006, p. A8.

22. Geoffrey Robertson, *Crimes against Humanity: The Struggle for Global Justice*, rev. ed. (New York: New Press, 2002), p. 37.

23. Howard Ball, *War Crimes and Justice* (Santa Barbara, CA: ABC-CLIO, 2002), p. 57.

24. Barbara Crossette, "A Reality: a New Global Criminal Tribunal," International Herald Tribune, April 12, 2002, p. 1A.

25. Norbert Ehrenfreund, *The Nuremberg Legacy: How the Nazi War Crimes Trials Changed the Course of History* (New York: Palgrave Macmillan, 2007), p. 128.

26. Fulvio Maria Palombino, "Universal Jurisdiction in Absentia over Genocide: Some Critical Remarks in Light of Recent Spanish Jurisprudence," *Journal of Genocide Research* 9, no. 2 (June 2007): 243–249.

27. Jonathan Dedarbaum, "The Rome Statute of the International Criminal Court: A Commentary," *Journal of Genocide Research* 6, no. 4 (December 2004): 601–604.

28. Meron, "Reflections on the Prosecution of War Crimes by International Tribunals," p. 556.

29. Crossette, "A Reality."

30. Marjorie Cohn, "How the Bush Administration's Opposition to the International Criminal Court Has Put Peacekeepers and Others in Danger," FindLaw for Legal Professionals, September 8, 2003, http://writ.lp.findlaw.com/commentary/20030908_cohn.html.

31. Jürgen Todenhöfer, *Warum tötest du, Zaid?* [*Why do you kill, Zaid?*] (Munich: C. Bertelsmann Verlag, 2008).

32. Cited, at length, in Arnold Krammer, *Prisoners of War: A Reference Handbook* (Westport, CT: Praeger Security International, 2008), pp. 68–69.

33. Andrew Sullivan, "Atrocities in Plain Sight," *New York Times Book Review*, January 23, 2005, p. 7.1, http://query.nytimes.com/gst/fullpage.html?res=9C0CE0D81738F930A15752C0A9639C8B63&sec=&spon=&pagewanted=2.

34. "A Guide to the Memos on Torture," *New York Times International Online*, http://www.nytimes.com/ref/international/24MEMO-GUIDE.html.

To make up for the lack of translators, the Bush administration outsourced translation services to questionable private contractors. Called "linguistic support," these companies, two of the largest of which are Titan Corporation and DynCorp International, received billions of dollars to provide language interpreters to the Iraq reconstruction effort, although many of the supposed "translators" sent to Iraq had poor language skills or couldn't speak Arabic at all.

35. Memo, George Bush to Secretaries of State and Defense, Attorney General, and Joint Chiefs of Staff, February 7, 2002. Available at http://WashingtonPost.com/wp-srv/nation/documents/020702bush.pdf. The president nonetheless assured his listeners that American military forces would live up to the highest level of civilized conduct, saying, "As a matter of policy, the United States Armed Forces shall continue to treat detainees humanely and, to the extent appropriate and consistent with military necessity, in a manner consistent with the principles of Geneva."

36. Sullivan, "Atrocities in Plain Sight."

37. Krammer, *Prisoners of War*, pp. 63–77. Vessey quotation is from *Meet the Press*, December 4, 2005, NBC News, p. 9. The transcript is available at http://www.msnbc.msn.com/id/10266650/.

38. Colby Buzzell, *My War: Killing Time in Iraq* (New York: G. P. Putnam's Sons, 2005), pp. 237–239.

39. Mark Danner, *Torture and Truth: America, Abu Ghraib, and the War on Terror* (New York: New York Review of Books, 2004), p. 31. General Fay's report, *Investigation*

of the Abu Ghraib Detention Facility and the 205th Military Intelligence Brigade (AR 15-6), is reproduced at the back of the Danner book, beginning on page 329.

40. Mark Danner, *Torture and Truth: America, Abu Ghraib, and the War on Terror* (New York: New York Review of Books, 2004), p. 1.

41. *Report of the International Committee of the Red Cross (ICRC) on the Treatment by the Coalition Forces of Prisoners of War and Other Protected Persons By the Geneva Conventions in Iraq during Arrest, Internment, and Interrogation*, February 2004, http://www.globalsecurity.org/military/library/report/2004/icrc_report_iraq_feb2004.pdf.

42. Peter Phillips, "Death by Torture: US Media Ignores Hard Evidence," *CounterPunch* (Petrolia, CA), December 2, 2005. For copies of the actual autopsies, see http://action.aclu.org/torturefoia/released/102405, 2005, p. 116, note 3.

43. See autopsies at http://action.aclu.org/torturefoia/released/102405, note 3, 110. See, especially, Joseph F. C. DiMento and Gilbert Geis, "The Extraordinary Condition of Extraordinary Rendition: The C.I.A., the D.E.A., Kidnaping [*sic*], Torture, and the Law," in *War Crimes, Genocide and Crimes against Humanity*, ed. L. Edward Day, Vol. 2 (Altoona, PA: Criminal Justice Program at Penn State Altoona, 2006), pp. 35–64. Available at http://www.war-crimes.org/.

44. Jane Mayer, "Outsourcing Torture: The Secret History of America's 'Extraordinary Rendition' Program," *The New Yorker*, February 14, 2005, pp. 106–123.

45. Simon Petermann, *Guantánamo: Les dérives de la guerre contre le terrorisme* (Paris: André Versaille, 2009), pp. 59–68.

46. Lisa Chedekel and Matthew Kauffman, "Army Sees Record Number of Suicides in Iraq," *Hartford Courant*, May 30, 2008, A1. Also available at http://pqasb.pqarchiver.com/courant/access/1487225291.html?dids=1487225291:1487225291&FMT=ABS&FMTS=ABS:FT&type=current&date=May+30%2C+2008&author=LISA+CHEDEKEL%3BMATTHEW+KAUFFMAN&pub=Hartford+Courant&edition=&startpage=A.1&desc=ARMY%3A+SUICIDES+IN+IRAQ+INCREASE.

47. Josh White, "Ex-Soldier Charged in Killing of Iraqi Family," *Washington Post*, July 4, 2006, p. A01.

48. Jim Frederick, "When a Soldier Murders: Steven Green Gets Life," *Time*, May 21, 2009. http://www.time.com/time/nation/article/0,8599,1900389,00.html; "Ex-Soldier Gets Life in Prison for Iraqi Slayings," *Wall Street Journal*, June 30, 2009. http://online.wsj.com/article/SB100014240529702037719045741813728381020 50.html.

49. Frederick, "When a Soldier Murders."

50. Scott Horton, "An Idea Whose Time Has Come—and Gone?" *The Economist*, July 25, 2009, pp. 58–59.

51. Genocide Watch, "Current Countries at Risk, 1 November 2008," http://genocidewatch.org/aboutgenocide/countriesatrisk2008.html.

APPENDIX

Primary Documents

Laws and Customs of War on Land (Hague IV), October 18, 1907

Entered into Force: 26 January 1910 IV Convention Respecting the Laws and Customs of War on Land . . .

Until a more complete code of the laws of war has been issued, the High Contracting Parties deem it expedient to declare that, in cases not included in the Regulations adopted by them, the inhabitants and the belligerents remain under the protection and the rule of the principles of the law of nations, as they result from the usages established among civilized peoples, from the laws of humanity, and the dictates of the public conscience. They declare that it is in this sense especially that Articles 1 and 2 of the Regulations adopted must be understood.

Who, after having deposited their full powers, found in good and due form, have agreed upon the following:

Article 1

The Contracting Powers shall issue instructions to their armed land forces which shall be in conformity with the Regulations respecting the laws and customs of war on land, annexed to the present Convention.

. . .

Article 3

A belligerent party which violates the provisions of the said Regulations shall, if the case demands, be liable to pay compensation. It shall be responsible for all acts committed by persons forming part of its armed forces.

(List of Signatories)
Annex to the Convention

Regulations Respecting the Laws and Customs of War on Land
Section I
On Belligerents

The Qualifications of Belligerents

Article 1

The laws, rights, and duties of war apply not only to armies, but also to militia and volunteer corps fulfilling the following conditions: To be commanded by a person responsible for his subordinates; To have a fixed distinctive emblem recognizable at a distance; To carry arms openly; and To conduct their operations in accordance with the laws and customs of war.

Article 2

The inhabitants of a territory which has not been occupied, who, on the approach of the enemy, spontaneously take up arms to resist the invading troops without having had time to organize themselves in accordance with Article 1, shall be regarded as belligerents if they carry arms openly and if they respect the laws and customs of war.

Article 3

The armed forces of the belligerent parties may consist of combatants and non-combatants. In the case of capture by the enemy, both have a right to be treated as prisoners of war.

Chapter II
Prisoners of War

Article 4

Prisoners of war are in the power of the hostile Government, but not of the individuals or corps who capture them.

They must be humanely treated.

All their personal belongings, except arms, horses, and military papers, remain their property.

Article 5

Prisoners of war may be interned in a town, fortress, camp, or other place, and bound not to go beyond certain fixed limits, but they cannot be confined except as in indispensable measure of safety and only while the circumstances which necessitate the measure continue to exist.

Article 6

The State may utilize the labour of prisoners of war according to their rank and aptitude, officers excepted. The tasks shall not be excessive and shall have no connection with the operations of the war.

Prisoners may be authorized to work for the public service, for private persons, or on their own account.

Work done for the State is paid for at the rates in force for work of a similar kind done by soldiers of the national army, or, if there are none in force, at a rate according to the work executed.

When the work is for other branches of the public service or for private persons the conditions are settled in agreement with the military authorities.

The wages of the prisoners shall go towards improving their position, and the balance shall be paid them on their release, after deducting the cost of their maintenance.

Article 7

The Government into whose hands prisoners of war have fallen is charged with their maintenance.

In the absence of a special agreement between the belligerents, prisoners of war shall be treated as regards board, lodging, and clothing on the same footing as the troops of the Government who captured them.

Article 8

Prisoners of war shall be subject to the laws, regulations, and orders in force in the army of the State in whose power they are. Any act of insubordination justifies the adoption towards them of such measures of severity as may be considered necessary.

Escaped prisoners who are retaken before being able to rejoin their own army or before leaving the territory occupied by the army which captured them are liable to disciplinary punishment.

Prisoners who, after succeeding in escaping, are again taken prisoners, are not liable to any punishment on account of the previous flight.

Article 9

Every prisoner of war is bound to give, if he is questioned on the subject, his true name and rank, and if he infringes this rule, he is liable to have the advantages given to prisoners of his class curtailed.

Article 10

Prisoners of war may be set at liberty on parole if the laws of their country allow, and, in such cases, they are bound, on their personal honour, scrupulously to fulfill, both towards their own Government and the

Government by whom they were made prisoners, the engagements they have contracted.

In such cases their own Government is bound neither to require of nor accept from them any service incompatible with the parole given.

Article 11

A prisoner of war cannot be compelled to accept his liberty on parole; similarly the hostile Government is not obliged to accede to the request of the prisoner to be set at liberty on parole.

Article 12

Prisoners of war liberated on parole and recaptured bearing arms against the Government to whom they had pledged their honour, or against the allies of that Government, forfeit their right to be treated as prisoners of war, and can be brought before the courts.

Article 13

Individuals who follow an army without directly belonging to it, such as newspaper correspondents and reporters, sutlers and contractors, who fall into the enemy's hands and whom the latter thinks expedient to detain, are entitled to be treated as prisoners of war, provided they are in possession of a certificate from the military authorities of the army which they were accompanying.

Article 14

An inquiry office for prisoners of war is instituted on the commencement of hostilities in each of the belligerent States, and, when necessary, in neutral countries which have received belligerents in their territory. It is the function of this office to reply to all inquiries about the prisoners. It receives from the various services concerned full information respecting internments and transfers, releases on parole, exchanges, escapes, admissions into hospital, deaths, as well as other information necessary to enable it to make out and keep up to date an individual return for each prisoner of war. The office must state in this return the regimental number, name and surname, age, place of origin, rank, unit, wounds, date and place of capture, internment, wounding, and death, as well as any observations of a special character. The individual return shall be sent to the Government of the other belligerent after the conclusion of peace.

It is likewise the function of the inquiry office to receive and collect all objects of personal use, valuables, letters, etc., found on the field of battle or left by prisoners who have been released on parole, or exchanged, or who have escaped, or died in hospitals or ambulances, and to forward them to those concerned.

Article 15

Relief societies for prisoners of war, which are properly constituted in accordance with the laws of their country and with the object of serving as the channel for charitable effort shall receive from the belligerents, for themselves and their duly accredited agents every facility for the efficient performance of their humane task within the bounds imposed by military necessities and administrative regulations. Agents of these societies may be admitted to the places of internment for the purpose of distributing relief, as also to the halting places of repatriated prisoners, if furnished with a personal permit by the military authorities, and on giving an undertaking in writing to comply with all measures of order and police which the latter may issue.

Article 16

Inquiry offices enjoy the privilege of free postage. Letters, money orders, and valuables, as well as parcels by post, intended for prisoners of war, or dispatched by them, shall be exempt from all postal duties in the countries of origin and destination, as well as in the countries they pass through. Presents and relief in kind for prisoners of war shall be admitted free of all import or other duties, as well as of payments for carriage by the State railways.

Article 17

Officers taken prisoners shall receive the same rate of pay as officers of corresponding rank in the country where they are detained, the amount to be ultimately refunded by their own Government.

Article 18

Prisoners of war shall enjoy complete liberty in the exercise of their religion, including attendance at the services of whatever church they may belong to, on the sole condition that they comply with the measures of order and police issued by the military authorities.

Article 19

The wills of prisoners of war are received or drawn up in the same way as for soldiers of the national army.

The same rules shall be observed regarding death certificates as well as for the burial of prisoners of war, due regard being paid to their grade and rank.

Article 20

After the conclusion of peace, the repatriation of prisoners of war shall be carried out as quickly as possible.

The Sick and Wounded

Article 21

The obligations of belligerents with regard to the sick and wounded are governed by the Geneva Convention.

Hostilities

Chapter I
Means of Injuring the Enemy

Article 22

The right of belligerents to adopt means of injuring the enemy is not unlimited.

Article 23

In addition to the prohibitions provided by special Conventions, it is especially forbidden—To employ poison or poisoned weapons; To kill or wound treacherously individuals belonging to the hostile nation or army; To kill or wound an enemy who, having laid down his arms, or having no longer means of defence, has surrendered at discretion; To declare that no quarter will be given; To employ arms, projectiles, or material calculated to cause unnecessary suffering; To make improper use of a flag of truce, of the national flag or of the military insignia and uniform of the enemy, as well as the distinctive badges of the Geneva Convention; To destroy or seize the enemy's property, unless such destruction or seizure be imperatively demanded by the necessities of war; To declare abolished, suspended, or inadmissible in a court of law the rights and actions of the nationals of the hostile party. A belligerent is likewise forbidden to compel the nationals of the hostile party to take part in the operations of war directed against their own country, even if they were in the belligerent's service before the commencement of the war.

Article 24

Ruses of war and the employment of measures necessary for obtaining information about the enemy and the country are considered permissible.

Article 25

The attack or bombardment, by whatever means, of towns, villages, dwellings, or buildings which are undefended is prohibited.

Article 26

The officer in command of an attacking force must, before commencing a bombardment, except in cases of assault, do all in his power to warn the authorities.

Article 27

In sieges and bombardments all necessary steps must be taken to spare, as far as possible, buildings dedicated to religion, art, science, or charitable purposes, historic monuments, hospitals, and places where the sick and wounded are collected, provided they are not being used at the time for military purposes.

It is the duty of the besieged to indicate the presence of such buildings or places by distinctive and visible signs, which shall be notified to the enemy beforehand.

Article 28

The pillage of a town or place, even when taken by assault, is prohibited.

Chapter II
Spies

Article 29

A person can only be considered a spy when, acting clandestinely or on false pretences, he obtains or endeavours to obtain information in the zone of operations of a belligerent, with the intention of communicating it to the hostile party.

Thus, soldiers not wearing a disguise who have penetrated into the zone of operations of the hostile army, for the purpose of obtaining information, are not considered spies. Similarly, the following are not considered spies: Soldiers and civilians, carrying out their mission openly, entrusted with the delivery of despatches intended either for their own army or for the enemy's army. To this class belong likewise persons sent in balloons for the purpose of carrying despatches and, generally, of maintaining communications between the different parts of an army or a territory.

Article 30

A spy taken in the act shall not be punished without previous trial.

Article 31

A spy who, after rejoining the army to which he belongs, is subsequently captured by the enemy, is treated as a prisoner of war, and incurs no responsibility for his previous acts of espionage.

Chapter III
Flags of Truce

Article 32

A person is regarded as a parlementaire who has been authorized by one of the belligerents to enter into communication with the other, and who advances bearing a white flag. He has a right to inviolability, as well as the trumpeter, bugler or drummer, the flag-bearer and interpreter who may accompany him.

Article 33

The commander to whom a parlementaire is sent is not in all cases obliged to receive him. He may take all the necessary steps to prevent the parlementaire taking advantage of his mission to obtain information. In case of abuse, he has the right to detain the parlementaire temporarily.

Article 34

The parlementaire loses his rights of inviolability if it is proved in a clear and incontestable manner that he has taken advantage of his privileged position to provoke or commit an act of treason.

Chapter IV
Capitulations

Article 35

Capitulations agreed upon between the Contracting Parties must take into account the rules of military honour. Once settled, they must be scrupulously observed by both parties.

. . .

Article 40

Any serious violation of the armistice by one of the parties gives the other party the right of denouncing it, and even, in cases of urgency, of recommencing hostilities immediately.

. . .

Military Authority Over the Territory of the Hostile State

. . .

Article 44

A belligerent is forbidden to force the inhabitants of territory occupied by it to furnish information about the army of the other belligerent, or about its means of defense.

Article 45

It is forbidden to compel the inhabitants of occupied territory to swear allegiance to the hostile Power.

Article 46

Family honour and rights, the lives of persons, and private property, as well as religious convictions and practice, must be respected.

Private property cannot be confiscated.

Article 47

Pillage is formally forbidden.

Article 48

If, in the territory occupied, the occupant collects the taxes, dues, and tolls imposed for the benefit of the State, he shall do so, as far as is possible, in accordance with the rules of assessment and incidence in force, and shall in consequence be bound to defray the expenses of the administration of the occupied territory to the same extent as the legitimate Government was so bound . . .

Article 50

No general penalty, pecuniary or otherwise, shall be inflicted upon the population on account of the acts of individuals for which they cannot be regarded as jointly and severally responsible. For every contribution a receipt shall be given to the contributors.

. . .

Article 52

Requisitions in kind and services shall not be demanded from municipalities or inhabitants except for the needs of the army of occupation. They shall be in proportion to the resources of the country, and of such a nature as not to involve the inhabitants in the obligation of taking part in military operations against their own country.

Such requisitions and services shall only be demanded on the authority of the commander in the locality occupied.

Contributions in kind shall as far as possible be paid for in cash; if not, a receipt shall be given and the payment of the amount due shall be made as soon as possible.

Article 53

An army of occupation can only take possession of cash, funds, and realizable securities which are strictly the property of the State, depots of arms, means of transport, stores and supplies, and, generally, all movable property belonging to the State which may be used for military operations. All appliances, whether on land, at sea, or in the air, adapted for the transmission of news, or for the transport of persons or things, exclusive of cases governed by naval law, depots of arms, and, generally, all kinds of munitions of war, may be seized, even if they belong to private individuals, but must be restored and compensation fixed when peace is made.

Article 54

Submarine cables connecting an occupied territory with a neutral territory shall not be seized or destroyed except in the case of absolute necessity. They must likewise be restored and compensation fixed when peace is made.

Article 55

The occupying State shall be regarded only as administrator and usufructuary of public buildings, real estate, forests, and agricultural estates belonging to the hostile State, and situated in the occupied country. It must safeguard the capital of these properties, and administer them in accordance with the rules of usufruct.

Article 56

The property of municipalities, that of institutions dedicated to religion, charity and education, the arts and sciences, even when State property, shall be treated as private property.

All seizure of, destruction or wilful damage done to institutions of this character, historic monuments, works of art and science, is forbidden, and should be made the subject of legal proceedings.

Assistant Legal Advisor Department of State
Volume 1 Multilateral 1776–1917
Department of State Publication 8407
Washington, DC : Government Printing Office, 1968

Source: Volume 1 Multilateral 1776–1917. Department of State Publication 8407, Washington, DC: GPO, 1968.

International Convention Relative to the Treatment of Prisoners of War, Geneva, July 27, 1929

. . .

Part I
General Provisions

Article 1

The present Convention shall apply without prejudice to the stipulations of Part VII:

(1) To all persons referred to in Articles 1, 2 and 3 of the Regulations annexed to the Hague Convention (IV) of 18 October 1907, concerning the Laws and Customs of War on Land, who are captured by the enemy.
(2) To all persons belonging to the armed forces of belligerents who are captured by the enemy in the course of operations of maritime or aerial war, subject to such exceptions (derogations) as the conditions of such capture render inevitable. Nevertheless these exceptions shall not infringe the fundamental principles of the present Convention; they shall cease from the moment when the captured persons shall have reached a prisoners of war camp.

Article 2

Prisoners of war are in the power of the hostile Government, but not of the individuals or formation which captured them. They shall at all times be humanely treated and protected, particularly against acts of violence, from insults and from public curiosity. Measures of reprisal against them are forbidden.

Article 3

Prisoners of war are entitled to respect for their persons and honour. Women shall be treated with all consideration due to their sex. Prisoners retain their full civil capacity.

Article 4

The detaining Power is required to provide for the maintenance of prisoners of war in its charge. Differences of treatment between prisoners are permissible only if such differences are based on the military rank, the state of physical or mental health, the professional abilities, or the sex of those who benefit from them.

Part II
Capture

Article 5

Every prisoner of war is required to declare, if he is interrogated on the subject, his true names and rank, or his regimental number. If he infringes this rule, he exposes himself to a restriction of the privileges accorded to prisoners of his category. No pressure shall be exercised on prisoners to obtain information regarding the situation in their armed forces or their country. Prisoners who refuse to reply may not be threatened, insulted, or exposed to unpleasantness or disadvantages of any kind whatsoever. If, by reason of his physical or mental condition, a prisoner is incapable of stating his identity, he shall be handed over to the Medical Service.

Article 6

All personal effects and articles in personal use—except arms, horses, military equipment and military papers—shall remain in the possession of prisoners of war, as well as their metal helmets and gas-masks. Sums of money carried by prisoners may only be taken from them on the order of an officer and after the amount has been recorded. A receipt shall be given for them. Sums thus impounded shall be placed to the account of each prisoner. Their identity tokens, badges of rank, decorations and articles of value may not be taken from prisoners.

Part III
Captivity

Section I
Evacuation of Prisoners of War

Article 7

As soon as possible after their capture, prisoners of war shall be evacuated to depots sufficiently removed from the fighting zone for them to be out of danger. Only prisoners who, by reason of their wounds or maladies, would run greater risks by being evacuated than by remaining may be kept temporarily in a dangerous zone. Prisoners shall not be unnecessarily exposed to danger while awaiting evacuation from a fighting zone. The evacuation of prisoners on foot shall in normal circumstances be effected by stages of not more than 20 kilometres per day, unless the necessity for reaching water and food depôts requires longer stages.

Article 8

Belligerents are required to notify each other of all captures of prisoners as soon as possible, through the intermediary of the Information Bureaux organised in accordance with Article 77. They are likewise required to inform each other of the official addresses to which letter from the prisoners' families may be addressed to the prisoners of war. As soon as possible, every prisoner shall be enabled to correspond personally with his family, in accordance with the conditions prescribed in Article 36 and the following Articles. As regards prisoners captured at sea, the provisions of the present article shall be observed as soon as possible after arrival in port.

Section II
Prisoners of War Camps

Article 9

Prisoners of war may be interned in a town, fortress or other place, and may be required not to go beyond certain fixed limits. They may also be interned in fenced camps; they shall not be confined or imprisoned except as a measure indispensable for safety or health, and only so long as circumstances exist which necessitate such a measure. Prisoners captured in districts which are unhealthy or whose climate is deleterious to persons coming from temperate climates shall be removed as soon as possible to a more favourable climate. Belligerents shall as far as possible avoid bringing together in the same camp prisoners of different races or nationalities. No prisoner may at any time be sent to an area where he would be exposed to the fire of the fighting zone, or be employed to render by his presence certain points or areas immune from bombardment.

CHAPTER 1
Installation of Camps
Article 10

Prisoners of war shall be lodged in buildings or huts which afford all possible safeguards as regards hygiene and salubrity. The premises must be entirely free from damp, and adequately heated and lighted. All precautions shall be taken against the danger of fire. As regards dormitories, their total area, minimum cubic air space, fittings and bedding material, the conditions shall be the same as for the depot troops of the detaining Power.

CHAPTER 2
Food and Clothing of Prisoners of War
Article 11

The food ration of prisoners of war shall be equivalent in quantity and quality to that of the depot troops. Prisoners shall also be afforded the means of preparing for themselves such additional articles of food as they may possess. Sufficient drinking water shall be supplied to them. The use of tobacco shall be authorized. Prisoners may be employed in the kitchens. All collective disciplinary measures affecting food are prohibited.

Article 12

Clothing, underwear and footwear shall be supplied to prisoners of war by the detaining Power. The regular replacement and repair of such articles shall be assured. Workers shall also receive working kit wherever the nature of the work requires it. In all camps, canteens shall be installed at which prisoners shall be able to procure, at the local market price, food commodities and ordinary articles. The profits accruing to the administrations of the camps from the canteens shall be utilised for the benefit of the prisoners.

CHAPTER 3
Hygiene in Camps
Article 13

Belligerents shall be required to take all necessary hygienic measures to ensure the cleanliness and salubrity of camps and to prevent epidemics. Prisoners of war shall have for their use, day and night, conveniences which conform to the rules of hygiene and are maintained in a constant state of cleanliness. In addition and without prejudice to the provision as far as possible of baths and shower-baths in the camps, the prisoners shall be provided with a sufficient quantity of water for their bodily cleanliness. They shall have facilities for engaging in physical exercises and obtaining the benefit of being out of doors.

Article 14

Each camp shall possess an infirmary, where prisoners of war shall receive attention of any kind of which they may be in need. If necessary, isolation establishments shall be reserved for patients suffering from infectious and contagious diseases. The expenses of treatment, including those of temporary remedial apparatus, shall be borne by the detaining Power. Belligerents shall be required to issue, on demand, to any prisoner treated, an official statement indicating the nature and duration of his illness and of the treatment received. It shall be permissible for belligerents mutually to authorize each other, by means of special agreements, to retain in the camps doctors and medical orderlies for the purpose of caring for their prisoner compatriots. Prisoners who have contracted a serious malady, or whose condition necessitates important surgical treatment, shall be admitted, at the expense of the detaining Power, to any military or civil institution qualified to treat them.

Article 15

Medical inspections of prisoners of war shall be arranged at least once a month. Their object shall be the supervision of the general state of health and cleanliness, and the detection of infectious and contagious diseases., particularly tuberculosis and venereal complaints.

CHAPTER 4

Intellectual and Moral Needs of Prisoners of War

Article 16

Prisoners of war shall be permitted complete freedom in the performance of their religious duties, including attendance at the services of their faith, on the sole condition that they comply with the routine and police regulations prescribed by the military authorities. Ministers of religion, who are prisoners of war, whatever may be their denomination, shall be allowed freely to minister to their co-religionists.

Article 17

Belligerents shall encourage as much as possible the organization of intellectual and sporting pursuits by the prisoners of war.

CHAPTER 5

Internal Discipline of Camps

Article 18

Each prisoners of war camp shall be placed under the authority of a responsible officer. In addition to external marks of respect required by the regulations in force in their own armed forces with regard to their nationals, prisoners of war shall be required to salute all officers of the detaining Power. Officer prisoners of war shall be required to salute only officers of that Power who are their superiors or equals in rank.

Article 19

The wearing of badges of rank and decorations shall be permitted.

Article 20

Regulations, orders, announcements and publications of any kind shall be communicated to prisoners of war in a language which they understand. The same principle shall be applied to questions.

CHAPTER 6

Special Provisions Concerning Officers and Persons of Equivalent Status

Article 21

At the commencement of hostilities, belligerents shall be required reciprocally to inform each other of the titles and ranks in use in their respective armed forces, with the view of ensuring equality of treatment between the corresponding ranks of officers and persons of equivalent status. Officers and persons of equivalent status who are prisoners of war shall be treated with due regard to their rank and age.

Article 22

In order to ensure the service of officers' camps, soldier prisoners of war of the same armed forces, and as far as possible speaking the same language, shall be detached for service therein in sufficient number, having regard to the rank of the officers and persons of equivalent status. Officers and persons of equivalent status shall procure their food and clothing from the pay to be paid to them by the detaining Power. The management of a mess by officers themselves shall be facilitated in every way. . . .

CHAPTER 8

Transfer of Prisoners of War

Article 25

Unless the course of military operations demands it, sick and wounded prisoners of war shall not be transferred if their recovery might be prejudiced by the journey.

Article 26

In the event of transfer, prisoners of war shall be officially informed in advance of their new destination; they shall be authorized to take with them their personal effects, their correspondence and parcels which have arrived for them. All necessary arrangements shall be made so that correspondence and parcels addressed to their former camp shall be sent on to them without delay. The sums credited to the account of transferred prisoners shall be transmitted to the competent authority of their new place of residence. Expenses incurred by the transfers shall be borne by the detaining Power.

Section III
Work of Prisoners of War

CHAPTER 1
General
Article 27

Belligerents may employ as workmen prisoners of war who are physically fit, other than officers and persons of equivalent statue, according to their rink and their ability. Nevertheless, if officers or persons of equivalent status ask for suitable work, this shall be found for them as far as possible. Non-commissioned officers who are prisoners of war may be compelled to undertake only supervisory work, unless they expressly request remunerative occupation. During the whole period of captivity, belligerents are required to admit prisoners of war who are victims of accidents at work to the benefit of provisions applicable to workmen of the same category under the legislation of the detaining Power. As regards prisoners of war to whom these legal provisions could not be applied by reason of the legislation of that Power, the latter undertakes to recommend to its legislative body all proper measures for the equitable compensation of the victims.

CHAPTER 2
Organization of Work
Article 28

The detaining Power shall assume entire responsibility for the maintenance, care, treatment and the payment of the wages of prisoners of war working for private individuals.

Article 29

No prisoner of war may be employed on work for which he is physically unsuited.

Article 30

The duration of the daily work of prisoners of war, including the time of the journey to and from work, shall not be excessive and shall in no case exceed that permitted for civil workers of the locality employed on the same work. Each prisoner shall be allowed a rest of twenty-four consecutive hours each week, preferably on Sunday.

CHAPTER 3
Prohibited Work
Article 31

Work done by prisoners of war shall have no direct connection with the operations of the war. In particular, it is forbidden to employ prisoners in the manufacture or transport of arms or munitions of any kind, or on the transport of material destined for combatant units. In the event of violation of the provisions of the preceding paragraph, prisoners are at liberty, after performing or commencing to perform the order, to have their complaints presented through the intermediary of the prisoners' representatives whose functions are described in Articles 43 an 44, or, in the absence of a prisoners' representative, through the intermediary of the representatives of the protecting Power.

Article 32

It is forbidden to employ prisoners of war on unhealthy or dangerous work. Conditions of work shall not be rendered more arduous by disciplinary measures.

CHAPTER 4

Labour Detachments

Article 33

Conditions governing labour detachments shall be similar to those of prisoners-of-war camps, particularly as concerns hygienic conditions, food, care in case of accidents or sickness, correspondence, and the reception of parcels. Every labour detachment shall be attached to a prisoners' camp. The commander of this camp shall be responsible for the observance in the labour detachment of the provisions of the present Convention . . .

Section IV

Relations of Prisoners of War with the Exterior

Article 35

On the commencement of hostilities, belligerents shall publish the measures prescribed for the execution of the provisions of the present section.

Article 36

Each of the belligerents shall fix periodically the number of letters and postcards which prisoners of war of different categories shall be permitted to send per month, and shall notify that number to the other belligerent. These letters and cards shall be sent by post by the shortest route. They may not be delayed or withheld for disciplinary motives. Not later than one week after his arrival in camp, and similarly in case of sickness, each prisoner shall be enabled to send a postcard to his family informing them of his capture and the state of his health. The said postcards shall be forwarded as quickly as possible and shall not be delayed in any manner. As a general rule, the correspondence of prisoners shall be written in their native language. Belligerents may authorize correspondence in other languages.

Article 37

Prisoners of war shall be authorized to receive individually postal parcels containing foodstuffs and other articles intended for consumption or clothing. The parcels shall be delivered to the addressees and a receipt given.

Article 38

Letters and remittances of money or valuables, as well as postal parcels addressed to prisoners of war, or despatched by them, either directly or through the intermediary of the information bureaux mentioned in Article 77, shall be exempt from all postal charges in the countries of origin and destination and in the countries through which they pass. Presents and relief in kind intended for prisoners of war shall also be exempt from all import or other duties, as well as any charges for carriage on railways operated by the State. Prisoners may, in cases of recognized urgency, be authorized to send telegrams on payment of the usual charges.

Article 39

Prisoners of war shall be permitted to receive individually consignments of books which may be subject to censorship. Representatives of the protecting Powers and of duly recognized and authorized relief societies may send works and collections of books to the libraries of prisoners, camps. The transmission of such consignments to libraries may not be delayed under pretext of difficulties of censorship.

Article 40

The censoring of correspondence shall be accomplished as quickly as possible. The examination of postal parcels shall, moreover, be effected under such conditions as will ensure the preservation of any foodstuffs which they may contain, and, if possible, be done in the presence of the addressee or of a representative duly recognized by him. Any prohibition of correspondence ordered by the belligerents, for military or political reasons, shall only be of a temporary character and shall also be for as brief a time as possible.

Article 41

Belligerents shall accord all facilities for the transmission of documents destined for prisoners of war or signed by them, in particular powers of attorney and wills. They shall take the necessary measures to secure, in case of need, the legalisation of signatures of prisoners.

Section V
Relations between Prisoners of War and the Authorities

CHAPTER 1
Complaints of Prisoners of War Respecting the Conditions of Captivity
Article 42

Prisoners of war shall have the right to bring to the notice of the military authorities, in whose hands they are, their petitions concerning the conditions of captivity to which they are subjected. They shall also have the right to communicate with the representatives of the protecting Powers in order to draw their attention to the points on which they have complaints to make with regard to the conditions of captivity. Such petitions and complaints shall be transmitted immediately. Even though they are found to be groundless, they shall not give rise to any punishment. . . .

CHAPTER 3
Penal Sanctions with Regard to Prisoners of War
I. General Provisions
Article 45

Prisoners of war shall be subject to the laws, regulations and orders in force in the armed forces of the detaining Power. Any act of insubordination shall render them liable to the measures prescribed by such laws, regulations, and orders, except as otherwise provided in this Chapter.

Article 46

Prisoners of war shall not be subjected by the military authorities or the tribunals of the detaining Power to penalties other than those which are prescribed for similar acts by members of the national forces. Officers, non-commissioned officers or private soldiers, prisoners of war, undergoing disciplinary punishment shall not be subjected to treatment less favourable than that prescribed, as regards the same punishment, for similar ranks in the armed forces of the detaining Power. All forms of corporal punishment, confinement in premises not lighted by daylight and, in general, all forms of cruelty whatsoever are prohibited. Collective penalties for individual acts are also prohibited.

Article 47

A statement of the facts in cases of acts constituting a breach of discipline, and particularly an attempt to escape, shall be drawn up in writing without delay. The period during which prisoners of war of whatever rank are detained in custody (pending the investigation of such offences) shall be reduced to a strict minimum. The judicial proceedings against a prisoner of war shall be conducted as quickly as circumstances will allow. The period during which prisoners shall be detained in custody shall be as short as possible. In all cases the period during which a prisoner is under arrest (awaiting punishment or trial) shall be deducted from the sentence, whether disciplinary or judicial, provided such deduction is permitted in the case of members of the national forces.

Article 48

After undergoing the judicial or disciplinary punishment which has been inflicted on them, prisoners of war shall not be treated differently from other prisoners. Nevertheless, prisoners who have been punished as the result of an attempt to escape may be subjected to a special régime of surveillance, but this shall not involve the suppression of any of the safeguards accorded to prisoners by the present Convention.

Article 49

No prisoner of war may be deprived of his rank by the detaining Power. Prisoners on whom disciplinary punishment is inflicted shall not be deprived of the privileges attaching to their rank. In particular, officers and persons of equivalent status who suffer penalties entailing deprivation of liberty shall not be placed in the same premises as non-commissioned officers or private soldiers undergoing punishment.

Article 50

Escaped prisoners of war who are re-captured before they have been able to rejoin their own armed forces or to leave the territory occupied by the armed forces which captured them shall be liable only to disciplinary punishment. Prisoners who, after succeeding in rejoining their armed forces or in leaving the territory occupied by the armed forces which captured them, are again taken prisoner shall not be liable to any punishment for their previous escape.

Article 51

Attempted escape, even if it is not a first offence, shall not be considered as an aggravation of the offence in the event of the prisoner of war being brought before the courts for crimes or offences against persons or property committed in the course of such attempt. After an attempted or successful escape, the comrades of the escaped person who aided the escape shall incur only disciplinary punishment therefore.

Article 52

Belligerents shall ensure that the competent authorities exercize the greatest leniency in considering the question whether an offence committed by a prisoner of war should be punished by disciplinary or by judicial measures. This provision shall be observed in particular in appraising facts in connexion with escape or attempted escape. A prisoner shall not be punished more than once for the same act or on the same charge.

Article 53

No prisoner who has been awarded any disciplinary punishment for an offence and who fulfils the conditions laid down for repatriation shall be retained on the ground that he has not undergone his punishment. Prisoners qualified for repatriation against whom any prosecution for a criminal offence has been brought may be excluded from repatriation until the termination of the proceedings and until fulfilment of their sentence, if any; prisoners already serving a sentence of imprisonment may be retained until the expiry of the sentence. Belligerents shall communicate to each other lists of those who cannot be repatriated for the reasons indicated in the preceding paragraph.

II. Disciplinary Punishments

Article 54

Imprisonment is the most severe disciplinary punishment which may be inflicted on a prisoner of war. The duration of any single punishment shall not exceed thirty days. This maximum of thirty days shall, moreover, not be exceeded in the event of there being several acts for which the prisoner is answerable to discipline at the time when his case is disposed of, whether such acts are connected or not. Where, during the course or after the termination of a period of imprisonment, a prisoner is sentenced to a fresh disciplinary penalty, a period of at least three days shall intervene between each of the periods of imprisonment, if one of such periods is of ten days or over.

Article 55

Subject to the provisions of the last paragraph of Article 11, the restrictions in regard to food permitted in the armed forces of the detaining Power may be applied, as an additional penalty, to prisoners of war undergoing disciplinary punishment. Such restrictions shall, however, only be ordered if the state of the prisoner's health permits.

Article 56

In no case shall prisoners of war be transferred to penitentiary establishments (prisoners, penitentiaries, convict establishments, etc.) in order to undergo disciplinary sentence there. Establishments in which disciplinary sentences are undergone shall conform to the requirements of hygiene. Facilities shall be afforded to prisoners undergoing sentence to keep themselves in a state of cleanliness. Every day, such prisoners shall have facilities for taking exercise or for remaining out of doors for at least two hours.

Article 57

Prisoners of war undergoing disciplinary punishment shall be permitted to read and write and to send and receive letters. On the other hand, it shall be permissible not to deliver parcels and remittances of money to the addressees until the expiration of the sentence. If the undelivered parcels contain perishable foodstuffs, these shall be handed over to the infirmary or to the camp kitchen.

Article 58

Prisoners of war undergoing disciplinary punishment shall be permitted, on their request, to present themselves for daily medical inspection. They shall receive such attention as the medical officers may consider necessary, and, if need be, shall be evacuated to the camp infirmary or to hospital.

Article 59

Without prejudice to the competency of the courts and the superior military authorities, disciplinary sentences may only be awarded by an officer vested with disciplinary powers in his capacity as commander of the camp or detachment, or by the responsible officer acting as his substitute.

III. Judicial Proceedings

Article 60

At the commencement of a judicial hearing against a prisoner of war, the detaining Power shall notify the representative of the protecting Power as soon as possible, and in any case before the date fixed for the opening of the hearing. The said notification shall contain the following particulars:

(a) Civil status and rank of the prisoner.
(b) Place of residence or detention.
(c) Statement of the charge or charges, and of the legal provisions applicable.

If it is not possible in this notification to indicate particulars of the court which will try the case, the date of the opening of the hearing and the place where it will take place, these particulars shall be furnished to the representative of the protecting Power at a later date, but as soon as possible and in any case at least three weeks before the opening of the hearing.

Article 61

No prisoner of war shall be sentenced without being given the opportunity to defend himself. No prisoner shall be compelled to admit that he is guilty of the offence of which he is accused.

Article 62

The prisoner of war shall have the right to be assisted by a qualified. advocate of his own choice and, if necessary, to have recourse to the offices of a competent interpreter. He shall be informed of his right by the detaining Power in good time before the hearing. Failing a choice on the part of the prisoner, the protecting Power may procure an advocate for him. The detaining Power shall, on the request of the protecting Power, furnish to the latter a list of persons qualified to conduct the defence. The representatives of the protecting Power shall have the right to attend the hearing of the case. The only exception to this rule is where the hearing has to be kept secret in the interests of the safety of the State. The detaining Power would then notify the protecting Power accordingly.

Article 63

A sentence shall only be pronounced on a prisoner of war by the same tribunals and in accordance with the same procedure as in the case of persons belonging to the armed forces of the detaining Power.

Article 64

Every prisoner of war shall have the right of appeal against any sentence against him in the same manner as persons belonging to the armed forces of the detaining Power.

Article 65

Sentences pronounced against prisoners of war shall be communicated immediately to the protecting Power.

Article 66

If sentence of death is passed on a prisoner of war, a communication setting forth in detail the nature and the circumstances of the offence shall be addressed as soon as possible to the representative of the protecting Power for transmission to the Power in whose armed forces the prisoner served. The sentence shall not be carried out before the expiration of a period of at least three months from the date of the receipt of this communication by the protecting Power.

Article 67

No prisoner of war may be deprived of the benefit of the provisions of Article 42 of the present Convention as the result of a judgment or otherwise.

Part IV
End of Captivity

. . .

Article 71

Prisoners of war who meet with accidents at work, unless the injury is self-inflicted, shall have the benefit of the same provisions as regards repatriation or accommodation in a neutral country.

Article 72

During the continuance of hostilities, and for humanitarian reasons, belligerents may conclude agreements with a view to the direct repatriation or accommodation in a neutral country of prisoners of war in good health who have been in captivity for a long time.

Article 73

The expenses of repatriation or transport to a neutral country of prisoners of war shall be borne, as from the frontier of the detaining Power, by the Power in whose armed forces such prisoners served.

Article 74

No repatriated person shall be employed on active military service.

. . .

Part V
Deaths of Prisoners of War

Article 76

The wills of prisoners of war shall be received and drawn up under the same conditions as for soldiers of the national armed forces. The same rules shall be followed as regards the documents relative to the certification of the death. The belligerents shall ensure that prisoners of war who have died in captivity are honourably buried, and that the graves bear the necessary indications and are treated with respect and suitably maintained.

. . .

Annex to the Convention of 27 July 1929, Relative to the Treatment of Prisoners of War

Model draft agreement concerning the direct repatriation or accommodation in a neutral country of prisoners of war for reasons of health

I. Guiding Principles for Direct Repatriation or Accommodation in a Neutral Country

A. 'Guiding Principles for Direct Repatriation'

The following shall be repatriated directly:

1. Sick and wounded whose recovery within one year is not probable according to medical prognosis, whose condition requires treatment, and whose intellectual or bodily powers appear to have undergone a considerable diminution.
2. Incurable sick and wounded whose intellectual or bodily powers appear to have undergone a considerable diminution.
3. Convalescent sick and wounded, whose intellectual or bodily powers appear to have undergone a considerable diminution.

B. 'Guiding Principles for Accommodation in a Neutral Country'

The following shall be accommodated in a neutral country:

1. Sick and wounded whose recovery is presumable within the period of one year, when it appears that such recovery would be more certain and more rapid if the sick and wounded were given the benefit of the resources offered by the neutral country than if their captivity, properly so called, were prolonged.
2. Prisoners of war whose intellectual or physical health appears, according to medical opinion, to be seriously threatened by continuance in captivity, while accommodation in a neutral country would probably diminish that risk.

C. 'Guiding Principles for the Repatriation of Prisoners in a Neutral Country'

Prisoners of war who have been accommodated in a neutral country, and belong to the following categories, shall be repatriated:

1. Those whose state of health appears to be, or likely to become such that they would fall into the categories of those to be repatriated for reasons of health.
2. Those who are convalescent, whose intellectual or physical powers appear to have undergone a considerable diminution.

II. Special Principles for Direct Repatriation or Accommodation in a Neutral Country

A. 'Special Principles for Repatriation'

The following shall be repatriated:

1. All prisoners of war suffering the following effective or functional disabilities as the result of organic injuries: loss of a limb, paralysis, articular or other disabilities, when the defect is at least the loss of a foot or a hand, or the equivalent of the loss of a foot or a hand.
2. All wounded or injured prisoners of war whose condition is such as to render them invalids whose cure within a year cannot be medically foreseen.
3. All sick prisoners whose condition is such as to render them invalids whose cure within a year cannot be medically foreseen.

The following in particular belong to this category:

(a) Progressive tuberculosis of any organ which, according to medical prognosis, cannot be cured or at least considerably improved by treatment in a neutral country;
(b) Non-tubercular affections of the respiratory organs which are presumed to be incurable (in particular, strongly developed pulmonary emphysema, with or without bronchitis, bronchiectasis, serious asthma, gas poisoning, etc.):
(c) Grave chronic affections of the circulatory organs (for example: valvular affections with a tendency to compensatory troubles, relatively grave affections of the myocardium, pericardium or the vessels, in particular, aneurism of the larger vessels which cannot be operated on, etc.);
(d) Grave chronic affections of the digestive organs;
(e) Grave chronic affections of the urinary and sexual organs, in particular, for example: any case of chronic nephritis, confirmed by symptoms, and especially when cardiac and vascular deterioration already exists; the same applies to chronic pyelitis and cystitis, etc.;
(f) Grave chronic maladies of the central and peripheral nervous system; in particular grave neurasthenia and hysteria, any indisputable case of epilepsy, grave Basedow's disease, etc.;
(g) Blindness of both eyes, or of one eye when the vision of the other is less than 1 in spite of the use of corrective glasses. Diminution of visual acuteness in cases where it is impossible to restore it by correction to an acuteness of 1/2 in at least one eye. The other ocular affections falling within the present category (glaucoma, iritis, choroiditis, etc.);
(h) Total bilateral deafness, and total unilateral deafness in cases where the ear which is not completely deaf cannot hear ordinary speaking voice at a distance of one metre;
(i) Any indisputable case of mental affection;
(k) Grave cases of chronic poisoning by metals or other causes (lead poisoning, mercury poisoning, morphinism, cocainism, alcoholism, gas poisoning, etc.);
(l) Chronic affections of the locomotive organs (arthritis deformans, gout, or rheumatism with impairment, which can be ascertained clinically), provided that they are serious;

(m) Malignant growths, if they are not amenable to relatively mild operations without danger to the life of the person operated upon;
(n) All cases of malaria with appreciable organic deterioration (serious chronic enlargement of the liver or spleen, cachexy, etc.);
(o) Grave chronic cutaneous affections, when their nature does not constitute a medical reason for treatment in a neutral country;
(p) Serious avitaminosis (beri-beri, pellagra, chronic scurvy).

B. 'Special Principles for Accommodation in a Neutral Country'

Prisoners of war shall be accommodated in a neutral country if they suffer from the following affections:

1. All forms of tuberculosis of any organ, if, according to present medical knowledge, they can be cured or their condition considerably improved by methods applicable in a neutral country(altitude, treatment in sanatoria, etc.).
2. All forms necessitating treatment of affections of the respiratory, circulatory, digestive, genito-urinary, or nervous organs, of the organs of the senses, or of the locomotive or cutaneous functions, provided that such forms of affection do not belong to the categories necessitating direct repatriation, or that they are not acute maladies (properly so called) susceptible of complete cure. The affections referred to in this paragraph are such as admit, by the application of methods of treatment available in the neutral country, of really better chances of the patient's recovery than if he were treated in captivity.
   Special consideration should be given to nervous troubles, the effective or determining causes of which are the effects of the war or of captivity, such as psychasthenia of prisoners of war or other analogous cases. All duly established cases of this nature must be treated in neutral countries when their gravity or their constitutional character does not render them cases for direct repatriation.
   Cases of psychasthenia of prisoners of war who are not cured after three months' sojourn in a neutral country, or which after that period are not manifestly on the way to complete recovery, shall be repatriated.
3. All cases of wounds or injuries or their consequences which offer better prospects of cure in a neutral country than in captivity, provided that such cases are neither such as justify direct repatriation, nor insignificant cases.
4. All duly established cases of malaria which do not show organic deterioration clinically ascertainable (chronic enlargement of the liver or spleen, cachexy, etc.), if sojourn in a neutral country offers particularly favourable prospects of final cure.
5. All cases of poisoning (in particular by gas, metals, or alkaloids) for which the prospects of cure in a neutral country are especially favourable.

The following are excluded from accommodation in a neutral country:

1. All cases of duly established mental affections.
2. All organic or functional nervous affections which are reputed to be incurable. (These two categories belong to those which entitle direct repatriation.)

3. Grave chronic alcoholism.
4. All contagious affections during the period when they are transmissible (acute infectious diseases, primary and secondary (syphilis, trachoma, leprosy, etc.).

Source: U.S. Statutes at Large 47, Stat. 2021.

Universal Declaration of Human Rights, United Nations, 1948

Preamble

WHEREAS recognition of the inherent dignity and of the equal and inalienable rights of all members of the human family is the foundation of freedom, justice and peace in the world,

WHEREAS disregard and contempt for human rights have resulted in barbarous acts which have outraged the conscience of mankind, and the advent of a world in which human beings shall enjoy freedom of speech and belief and freedom from fear and want has been proclaimed as the highest aspiration of the common people,

WHEREAS it is essential, if man is not to be compelled to have recourse, as a last resort, to rebellion against tyranny and oppression, that human rights should be protected by the rule of law,

WHEREAS it is essential to promote the development of friendly relations between nations,

WHEREAS the peoples of the United Nations have in the Charter reaffirmed their faith in fundamental human rights, in the dignity and worth of the human person and in the equal rights of men and women and have determined to promote social progress and better standards of life in larger freedom,

WHEREAS Member States have pledged themselves to achieve, in co-operation with the United Nations, the promotion of universal respect for and observance of human rights and fundamental freedoms,

WHEREAS a common understanding of these rights and freedoms is of the greatest importance for the full realization of this pledge,

Now, Therefore,
The General Assembly
Proclaims
This Universal Declaration of Human Rights

as a common standard of achievement for all peoples and all nations, to the end that every individual and every organ of society, keeping this Declaration constantly in mind, shall strive by teaching and education to promote respect for these rights and freedoms and by progressive measures, national and international, to secure their universal and effective recognition and observance, both among the peoples of Member States themselves and among the peoples of territories under their jurisdiction.

Article 1

All human beings are born free and equal in dignity and rights. They are endowed with reason and conscience and should act towards one another in a spirit of brotherhood.

Article 2

Everyone is entitled to all the rights and freedoms set forth in this Declaration, without distinction of any kind, such as race, colour, sex, language, religion, political or other opinion, national or social origin, property, birth or other status.

Furthermore, no distinction shall be made on the basis of the political, jurisdictional or international status of the country or territory to which a person belongs, whether it be independent, trust, nonselfgoverning or under any other limitation of sovereignty.

Article 3

Everyone has the right to life, liberty and security of person.

Article 4

No one shall be held in slavery or servitude; slavery and the slave trade shall be prohibited in all their forms.

Article 5

No one shall be subjected to torture or to cruel, inhuman or degrading treatment or punishment.

Article 6

Everyone has the right to recognition everywhere as a person before the law.

Article 7

All are equal before the law and are entitled without any discrimination to equal protection of the law. All are entitled to equal protection against any discrimination in violation of this Declaration and against any incitement to such discrimination.

Article 8

Everyone has the right to an effective remedy by the competent national tribunals for acts violating the fundamental rights granted him by the constitution or by law.

Article 9

No one shall be subjected to arbitrary arrest, detention or exile.

Article 10

Everyone is entitled in full equality to a fair and public hearing by an independent and impartial tribunal, in the determination of his rights and obligations and of any criminal charge against him.

Article 11

(1) Everyone charged with a penal offence has the right to be presumed innocent until proved guilty according to law in a public trial at which he has had all the guarantees necessary for his defence.

(2) No one shall be held guilty of any penal offence on account of any act or omission which did not constitute a penal offence, under national or international law, at the time when it was committed. Nor shall a heavier penalty be imposed than the one that was applicable at the time the penal offence was committed.

Article 12

No one shall be subjected to arbitrary interference with his privacy, family, home or correspondence, nor to attacks upon his honour and reputation. Everyone has the right to the protection of the law against such interference or attacks.

Article 13

(1) Everyone has the right to freedom of movement and residence within the borders of each State.

(2) Everyone has the right to leave any country, including his own, and to return to his country.

Article 14

(1) Everyone has the right to seek and to enjoy in other countries asylum from persecution.

(2) This right may not be invoked in the case of prosecutions genuinely arising from non-political crimes or from acts contrary to the purposes and principles of the United Nations.

Article 15

(1) Everyone has the right to a nationality.
(2) No one shall be arbitrarily deprived of his nationality nor denied the right to change his nationality.

Article 16

(1) Men and women of full age, without any limitation due to race, nationality or religion, have the right to marry and to found a family. They are entitled to equal rights as a marriage, during marriage and at its dissolution.
(2) Marriage shall be entered into only with the free and full consent of the intending spouses.
(3) The family is the natural and fundamental group unit of society and is entitled to protection by society and the State.

Article 17

(1) Everyone has the right to own property alone as well as in association with others.
(2) No one shall be arbitrarily deprived of his property.

Article 18

Everyone has the right to freedom of thought, conscience and religion; this right includes freedom to change his religion or belief, and freedom, either alone or in community with others and in public or private, to manifest his religion or belief in teaching, practice, worship and observance.

Article 19

Everyone has the right to freedom of opinion and expression; this right includes freedom to hold opinions without interference and to seek, receive and impart information and ideas through any media and regardless of frontiers.

Article 20

(1) Everyone has the right to freedom of peaceful assembly and association.
(2) No one may be compelled to belong to an association.

Article 21

(1) Everyone has the right to take part in the government of his country, directly or through freely chosen representatives.
(2) Everyone has the right of equal access to public service in his country.
(3) The will of the people shall be the basis of the authority of the government; this will shall be expressed in periodic and genuine elections which shall be

by universal and equal suffrage and shall be held by secret vote or by equivalent free voting procedures.

Article 22

Everyone, as a member of society, has the right to social security and is entitled to realization, through national effort and international co-operation and in accordance with the organization and resources of each State, of the economic, social and cultural rights indispensible for his dignity and the free development of his personality.

Article 23

(1) Everyone has the right to work, to free choice of employment, to just and favourable conditions of work and to protection against unemployment.
(2) Everyone, without any discrimination, has the right to equal pay for equal work.
(3) Everyone who works has the right to just and favourable remuneration ensuring for himself and his family an existence worthy of human dignity, and supplemented, if necessary, by other means of social protection.
(4) Everyone has the right to form and to join trade unions for the protection of his interests.

Article 24

Everyone has the right to rest and leisure, including reasonable limitation of working hours and periodic holidays with pay.

Article 25

(1) Everyone has the right to a standard of living adequate for the health and well-being of himself and of his family, including food, clothing, housing, and medical care and necessary social services, and the right to security in the event of unemployment, sickness, disability, widowhood, old age, or other lack of livelihood in circumstances beyond his control.
(2) Motherhood and childhood are entitled to special care and assistance. All children, whether born in or out of wedlock, shall enjoy the same social protection.

Article 26

(1) Everyone has the right to education. Education shall be free, at least in the elementary and fundamental stages. Elementary education shall be compulsory. Technical and professional education shall be made generally available and higher education shall be equally accessible to all on the basis of merit.
(2) Education shall be directed to the full development of the human personality and to the strengthening of respect for human rights and fundamental freedoms. It shall promote understanding, tolerance and friendship among all nations, racial or religious groups, and shall further the activities of the United Nations for the maintenance of peace.

(3) Parents have a prior right to choose the kind of education that shall be given to their children.

Article 27

(1) Everyone has the right freely to participate in the cultural life of the community, to enjoy the arts and to share in scientific advancement and its benefits.
(2) Everyone has the right to the protection of the moral and material interests resulting from any scientific, literary or artistic production of which he is the author.

Article 28

Everyone is entitled to a social and international order in which the rights and freedoms set forth in this Declaration can be fully realized.

Article 29

(1) Everyone has duties to the community in which alone the free and full development of his personality is possible.
(2) In the exercise of his rights and freedoms, everyone shall be subject only to such limitations as are determined by law solely for the purpose of securing due recognition and respect for the rights and freedoms and others and of meeting the just requirements of morality, public order and the general welfare in a democratic society.
(3) These rights and freedoms may in no case be exercised contrary to the purposes and principles of the United Nations.

Article 30

Nothing in this Declaration may be interpreted as implying for any State, group or person any right to engage in any activity or to perform any act aimed at the destruction of any of the rights and freedoms set forth herein.

Source: UN General Assembly Resolution 217A (III), A/810 at 71, 1948. (© United Nations, 1948. Reproduced with permission.)

Geneva Convention Relative to the Treatment of Prisoners of War, August 12, 1949 (Geneva Convention III)

Entry into Force: 21 October 1950

The undersigned Plenipotentiaries of the Governments represented at the Diplomatic Conference held at Geneva from April 21 to August 12, 1949, for the purpose of revising the Convention concluded at Geneva on July 27, 1929 relative to the Treatment of Prisoners of War, have agreed as follows:

Part I
General Provisions

Article 1

The High Contracting Parties undertake to respect and to ensure respect for the present Convention in all circumstances.

Article 2

In addition to the provisions which shall be implemented in peace time, the present Convention shall apply to all cases of declared war or of any other armed conflict which may arise between two or more of the High Contracting Parties, even if the state of war is not recognized by one of them.

The Convention shall also apply to all cases of partial or total occupation of the territory of a High Contracting Party, even if the said occupation meets with no armed resistance.

Although one of the Powers in conflict may not be a party to the present Convention, the Powers who are parties thereto shall remain bound by it in their mutual relations. They shall furthermore be bound by the Convention in relation to the said Power, if the latter accepts and applies the provisions thereof.

Article 3

In the case of armed conflict not of an international character occurring in the territory of one of the High Contracting Parties, each Party to the conflict shall be bound to apply, as a minimum, the following provisions:

(1) Persons taking no active part in the hostilities, including members of armed forces who have laid down their arms and those placed hors de combat by sickness, wounds, detention, or any other cause, shall in all circumstances be treated humanely, without any adverse distinction founded on race, colour, religion or faith, sex, birth or wealth, or any other similar criteria.
To this end the following acts are and shall remain prohibited at any time and in any place whatsoever with respect to the above-mentioned persons:

 (a) violence to life and person, in particular murder of all kinds, mutilation, cruel treatment and torture;
 (b) taking of hostages;
 (c) outrages upon personal dignity, in particular, humiliating and degrading treatment;
 (d) he passing of sentences and the carrying out of executions without previous judgment pronounced by a regularly constituted court affording all the judicial guarantees which are recognized as indispensable by civilized peoples.

(2) The wounded and sick shall be collected and cared for.

An impartial humanitarian body, such as the International Committee of the Red Cross, may offer its services to the Parties to the conflict.

The Parties to the conflict should further endeavour to bring into force, by means of special agreements, all or part of the other provisions of the present Convention.

The application of the preceding provisions shall not affect the legal status of the Parties to the conflict.

Article 4

A. Prisoners of war, in the sense of the present Convention, are persons belonging to one of the following categories, who have fallen into the power of the enemy:

(1) Members of the armed forces of a Party to the conflict, as well as members of militias or volunteer corps forming part of such armed forces.
(2) Members of other militias and members of other volunteer corps, including those of organized resistance movements, belonging to a Party to the conflict and operating in or outside their own territory, even if this territory is occupied, provided that such militias or volunteer corps, including such organized resistance movements, fulfil the following conditions:

(a) that of being commanded by a person responsible for his subordinates;
(b) that of having a fixed distinctive sign recognizable at a distance;
(c) that of carrying arms openly;
(d) that of conducting their operations in accordance with the laws and customs of war.

(3) Members of regular armed forces who profess allegiance to a government or an authority not recognized by the Detaining Power.
(4) Persons who accompany the armed forces without actually being members thereof, such as civilian members of military aircraft crews, war correspondents, supply contractors, members of labour units or of services responsible for the welfare of the armed forces, provided that they have received authorization, from the armed forces which they accompany, who shall provide them for that purpose with an identity card similar to the annexed model.
(5) Members of crews, including masters, pilots and apprentices, of the merchant marine and the crews of civil aircraft of the Parties to the conflict, who do not benefit by more favourable treatment under any other provisions of international law.
(6) Inhabitants of a non-occupied territory, who on the approach of the enemy spontaneously take up arms to resist the invading forces, without having had time to form themselves into regular armed units, provided they carry arms openly and respect the laws and customs of war.

B. The following shall likewise be treated as prisoners of war under the present Convention:

(1) Persons belonging, or having belonged, to the armed forces of the occupied country, if the occupying Power considers it necessary by reason of such allegiance to intern them, even though it has originally liberated them while hostilities were going on outside the territory it occupies, in particular where such persons have made an unsuccessful attempt to rejoin the armed forces to which they belong and which are engaged in combat, or where they fail to comply with a summons made to them with a view to internment.
(2) The persons belonging to one of the categories enumerated in the present Article, who have been received by neutral or non-belligerent Powers on their territory and whom these Powers are required to intern under international law, without prejudice to any more favourable treatment which these Powers may choose to give and with the exception of Articles 8, 10, 15, 30, fifth paragraph, 58–67, 92, 126 and, where diplomatic relations exist between the Parties to the conflict and the neutral or non-belligerent Power concerned, those Articles concerning the Protecting Power. Where such diplomatic relations exist, the Parties to a conflict on whom these persons depend shall be allowed to perform towards them the functions of a Protecting Power as provided in the present Convention, without prejudice to the functions which these Parties normally exercise in conformity with diplomatic and consular usage and treaties.

C. This Article shall in no way affect the status of medical personnel and chaplains as provided for in Article 33 of the present Convention.

. . .

Article 7

Prisoners of war may in no circumstances renounce in part or in entirety the rights secured to them by the present Convention, and by the special agreements referred to in the foregoing Article, if such there be.

. . .

Part II
General Protection of Prisoners of War

Article 12

Prisoners of war are in the hands of the enemy Power, but not of the individuals or military units who have captured them. Irrespective of the individual responsibilities that may exist, the Detaining Power is responsible for the treatment given them.

Prisoners of war may only be transferred by the Detaining Power to a Power which is a party to the Convention and after the Detaining Power has satisfied itself of the willingness and ability of such transferee Power to apply the Convention. When prisoners of war are transferred under such circumstances, responsibility for the application of the Convention rests on the Power accepting them while they are in its custody.

Nevertheless, if that Power fails to carry out the provisions of the Convention in any important respect, the Power by whom the prisoners of war were transferred shall, upon being notified by the Protecting Power, take effective measures to correct the situation or shall request the return of the prisoners of war. Such requests must be complied with.

Article 13

Prisoners of war must at all times be humanely treated. Any unlawful act or omission by the Detaining Power causing death or seriously endangering the health of a prisoner of war in its custody is prohibited, and will be regarded as a serious breach of the present Convention. In particular, no prisoner of war may be subjected to physical mutilation or to medical or scientific experiments of any kind which are not justified by the medical, dental or hospital treatment of the prisoner concerned and carried out in his interest.

Likewise, prisoners of war must at all times be protected, particularly against acts of violence or intimidation and against insults and public curiosity.

Measures of reprisal against prisoners of war are prohibited.

Article 14

Prisoners of war are entitled in all circumstances to respect for their persons and their honour.

Women shall be treated with all the regard due to their sex and shall in all cases benefit by treatment as favourable as that granted to men.

Prisoners of war shall retain the full civil capacity which they enjoyed at the time of their capture. The Detaining Power may not restrict the exercise, either within or without its own territory, of the rights such capacity confers except in so far as the captivity requires.

Article 15

The Power detaining prisoners of war shall be bound to provide free of charge for their maintenance and for the medical attention required by their state of health.

Article 16

Taking into consideration the provisions of the present Convention relating to rank and sex, and subject to any privileged treatment which may be accorded to them by reason of their state of health, age or professional qualifications, all prisoners of war shall be treated alike by the Detaining Power, without any adverse distinction based on race, nationality, religious belief or political opinions, or any other distinction founded on similar criteria.

Part III
Captivity

Section I
Beginning of Captivity

Article 17

Every prisoner of war, when questioned on the subject, is bound to give only his surname, first names and rank, date of birth, and army, regimental, personal or serial number, or failing this, equivalent information.

If he wilfully infringes this rule, he may render himself liable to a restriction of the privileges accorded to his rank or status.

Each Party to a conflict is required to furnish the persons under its jurisdiction who are liable to become prisoners of war, with an identity card showing the owner's surname, first names, rank, army, regimental, personal or serial number or equivalent information, and date of birth. The identity card may, furthermore, bear the signature or the fingerprints, or both, of the owner, and may bear, as well, any other information the Party to the conflict may wish to add concerning persons belonging to its armed forces. As far as possible the card shall measure 6.5 x 10 cm. and shall be issued in duplicate. The identity card shall be shown by the prisoner of war upon demand, but may in no case be taken away from him.

No physical or mental torture, nor any other form of coercion, may be inflicted on prisoners of war to secure from them information of any kind whatever. Prisoners of war who refuse to answer may not be threatened, insulted, or exposed to unpleasant or disadvantageous treatment of any kind.

Prisoners of war who, owing to their physical or mental condition, are unable to state their identity, shall be handed over to the medical service. The identity of such prisoners shall be established by all possible means, subject to the provisions of the preceding paragraph.

The questioning of prisoners of war shall be carried out in a language which they understand.

Article 18

All effects and articles of personal use, except arms, horses, military equipment and military documents, shall remain in the possession of prisoners of war, likewise their metal helmets and gas masks and like articles issued for personal protection. Effects and articles used for their clothing or feeding shall likewise remain in their possession, even if such effects and articles belong to their regulation military equipment.

At no time should prisoners of war be without identity documents. The Detaining Power shall supply such documents to prisoners of war who possess none.

Badges of rank and nationality, decorations and articles having above all a personal or sentimental value may not be taken from prisoners of war.

Sums of money carried by prisoners of war may not be taken away from them except by order of an officer, and after the amount and particulars of the owner have been recorded in a special register and an itemized receipt has been given, legibly inscribed with the name, rank and unit of the person issuing the said receipt. Sums in the currency of the Detaining Power, or which are changed into such currency at the prisoner's request, shall be placed to the credit of the prisoner's account as provided in Article 64.

The Detaining Power may withdraw articles of value from prisoners of war only for reasons of security; when such articles are withdrawn, the procedure laid down for sums of money impounded shall apply.

Such objects, likewise sums taken away in any currency other than that of the Detaining Power and the conversion of which has not been asked for by the owners, shall be kept in the custody of the Detaining Power and shall be returned in their initial shape to prisoners of war at the end of their captivity.

Article 19

Prisoners of war shall be evacuated, as soon as possible after their capture, to camps situated in an area far enough from the combat zone for them to be out of danger.

Only those prisoners of war who, owing to wounds or sickness, would run greater risks by being evacuated than by remaining where they are, may be temporarily kept back in a danger zone.

Prisoners of war shall not be unnecessarily exposed to danger while awaiting evacuation from a fighting zone.

Article 20

The evacuation of prisoners of war shall always be effected humanely and in conditions similar to those for the forces of the Detaining Power in their changes of station.

The Detaining Power shall supply prisoners of war who are being evacuated with sufficient food and potable water, and with the necessary clothing and medical attention. The Detaining Power shall take all suitable precautions to ensure their safety during evacuation, and shall establish as soon as possible a list of the prisoners of war who are evacuated.

If prisoners of war must, during evacuation, pass through transit camps, their stay in such camps shall be as brief as possible.

Section II
Internment of Prisoners of War

CHAPTER I
General Observations

Article 21

The Detaining Power may subject prisoners of war to internment. It may impose on them the obligation of not leaving, beyond certain limits, the camp where they are interned, or if the said camp is fenced in, of not going outside its perimeter. Subject to the provisions of the present Convention relative to penal and disciplinary sanctions, prisoners of war may not be held in close confinement except where necessary to safeguard their health and then only during the continuation of the circumstances which make such confinement necessary.

Prisoners of war may be partially or wholly released on parole or promise, in so far as is allowed by the laws of the Power on which they depend. Such measures shall be taken particularly in cases where this may contribute to the improvement of their state of health. No prisoner of war shall be compelled to accept liberty on parole or promise.

Upon the outbreak of hostilities, each Party to the conflict shall notify the adverse Party of the laws and regulations allowing or forbidding its own nationals to accept liberty on parole or promise. Prisoners of war who are paroled or who have given their promise in conformity with the laws and regulations so notified, are bound on their personal honour scrupulously to fulfil, both towards the Power on which they depend and towards the Power which has captured them, the engagements of their paroles or promises. In such cases, the Power on which they depend is bound neither to require nor to accept from them any service incompatible with the parole or promise given.

Article 22

Prisoners of war may be interned only in premises located on land and affording every guarantee of hygiene and healthfulness. Except in particular cases which are justified by the interest of the prisoners themselves, they shall not be interned in penitentiaries.

Prisoners of war interned in unhealthy areas, or where the climate is injurious for them, shall be removed as soon as possible to a more favourable climate.

The Detaining Power shall assemble prisoners of war in camps or camp compounds according to their nationality, language and customs, provided that such prisoners shall not be separated from prisoners of war belonging to the armed forces with which they were serving at the time of their capture, except with their consent.

Article 23

No prisoner of war may at any time be sent to, or detained in areas where he may be exposed to the fire of the combat zone, nor may his presence be used to render certain points or areas immune from military operations.

Prisoners of war shall have shelters against air bombardment and other hazards of war, to the same extent as the local civilian population. With the exception of those engaged in the protection of their quarters against the aforesaid hazards, they may enter such shelters as soon as possible after the giving of the alarm. Any other protective measure taken in favour of the population shall also apply to them.

Detaining Powers shall give the Powers concerned, through the intermediary of the Protecting Powers, all useful information regarding the geographical location of prisoner of war camps.

Whenever military considerations permit, prisoner of war camps shall be indicated in the day-time by the letters PW or PG, placed so as to be clearly visible from the air. The Powers concerned may, however, agree upon any other system of marking. Only prisoner of war camps shall be marked as such.

Article 24

Transit or screening camps of a permanent kind shall be fitted out under conditions similar to those described in the present Section, and the prisoners therein shall have the same treatment as in other camps.

CHAPTER II
Quarters, Food and Clothing of Prisoners of War

Article 25

Prisoners of war shall be quartered under conditions as favourable as those for the forces of the Detaining Power who are billeted in the same area. The said conditions shall make allowance for the habits and customs of the prisoners and shall in no case be prejudicial to their health.

The foregoing provisions shall apply in particular to the dormitories of prisoners of war as regards both total surface and minimum cubic space, and the general installations, bedding and blankets.

The premises provided for the use of prisoners of war individually or collectively, shall be entirely protected from dampness and adequately heated and lighted, in particular between dusk and lights out. All precautions must be taken against the danger of fire.

In any camps in which women prisoners of war, as well as men, are accommodated, separate dormitories shall be provided for them.

Article 26

The basic daily food rations shall be sufficient in quantity, quality and variety to keep prisoners of war in good health and to prevent loss of weight or the development of nutritional deficiencies. Account shall also be taken of the habitual diet of the prisoners.

The Detaining Power shall supply prisoners of war who work with such additional rations as are necessary for the labour on which they are employed.

Sufficient drinking water shall be supplied to prisoners of war. The use of tobacco shall be permitted.

Prisoners of war shall, as far as possible, be associated with the preparation of their meals; they may be employed for that purpose in the kitchens. Furthermore, they shall be given the means of preparing, themselves, the additional food in their possession.

Adequate premises shall be provided for messing.

Collective disciplinary measures affecting food are prohibited.

Article 27

Clothing, underwear and footwear shall be supplied to prisoners of war in sufficient quantities by the Detaining Power, which shall make allowance for the climate of the region where the prisoners are detained. Uniforms of enemy armed forces captured by the Detaining Power should, if suitable for the climate, be made available to clothe prisoners of war.

The regular replacement and repair of the above articles shall be assured by the Detaining Power. In addition, prisoners of war who work shall receive appropriate clothing, wherever the nature of the work demands.

Article 28

Canteens shall be installed in all camps, where prisoners of war may procure foodstuffs, soap and tobacco and ordinary articles in daily use. The tariff shall never be in excess of local market prices.

The profits made by camp canteens shall be used for the benefit of the prisoners; a special fund shall be created for this purpose. The prisoners' representative shall have the right to collaborate in the management of the canteen and of this fund.

When a camp is closed down, the credit balance of the special fund shall be handed to an international welfare organization, to be employed for the benefit of prisoners of war of the same nationality as those who have contributed to the fund. In case of a general repatriation, such profits shall be kept by the Detaining Power, subject to any agreement to the contrary between the Powers concerned.

CHAPTER III
Hygiene and Medical Attention

Article 29

The Detaining Power shall be bound to take all sanitary measures necessary to ensure the cleanliness and healthfulness of camps and to prevent epidemics.

Prisoners of war shall have for their use, day and night, conveniences which conform to the rules of hygiene and are maintained in a constant state of cleanliness. In any camps in which women prisoners of war are accommodated, separate conveniences shall be provided for them.

Also, apart from the baths and showers with which the camps shall be furnished prisoners of war shall be provided with sufficient water and soap for their personal toilet and for washing their personal laundry; the necessary installations, facilities and time shall be granted them for that purpose.

Article 30

Every camp shall have an adequate infirmary where prisoners of war may have the attention they require, as well as appropriate diet. Isolation wards shall, if necessary, be set aside for cases of contagious or mental disease.

Prisoners of war suffering from serious disease, or whose condition necessitates special treatment, a surgical operation or hospital care, must be admitted to any military or civilian medical unit where such treatment can be given, even if their repatriation is contemplated in the near future. Special facilities shall be afforded for the care to be given to the disabled, in particular to the blind, and for their. rehabilitation, pending repatriation.

Prisoners of war shall have the attention, preferably, of medical personnel of the Power on which they depend and, if possible, of their nationality.

Prisoners of war may not be prevented from presenting themselves to the medical authorities for examination. The detaining authorities shall, upon request, issue to every prisoner who has undergone treatment, an official certificate indicating the nature of his illness or injury, and the duration and kind of treatment received. A duplicate of this certificate shall be forwarded to the Central Prisoners of War Agency.

The costs of treatment, including those of any apparatus necessary for the maintenance of prisoners of war in good health, particularly dentures and other artificial appliances, and spectacles, shall be borne by the Detaining Power.

Article 31

Medical inspections of prisoners of war shall be held at least once a month. They shall include the checking and the recording of the weight of each prisoner of war.

Their purpose shall be, in particular, to supervise the general state of health, nutrition and cleanliness of prisoners and to detect contagious diseases, especially tuberculosis, malaria and venereal disease. For this purpose the most efficient methods available shall be employed, e.g. periodic mass miniature radiography for the early detection of tuberculosis.

Article 32

Prisoners of war who, though not attached to the medical service of their armed forces, are physicians, surgeons, dentists, nurses or medical orderlies, may be required by the Detaining Power to exercise their medical functions in the interests of prisoners of war dependent on the same Power. In that case they shall continue to be prisoners of war, but shall receive the same treatment as corresponding medical personnel retained by the Detaining Power. They shall be exempted from any other work under Article 49.

. . .

CHAPTER V
Religious, Intellectual and Physical Activities

Article 34

Prisoners of war shall enjoy complete latitude in the exercise of their religious duties, including attendance at the service of their faith, on condition that they comply with the disciplinary routine prescribed by the military authorities.

Adequate premises shall be provided where religious services may be held.

. . .

Article 38

While respecting the individual preferences of every prisoner, the Detaining Power shall encourage the practice of intellectual, educational, and recreational pursuits, sports and games amongst prisoners, and shall take the measures necessary to ensure the exercise thereof by providing them with adequate premises and necessary equipment.

Prisoners shall have opportunities for taking physical exercise, including sports and games, and for being out of doors. Sufficient open spaces shall be provided for this purpose in all camps.

CHAPTER VI
Discipline

Article 39

Every prisoner of war camp shall be put under the immediate authority of a responsible commissioned officer belonging to the regular armed forces of the Detaining Power. Such officer shall have in his possession a copy of the present Convention; he shall ensure that its provisions are known to the camp staff and the guard and shall be responsible, under the direction of his government, for its application.

Prisoners of war, with the exception of officers, must salute and show to all officers of the Detaining Power the external marks of respect provided for by the regulations applying in their own forces.

Officer prisoners of war are bound to salute only officers of a higher rank of the Detaining Power; they must, however, salute the camp commander regardless of his rank.

Article 40

The wearing of badges of rank and nationality, as well as of decorations, shall be permitted.

Article 41

In every camp the text of the present Convention and its Annexes and the contents of any special agreement provided for in Article 6, shall be posted, in the prisoners' own language, in places where all may read them. Copies shall be supplied, on request, to the prisoners who cannot have access to the copy which has been posted.

Regulations, orders, notices and publications of every kind relating to the conduct of prisoners of war shall be issued to them in a language which they understand. Such regulations, orders and publications shall be posted in the manner described above and copies shall be handed to the prisoners' representative. Every order and command addressed to prisoners of war individually must likewise be given in a language which they understand.

Article 42

The use of weapons against prisoners of war, especially against those who are escaping or attempting to escape, shall constitute an extreme measure, which shall always be preceded by warnings appropriate to the circumstances.

CHAPTER VII
Rank of Prisoners of War

Article 43

Upon the outbreak of hostilities, the Parties to the conflict shall communicate to one another the titles and ranks of all the persons mentioned in Article 4 of the present Convention, in order to ensure equality of treatment between prisoners of equivalent rank. Titles and ranks which are subsequently created shall form the subject of similar communications.

The Detaining Power shall recognize promotions in rank which have been accorded to prisoners of war and which have been duly notified by the Power on which these prisoners depend.

Article 44

Officers and prisoners of equivalent status shall be treated with the regard due to their rank and age.

In order to ensure service in officers' camps, other ranks of the same armed forces who, as far as possible, speak the same language, shall be assigned in sufficient numbers, account being taken of the rank of officers and prisoners of equivalent status. Such orderlies shall not be required to perform any other work.

Supervision of the mess by the officers themselves shall be facilitated in every way.

Article 45

Prisoners of war other than officers and prisoners of equivalent status shall be treated with the regard due to their rank and age.

Supervision of the mess by the prisoners themselves shall be facilitated in every way.

. . .

Section III
Labour of Prisoners of War

Article 49

The Detaining Power may utilize the labour of prisoners of war who are physically fit, taking into account their age, sex, rank and physical aptitude, and with a view particularly to maintaining them in a good state of physical and mental health.

Non-commissioned officers who are prisoners of war shall only be required to do supervisory work. Those not so required may ask for other suitable work which shall, so far as possible, be found for them.

If officers or persons of equivalent status ask for suitable work, it shall be found for them, so far as possible, but they may in no circumstances be compelled to work.

Article 50

Besides work connected with camp administration, installation or maintenance, prisoners of war may be compelled to do only such work as is included in the following classes:

(a) agriculture;
(b) industries connected with the production or the extraction of raw materials, and manufacturing industries, with the exception of metallurgical, machinery and chemical industries; public works and building operations which have no military character or purpose;
(c) transport and handling of stores which are not military in character or purpose;
(d) commercial business, and arts and crafts;
(e) domestic service;
(f) public utility services having no military character or purpose.

Should the above provisions be infringed, prisoners of war shall be allowed to exercise their right of complaint, in conformity with Article 78.

Article 51

Prisoners of war must be granted suitable working conditions, especially as regards accommodation, food, clothing and equipment; such conditions shall not be inferior to those enjoyed by nationals of the Detaining Power employed in similar work; account shall also be taken of climatic conditions.

The Detaining Power, in utilizing the labour of prisoners of war, shall ensure that in areas in which such prisoners are employed, the national legislation concerning the protection of labour, and, more particularly, the regulations for the safety of workers, are duly applied.

Prisoners of war shall receive training and be provided with the means of protection suitable to the work they will have to do and similar to those accorded to the nationals of the Detaining Power. Subject to the provisions of Article 52, prisoners may be submitted to the normal risks run by these civilian workers.

Conditions of labour shall in no case be rendered more arduous by disciplinary measures.

Article 52

Unless he be a volunteer, no prisoner of war may be employed on labour which is of an unhealthy or dangerous nature.

No prisoner of war shall be assigned to labour which would be looked upon as humiliating for a member of the Detaining Power's own forces.

The removal of mines or similar devices shall be considered as dangerous labour.

Article 53

The duration of the daily labour of prisoners of war, including the time of the journey to and from, shall not be excessive, and must in no case exceed that permitted for civilian workers in the district, who are nationals of the Detaining Power and employed on the same work.

Prisoners of war must be allowed, in the middle of the day's work, a rest of not less than one hour. This rest will be the same as that to which workers of the Detaining Power are entitled, if the latter is of longer duration. They shall be allowed in addition a rest of twenty-four consecutive hours every week, preferably on Sunday or the day of rest in their country of origin. Furthermore, every prisoner who has worked for one year shall be granted a rest of eight consecutive days, during which his working pay shall be paid him.

If methods of labour such as piece work are employed, the length of the working period shall not be rendered excessive thereby.

Article 54

The working pay due to prisoners of war shall be fixed in accordance with the provisions of Article 62 of the present Convention.

Prisoners of war who sustain accidents in connection with work, or who contract a disease in the course, or in consequence of their work, shall receive all the care their condition may require. The Detaining Power shall furthermore deliver to such prisoners of war a medical certificate enabling them to submit their claims to the Power on which they depend, and shall send a duplicate to the Central Prisoners of War Agency provided for in Article 123.

Article 55

The fitness of prisoners of war for work shall be periodically verified by medical examinations at least once a month. The examinations shall have particular regard to the nature of the work which prisoners of war are required to do.

If any prisoner of war considers himself incapable of working, he shall be permitted to appear before the medical authorities of his camp. Physicians or surgeons may recommend that the prisoners who are, in their opinion, unfit for work, be exempted therefrom.

Article 56

The organization and administration of labour detachments shall be similar to those of prisoner of war camps.

Every labour detachment shall remain under the control of and administratively part of a prisoner of war camp. The military authorities and the commander of the said camp shall be responsible, under the direction of their government, for the observance of the provisions of the present Convention in labour detachments.

The camp commander shall keep an up-to-date record of the labour detachments dependent on his camp, and shall communicate it to the delegates of the Protecting Power, of the International Committee of the Red Cross, or of other agencies giving relief to prisoners of war, who may visit the camp.

Article 57

The treatment of prisoners of war who work for private persons, even if the latter are responsible for guarding and protecting them, shall not be inferior to that which is provided for by the present Convention. The Detaining Power, the military authorities and the commander of the camp to which such prisoners belong shall be entirely responsible for the maintenance, care, treatment, and payment of the working pay of such prisoners of war.

Such prisoners of war shall have the right to remain in communication with the prisoners' representatives in the camps on which they depend.

Section IV
Financial Resources of Prisoners of War

Article 58

Upon the outbreak of hostilities, and pending an arrangement on this matter with the Protecting Power, the Detaining Power may determine the maximum amount of money in cash or in any similar form, that prisoners may have in their possession. Any amount in excess, which was properly in their possession and which has been taken or withheld from them, shall be placed to their account, together with any monies deposited by them, and shall not be converted into any other currency without their consent.

If prisoners of war are permitted to purchase services or commodities outside the camp against payment in cash, such payments shall be made by the prisoner himself or by the camp administration who will charge them to the accounts of the prisoners concerned. The Detaining Power will establish the necessary rules in this respect.

Article 59

Cash which was taken from prisoners of war, in accordance with Article 18, at the time of their capture, and which is in the currency of the Detaining Power, shall be placed to their separate accounts, in accordance with the provisions of Article 64 of the present Section.

The amounts, in the currency of the Detaining Power, due to the conversion of sums in other currencies that are taken from the prisoners of war at the same time, shall also be credited to their separate accounts.

Article 60

The Detaining Power shall grant all prisoners of war a monthly advance of pay, the amount of which shall be fixed by conversion, into the currency of the said Power, of the following amounts:

Category I : Prisoners ranking below sergeants: eight Swiss francs.

Category II : Sergeants and other non-commissioned officers, or prisoners of equivalent rank: twelve Swiss francs.

Category III: Warrant officers and commissioned officers below the rank of major or prisoners of equivalent rank: fifty Swiss francs.

Category IV : Majors, lieutenant-colonels, colonels or prisoners of equivalent rank: sixty Swiss francs.

Category V : General officers or prisoners of war of equivalent rank: seventy-five Swiss francs.

However, the Parties to the conflict concerned may by special agreement modify the amount of advances of pay due to prisoners of the preceding categories.

Furthermore, if the amounts indicated in the first paragraph above would be unduly high compared with the pay of the Detaining Power's armed forces or would, for any reason, seriously embarrass the Detaining Power, then, pending the conclusion of a special agreement with the Power on which the prisoners depend to vary the amounts indicated above, the Detaining Power:

(a) shall continue to credit the accounts of the prisoners with the amounts indicated in the first paragraph above;

(b) may temporarily limit the amount made available from these advances of pay to prisoners of war for their own use, to sums which are reasonable, but which, for Category I, shall never be inferior to the amount that the Detaining Power gives to the members of its own armed forces.

The reasons for any limitations will be given without delay to the Protecting Power.

Article 61

The Detaining Power shall accept for distribution as supplementary pay to prisoners of war sums which the Power on which the prisoners depend may forward to them, on condition that the sums to be paid shall be the same for each prisoner of the same category, shall be payable to all prisoners of that category depending on that Power, and shall be placed in their separate accounts, at the earliest opportunity, in accordance with the provisions of Article 64. Such supplementary pay shall not relieve the Detaining Power of any obligation under this Convention.

Article 62

Prisoners of war shall be paid a fair working rate of pay by the detaining authorities direct. The rate shall be fixed by the said authorities, but shall at no time be less than one-fourth of one Swiss franc for a full working day. The Detaining Power shall inform prisoners of war, as well as the Power on which they depend, through the intermediary of the Protecting Power, of the rate of daily working pay that it has fixed.

Working pay shall likewise be paid by the detaining authorities to prisoners of war permanently detailed to duties or to a skilled or semi-skilled occupation in connection with the administration, installation or maintenance of camps, and to the prisoners who are required to carry out spiritual or medical duties on behalf of their comrades.

The working pay of the prisoners' representative, of his advisers, if any, and of his assistants, shall be paid out of the fund maintained by canteen profits. The scale of this working pay shall be fixed by the prisoners' representative and approved by the camp commander. If there is no such fund, the detaining authorities shall pay these prisoners a fair working rate of pay.

Article 63

Prisoners of war shall be permitted to receive remittances of money addressed to them individually or collectively.

Every prisoner of war shall have at his disposal the credit balance of his account as provided for in the following Article, within the limits fixed by the Detaining Power, which shall make such payments as are requested. Subject to financial or monetary restrictions which the Detaining Power regards as essential, prisoners of war may also have payments made abroad. In this case payments addressed by prisoners of war to dependents shall be given priority.

In any event, and subject to the consent of the Power on which they depend, prisoners may have payments made in their own country, as follows: the Detaining Power shall send to the aforesaid Power through the Protecting Power, a notification giving all the necessary particulars concerning the prisoners of war, the beneficiaries of the payments, and the amount of the sums to be paid, expressed in the Detaining Power's currency. The said notification shall be signed by the prisoners and countersigned by the camp commander. The Detaining Power shall debit the prisoners' account by a corresponding amount; the sums thus debited shall be placed by it to the credit of the Power on which the prisoners depend.

To apply the foregoing provisions, the Detaining Power may usefully consult the Model Regulations in Annex V of the present Convention.

Article 64

The Detaining Power shall hold an account for each prisoner of war, showing at least the following:

(1) The amounts due to the prisoner or received by him as advances of pay, as working pay or derived from any other source; the sums in the currency of the Detaining Power which were taken from him; the sums taken from him and converted at his request into the currency of the said Power.
(2) The payments made to the prisoner in cash, or in any other similar form; the payments made on his behalf and at his request; the sums transferred under Article 63, third paragraph.

Article 65

Every item entered in the account of a prisoner of war shall be countersigned or initialled by him, or by the prisoners' representative acting on his behalf.

Prisoners of war shall at all times be afforded reasonable facilities for consulting and obtaining copies of their accounts, which may likewise be inspected by the representatives of the Protecting Powers at the time of visits to the camp.

When prisoners of war are transferred from one camp to another, their personal accounts will follow them. In case of transfer from one Detaining Power to another, the monies which are their property and are not in the currency of the Detaining Power will follow them. They shall be given certificates for any other monies standing to the credit of their accounts.

The Parties to the conflict concerned may agree to notify to each other at specific intervals through the Protecting Power, the amount of the accounts of the prisoners of war.

Article 66

On the termination of captivity, through the release of a prisoner of war or his repatriation, the Detaining Power shall give him a statement, signed by an authorized officer of that Power, showing the credit balance then due to him. The Detaining Power shall also send through the Protecting Power to the government upon which the prisoner of war depends, lists giving all appropriate particulars of all prisoners of war whose captivity has been terminated by repatriation, release, escape, death or any other means, and showing the amount of their credit balances. Such lists shall be certified on each sheet by an authorized representative of the Detaining Power.

Any of the above provisions of this Article may be varied by mutual agreement between any two Parties to the conflict.

The Power on which the prisoner of war depends shall be responsible for settling with him any credit balance due to him from the Detaining Power on the termination of his captivity.

Article 67

Advances of pay, issued to prisoners of war in conformity with Article 60, shall be considered as made on behalf of the Power on which they depend. Such advances of pay, as well as all payments made by the said Power under Article 63, third paragraph, and Article 68, shall form the subject of arrangements between the Powers concerned, at the close of hostilities.

Article 68

Any claim by a prisoner of war for compensation in respect of any injury or other disability arising out of work shall be referred to the Power on which he depends, through the Protecting Power. In accordance with Article 54, the Detaining Power will, in all cases, provide the prisoner of war concerned with a statement showing the nature of the injury or disability, the circumstances in which it arose and particulars of medical or hospital treatment given for it. This statement will be signed by a responsible officer of the Detaining Power and the medical particulars certified by a medical officer.

Any claim by a prisoner of war for compensation in respect of personal effects monies or valuables impounded by the Detaining Power under Article 18 and not forthcoming on his repatriation, or in respect of loss alleged to be due to the fault of the Detaining Power or any of its servants, shall likewise be referred to the Power on which he depends. Nevertheless, any such personal effects required for use by the prisoners of war whilst in captivity shall be replaced at the expense of the Detaining Power. The Detaining Power will, in all cases, provide the prisoner of war with a statement, signed by a responsible officer, showing all available information regarding the reasons why such effects, monies or valuables have not been restored to him. A copy of this statement will be forwarded to the Power on which he depends through the Central Prisoners of War Agency provided for in Article 123.

Section V
Relations of Prisoners of War with the Exterior

. . .

Article 71

Prisoners of war shall be allowed to send and receive letters and cards. If the Detaining Power deems it necessary to limit the number of letters and cards sent by each prisoner of war, the said number shall not be less than two letters and four cards monthly, exclusive of the capture cards provided for in Article 70, and conforming as closely as possible to the models annexed to the present Convention. Further limitations may be imposed only if the Protecting Power is satisfied that it would be in the interests of the prisoners of war concerned to do so owing to difficulties of translation caused by the Detaining Power's inability to find sufficient qualified linguists to carry out the necessary censorship. If limitations must be placed on the correspondence addressed to prisoners of war, they may be ordered only by the Power on which the prisoners depend, possibly at the request of the Detaining Power. Such letters and cards must be conveyed by the most rapid method at the disposal of the Detaining Power; they may not be delayed or retained for disciplinary reasons.

Prisoners of war who have been without news for a long period, or who are unable to receive news from their next of kin or to give them news by the ordinary postal route, as well as those who are at a great distance from their homes, shall be permitted to send telegrams, the fees being charged against the prisoners of war's accounts with the Detaining Power or paid in the currency at their disposal. They shall likewise benefit by this measure in cases of urgency.

As a general rule, the correspondence of prisoners of war shall be written in their native language. The Parties to the conflict may allow correspondence in other languages.

Sacks containing prisoner of war mail must be securely sealed and labelled so as clearly to indicate their contents, and must be addressed to offices of destination.

Article 72

Prisoners of war shall be allowed to receive by post or by any other means individual parcels or collective shipments containing, in particular, foodstuffs, clothing, medical supplies and articles of a religious, educational or recreational character which may meet their needs, including books, devotional articles, scientific equipment, examination papers, musical instruments, sports outfits and materials allowing prisoners of war to pursue their studies or their cultural activities.

Such shipments shall in no way free the Detaining Power from the obligations imposed upon it by virtue of the present Convention.

The only limits which may be placed on these shipments shall be those proposed by the Protecting Power in the interest of the prisoners themselves, or by the International Committee of the Red Cross or any other organization giving assistance to the prisoners, in respect of their own shipments only, on account of exceptional strain on transport or communications.

The conditions for the sending of individual parcels and collective relief shall, if necessary, be the subject of special agreements between the Powers concerned, which may in no case delay the receipt by the prisoners of relief supplies. Books may not be included in parcels of clothing and foodstuffs. Medical supplies shall, as a rule, be sent in collective parcels.

. . .

Article 76

The censoring of correspondence addressed to prisoners of war or despatched by them shall be done as quickly as possible. Mail shall be censored only by the despatching State and the receiving State, and once only by each.

The examination of consignments intended for prisoners of war shall not be carried out under conditions that will expose the goods contained in them to deterioration; except in the case of written or printed matter, it shall be done in the presence of the addressee, or of a fellow-prisoner duly delegated by him. The delivery to prisoners of individual or collective consignments shall not be delayed under the pretext of difficulties of censorship.

Any prohibition of correspondence ordered by Parties to the conflict, either for military or political reasons, shall be only temporary and its duration shall be as short as possible.

. . .

Section VI
Relations between Prisoners of War and the Authorities

CHAPTER I
Complaints of Prisoners of War Respecting the Conditions of Captivity

Article 78

Prisoners of war shall have the right to make known to the military authorities in whose power they are, their requests regarding the conditions of captivity to which they are subjected.

They shall also have the unrestricted right to apply to the representatives of the Protecting Powers either through their prisoners' representative or, if they consider it necessary, direct, in order to draw their attention to any points on which they may have complaints to make regarding their conditions of captivity.

These requests and complaints shall not be limited nor considered to be a part of the correspondence quota referred to in Article 71. They must be transmitted immediately. Even if they are recognized to be unfounded, they may not give rise to any punishment.

Prisoners' representatives may send periodic reports on the situation in the camps and the needs of the prisoners of war to the representatives of the Protecting Powers.

CHAPTER II
Prisoner of War Representatives

Article 79

In all places where there are prisoners of war, except in those where there are officers, the prisoners shall freely elect by secret ballot, every six months, and also in case of vacancies, prisoners' representatives entrusted with representing them before the military authorities, the Protecting Powers, the International Committee of the Red Cross and any other organization which may assist them. These prisoners' representatives shall be eligible for re-election.

In camps for officers and persons of equivalent status or in mixed camps, the senior officer among the prisoners of war shall be recognized as the camp prisoners' representative. In camps for officers, he shall be assisted by one or more advisers chosen by the officers; in mixed camps, his assistants shall be chosen from among the prisoners of war who are not officers and shall be elected by them.

Officer prisoners of war of the same nationality shall be stationed in labour camps for prisoners of war, for the purpose of carrying out the camp administration duties for which the prisoners of war are responsible. These officers may be elected as prisoners' representatives under the first paragraph of this Article. In such a case the assistants to the prisoners' representatives shall be chosen from among those prisoners of war who are not officers.

Every representative elected must be approved by the Detaining Power before he has the right to commence his duties. Where the Detaining Power refuses to approve a prisoner of war elected by his fellow prisoners of war, it must inform the Protecting Power of the reason for such refusal.

In all cases the prisoners' representative must have the same nationality, language and customs as the prisoners of war whom he represents. Thus, prisoners of war distributed in different sections of a camp, according to their nationality, language or customs, shall have for each section their own prisoners' representative, in accordance with the foregoing paragraphs.

Article 80

Prisoners' representatives shall further the physical, spiritual and intellectual wellbeing of prisoners of war.

In particular, where the prisoners decide to organize amongst themselves a system of mutual assistance, this organization will be within the province of the prisoners' representative, in addition to the special duties entrusted to him by other provisions of the present Convention.

Prisoners' representatives shall not be held responsible, simply by reason of their duties, for any offences committed by prisoners of war.

Article 81

Prisoners' representatives shall not be required to perform any other work, if the accomplishment of their duties is thereby made more difficult.

Prisoners' representatives may appoint from amongst the prisoners such assistants as they may require. All material facilities shall be granted them, particularly a certain freedom of movement necessary for the accomplishment of their duties (inspection of labour detachments, receipt of supplies, etc.).

Prisoners' representatives shall be permitted to visit premises where prisoners of war are detained, and every prisoner of war shall have the right to consult freely his prisoners' representative.

All facilities shall likewise be accorded to the prisoners' representatives for communication by post and telegraph with the detaining authorities, the Protecting Powers, the International Committee of the Red Cross and their delegates, the Mixed Medical Commissions and the bodies which give assistance to prisoners of war. Prisoners' representatives of labour detachments shall enjoy the same facilities for communication with the prisoners' representatives of the principal camp. Such communications shall not be restricted, nor considered as forming a part of the quota mentioned in Article 71.

Prisoners' representatives who are transferred shall be allowed a reasonable time to acquaint their successors with current affairs.

In case of dismissal, the reasons therefor shall be communicated to the Protecting Power.

CHAPTER III
Penal and Disciplinary Sanctions
I. General Provisions

Article 82

A prisoner of war shall be subject to the laws, regulations and orders in force in the armed forces of the Detaining Power; the Detaining Power shall be justified in taking judicial or disciplinary measures in respect of any offence committed by a prisoner of war against such laws, regulations or orders. However, no proceedings or punishments contrary to the provisions of this Chapter shall be allowed.

If any law, regulation or order of the Detaining Power shall declare acts committed by a prisoner of war to be punishable, whereas the same acts would not be punishable if committed by a member of the forces of the Detaining Power, such acts shall entail disciplinary punishments only.

Article 83

In deciding whether proceedings in respect of an offence alleged to have been committed by a prisoner of war shall be judicial or disciplinary, the Detaining Power shall ensure that the competent authorities exercise the greatest leniency and adopt, wherever possible, disciplinary rather than judicial measures.

Article 84

A prisoner of war shall be tried only by a military court, unless the existing laws of the Detaining Power expressly permit the civil courts to try a member of the armed forces of the Detaining Power in respect of the particular offence alleged to have been committed by the prisoner of war.

In no circumstances whatever shall a prisoner of war be tried by a court of any kind which does not offer the essential guarantees of independence and impartiality as generally recognized, and, in particular, the procedure of which does not afford the accused the rights and means of defence provided for in Article 105.

Article 85

Prisoners of war prosecuted under the laws of the Detaining Power for acts committed prior to capture shall retain, even if convicted, the benefits of the present Convention.

Article 86

No prisoner of war may be punished more than once for the same act or on the same charge.

Article 87

Prisoners of war may not be sentenced by the military authorities and courts of the Detaining Power to any penalties except those provided for in respect of members of the armed forces of the said Power who have committed the same acts.

When fixing the penalty, the courts or authorities of the Detaining Power shall take into consideration, to the widest extent possible, the fact that the accused, not being a national of the Detaining Power, is not bound to it by any duty of allegiance, and that he is in its power as the result of circumstances independent of his own will. The said courts or authorities shall be at liberty to reduce the penalty provided for the violation of which the prisoner of war is accused, and shall therefore not be bound to apply the minimum penalty prescribed.

Collective punishment for individual acts, corporal punishment, imprisonment in premises without daylight and, in general, any form of torture or cruelty, are forbidden.

No prisoner of war may be deprived of his rank by the Detaining Power, or prevented from wearing his badges.

Article 88

Officers, non-commissioned officers and men who are prisoners of war undergoing a disciplinary or judicial punishment, shall not be subjected to more severe treatment than that applied in respect of the same punishment to members of the armed forces of the Detaining Power of equivalent rank.

A woman prisoner of war shall not be awarded or sentenced to a punishment more severe, or treated whilst undergoing punishment more severely, than a woman member of the armed forces of the Detaining Power dealt with for a similar offence.

In no case may a woman prisoner of war be awarded or sentenced to a punishment more severe, or treated whilst undergoing punishment more severely, than a male member of the armed forces of the Detaining Power dealt with for a similar offence.

Prisoners of war who have served disciplinary or judicial sentences may not be treated differently from other prisoners of war.

II. Disciplinary Sanctions

Article 89

The disciplinary punishments applicable to prisoners of war are the following:

(1) A fine which shall not exceed 50 per cent of the advances of pay and working pay which the prisoner of war would otherwise receive under the provisions of Articles 60 and 62 during a period of not more than thirty days.
(2) Discontinuance of privileges granted over and above the treatment provided for by the present Convention.
(3) Fatigue duties not exceeding two hours daily.
(4) Confinement.

The punishment referred to under (3) shall not be applied to officers.

In no case shall disciplinary punishments be inhuman, brutal or dangerous to the health of prisoners of war.

Article 90

The duration of any single punishment shall in no case exceed thirty days. Any period of confinement awaiting the hearing of a disciplinary offence or the award of disciplinary punishment shall be deducted from an award pronounced against a prisoner of war.

The maximum of thirty days provided above may not be exceeded, even if the prisoner of war is answerable for several acts at the same time when he is awarded punishment, whether such acts are related or not.

The period between the pronouncing of an award of disciplinary punishment and its execution shall not exceed one month.

When a prisoner of war is awarded a further disciplinary punishment, a period of at least three days shall elapse between the execution of any two of the punishments, if the duration of one of these is ten days or more.

Article 91

The escape of a prisoner of war shall be deemed to have succeeded when:

(1) he has joined the armed forces of the Power on which he depends, or those of an allied Power;
(2) he has left the territory under the control of the Detaining Power, or of an ally of the said Power;
(3) he has joined a ship flying the flag of the Power on which he depends, or of an allied Power, in the territorial waters of the Detaining Power, the said ship not being under the control of the last named Power.

Prisoners of war who have made good their escape in the sense of this Article and who are recaptured, shall not be liable to any punishment in respect of their previous escape.

Article 92

A prisoner of war who attempts to escape and is recaptured before having made good his escape in the sense of Article 91 shall be liable only to a disciplinary punishment in respect of this act, even if it is a repeated offence.

A prisoner of war who is recaptured shall be handed over without delay to the competent military authority.

Article 88, fourth paragraph, notwithstanding, prisoners of war punished as a result of an unsuccessful escape may be subjected to special surveillance. Such surveillance must not affect the state of their health, must be undergone in a prisoner of war camp, and must not entail the suppression of any of the safeguards granted them by the present Convention.

Article 93

Escape or attempt to escape, even if it is a repeated offence, shall not be deemed an aggravating circumstance if the prisoner of war is subjected to trial by judicial proceedings in respect of an offence committed during his escape or attempt to escape.

In conformity with the principle stated in Article 83, offences committed by prisoners of war with the sole intention of facilitating their escape and which do not entail any violence against life or limb, such as offences against public property, theft without intention of self-enrichment, the drawing up or use of false papers, or the wearing of civilian clothing, shall occasion disciplinary punishment only.

Prisoners of war who aid or abet an escape or an attempt to escape shall be liable on this count to disciplinary punishment only.

Article 94

If an escaped prisoner of war is recaptured, the Power on which he depends shall be notified thereof in the manner defined in Article 122, provided notification of his escape has been made.

Article 95

A prisoner of war accused of an offence against discipline shall not be kept in confinement pending the hearing unless a member of the armed forces of the Detaining Power would be so kept if he were accused of a similar offence, or if it is essential in the interests of camp order and discipline.

Any period spent by a prisoner of war in confinement awaiting the disposal of an offence against discipline shall be reduced to an absolute minimum and shall not exceed fourteen days.

The provisions of Articles 97 and 98 of this Chapter shall apply to prisoners of war who are in confinement awaiting the disposal of offences against discipline.

Article 96

Acts which constitute offences against discipline shall be investigated immediately.

Without prejudice to the competence of courts and superior military authorities, disciplinary punishment may be ordered only by an officer having disciplinary powers in his capacity as camp commander, or by a responsible officer who replaces him or to whom he has delegated his disciplinary powers.

In no case may such powers be delegated to a prisoner of war or be exercised by a prisoner of war.

Before any disciplinary award is pronounced, the accused shall be given precise information regarding the offences of which he is accused, and given an opportunity of explaining his conduct and of defending himself. He shall be permitted, in particular, to call witnesses and to have recourse, if necessary, to the services of a qualified interpreter. The decision shall be announced to the accused prisoner of war and to the prisoners' representative.

A record of disciplinary punishments shall be maintained by the camp commander and shall be open to inspection by representatives of the Protecting Power.

Article 97

Prisoners of war shall not in any case be transferred to penitentiary establishments (prisons, penitentiaries, convict prisons, etc.) to undergo disciplinary punishment therein.

All premises in which disciplinary punishments are undergone shall conform to the sanitary requirements set forth in Article 25. A prisoner of war undergoing punishment shall be enabled to keep himself in a state of cleanliness, in conformity with Article 29.

Officers and persons of equivalent status shall not be lodged in the same quarters as non-commissioned officers or men.

Women prisoners of war undergoing disciplinary punishment shall be confined in separate quarters from male prisoners of war and shall be under the immediate supervision of women.

Article 98

A prisoner of war undergoing confinement as a disciplinary punishment, shall continue to enjoy the benefits of the provisions of this Convention except in so far as these are necessarily rendered inapplicable by the mere fact that he is confined. In no case may he be deprived of the benefits of the provisions of Articles 78 and 126.

A prisoner of war awarded disciplinary punishment may not be deprived of the prerogatives attached to his rank.

Prisoners of war awarded disciplinary punishment shall be allowed to exercise and to stay in the open air at least two hours daily.

They shall be allowed, on their request, to be present at the daily medical inspections. They shall receive the attention which their state of health requires and, if necessary, shall be removed to the camp infirmary or to a hospital.

They shall have permission to read and write, likewise to send and receive letters. Parcels and remittances of money, however, may be withheld from them until the completion of the punishment; they shall meanwhile be entrusted to the prisoners' representative, who will hand over to the infirmary the perishable goods contained in such parcels.

III. Judicial Proceedings

Article 99

No prisoner of war may be tried or sentenced for an act which is not forbidden by the law of the Detaining Power or by international law, in force at the time the said act was committed.

No moral or physical coercion may be exerted on a prisoner of war in order to induce him to admit himself guilty of the act of which he is accused.

No prisoner of war may be convicted without having had an opportunity to present his defence and the assistance of a qualified advocate or counsel.

Article 100

Prisoners of war and the Protecting Powers shall be informed as soon as possible of the offences which are punishable by the death sentence under the laws of the Detaining Power.

Other offences shall not thereafter be made punishable by the death penalty without the concurrence of the Power on which the prisoners of war depend.

The death sentence cannot be pronounced on a prisoner of war unless the attention of the court has, in accordance with Article 87, second paragraph, been particularly called to the fact that since the accused is not a national of the Detaining Power, he is not bound to it by any duty of allegiance, and that he is in its power as the result of circumstances independent of his own will.

Article 101

If the death penalty is pronounced on a prisoner of war, the sentence shall not be executed before the expiration of a period of at least six months from the date when the Protecting Power receives, at an indicated address, the detailed communication provided for in Article 107.

Article 102

A prisoner of war can be validly sentenced only if the sentence has been pronounced by the same courts according to the same procedure as in the case of members of the armed forces of the Detaining Power, and if, furthermore, the provisions of the present Chapter have been observed.

Article 103

Judicial investigations relating to a prisoner of war shall be conducted as rapidly as circumstances permit and so that his trial shall take place as soon as possible. A prisoner of war shall not be confined while awaiting trial unless a member of the armed forces of the Detaining Power would be so confined if he were accused of a similar offence, or if it is essential to do so in the interests of national security. In no circumstances shall this confinement exceed three months.

Any period spent by a prisoner of war in confinement awaiting trial shall be deducted from any sentence of imprisonment passed upon him and taken into account in fixing any penalty.

The provisions of Articles 97 and 98 of this Chapter shall apply to a prisoner of war whilst in confinement awaiting trial.

Article 104

In any case in which the Detaining Power has decided to institute judicial proceedings against a prisoner of war, it shall notify the Protecting Power as soon as possible and at least three weeks before the opening of the trial. This period of three weeks shall run as from the day on which such notification reaches the Protecting Power at the address previously indicated by the latter to the Detaining Power.

The said notification shall contain the following information:

(1) Surname and first names of the prisoner of war, his rank, his army, regimental, personal or serial number, his date of birth, and his profession or trade, if any;
(2) Place of internment or confinement;
(3) Specification of the charge or charges on which the prisoner of war is to be arraigned, giving the legal provisions applicable;
(4) Designation of the court which will try the case, likewise the date and place fixed for the opening of the trial.

The same communication shall be made by the Detaining Power to the prisoners' representative.

If no evidence is submitted, at the opening of a trial, that the notification referred to above was received by the Protecting Power, by the prisoner of war and by the prisoners' representative concerned, at least three weeks before the opening of the trial, then the latter cannot take place and must be adjourned.

Article 105

The prisoner of war shall be entitled to assistance by one of his prisoner comrades, to defence by a qualified advocate or counsel of his own choice, to the calling of witnesses and, if he deems necessary, to the services of a competent interpreter. He shall be advised of these rights by the Detaining Power in due time before the trial.

Failing a choice by the prisoner of war, the Protecting Power shall find him an advocate or counsel, and shall have at least one week at its disposal for the purpose. The Detaining Power shall deliver to the said Power, on request, a list of persons qualified to present the defence. Failing a choice of an advocate or counsel by the prisoner of war or the Protecting Power, the Detaining Power shall appoint a competent advocate or counsel to conduct the defence.

The advocate or counsel conducting the defence on behalf of the prisoner of war shall have at his disposal a period of two weeks at least before the opening of the trial, as well as the necessary facilities to prepare the defence of the accused. He may, in particular, freely visit the accused and interview him in private. He may also confer with any witnesses for the defence, including prisoners of war. He shall have the benefit of these facilities until the term of appeal or petition has expired.

Particulars of the charge or charges on which the prisoner of war is to be arraigned, as well as the documents which are generally communicated to the accused by virtue of the laws in force in the armed forces of the Detaining Power, shall be communicated to the accused prisoner of war in a language which he understands, and in good time before the opening of the trial. The same communication in the same circumstances shall be made to the advocate or counsel conducting the defence on behalf of the prisoner of war.

The representatives of the Protecting Power shall be entitled to attend the trial of the case, unless, exceptionally, this is held in camera in the interest of State security. In such a case the Detaining Power shall advise the Protecting Power accordingly.

Article 106

Every prisoner of war shall have, in the same manner as the members of the armed forces of the Detaining Power, the right of appeal or petition from any sentence pronounced upon him, with a view to the quashing or revising of the sentence or the reopening of the trial. He shall be fully informed of his right to appeal or petition and of the time limit within which he may do so.

Article 107

Any judgment and sentence pronounced upon a prisoner of war shall be immediately reported to the Protecting Power in the form of a summary communication, which shall also indicate whether he has the right of appeal with a view to the quashing of the sentence or the reopening of the trial. This communication shall likewise be sent to the prisoners' representative concerned. It shall also be sent to the accused prisoner of war in a language he understands, if the sentence was not pronounced in his presence. The Detaining Power shall also immediately communicate to the Protecting Power the decision of the prisoner of war to use or to waive his right of appeal.

Furthermore, if a prisoner of war is finally convicted or if a sentence pronounced on a prisoner of war in the first instance is a death sentence, the Detaining Power shall as soon as possible address to the Protecting Power a detailed communication containing:

(1) the precise wording of the finding and sentence;
(2) a summarized report of any preliminary investigation and of the trial, emphasizing in particular the elements of the prosecution and the defence;
(3) notification, where applicable, of the establishment where the sentence will be served.

The communications provided for in the foregoing sub-paragraphs shall be sent to the Protecting Power at the address previously made known to the Detaining Power.

Article 108

Sentences pronounced on prisoners of war after a conviction has become duly enforceable, shall be served in the same establishments and under the same conditions as in the case of members of the armed forces of the Detaining Power. These conditions shall in all cases conform to the requirements of health and humanity.

A woman prisoner of war on whom such a sentence has been pronounced shall be confined in separate quarters and shall be under the supervision of women.

In any case, prisoners of war sentenced to a penalty depriving them of their liberty shall retain the benefit of the provisions of Articles 78 and 126 of the present Convention. Furthermore, they shall be entitled to receive and despatch correspondence, to receive at least one relief parcel monthly, to take regular exercise in the open air, to have the medical care required by their state of health, and the spiritual assistance they may desire. Penalties to which they may be subjected shall be in accordance with the provisions of Article 87, third paragraph.

Part IV
Termination of Captivity

Section I
Direct Repatriation and Accommodation in Neutral Countries

. . .

Article 110

The following shall be repatriated direct:

(1) Incurably wounded and sick whose mental or physical fitness seems to have been gravely diminished.
(2) Wounded and sick who, according to medical opinion, are not likely to recover within one year, whose condition requires treatment and whose mental or physical fitness seems to have been gravely diminished.
(3) Wounded and sick who have recovered, but whose mental or physical fitness seems to have been gravely and permanently diminished.

The following may be accommodated in a neutral country:

(1) Wounded and sick whose recovery may be expected within one year of the date of the wound or the beginning of the illness, if treatment in a neutral country might increase the prospects of a more certain and speedy recovery.
(2) Prisoners of war whose mental or physical health, according to medical opinion, is seriously threatened by continued captivity, but whose accommodation in a neutral country might remove such a threat.

The conditions which prisoners of war accommodated in a neutral country must fulfil in order to permit their repatriation shall be fixed, as shall likewise their status, by agreement between the Powers concerned. In general, prisoners of war who have been accommodated in a neutral country, and who belong to the following categories, should be repatriated:

(1) Those whose state of health has deteriorated so as to fulfil the condition laid down for direct repatriation;
(2) Those whose mental or physical powers remain, even after treatment, considerably impaired.

If no special agreements are concluded between the Parties to the conflict concerned, to determine the cases of disablement or sickness entailing direct repatriation or accommodation in a neutral country, such cases shall be settled in accordance with the principles laid down in the Model Agreement concerning direct repatriation and accommodation in neutral countries of wounded and sick prisoners of war and in the Regulations concerning Mixed Medical Commissions annexed to the present Convention.

. . .

Article 115

No prisoner of war on whom a disciplinary punishment has been imposed and who is eligible for repatriation or for accommodation in a neutral country, may be kept back on the plea that he has not undergone his punishment.

Prisoners of war detained in connection with a judicial prosecution or conviction, and who are designated for repatriation or accommodation in a neutral country, may benefit by such measures before the end of the proceedings or the completion of the punishment, if the Detaining Power consents.

Parties to the conflict shall communicate to each other the names of those who will be detained until the end of the proceedings or the completion of the punishment.

. . .

Article 117

No repatriated person may be employed on active military service.

Section II
Release and Repatriation of Prisoners of War at the Close of Hostilities

Article 118

Prisoners of war shall be released and repatriated without delay after the cessation of active hostilities.

. . .

Section III
Death of Prisoners of War

Article 120

Wills of prisoners of war shall be drawn up so as to satisfy the conditions of validity required by the legislation of their country of origin, which will take steps to inform the Detaining Power of its requirements in this respect. At the request of the prisoner of war and, in all cases, after death, the will shall be transmitted without delay to the Protecting Power; a certified copy shall be sent to the Central Agency.

Death certificates, in the form annexed to the present Convention, or lists certified by a responsible officer, of all persons who die as prisoners of war shall be forwarded as rapidly as possible to the Prisoner of War Information Bureau established in accordance with Article 122. The death certificates or certified lists shall show particulars of identity as set out in the third paragraph of Article 17, and also the date and place of death, the cause of death, the date and place of burial and all particulars necessary to identify the graves.

The burial or cremation of a prisoner of war shall be preceded by a medical examination of the body with a view to confirming death and enabling a report to be made and, where necessary, establishing identity.

The detaining authorities shall ensure that prisoners of war who have died in captivity are honourably buried, if possible according to the rites of the religion to which they belonged, and that their graves are respected, suitably maintained and marked so as to be found at any time. Wherever possible, deceased prisoners of war who depended on the same Power shall be interred in the same place.

Deceased prisoners of war shall be buried in individual graves unless unavoidable circumstances require the use of collective graves. Bodies may be cremated only for imperative reasons of hygiene, on account of the religion of the deceased or in accordance with his express wish to this effect. In case of cremation, the fact shall be stated and the reasons given in the death certificate of the deceased.

In order that graves may always be found, all particulars of burials and graves shall be recorded with a Graves Registration Service established by the Detaining Power. Lists of graves and particulars of the prisoners of war interred in cemeteries and elsewhere shall be transmitted to the Power on which such prisoners of war depended. Responsibility for the care of these graves and for records of any subsequent moves of the bodies shall rest on the Power controlling the territory, if a Party to the present Convention. These provisions shall also apply to the ashes, which shall be kept by the Graves Registration Service until proper disposal thereof in accordance with the wishes of the home country.

Article 121

Every death or serious injury of a prisoner of war caused or suspected to have been caused by a sentry, another prisoner of war, or any other person, as well as any death the cause of which is unknown, shall be immediately followed by an official enquiry by the Detaining Power.

A communication on this subject shall be sent immediately to the Protecting Power. Statements shall be taken from witnesses, especially from those who are prisoners of war, and a report including such statements shall be forwarded to the Protecting Power.

If the enquiry indicates the guilt of one or more persons, the Detaining Power shall take all measures for the prosecution of the person or persons responsible.

. . .

Protocol Additional to the Geneva Conventions of August 12, 1949, and Relating to the Protection of Victims of International Armed Conflicts (Protocol I), Geneva, July 1977

Preamble

The High Contracting Parties,

Proclaiming their earnest wish to see peace prevail among peoples,

Recalling that every State has the duty, in conformity with the Charter of the United Nations, to refrain in its international relations from the threat or use of force against the sovereignty, territorial integrity or political independence of any State, or in any other manner inconsistent with the purposes of the United Nations,

Believing it necessary nevertheless to reaffirm and develop the provisions protecting the victims of armed conflicts and to supplement measures intended to reinforce their application,

Expressing their conviction that nothing in this Protocol or in the Geneva Conventions of 12 August 1949 can be construed as legitimizing or authorizing any act of aggression or any other use of force inconsistent with the Charter of the United Nations,

Reaffirming further that the provisions of the Geneva Conventions of 12 August 1949 and of this Protocol must be fully applied in all circumstances to all persons who are protected by those instruments, without any adverse distinction based on the nature or origin of the armed conflict or on the causes espoused by or attributed to the Parties to the conflict,

Have agreed on the following:

Article 1—General Principles and Scope of Application

1. The High Contracting Parties undertake to respect and to ensure respect for this Protocol in all circumstances.
2. In cases not covered by this Protocol or by other international agreements, civilians and combatants remain under the protection and authority of the principles of international law derived from established custom, from the principles of humanity and from the dictates of public conscience.
3. This Protocol, which supplements the Geneva Conventions of 12 August 1949 for the protection of war victims, shall apply in the situations referred to in Article 2 common to those Conventions.
4. The situations referred to in the preceding paragraph include armed conflicts in which peoples are fighting against colonial domination and alien occupation and against racist regimes in the exercise of their right of self-determination, as enshrined in the Charter of the United Nations and the Declaration on Principles of International Law concerning Friendly Relations and Co-operation among States in accordance with the Charter of the United Nations.

Article 2—Definitions

For the purposes of this Protocol:

(a) "First Convention," "Second Convention," "Third Convention" and "Fourth Convention" mean, respectively, the Geneva Convention for the Amelioration of the Condition of the Wounded and Sick in Armed Forces in the Field of 12 August 1949; the Geneva Convention for the Amelioration of the Condition of Wounded, Sick and Shipwrecked Members of Armed Forces at Sea of 12 August 1949; the Geneva Convention relative to the Treatment of Prisoners of War of 12 August 1949; the Geneva Convention relative to the Protection of Civilian Persons in Time of War of 12 August 1949; "the Conventions" means the four Geneva Conventions of 12 August 1949 for the protection of war victims;

(b) "rules of international law applicable in armed conflict" means the rules applicable in armed conflict set forth in international agreements to which the Parties to the conflict are Parties and the generally recognized principles and rules of international law which are applicable to armed conflict;

(c) "Protecting Power" means a neutral or other State not a Party to the conflict which has been designated by a Party to the conflict and accepted by the adverse Party and has agreed to carry out the functions assigned to a Protecting Power under the Conventions and this Protocol;

(d) "substitute" means an organization acting in place of a Protecting Power in accordance with Article 5.

. . .

Article 32—General Principle

In the implementation of this Section, the activities of the High Contracting Parties, of the Parties to the conflict and of the international humanitarian organizations mentioned in the Conventions and in this Protocol shall be prompted mainly by the right of families to know the fate of their relatives.

. . .

Article 35—Basic Rules

1. In any armed conflict, the right of the Parties to the conflict to choose methods or means of warfare is not unlimited.
2. It is prohibited to employ weapons, projectiles and material and methods of warfare of a nature to cause superfluous injury or unnecessary suffering.
3. It is prohibited to employ methods or means of warfare which are intended, or may be expected, to cause widespread, long-term and severe damage to the natural environment.

Article 36—New Weapons

In the study, development, acquisition or adoption of a new weapon, means or method of warfare, a High Contracting Party is under an obligation to determine whether its employment would, in some or all circumstances, be prohibited by this Protocol or by any other rule of international law applicable to the High Contracting Party.

. . .

Article 40—Quarter

It is prohibited to order that there shall be no survivors, to threaten an adversary therewith or to conduct hostilities on this basis.

Article 41—Safeguard of an Enemy *Hors De Combat*

1. A person who is recognized or who, in the circumstances, should be recognized to be *hors de combat* shall not be made the object of attack.
2. A person is *hors de combat* if:
   (a) he is in the power of an adverse Party,
   (b) he clearly expresses an intention to surrender, or
   (c) he has been rendered unconscious or is otherwise incapacitated by wounds or sickness, and therefore is incapable of defending himself, provided that in any of these cases he abstains from any hostile act and does not attempt to escape.
3. When persons entitled to protection as prisoners of war have fallen into the power of an adverse Party under unusual conditions of combat which prevent their evacuation as provided for in Part III, Section I, of the Third Convention, they shall be released and all feasible precautions shall be taken to ensure their safety.

. . .

Article 44—Combatants and Prisoners of War

1. Any combatant, as defined in Article 43, who falls into the power of an adverse Party shall be a prisoner of war.
2. While all combatants are obliged to comply with the rules of international law applicable in armed conflict, violations of these rules shall not deprive a combatant of his right to be a combatant or, if he falls into the power of an adverse Party, of his right to be a prisoner of war, except as provided in paragraphs 3 and 4.
3. In order to promote the protection of the civilian population from the effects of hostilities, combatants are obliged to distinguish themselves from the civilian population while they are engaged in an attack or in a military operation preparatory to an attack. Recognizing, however, that there are situations in armed conflicts where, owing to the nature of the hostilities an armed combatant cannot so distinguish himself, he shall retain his status as a combatant, provided that, in such situations, he carries his arms openly:

   (a) during each military engagement, and
   (b) during such time as he is visible to the adversary while he is engaged in a military deployment preceding the launching of an attack in which he is to participate.
   Acts which comply with the requirements of this paragraph shall not be considered as perfidious within the meaning of Article 37, paragraph 1 (c).

4. A combatant who falls into the power of an adverse Party while failing to meet the requirements set forth in the second sentence of paragraph 3 shall forfeit his right to be a prisoner of war, but he shall, nevertheless, be given protections equivalent in all respects to those accorded to prisoners of war by the Third Convention and by this Protocol. This protection includes protections equivalent to those accorded to prisoners of war by the Third Convention in the case where such a person is tried and punished for any offenses he has committed.
5. Any combatant who falls into the power of an adverse Party while not engaged in an attack or in a military operation preparatory to an attack shall not forfeit his rights to be a combatant and a prisoner of war by virtue of his prior activities.
6. This Article is without prejudice to the right of any person to be a prisoner of war pursuant to Article 4 of the Third Convention.
7. This Article is not intended to change the generally accepted practice of States with respect to the wearing of the uniform by combatants assigned to the regular, uniformed armed units of a Party to the conflict.
8. In addition to the categories of persons mentioned in Article 13 of the First and Second Conventions, all members of the armed forces of a Party to the conflict, as defined in Article 43 of this Protocol, shall be entitled to protection under those Conventions if they are wounded or sick or, in the case of the Second Convention, shipwrecked at sea or in other waters.

Article 45—Protection of Persons Who Have Taken Part in Hostilities

1. A person who takes part in hostilities and falls into the power of an adverse Party shall be presumed to be a prisoner of war, and therefore shall be protected by the Third Convention, if he claims the status of prisoner of war, or if he appears to be entitled to such status, or if the Party on which he depends claims such status on his behalf by notification to the detaining Power or to the Protecting Power. Should any doubt arise as to whether any such person is entitled to the status of prisoner of war, he shall continue to have such status and, therefore, to be protected by the Third Convention and this Protocol until such time as his status has been determined by a competent tribunal.
2. If a person who has fallen into the power of an adverse Party is not held as a prisoner of war and is to be tried by that Party for an offence arising out of the hostilities, he shall have the right to assert his entitlement to prisoner-of-war status before a judicial tribunal and to have that question adjudicated. Whenever possible under the applicable procedure, this adjudication shall occur before the trial for the offence. The representatives of the Protecting Power shall be entitled to attend the proceedings in which that question is adjudicated, unless, exceptionally, the proceedings are held *in* camera in the interest of State security. In such a case the detaining Power shall advise the Protecting Power accordingly.
3. Any person who has taken part in hostilities, who is not entitled to prisoner-of-war status and who does not benefit from more favorable treatment in accordance with the Fourth Convention shall have the right at all times to the protection of Article 75 of this Protocol. In occupied territory, any such person, unless he is held as a spy, shall also be entitled, notwithstanding Article 5 of the Fourth Convention, to his rights of communication under that Convention.

. . .

Article 47—Mercenaries

1. A mercenary shall not have the right to be a combatant or a prisoner of war.
2. A mercenary is any person who:

   (a) is specially recruited locally or abroad in order to fight in an armed conflict;
   (b) does, in fact, take a direct part in the hostilities;
   (c) is motivated to take part in the hostilities essentially by the desire for private gain and, in fact, is promised, by or on behalf of a Party to the conflict, material compensation substantially in excess of that promised or paid to combatants of similar ranks and functions in the armed forces of that Party;
   (d) is neither a national of a Party to the conflict nor a resident of territory controlled by a Party to the conflict,
   (e) is not a member of the armed forces of a Party to the conflict, and

(f) has not been sent by a State which is not a Party to the conflict on official duty as a member of its armed forces.

. . .

Article 51—Protection of the Civilian Population

1. The civilian population and individual civilians shall enjoy general protection against dangers arising from military operations. To give effect to this protection, the following rules, which are additional to other applicable rules of international law, shall be observed in all circumstances.
2. The civilian population as such, as well as individual civilians, shall not be the object of attack. Acts or threats of violence the primary purpose of which is to spread terror among the civilian population are prohibited.
3. Civilians shall enjoy the protection afforded by this Section, unless and for such time as they take a direct part in hostilities.
4. Indiscriminate attacks are prohibited. indiscriminate attacks are:

   (a) those which are not directed at a specific military objective;
   (b) those which employ a method or means of combat which cannot be directed at a specific military objective; or
   (c) those which employ a method or means of combat the effects of which cannot be limited as required by this Protocol; and consequently, in each such case, are of a nature to strike military objectives and civilians or civilian objects without distinction.

5. Among others, the following types of attacks are to be considered as indiscriminate:

   (a) an attack by bombardment by any methods or means which treats as a single military objective a number of clearly separated and distinct military objectives located in a city, town, village or other area containing a similar concentration of civilians or civilian objects; and
   (b) an attack which may be expected to cause incidental loss of civilian life, injury to civilians, damage to civilian objects, or a combination thereof, which would be excessive in relation to the concrete and direct military advantage anticipated.

6. Attacks against the civilian population or civilians by way of reprisals are prohibited.
7. The presence or movements of the civilian population or individual civilians shall not be used to render certain points or areas immune from military operations, in particular in attempts to shield military objectives from attacks or to shield, favor or impede military operations. The Parties to the conflict shall not direct the movement of the civilian population or individual civilians in order to attempt to shield military objectives from attacks or to shield military operations.
8. Any violation of these prohibitions shall not release the Parties to the conflict from their legal obligations with respect to the civilian population and

civilians, including the obligation to take the precautionary measures provided for in Article 57.

Article 52—General Protection of Civilian Objects

1. Civilian objects shall not be the object of attack or of reprisals. Civilian objects are all objects which are not military objectives as defined in paragraph 2.
2. Attacks shall be limited strictly to military objectives. In so far as objects are concerned, military objectives are limited to those objects which by their nature, location, purpose or use make an effective contribution to military action and whose total or partial destruction, capture or neutralization, in the circumstances ruling at the time, offers a definite military advantage.
3. In case of doubt whether an object which is normally dedicated to civilian purposes, such as a place of worship, a house or other dwelling or a school, is being used to make an effective contribution to military action, it shall be presumed not to be so used.

Article 53—Protection of Cultural Objects and of Places of Worship

Without prejudice to the provisions of the Hague Convention for the Protection of Cultural Property in the Event of Armed Conflict of 14 May 1954, and of other relevant international instruments, it is prohibited:

(a) to commit any acts of hostility directed against the historic monuments, works of art or places of worship which constitute the cultural or spiritual heritage of peoples;
(b) to use such objects in support of the military effort;
(c) to make such objects the object of reprisals.

Article 54—Protection of Objects Indispensable to the Survival of the Civilian Population

1. Starvation of civilians as a method of warfare is prohibited.
2. It is prohibited to attack, destroy, remove or render useless objects indispensable to the survival of the civilian population, such as foodstuffs, agricultural areas for the production of foodstuffs, crops, livestock, drinking water installations and supplies and irrigation works, for the specific purpose of denying them for their sustenance value to the civilian population or to the adverse Party, whatever the motive, whether in order to starve out civilians, to cause them to move away, or for any other motive.
3. The prohibitions in paragraph 2 shall not apply to such of the objects covered by it as are used by an adverse Party:

   (a) as sustenance solely for the members of its armed forces; or
   (b) if not as sustenance, then in direct support of military action, provided, however, that in no event shall actions against these objects be taken which may be expected to leave the civilian population with such inadequate food or water as to cause its starvation or force its movement.

4. These objects shall not be made the object of reprisals.
5. In recognition of the vital requirements of any Party to the conflict in the defense of its national territory against invasion, derogation from the prohibitions contained in paragraph 2 may be made by a Party to the conflict within such territory under its own control where required by imperative military necessity.

Article 55—Protection of the Natural Environment

1. Care shall be taken in warfare to protect the natural environment against widespread, long-term and severe damage. This protection includes a prohibition of the use of methods or means of warfare which are intended or may be expected to cause such damage to the natural environment and thereby to prejudice the health or survival of the population.
2. Attacks against the natural environment by way of reprisals are prohibited.

Article 56—Protection of Works and Installations Containing Dangerous Forces

1. Works or installations containing dangerous forces, namely dams, dykes and nuclear electrical generating stations, shall not be made the object of attack, even where these objects are military objectives, if such attack may cause the release of dangerous forces and consequent severe losses among the civilian population. Other military objectives located at or in the vicinity of these works or installations shall not be made the object of attack if such attack may cause the release of dangerous forces from the works or installations and consequent severe losses among the civilian population.
2. The special protection against attack provided by paragraph 1 shall cease:

   (a) for a dam or a dyke only if it is used for other than its normal function and in regular, significant and direct support of military operations and if such attack is the only feasible way to terminate such support;
   (b) for a nuclear electrical generating station only if it provides electric power in regular, significant and direct support of military operations and if such attack is the only feasible way to terminate such support;
   (c) for other military objectives located at or in the vicinity of these works or installations only if they are used in regular, significant and direct support of military operations and if such attack is the only feasible way to terminate such support.

3. In all cases, the civilian population and individual civilians shall remain entitled to all the protection accorded them by international law, including the protection of the precautionary measures provided for in Article 57. If the protection ceases and any of the works, installations or military objectives mentioned in paragraph 1 is attacked, all practical precautions shall be taken to avoid the release of the dangerous forces.
4. It is prohibited to make any of the works, installations or military objectives mentioned in paragraph 1 the object of reprisals.

5. The Parties to the conflict shall endeavor to avoid locating any military objectives in the vicinity of the works or installations mentioned in paragraph 1. Nevertheless, installations erected for the sole purpose of defending the protected works or installations from attack are permissible and shall not themselves be made the object of attack, provided that they are not used in hostilities except for defensive actions necessary to respond to attacks against the protected works or installations and that their armament is limited to weapons capable only of repelling hostile action against the protected works or installations.
6. The High Contracting Parties and the Parties to the conflict are urged to conclude further agreements among themselves to provide additional protection for objects containing dangerous forces.
7. In order to facilitate the identification of the objects protected by this article, the Parties to the conflict may mark them with a special sign consisting of a group of three bright orange circles placed on the same axis, as specified in Article 16 of Annex I to this Protocol. The absence of such marking in no way relieves any Party to the conflict of its obligations under this Article.

Article 57—Precautions in Attack

1. In the conduct of military operations, constant care shall be taken to spare the civilian population, civilians and civilian objects.
2. With respect to attacks, the following precautions shall be taken:

   (a) those who plan or decide upon an attack shall:

      (i) do everything feasible to verify that the objectives to be attacked are neither civilians nor civilian objects and are not subject to special protection but are military objectives within the meaning of paragraph 2 of Article 52 and that it is not prohibited by the provisions of this Protocol to attack them;

      (ii) take all feasible precautions in the choice of means and methods of attack with a view to avoiding, and in any event to minimizing, incidental loss of civilian life, injury to civilians and damage to civilian objects;

      (iii) refrain from deciding to launch any attack which may be expected to cause incidental loss of civilian life, injury to civilians, damage to civilian objects, or a combination thereof, which would be excessive in relation to the concrete and direct military advantage anticipated;

   (b) an attack shall be cancelled or suspended if it becomes apparent that the objective is not a military one or is subject to special protection or that the attack may be expected to cause incidental loss of civilian life, injury to civilians, damage to civilian objects, or a combination thereof, which would be excessive in relation to the concrete and direct military advantage anticipated;

   (c) effective advance warning shall be given of attacks which may affect the civilian population, unless circumstances do not permit.

3. When a choice is possible between several military objectives for obtaining a similar military advantage, the objective to be selected shall be that [target] the attack on which may be expected to cause the least danger to civilian lives and to civilian objects.
4. In the conduct of military operations at sea or in the air, each Party to the conflict shall, in conformity with its rights and duties under the rules of international law applicable in armed conflict, take all reasonable precautions to avoid losses of civilian lives and damage to civilian objects.
5. No provision of this article may be construed as authorizing any attacks against the civilian population, civilians or civilian objects.

. . .

Article 75—Fundamental Guarantees

1. In so far as they are affected by a situation referred to in Article 1 of this Protocol, persons who are in the power of a Party to the conflict and who do not benefit from more favorable treatment under the Conventions or under this Protocol shall be treated humanely in all circumstances and shall enjoy, as a minimum, the protection provided by this Article without any adverse distinction based upon race, color, sex, language, religion or belief, political or other opinion, national or social origin, wealth, birth or other status, or on any other similar criteria. Each Party shall respect the person, honor, convictions and religious practices of all such persons.
2. The following acts are and shall remain prohibited at any time and in any place whatsoever, whether committed by civilian or by military agents:
   - (a) violence to the life, health, or physical or mental well-being of persons, in particular:
     - (i) murder;
     - (ii) torture of all kinds, whether physical or mental;
     - (iii) corporal punishment; and
     - (iv) mutilation;
   - (b) outrages upon personal dignity, in particular humiliating and degrading treatment, enforced prostitution and a form of indecent assault;
   - (c) the taking of hostages;
   - (d) collective punishments; and
   - (e) threats to commit any of the foregoing acts.
3. Any person arrested, detained or interned for actions related to the armed conflict shall be informed promptly, in a language he understands, of the reasons why these measures have been taken. Except in cases of arrest or detention for penal offences, such persons shall be released with the minimum possible delay and in any event as soon as the circumstances justifying the arrest, detention or internment have ceased to exist.
4. No sentence may be passed and no penalty may be executed on a person found guilty of a penal offence related to the armed conflict except pursuant to a conviction pronounced by an impartial and regularly constituted court respecting

the generally recognized principles of regular judicial procedure, which include the following:

(a) the procedure shall provide for an accused to be informed without delay of the particulars of the offence alleged against him and shall afford the accused before and during his trial all necessary rights and means of defense;
(b) no one shall be convicted of an offence except on the basis of individual penal responsibility;
(c) no one shall be accused or convicted of a criminal offence on account of any act or omission which did not constitute a criminal offence under the national or international law to which he was subject at the time when it was committed; nor shall a heavier penalty be imposed than that which was applicable at the time when the criminal offence was committed; if, after the commission of the offence, provision is made by law for the imposition of a lighter penalty, the offender shall benefit thereby;
(d) anyone charged with an offence is presumed innocent until proved guilty according to law;
(e) anyone charged with an offence shall have the right to be tried in his presence;
(f) no one shall be compelled to testify against himself or to confess guilt;
(g) anyone charged with an offence shall have the right to examine, or have examined, the witnesses against him and to obtain the attendance and examination of witnesses on his behalf under the same conditions as witnesses against him;
(h) no one shall be prosecuted or punished by the same Party for an offence in respect of which a final judgment acquitting or convicting that person has been previously pronounced under the same law and judicial procedure;
(i) anyone prosecuted for an offence shall have the right to have the judgment pronounced publicly; and
(j) a convicted person shall be advised on conviction of his judicial and other remedies and of the time-limits within which they may be exercised.

5. Women whose liberty has been restricted for reasons related to the armed conflict shall be held in quarters separated from men's quarters. They shall be under the immediate supervision of women. Nevertheless, in cases where families are detained or interned, they shall, whenever possible, be held in the same place and accommodated as family units.
6. Persons who are arrested, detained or interned for reasons related to the armed conflict shall enjoy the protection provided by this Article until their final release, repatriation or re-establishment, even after the end of the armed conflict.
7. In order to avoid any doubt concerning the prosecution and trial of persons accused of war crimes or crimes against humanity, the following principles shall apply:

(a) persons who are accused of such crimes should be submitted for the purpose of prosecution and trial in accordance with the applicable rules of international law; and

(b) any such persons who do not benefit from more favorable treatment under the Conventions or this Protocol shall be accorded the treatment provided by this Article, whether or not the crimes of which they are accused constitute grave breaches of the Conventions or of this Protocol.

8. No provision of this Article may be construed as limiting or infringing any other more favorable provision granting greater protection, under any applicable rules of international law, to persons covered by paragraph 1.

. . .

Article 82—Legal Advisers in Armed Forces

The High Contracting Parties at all times, and the Parties to the conflict in time of armed conflict, shall ensure that legal advisers are available, when necessary, to advise military commanders at the appropriate level on the application of the Conventions and this Protocol and on the appropriate instruction to be given to the armed forces on this subject.

Article 83—Dissemination

1. The High Contracting Parties undertake, in time of peace as in time of armed conflict, to disseminate the Conventions and this Protocol as widely as possible in their respective countries and, in particular, to include the study thereof in their programs of military instruction and to encourage the study thereof by the civilian population, so that those instruments may become known to the armed forces and to the civilian population.
2. Any military or civilian authorities who, in time of armed conflict, assume responsibilities in respect of the application of the Conventions and this Protocol shall be fully acquainted with the text. The armed forces under their command and other persons under their control, may be called upon to prevent and, where necessary, to suppress and to report to competent authorities breaches of the Conventions and of this Protocol.
2. In order to prevent and suppress breaches, High Contracting Parties and Parties to the conflict shall require that, commensurate with their level of responsibility, commanders ensure that members of the armed forces under their command are aware of their obligations under the Conventions and this Protocol.

Protocol Additional to the Geneva Conventions of 12 August 1949, and Relating to the Protection of Victims of Non-International Armed Conflicts (Protocol II) Geneva, July 1977

. . .

Article 86—Failure to Act

1. The High Contracting Parties and the Parties to the conflict shall repress grave breaches, and take measures necessary to suppress all other breaches,

of the Conventions or of this Protocol which result from a failure to act when under a duty to do so.

2. The fact that a breach of the Conventions or of this Protocol was committed by a subordinate does not absolve his superiors from penal or disciplinary responsibility, as the case may be, if they knew, or had information which should have enabled them to conclude in the circumstances at the time, that he was committing or was going to commit such a breach and if they did not take all feasible measures within their power to prevent or repress the breach.

. . .

Part I
Scope of this Protocol
Article 1—Material Field of Application

1. This Protocol, which develops and supplements Article 3 common to the Geneva Conventions of 12 August 1949 without modifying its existing conditions of application, shall apply to all armed conflicts which are not covered by Article 1 of the Protocol Additional to the Geneva Conventions of 12 August 1949, and relating to the Protection of Victims of International Armed Conflicts (Protocol I) and which take place in the territory of a High Contracting Party between its armed forces and dissident armed forces or other organized armed groups which, under responsible command, exercise such control over a part of its territory as to enable them to carry out sustained and concerted military operations and to implement this Protocol.
2. This Protocol shall not apply to situations of internal disturbances and tensions, such as riots, isolated and sporadic acts of violence and other acts of a similar nature as not being armed conflicts.

. . .

Article 3—Non-Intervention

1. Nothing in this Protocol shall be invoked for the purpose of affecting the sovereignty of a State or the responsibility of the government, by all legitimate means, to maintain or re-establish law and order in the State or to defend the national unity and territorial integrity of the State.

Nothing in this Protocol shall be invoked as a justification for intervening, directly or indirectly, for any reason whatever, in the armed conflict or in the internal or external affairs of the High Contracting Party in the territory of which that conflict occurs.

United Nations Convention against Torture and Other Cruel, Inhuman, or Degrading Treatment or Punishment, 1984

The States Parties to this Convention,

Considering that, in accordance with the principles proclaimed in the Charter of the United Nations, recognition of the equal and inalienable rights of all members of the human family is the foundation of freedom, justice and peace in the world,

Recognizing that those rights derive from the inherent dignity of the human person,

Considering the obligation of States under the Charter, in particular Article 55, to promote universal respect for, and observance of, human rights and fundamental freedoms,

Having regard to article 5 of the Universal Declaration of Human Rights and article 7 of the International Covenant on Civil and Political Rights, both of which provide that no one may be subjected to torture or to cruel, inhuman or degrading treatment or punishment,

Having regard also to the Declaration on the Protection of All Persons from Being Subjected to Torture and Other Cruel, Inhuman or Degrading Treatment or Punishment, adopted by the General Assembly on 9 December 1975 (resolution 3452 (XXX)),

Desiring to make more effective the struggle against torture and other cruel, inhuman or degrading treatment or punishment throughout the world,

Have agreed as follows:

Part I

Article 1

1. For the purposes of this Convention, torture means any act by which severe pain or suffering, whether physical or mental, is intentionally inflicted on a person for such purposes as obtaining from him or a third person information

or a confession, punishing him for an act he or a third person has committed or is suspected of having committed, or intimidating or coercing him or a third person, or for any reason based on discrimination of any kind, when such pain or suffering is inflicted by or at the instigation of or with the consent or acquiescence of a public official or other person acting in an official capacity. It does not include pain or suffering arising only from, inherent in or incidental to lawful sanctions.

2. This article is without prejudice to any international instrument or national legislation which does or may contain provisions of wider application.

Article 2

1. Each State Party shall take effective legislative, administrative, judicial or other measures to prevent acts of torture in any territory under its jurisdiction.
2. No exceptional circumstances whatsoever, whether a state of war or a threat or war, internal political instability or any other public emergency, may be invoked as a justification of torture.
3. An order from a superior officer or a public authority may not be invoked as a justification of torture.

Article 3

1. No State Party shall expel, return . . . or extradite a person to another State where there are substantial grounds for believing that he would be in danger of being subjected to torture.
2. For the purpose of determining whether there are such grounds, the competent authorities shall take into account all relevant considerations including, where applicable, the existence in the State concerned of a consistent pattern of gross, flagrant or mass violations of human rights.

Article 4

1. Each State Party shall ensure that all acts of torture are offences under its criminal law. The same shall apply to an attempt to commit torture and to an act by any person which constitutes complicity or participation in torture.
2. Each State Party shall make these offences punishable by appropriate penalties which take into account their grave nature.

Article 5

1. Each State Party shall take such measures as may be necessary to establish its jurisdiction over the offences referred to in article 4 in the following cases:

    1. When the offences are committed in any territory under its jurisdiction or on board a ship or aircraft registered in that State;
    2. When the alleged offender is a national of that State;

3. When the victim was a national of that State if that State considers it appropriate.

2. Each State Party shall likewise take such measures as may be necessary to establish its jurisdiction over such offences in cases where the alleged offender is present in any territory under its jurisdiction and it does not extradite him pursuant to article 8 to any of the States mentioned in Paragraph 1 of this article.
3. This Convention does not exclude any criminal jurisdiction exercised in accordance with internal law.

Article 6

1. Upon being satisfied, after an examination of information available to it, that the circumstances so warrant, any State Party in whose territory a person alleged to have committed any offence referred to in article 4 is present, shall take him into custody or take other legal measures to ensure his presence. The custody and other legal measures shall be as provided in the law of that State but may be continued only for such time as is necessary to enable any criminal or extradition proceedings to be instituted.
2. Such State shall immediately make a preliminary inquiry into the facts.
3. Any person in custody pursuant to paragraph 1 of this article shall be assisted in communicating immediately with the nearest appropriate representative of the State of which he is a national, or, if he is a stateless person, to the representative of the State where he usually resides.
4. When a State, pursuant to this article, has taken a person into custody, it shall immediately notify the States referred to in article 5, paragraph 1, of the fact that such person is in custody and of the circumstances which warrant his detention. The State which makes the preliminary inquiry contemplated in paragraph 2 of this article shall promptly report its findings to the said State and shall indicate whether it intends to exercise jurisdiction.

Article 7

1. The State Party in territory under whose jurisdiction a person alleged to have committed any offence referred to in article 4 is found, shall in the cases contemplated in article 5, if it does not extradite him, submit the case to its competent authorities for the purpose of prosecution.
2. These authorities shall take their decision in the same manner as in the case of any ordinary offence of a serious nature under the law of that State. In the cases referred to in article 5, paragraph 2, the standards of evidence required for prosecution and conviction shall in no way be less stringent than those which apply in the cases referred to in article 5, paragraph 1.
3. Any person regarding whom proceedings are brought in connection with any of the offences referred to in article 4 shall be guaranteed fair treatment at all stages of the proceedings.

Article 8

1. The offences referred to in article 4 shall be deemed to be included as extraditable offences in any extradition treaty existing between States Parties. States Parties undertake to include such offences as extraditable offences in every extradition treaty to be concluded between them.
2. If a State Party which makes extradition conditional on the existence of a treaty receives a request for extradition from another State Party with which it has no extradition treaty, it may consider this Convention as the legal basis for extradition in respect of such offenses. Extradition shall be subject to the other conditions provided by the law of the requested State.
3. States Parties which do not make extradition conditional on the existence of a treaty shall recognize such offences as extraditable offences between themselves subject to the conditions provided by the law of the requested state.
4. Such offences shall be treated, for the purpose of extradition between States Parties, as if they had been committed not only in the place in which they occurred but also in the territories of the States required to establish their jurisdiction in accordance with article 5, paragraph 1.

Article 9

1. States Parties shall afford one another the greatest measure of assistance in connection with civil proceedings brought in respect of any of the offences referred to in article 4, including the supply of all evidence at their disposal necessary for the proceedings.
2. States Parties shall carry out their obligations under paragraph 1 of this article in conformity with any treaties on mutual judicial assistance that may exist between them.

Article 10

1. Each State Party shall ensure that education and information regarding the prohibition against torture are fully included in the training of law enforcement personnel, civil or military, medical personnel, public officials and other persons who may be involved in the custody, interrogation or treatment of any individual subjected to any form of arrest, detention or imprisonment.
2. Each State Party shall include this prohibition in the rules or instructions issued in regard to the duties and functions of any such persons.

Article 11

Each State Party shall keep under systematic review interrogation rules, instructions, methods and practices as well as arrangements for the custody and treatment of persons subjected to any form of arrest, detention or imprisonment in any territory under its jurisdiction, with a view to preventing any cases of torture.

Article 12

Each State Party shall ensure that its competent authorities proceed to a prompt and impartial investigation, wherever there is reasonable ground to believe that an act of torture has been committee in any territory under its jurisdiction.

Article 13

Each State Party shall ensure that any individual who alleges he has been subjected to torture in any territory under its jurisdiction has the right to complain to and to have his case promptly and impartially examined its competent authorities. Steps shall be taken to ensure that the complainant and witnesses are protected against all ill-treatment or intimidation as a consequence of his complaint or any evidence given.

Article 14

1. Each State Party shall ensure in its legal system that the victim of an act of torture obtains redress and has an enforceable right to fair and adequate compensation including the means for as full rehabilitation as possible. In the event of the death of the victim as a result of an act of torture, his dependents shall be entitled to compensation.
2. Nothing in this article shall affect any right of the victim or other person to compensation which may exist under national law.

Article 15

Each State Party shall ensure that any statement which is established to have been made as a result of torture shall not be invoked as evidence in any proceedings, except against a person accused of torture as evidence that the statement was made.

Article 16

1. Each State Party shall undertake to prevent in any territory under its jurisdiction other acts of cruel, inhuman or degrading treatment or punishment which do not amount to torture as defined in article 1, when such acts are committed by or at the instigation of or with the consent or acquiescence of a public official or other person acting in an official capacity. In particular, the obligations contained in articles 10, 11, 12 and 13 shall apply with the substitution for references to torture or references to other forms of cruel, inhuman or degrading treatment or punishment.
2. The provisions of this Convention are without prejudice to the provisions of any other international instrument or national law which prohibit cruel, inhuman or degrading treatment or punishment or which relate to extradition or expulsion.

Part II

Article 17

1. There shall be established a Committee against Torture (hereinafter referred to as the Committee) which shall carry out the functions hereinafter provided. The Committee shall consist of 10 experts of high moral standing and recognized competence in the field of human rights, who shall serve in their personal capacity. The experts shall be elected by the States Parties, consideration being given to equitable geographical distribution and to the usefulness of the participation of some persons having legal experience.
2. The members of the Committee shall be elected by secret ballot from a list of persons nominated by States Parties. Each State Party may nominate one person from among its own nationals. States Parties shall bear in mind the usefulness of nominating persons who are also members of the Human Rights Committee established under the International Covenant on Civil and Political Rights and are willing to serve on the Committee against Torture.
3. Elections of the members of the Committee shall be held at biennial meetings of States Parties convened by the Secretary-General of the United Nations. At those meetings, for which two thirds of the States Parties shall constitute a quorum, the persons elected to the Committee shall be those who obtain the largest number of votes and an absolute majority of the votes of the representatives of States Parties present and voting.
4. The initial election shall be held no later than six months after the date of the entry into force of this Convention. At least four months before the date of each election, the Secretary-General of the United Nations shall address a letter to the States Parties inviting them to submit their nominations within three months. The Secretary-General shall prepare a list in alphabetical order of all persons thus nominated, indicating the States Parties which have nominated them, and shall submit it to the States Parties.
5. The members of the Committee shall be elected for a term of four years. They shall be eligible for re-election if renominated. However, the term of five of the members elected at the first election shall expire at the end of two years; immediately after the first election the names of these five members shall be chosen by lot by the chairman of the meeting referred to in paragraph 3.
6. If a member of the Committee dies or resigns or for any other cause can no longer perform his Committee duties, the State Party which nominated him shall appoint another expert from among its nationals to serve for the remainder of his term, subject to the approval of the majority of the States Parties. The approval shall be considered given unless half or more of the States Parties respond negatively within six weeks after having been informed by the Secretary-General of the United Nations of the proposed appointment.
7. States Parties shall be responsible for the expenses of the members of the Committee while they are in performance of Committee duties.

Article 18

1. The Committee shall elect its officers for a term of two years. They may be re-elected.
2. The Committee shall establish its own rules of procedure, but these rules shall provide, inter alia, that
   1. Six members shall constitute a quorum;
   2. Decisions of the Committee shall be made by a majority vote of the members present.
3. The Secretary-General of the United Nations shall provide the necessary staff and facilities for the effective performance of the functions of the Committee under this Convention.
4. The Secretary-General of the United Nations shall convene the initial meeting of the Committee. After its initial meeting, the Committee shall meet at such times as shall be provided in its rules of procedure.
5. The State Parties shall be responsible for expenses incurred in connection with the holding of meetings of the States Parties and of the Committee, including reimbursement of the United Nations for any expenses, such as the cost of staff and facilities, incurred by the United Nations pursuant to paragraph 3 above.

Article 19

1. The States Parties shall submit to the Committee, through the Secretary-General of the United Nations, reports on the measures they have taken to give effect to their undertakings under this Convention, within one year after the entry into force of this Convention for the State Party concerned. Thereafter the States Parties shall submit supplementary reports every four years on any new measures taken, and such other reports as the Committee may request.
2. The Secretary-General shall transmit the reports to all States Parties.
3. Each report shall be considered by the Committee which may make such comments or suggestions on the report as it considers appropriate, and shall forward these to the State Party concerned. That State Party may respond with any observations it chooses to the Committee.
4. The Committee may, at its discretion, decide to include any comments or suggestions made by it in accordance with paragraph 3, together with the observations thereon received from the State Party concerned, in its annual report made in accordance with article 24. If so requested by the State Party concerned, the Committee may also include a copy of the report submitted under paragraph 1.

Article 20

1. If the Committee receives reliable information which appears to it to contain well-founded indications that torture is being systematically practised in the territory of a State Party, the Committee shall invite that State Party to

co-operate in the examination of the information and to this end to submit observations with regard to the information concerned.

2. Taking into account any observations which may have been submitted by the State Party concerned as well as any other relevant information available to it, the Committee may, if it decides that this is warranted, designate one or more of its members to make a confidential inquiry and to report to the Committee urgently.
3. If an inquiry is made in accordance with paragraph 2, the Committee shall seek the co-operation of the State Party concerned. In agreement with that State Party, such an inquiry may include a visit to its territory.
4. After examining the findings of its member or members submitted in accordance with paragraph 2, the Committee shall transmit these findings to the State Party concerned together with any comments or suggestions which seem appropriate in view of the situation.
5. All the proceedings of the Committee referred to in paragraphs 1 to 4 of this article shall be confidential, and at all stages of the proceedings the co-operation of the State Party shall be sought. After such proceedings have been completed with regard to an inquiry made in accordance with paragraph 2, the Committee may, after consultations with the State Party concerned, decide to include a summary account of the results of the proceedings in its annual report made in accordance with article 24.

Article 21

1. A State Party to this Convention may at any time declare under this article 3 that it recognizes the competence of the Committee to receive and consider communications to the effect that a State Party claims that another State Party is not fulfilling its obligations under this Convention. Such communications may be received and considered according to the procedures laid down in this article only if submitted by a State Party which has made a declaration recognizing in regard to itself the competence of the Committee. No communication shall be dealt with by the Committee under this article if it concerns a State Party which has not made such a declaration. Communications received under this article shall be dealt with in accordance with the following procedure:

    1. If a State Party considers that another State Party is not giving effect to the provisions of this Convention, it may, by written communication, bring the matter to the attention of that State Party. Within three months after the receipt of the communication the receiving State shall afford the State which sent the communication an explanation or any other statement in writing clarifying the matter which should include, to the extent possible and pertinent, references to domestic procedures and remedies taken, pending, or available in the matter.
    2. If the matter is not adjusted to the satisfaction of both States Parties concerned within six months after the receipt by the receiving State of the

initial communication, either State shall have the right to refer the matter to the Committee by notice given to the Committee and to the other State.

3. The Committee shall deal with a matter referred to it under this article only after it has ascertained that all domestic remedies have been invoked and exhausted in the matter, in conformity with the generally recognized principles of international law. This shall not be the rule where the application of the remedies is unreasonably prolonged or is unlikely to bring effective relief to the person who is the victim of the violation of this Convention.
4. The Committee shall hold closed meetings when examining communications under this article.
5. Subject to the provisions of subparagraph (c), the Committee shall make available its good offices to the States Parties concerned with a view to a friendly solution of the matter on the basis of respect for the obligations provided for in the present Convention. For this purpose, the Committee may, when appropriate, set up an ad hoc conciliation commission.
6. In any matter referred to it under this article, the Committee may call upon the States Parties concerned, referred to in subparagraph (b), to supply any relevant information.
7. The States Parties concerned, referred to in subparagraph (b), shall have the right to be represented when the matter is being considered by the Committee and to make submissions orally and/or in writing.
8. The Committee shall, within 12 months after the date of receipt of notice under subparagraph (b), submit a report.
    1. If a solution within the terms of subparagraph (e) is reached, the Committee shall confine its report to a brief statement of the facts and of the solution reached.
    2. If a solution within the terms of subparagraph (e) is not reached, the Committee shall confine its report to a brief statement of the facts; the written submissions and record of the oral submissions made by the States Parties concerned shall be attached to the report.

In every matter, the report shall be communicated to the States Parties concerned.

2. The provisions of this article shall come into force when five States Parties to this Convention have made declarations under paragraph 1 of this article. Such declarations shall be deposited by the States Parties with the Secretary-General of the United Nations, who shall transmit copies thereof to the other States Parties. A declaration may be withdrawn at any time by notification to the Secretary-General. Such a withdrawal shall not prejudice the consideration of any matter which is the subject of a communication already transmitted under this article; no further communication by any State Party shall be received under this article after the notification of withdrawal of the

declaration has been received by the Secretary-General, unless the State Party concerned has made a new declaration.

Article 22

1. A State Party to this Convention may at any time declare under this article that it recognizes the competence of the Committee to receive and consider communications from or on behalf of individuals subject to its jurisdiction who claim to be victims of a violation by a State Party of the provisions of the Convention. No communication shall be received by the Committee if it concerns a State Party to the Convention which has not made such a declaration.
2. The Committee shall consider inadmissible any communication under this article which is anonymous, or which it considers to be an abuse of the right of submission of such communications or to be incompatible with the provisions of this Convention.
3. Subject to the provisions of paragraph 2, the Committee shall bring any communication submitted to it under this article to the attention of the State Party to this Convention which has made a declaration under paragraph 1 and is alleged to be violating any provisions of the Convention. Within six months, the receiving State shall submit to the Committee written explanations or statements clarifying the matter and the remedy, if any, that may have been taken by that State.
4. The Committee shall consider communications received under this article in the light of all information made available to it by or on behalf of the individual and by the State Party concerned.
5. The Committee shall not consider any communication from an individual under this article unless it has ascertained that:

    1. The same matter has not been, and is not being examined under another procedure of international investigation or settlement;
    2. The individual has exhausted all available domestic remedies; this shall not be the rule where the application of the remedies is unreasonably prolonged or is unlikely to bring effective relief to the person who is the victim of the violation of this Convention.

6. The Committee shall hold closed meetings when examining communications under this article.
7. The Committee shall forward its views to the State Party concerned and to the individual.
8. The provisions of this article shall come into force when five States Parties to this Convention have made declarations under paragraph 1 of this article. Such declarations shall be deposited by the States Parties with the Secretary-General of the United Nations, who shall transmit parties thereof to the other States Parties. A declaration may be withdrawn at any time by notification to the Secretary-General. Such a withdrawal shall not prejudice the consideration

of any matter which is the subject of a communication already transmitted under this article; no further communication by or on behalf of an individual shall be received under this article after the notification of withdrawal of the declaration has been received by the Secretary-General, unless the State Party concerned has made a new declaration. . . .

Source: UN General Assembly Official Records. 39th Sess. G.A. Res. 39/46 (Meeting No. 93), December 10, 1984.

Memorandum for John A. Rizzo, Acting General Counsel of the Central Intelligence Agency, from Office of the Assistant Attorney General, August 1, 2002

You have asked for this Office's views on whether certain proposed conduct would violate the prohibition against torture found at Section 2340A of title 18 of the United States Code. You have asked for this advice in the course of conducting interrogations of Abu Zubaydah. As we understand it, Zubaydah is one of the highest ranking members of the al Qaeda terrorist organization, with which the United States is currently engaged in an international armed conflict following the attacks on the World Trade Center and the Pentagon on September 11, 2001. This letter memorializes our previous oral advice, given on July 24, 2002 and July 26, 2002, that the proposed conduct would not violate this prohibition.

I

Our advice is based upon the following facts, which you have provided to us. We also understand that you do not have any facts in your possession contrary to the facts outlined here, and this opinion is limited to these facts. If these facts were to change, this advice would not necessarily apply. Zubaydah is currently being held by the United States. The interrogation team is certain that he has additional information that he refuses to divulge. Specifically, he is withholding information regarding terrorist networks in the United States or in Saudi Arabia and information regarding plans to conduct attacks within the United States or against our interests overseas. Zubaydah has become accustomed to a certain level of treatment and displays no signs of willingness to disclose further information. Moreover, your intelligence indicates that there is currently a level of "chatter" equal to that which preceded the September 11 attacks. In light of the information you believe Zubaydah has and the high level of threat you believe now exists, you wish to move the interrogations into what you have described as an "increased pressure phase."

As part of this increased pressure phase, Zubaydah will have contact only with a new interrogation specialist, whom he has not met previously, and the Survival, Evasion, Resistance, Escape ("SERE") training psychologist who has been involved with the interrogations since they began. This phase will likely last no more than several days but could last up to thirty days. In this phase, you would like to employ ten techniques that you believe will dislocate his expectations regarding the treatment he believes he will receive and encourage him to disclose the crucial information mentioned above. These ten techniques are: (1) attention grasp, (2) walling, (3) facial hold, (4) facial slap (insult slap), (5) cramped confinement, (6) wall standing, (7) stress positions, (8) sleep deprivation, (9) insects placed in a confinement box, and (10) the waterboard. You have informed us that the use of these techniques would be on an as-needed basis and that not all of these techniques will necessarily be used. The interrogation team would use these techniques in some combination to convince Zubaydah that the only way he can influence his surrounding environment is through cooperation. You have, however, informed us that you expect these techniques to be used in some sort of escalating fashion, culminating with the waterboard, though not necessarily ending with this technique. Moreover, you have also orally informed us that although some of these techniques may be used with more than once, that repetition will not be substantial because the techniques generally lose their effectiveness after several repetitions. You have also informed us that Zubaydah sustained a wound during his capture, which is being treated.

Based on the facts you have given us, we understand each of these techniques to be as follows. The attention grasp consists of grasping the individual with both hands, one hand on each side of the collar opening, in a controlled and quick motion. In the same motion as the grasp, the individual is drawn toward the interrogator.

For walling, a flexible false wall will be constructed. The individual is placed with his heels touching the wall. The interrogator pulls the individual forward and then quickly and firmly pushes the individual into the wall. It is the individual's shoulder blades that hit the wall. During this motion, the head and neck are supported with a rolled hood or towel that provides a c-collar effect to help prevent whiplash. To further reduce the probability of injury, the individual is allowed to rebound from the flexible wall. You have orally informed us that the false wall is in part constructed to create a loud sound when the individual hits it, which will further shock or surprise in the individual. In part, the idea is to create a sound that will make the impact seem far worse than it is and that will be far worse than any injury that might result from the action.

The facial hold is used to hold the head immobile. One open palm is placed on either side of the individual's face. The fingertips are kept well away from the individual's eyes.

With the facial slap or insult slap, the interrogator slaps the individual's face with fingers slightly spread. The hand makes contact with the area directly between the tip of the individual's chin and the bottom of the corresponding earlobe. The interrogator invades the individual's personal space. The goal of the facial slap is not to inflict physical pain that is severe or lasting. Instead, the purpose of the facial slap is to induce shock, surprise, and/or humiliation.

Cramped confinement involves the placement of the individual in a confined space, the dimensions of which restrict the individual's movement. The confined space is usually dark. The duration of confinement varies based upon the size of the container. For the larger confined space, the individual can stand up or sit down; the smaller space is large enough for the subject to sit down. Confinement in the larger space can last up to eighteen hours; for the smaller space, confinement lasts for no more than two hours.

Wall standing is used to induce muscle fatigue. The individual stands about four to five feet from a wall, with his feet spread approximately to shoulder width. His arms are stretched out in front of him, with his fingers resting on the wall. His fingers support all of his body weight. The individual is not permitted to move or reposition his hands or feet.

A variety of stress positions may be used. You have informed us that these positions are not designed to produce the pain associated with contortions or twisting of the body. Rather, somewhat like walling, they are designed to produce the physical discomfort associated with muscle fatigue. Two particular stress positions are likely to be used on Zubaydah: (1) sitting on the floor with legs extended straight out in front of him with his arms raised above his head; and (2) kneeling on the floor while leaning back at a 45 degree angle. You have also orally informed us that through observing Zubaydah in captivity, you have noted that he appears to be quite flexible despite his wound.

Sleep deprivation may be used. You have indicated that your purpose in using this technique is to reduce the individual's ability to think on his feet and, through the discomfort associated with lack of sleep, to motivate him to cooperate. The effect of such sleep deprivation will generally remit after one or two nights of uninterrupted sleep. You have informed us that your research has revealed that, in rare instances, some individuals who are already predisposed to psychological problems may experience abnormal reactions to sleep deprivation. Even in those cases, however, reactions abate after the individual is permitted to sleep. Moreover, personnel with medical training are available to and will intervene in the unlikely event of an abnormal reaction. You have orally informed us that you would not deprive Zubaydah of sleep for more than eleven days at a time and that you have previously kept him awake for 72 hours, from which no mental or physical harm resulted.

You would like to place Zubaydah in a cramped confinement box with an insect. You have informed us that he appears to have a fear of insects. In particular, you would like to tell Zubaydah that you intend to place a stinging insect into the box with him. You would, however, place a harmless insect in the box. You have orally informed us that you would in fact place a harmless insect such as a caterpillar in the box with him . . .

Finally, you would like to use a technique called the "waterboard." In this procedure, the individual is bound securely to an inclined bench, which is approximately four feet by seven feet. The individual's feet are generally elevated. A cloth is placed over the forehead and eyes. Water is then applied to the cloth in a controlled manner. As this is done, the cloth is lowered until it covers both the nose and mouth. Once the cloth is saturated and completely covers the mouth and nose, air flow is slightly restricted for 20 to 40 seconds due to the presence of the cloth. This causes an increase in carbon dioxide level in the individual's blood. This increase in the carbon dioxide level stimulates increased effort to breathe. This effort plus the cloth produces the perception of "suffocation and incipient panic," i.e., the perception of drowning. The individual does not breathe any water into his lungs. During those 20 to 40 seconds, water is continuously applied from a height of twelve to twenty-four inches. After this period, the cloth is lifted, and the individual is allowed to breathe unimpeded for three or four full breaths. The sensation of drowning is immediately relieved by the removal of the cloth. The procedure may then be repeated. The water is usually applied from a canteen cup or small watering can with a spout. You have orally informed us that this procedure triggers an automatic physiological sensation of drowning that the individual cannot control even though he may be aware that he is in fact not drowning. You have also orally informed us that it is likely that this procedure would not last more than 20 minutes in any one application.

We also understand that a medical expert with SERE experience will be present throughout this phase and that the procedures will be stopped if deemed medically necessary to prevent severe mental or physical harm to Zubaydah. As mentioned above, Zubaydah suffered an injury during his capture. You have informed us that steps will be taken to ensure that this injury is not in any way exacerbated by the use of these methods and that adequate medical attention will be given to ensure that it will heal properly.

II

In this part, we review the context within which these procedures will be applied. You have informed us that you have taken various steps to ascertain what effect, if any, these techniques would have on Zubaydah's mental health. These same techniques, with the exception of the insect in the cramped confined space, have been used and continue to be used on some members of our military personnel during their SERE training. Because of the use of these procedures in training our own military personnel to resist interrogations, you have consulted with various individuals who have extensive experience in the use of these techniques. You have done so in order to ensure that no prolonged mental harm would result from the use of these proposed procedures.

Through your consultation with various individuals responsible for such training, you have learned that these techniques have been used as elements of a course of conduct without any reported incident of prolonged mental harm. ██████ of the SERE school, ██████ has reported that, during the seven-year period that he spent in those positions, there were two requests from Congress for information concerning alleged injuries resulting from the training. One of these inquiries was prompted by the temporary physical injury a trainee sustained as result of being placed in a confinement box. The other inquiry involved claims that the SERE training caused two individuals to engage in criminal behavior, namely, felony shoplifting and downloading child pornography onto a military computer. According to this official, these claims were found to be baseless. Moreover, he has indicated that during the three and a half years he spent as ██████ of the SERE program, he trained 10,000 students. Of those students, only two dropped out of the training following the use of these techniques. Although on rare occasions some students temporarily postponed the remainder of their training and received psychological counseling, those students were able to finish the program without any indication of subsequent mental health effects.

You have informed us that you have consulted with ██████ who has ten years of experience with SERE training ██████ He stated that, during those ten years, insofar as he is aware, none of the individuals who completed the program suffered any adverse mental health effects. He informed you that there was one person who did not complete the training. That person experienced an adverse mental health reaction that lasted only two hours. After those two hours, the individual's symptoms spontaneously dissipated without requiring treatment or counseling and no other symptoms were ever reported by this individual. According to the information you have provided to us, this assessment of the use of these procedures includes the use of the waterboard.

Additionally you received a memorandum from the which you supplied to us. has experience with the use of all of these procedures in a course of conduct, with the exception of the insect in the confinement box and the waterboard. This memorandum confirms that the use of these procedures has not resulted in any reported instances of prolonged mental harm, and very few instances of immediate and temporary adverse psychological responses to the training. reported that a small minority of students have had temporary adverse psychological reactions during training. Of the 26,829 students trained from 1992 through 2001 in the Air Force SERE training, 4.3 percent of those students had contact with psychology services. Of those 4.3 percent, only 3.2 percent were pulled from the program for psychological reasons. Thus, out of the students trained overall, only 0.14 percent were pulled from the program for psychological reasons. Furthermore, although indicated that surveys of students having completed this training are not done, he expressed confidence that the training did not cause any long-term psychological impact. He based his conclusion on the debriefing of students that is done after the training. More importantly, he based this assessment on the fact that although training is required to be extremely stressful in order to be effective, very few complaints have been made regarding the training. During his tenure, in which 10,000 students were trained, no congressional complaints have been made. While there was one Inspector General complaint, it was not due to psychological concerns. Moreover, he was aware of only one letter inquiring about the long-term impact of these techniques from an individual trained over twenty years ago. He found that it was impossible to attribute this individual's symptoms to his training. concluded that if there are any long-term psychological effects of the United States Air Force training using the procedures outlined above they "are certainly minimal."

With respect to the waterboard, you have also orally informed us that the Navy continues to use it in training. You have informed us that your on-site psychologists, who have extensive experience with the use of the waterboard in Navy training, have not encountered any significant long-term mental health consequences from its use. Your on-site psychologists have also indicated that JPRA has likewise not reported any significant long-term mental health consequences from the use of the waterboard. You have informed us that other services ceased use of the waterboard because it was not successful as an interrogation technique, but not because of any concerns over any harm, physical or mental, caused by it. It was also reported to be almost 100 percent effective in producing cooperation among the trainees.

[REDACTED] also indicated that he had observed the use of the waterboard in Navy training some ten to twelve times. Each time it resulted in cooperation but it did not result in any physical harm to the student.

You have also reviewed the relevant literature and found no empirical data on the effect of these techniques, with the exception of sleep deprivation. With respect to sleep deprivation, you have informed us that it is not uncommon for someone to be deprived of sleep for 72 hours and still perform excellently on visual-spatial motor tasks and short-term memory tests. Although some individuals may experience hallucinations, according to the literature you surveyed, those who experience such psychotic symptoms have almost always had such episodes prior to the sleep deprivation. You have indicated the studies of lengthy sleep deprivation showed no psychosis, loosening of thoughts, flattening of emotions, delusions, or paranoid ideas. In one case, even after eleven days of deprivation, no psychosis or permanent brain damaged occurred. In fact the individual reported feeling almost back to normal after one night's sleep. Further, based on the experiences with its use in military training (where it is induced for up to 48 hours), you found that rarely, if ever, will the individual suffer harm after the sleep deprivation is discontinued. Instead, the effects remit after a few good nights of sleep.

You have taken the additional step of consulting with U.S. interrogations experts, and other individuals with oversight over the SERE training process. None of these individuals was aware of any prolonged psychological effect caused by the use of any of the above techniques either separately or as a course of conduct. Moreover, you consulted with outside psychologists who reported that they were unaware of any cases where long-term problems have occurred as a result of these techniques.

Moreover, in consulting with a number of mental health experts, you have learned that the effect of any of these procedures will be dependant on the individual's personal history, cultural history and psychological tendencies. To that end, you have informed us that you have completed a psychological assessment of Zubaydah. This assessment is based on interviews with Zubaydah, observations of him, and information collected from other sources such as intelligence and press reports. Our understanding of Zubaydah's psychological profile, which we set forth below, is based on that assessment.

According to this assessment, Zubaydah, though only 31, rose quickly from very low level mujahedin to third or fourth man in al Qaeda. He has served as Usama Bin Laden's senior lieutenant. In that capacity, he has managed a network of training camps. He has been instrumental in the training of operatives for al Qaeda, the Egyptian Islamic Jihad, and other terrorist elements inside Pakistan and Afghanistan. He acted as the Deputy Camp Commander for al Qaeda training camp in Afghanistan, personally approving entry and graduation of all trainees during 1999–2000. From 1996 until 1999, he approved all individuals going in and out of Afghanistan to the training camps. Further, no one went in and out of Peshawar, Pakistan without his knowledge and approval. He also acted as al Qaeda's coordinator of external contacts and foreign communications. Additionally, he has acted as al Qaeda's counter-intelligence officer and has been trusted to find spies within the organization.

Zubaydah has been involved in every major terrorist operation carried out by al Qaeda. He was a planner for the Millennium plot to attack U.S. and Israeli targets during the Millennium celebrations in Jordan. Two of the central figures in this plot who were arrested have identified Zubaydah as the supporter of their cell and the plot. He also served as a planner for the Paris Embassy plot in 2001. Moreover, he was one of the planners of the September 11 attacks. Prior to his capture, he was engaged in planning future terrorist attacks against U.S. interests.

Your psychological assessment indicates that it is believed Zubaydah wrote al Qaeda's manual on resistance techniques. You also believe that his experiences in al Qaeda make him well-acquainted with and well-versed in such techniques. As part of his role in al Qaeda, Zubaydah visited individuals in prison and helped them upon their release. Through this contact and activities with other al Qaeda mujahedin, you believe that he knows many stories of capture, interrogation, and resistance to such interrogation. Additionally, he has spoken with Ayman al-Zawahiri, and you believe it is likely that the two discussed Zawahiri's experiences as a prisoner of the Russians and the Egyptians.

Zubaydah stated during interviews that he thinks of any activity outside of jihad as "silly." He has indicated that his heart and mind are devoted to serving Allah and Islam through jihad and he has stated that he has no doubts or regrets about committing himself to jihad. Zubaydah believes that the global victory of Islam is inevitable. You have informed us that he continues to express his unabated desire to kill Americans and Jews.

Your psychological assessment describes his personality as follows. He is "a highly self-directed individual who prizes his independence." He has "narcissistic features," which are evidenced in the attention he pays to his personal appearance and his "obvious 'efforts' to demonstrate that he is really a rather 'humble and regular guy.'" He is "somewhat compulsive" in how he organizes his environment and business. He is confident, self-assured, and possesses an air of authority. While he admits to at times wrestling with how to determine who is an "innocent," he has acknowledged celebrating the destruction of the World Trade Center. He is intelligent and intellectually curious. He displays "excellent self-discipline." The assessment describes him as a perfectionist, persistent, private, and highly capable in his social interactions. He is very guarded about opening up to others and your assessment repeatedly emphasizes that he tends not to trust others easily. He is also "quick to recognize and assess the moods and motivations of others." Furthermore, he is proud of his ability to lie and deceive others successfully. Through his deception he has, among other things, prevented the location of al Qaeda safehouses and even acquired a United Nations refugee identification card.

According to your reports, Zubaydah does not have any pre-existing mental conditions or problems that would make him likely to suffer prolonged mental harm from your proposed interrogation methods. Through reading his diaries and interviewing him, you have found no history of "mood disturbance or other psychiatric pathology[,]" "thought disorder[,] . . . enduring mood or mental health problems." He is in fact "remarkably resilient and confident that he can overcome adversity." When he encounters stress or low mood, this appears to last only for a short time. He deals with stress by assessing its source, evaluating the coping resources available to him, and then taking action. Your assessment notes that he is "generally self-sufficient and relies on his understanding and application of religious and psychological principles, intelligence and discipline to avoid and overcome problems." Moreover, you have found that he has a "reliable and durable support system" in his faith, "the blessings of religious leaders, and camaraderie of like-minded mujahedin brothers." During detention, Zubaydah has managed his mood, remaining at most points "circumspect, calm, controlled, and deliberate." He has maintained this demeanor during aggressive interrogations and reductions in sleep. You describe that in an initial confrontational incident, Zubaydah showed signs of sympathetic nervous system arousal, which you think was possibly fear. Although this incident led him to disclose intelligence information, he was able to quickly regain his composure, his air of confidence, and his "strong resolve" not to reveal any information.

Overall, you summarize his primary strengths as the following: ability to focus, goal-directed discipline, intelligence, emotional resilience, street savvy, ability to organize and manage people, keen observation skills, fluid adaptability (can anticipate and adapt under duress and with minimal resources), capacity to assess and exploit the needs of others, and ability to adjust goals to emerging opportunities.

You anticipate that he will draw upon his vast knowledge of interrogation techniques to cope with the interrogation. Your assessment indicates that Zubaydah may be willing to die to protect the most important information that he holds. Nonetheless, you are of the view that his belief that Islam will ultimately dominate the world and that this victory is inevitable may provide the chance that Zubaydah will give information and rationalize it solely as a temporary setback. Additionally, you believe he may be willing to disclose some information, particularly information he deems to not be critical, but which may ultimately be useful to us when pieced together with other intelligence information you have gained.

III

Section 2340A makes it a criminal offense for any person "outside of the United States [to] commit[] or attempt[] to commit torture." Section 2340(I) defines torture as:

> an act committed by a person acting under the color of law specifically intended to inflict severe physical or mental pain or suffering (other than pain or suffering incidental to lawful sanctions) upon another person within his custody of physical control.

18 U.S.C. § 2340(I). As we outlined in our opinion on standards of conduct under Section 2340A, a violation of 2340A requires a showing that: (1) the torture occurred outside the United States; (2) the defendant acted under the color of law; (3) the victim was within the defendant's custody or control; (4) the defendant specifically intended to inflict severe pain or suffering; and (5) that the acted inflicted severe pain or suffering. *See* Memorandum for John Rizzo, Acting General Counsel for the Central Intelligence Agency, from Jay S. Bybee, Assistant Attorney General, Office of Legal Counsel, *Re: Standards of Conduct for Interrogation under 18 U.S.C. §§ 2340–2340A* at 3 (August 1, 2002) ("Section 2340A Memorandum"). You have asked us to assume that Zubaydah is being held outside the United States, Zubaydah is within U.S. custody, and the interrogators are acting under the color of law. At issue is whether the last two elements would be met by the use of the proposed procedures, namely, whether those using these procedures would have the requisite mental state and whether these procedures would inflict severe pain or suffering within the meaning of the statute.

Severe Pain or Suffering. In order for pain or suffering to rise to the level of torture, the statute requires that it be severe. As we have previously explained, this reaches only extreme acts. *See id.* at 13. Nonetheless, drawing upon cases under the Torture Victim Protection Act (TVPA), which has a definition of torture that is similar to Section 2340's definition, we found that a single event of sufficiently intense pain may fall within this prohibition. *See id.* at 26. As a result, we have analyzed each of these techniques separately. In further drawing upon those cases, we also have found that courts tend to take a totality-of-the-circumstances approach and consider an entire course of conduct to determine whether torture has occurred. *See id.* at 27. Therefore, in addition to considering each technique separately, we consider them together as a course of conduct.

Section 2340 defines torture as the infliction of severe physical or mental pain or suffering. We will consider physical pain and mental pain separately *See* 18 U.S.C. § 2340(I). With respect to *physical* pain, we previously concluded that "severe pain" within the meaning of Section 2340 is pain that is difficult for the individual to endure and is of an intensity akin to the pain accompanying serious physical injury. *See* Section 2340A Memorandum at 6. Drawing upon the TVPA precedent, we have noted that examples of acts inflicting severe pain that typify torture are, among other things, severe beatings with weapons such as clubs, and the burning of prisoners. *See id.* at 24. We conclude below that none of the proposed techniques inflicts such pain.

The facial hold and the attention grasp involve no physical pain. In the absence of such pain it is obvious that they cannot be said to inflict severe physical pain or suffering. The stress positions and wall standing both may result in muscle fatigue. Each involves the sustained holding of a position. In wall standing, it will be holding a position in which all of the individual's body weight is placed on his finger tips. The stress positions will likely include sitting on the floor with legs extended straight out in front and arms raised above the head, and kneeling on the floor and leaning back at a 45 degree angle. Any pain associated with muscle fatigue is not of the intensity sufficient to amount to "severe physical pain or suffering" under the statute, nor, despite its discomfort, can it be said to be difficult to endure. Moreover, you have orally informed us that no stress position will be used that could interfere with the healing of Zubaydah's wound. Therefore, we conclude that these techniques involve discomfort that falls far below the threshold of severe physical pain.

Similarly, although the confinement boxes (both small and large) are physically uncomfortable because their size restricts movement, they are not so small as to require the individual to contort his body to sit (small box) or stand (large box). You have also orally informed us that despite his wound, Zubaydah remains quite flexible, which would substantially reduce any pain associated with being placed in the box. We have no information from the medical experts you have consulted that the limited duration for which the individual is kept in the boxes causes any substantial physical pain. As a result, we do not think the use of these boxes can be said to cause pain that is of the intensity associated with serious physical injury.

The use of one of these boxes with the introduction of an insect does not alter this assessment. As we understand it, no actually harmful insect will be placed in the box. Thus, though the introduction of an insect may produce trepidation in Zubaydah (which we discuss below), it certainly does not cause physical pain.

As for sleep deprivation, it is clear that depriving someone of sleep does not involve severe physical pain within the meaning of the statute. While sleep deprivation may involve some physical discomfort, such as the fatigue or the discomfort experienced in the difficulty of keeping one's eyes open, these effects remit after the individual is permitted to sleep. Based on the facts you have provided us, we are not aware of any evidence that sleep deprivation results in severe physical pain or suffering. As a result, its use does not violate Section 2340A.

Even those techniques that involve physical contact between the interrogator and the individual do not result in severe pain. The facial slap and walling contain precautions to ensure that no pain even approaching this level results. The slap is delivered with fingers slightly spread, which you have explained to us is designed to be less painful than a closed-hand slap. The slap is also delivered to the fleshy part of the face, further reducing any risk of physical damage or serious pain. The facial slap does not produce pain that is difficult to endure. Likewise, walling involves quickly pulling the person forward and then thrusting him against a flexible false wall. You have informed us that the sound of hitting the wall will actually be far worse than any possible injury to the individual. The use of the rolled towel around the neck also reduces any risk of injury. While it may hurt to be pushed against the wall, any pain experienced is not of the intensity associated with serious physical injury.

As we understand it, when the waterboard is used, the subject's body responds as if the subject were drowning—even though the subject may be well aware that he is in fact not drowning. You have informed us that this procedure does not inflict actual physical harm. Thus, although the subject may experience the fear or panic associated with the feeling of drowning, the waterboard does not inflict physical pain. As we explained in the Section 2340A Memorandum, "pain and suffering" as used in Section 2340 is best understood as a single concept, not distinct concepts of "pain" as distinguished from "suffering." *See* Section 2340A Memorandum at 6 n.3. The waterboard, which inflicts no pain or actual harm whatsoever, does not, in our view inflict "severe pain or suffering." Even if one were to parse the statute more finely to attempt to treat "suffering" as a distinct concept, the waterboard could not be said to inflict severe suffering. The waterboard is simply a controlled acute episode, lacking the connotation of a protracted period of time generally given to suffering.

Finally, as we discussed above, you have informed us that in determining which procedures to use and how you will use them, you have selected techniques that will not harm Zubaydah's wound. You have also indicated that numerous steps will be taken to ensure that none of these procedures in any way interferes with the proper healing of Zubaydah's wound. You have also indicated that, should it appear at any time that Zubaydah is experiencing severe pain or suffering, the medical personnel on hand will stop the use of any technique.

Even when all of these methods are considered combined in an overall course of conduct, they still would not inflict severe physical pain or suffering.

As discussed above, a number of these acts result in no physical pain, others produce only physical discomfort. You have indicated that these acts will not be used with substantial repetition, so that there is no possibility that severe physical pain could arise from such repetition. Accordingly, we conclude that these acts neither separately nor as part of a course of conduct would inflict severe physical pain or suffering within the meaning of the statute.

We next consider whether the use of these techniques would inflict severe *mental* pain or suffering within the meaning of Section 2340. Section 2340 defines severe mental pain or suffering as "the prolonged mental harm caused by or resulting from" one of several predicate acts. 18 U.S.C. § 2340(2). Those predicate acts are: (1) the intentional infliction or threatened infliction of severe physical pain or suffering; (2) the administration or application, or threatened administration or application of mind-altering substances or other procedures calculated to disrupt profoundly the senses or the personality; (3) the threat of imminent death; or (4) the threat that any of the preceding acts will be done to another person. *See* 18 U.S.C. § 2340(2)(A)–(D). As we have explained, this list of predicate acts is exclusive. *See* Section 2340A Memorandum at 8. No other acts can support a charge under Section 2340A based on the infliction of severe mental pain or suffering. *See id.* Thus, if the methods that you have described do not either in and of themselves constitute one of these acts or as a course of conduct fulfill the predicate act requirement, the prohibition has not been violated. *See id.* Before addressing these techniques, we note that it is plain that none of these procedures involves a threat to any third party, the use of any kind of drugs, or for the reasons described above, the infliction of severe physical pain. Thus, the question is whether any of these acts, separately or as a course of conduct, constitutes a threat of severe physical pain or suffering, a procedure designed to disrupt profoundly the senses, or a threat of imminent death. As we previously explained, whether an action constitutes a threat must be assessed from the standpoint of a reasonable person in the subject's position. *See id.* at 9.

No argument can be made that the attention grasp or the facial hold constitute threats of imminent death or are procedures designed to disrupt profoundly the senses or personality. In general the grasp and the facial hold will startle the subject, produce fear, or even insult him. As you have informed us, the use of these techniques is not accompanied by a specific verbal threat of severe physical pain or suffering. To the extent that these techniques could be considered a threat of severe physical pain or suffering, such a threat would have to be inferred from the acts themselves. Because these actions themselves involve no pain, neither could be interpreted by a reasonable person in Zubaydah's position to constitute a threat of severe pain or suffering. Accordingly, these two techniques are not predicate acts within the meaning of Section 2340.

The facial slap likewise falls outside the set of predicate acts. It plainly is not a threat of imminent death, under Section 2340(2)(C), or a procedure designed to disrupt profoundly the senses or personality, under Section 2340(2)(B). Though it may hurt, as discussed above, the effect is one of smarting or stinging and surprise or humiliation, but not severe pain. Nor does it alone constitute a threat of severe pain or suffering, under Section 2340(2)(A). Like the facial hold and the attention grasp, the use of this slap is not accompanied by a specific verbal threat of further escalating violence. Additionally, you have informed us that in one use this technique will typically involve at most two slaps. Certainly, the use of this slap may dislodge any expectation that Zubaydah had that he would not be touched in a physically aggressive manner. Nonetheless, this alteration in his expectations could hardly be construed by a reasonable person in his situation to be tantamount to a threat of severe physical pain or suffering. At most, this technique suggests that the circumstances of his confinement and interrogation have changed. Therefore, the facial slap is not within the statute's exclusive list of predicate acts.

Walling plainly is not a procedure calculated to disrupt profoundly the senses or personality. While walling involves what might be characterized as rough handling, it does not involve the threat of imminent death or, as discussed above, the infliction of severe physical pain. Moreover, once again we understand that use of this technique will not be accompanied by any specific verbal threat that violence will ensue absent cooperation. Thus, like the facial slap, walling can only constitute a threat of severe physical pain if a reasonable person would infer such a threat from the use of the technique itself. Walling does not in and of itself inflict severe pain or suffering. Like the facial slap, walling may alter the subject's expectation as to the treatment he believes he will receive. Nonetheless, the character of the action falls so far short of inflicting severe pain or suffering within the meaning of the statute that even if he inferred that greater aggressiveness was to follow, the type of actions that could be reasonably be anticipated would still fall below anything sufficient to inflict severe physical pain or suffering under the statute. Thus, we conclude that this technique falls outside the proscribed predicate acts.

Like walling, stress positions and wall-standing are not procedures calculated to disrupt profoundly the senses, nor are they threats of imminent death. These procedures, as discussed above, involve the use of muscle fatigue to encourage cooperation and do not themselves constitute the infliction of severe physical pain or suffering. Moreover, there is no aspect of violence to either technique that remotely suggests future severe pain or suffering from which such a threat of future harm could be inferred. They simply involve forcing the subject to remain in uncomfortable positions. While these acts may indicate to the subject that he may be placed in these positions again if he does not disclose information, the use of these techniques would not suggest to a reasonable person in the subject's position that he is being threatened with severe pain or suffering. Accordingly, we conclude that these two procedures do not constitute any of the predicate acts set forth in Section 2340(2).

As with the other techniques discussed so far, cramped confinement is not a threat of imminent death. It may be argued that, focusing in part on the fact that the boxes will be without light, placement in these boxes would constitute a procedure designed to disrupt profoundly the senses. As we explained in our recent opinion, however, to "disrupt profoundly the senses" a technique must produce an extreme effect in the subject. *See* Section 2340A Memorandum at 10–12. We have previously concluded that this requires that the procedure cause substantial interference with the individual's cognitive abilities or fundamentally alter his personality. *See id.* at 11. Moreover, the statute requires that such procedures must be calculated to produce this effect. *See id.* at 10; 18 U.S.C. § 2340(2)(B).

With respect to the small confinement box, you have informed us that he would spend at most two hours in this box. You have informed us that your purpose in using these boxes is not to interfere with his senses or his personality, but to cause him physical discomfort that will encourage him to disclose critical information. Moreover, your imposition of time limitations on the use of either of the boxes also indicates that the use of these boxes is not designed or calculated to disrupt profoundly the senses or personality. For the larger box, in which he can both stand and sit, he may be placed in this box for up to eighteen hours at a time, while you have informed us that he will never spend more than an hour at time in the smaller box. These time limits further ensure that no profound disruption of the senses or personality, were it even possible, would result. As such, the use of the confinement boxes does not constitute a procedure calculated to disrupt profoundly the senses or personality.

Nor does the use of the boxes threaten Zubaydah with severe physical pain or suffering. While additional time spent in the boxes may be threatened, their use is not accompanied by any express threats of severe physical pain or suffering. Like the stress positions and walling, placement in the boxes is physically uncomfortable but any such discomfort does not rise to the level of severe physical pain or suffering. Accordingly, a reasonable person in the subject's position would not infer from the use of this technique that severe physical pain is the next step in his interrogator's treatment of him. Therefore, we conclude that the use of the confinement boxes does not fall within the statute's required predicate acts.

In addition to using the confinement boxes alone, you also would like to introduce an insect into one of the boxes with Zubaydah. As we understand it, you plan to inform Zubaydah that you are going to place a stinging insect into the box, but you will actually place a harmless insect in the box, such as a caterpillar. If you do so, to ensure that you are outside the predicate act requirement, you must inform him that the insects will not have a sting that would produce death or severe pain. If, however, you were to place the insect in the box without informing him that you are doing so, then, in order to not commit a predicate act, you should not affirmatively lead him to believe that any insect is present which has a sting that could produce severe pain or suffering or even cause his death. [redacted] so long as you take either of the approaches we have described, the insect's placement in the box would not constitute a threat of severe physical pain or suffering to a reasonable person in his position. An individual placed in a box, even an individual with a fear of insects, would not reasonably feel threatened with severe physical pain or suffering if a caterpillar was placed in the box. Further, you have informed us that you are not aware that Zubaydah has any allergies to insects, and you have not informed us of any other factors that would cause a reasonable person in that same situation to believe that an unknown insect would cause him severe physical pain or death. Thus, we conclude that the placement of the insect in the confinement box with Zubaydah would not constitute a predicate act.

Sleep deprivation also clearly does not involve a threat of imminent death. Although it produces physical discomfort, it cannot be said to constitute a threat of severe physical pain or suffering from the perspective of a reasonable person in Zubaydah's position. Nor could sleep deprivation constitute a procedure calculated to disrupt profoundly the senses, so long as sleep deprivation (as you have informed us is your intent) is used for limited periods, before hallucinations or other profound disruptions of the senses would occur. To be sure, sleep deprivation may reduce the subject's ability to think on his feet. Indeed, you indicate that this is the intended result. His mere reduced ability to evade your questions and resist answering does not, however, rise to the level of disruption required by the statute. As we explained above, a disruption within the meaning of the statute is an extreme one, substantially interfering with an individual's cognitive abilities, for example, inducing hallucinations, or driving him to engage in uncharacteristic self-destructive behavior. *See infra* 13; Section 2340A Memorandum at 11. Therefore, the limited use of sleep deprivation does not constitute one of the required predicate acts.

We find that the use of the waterboard constitutes a threat of imminent death. As you have explained the waterboard procedure to us, it creates in the subject the uncontrollable physiological sensation that the subject is drowning. Although the procedure will be monitored by personnel with medical training and extensive SERE school experience with this procedure who will ensure the subject's mental and physical safety, the subject is not aware of any of these precautions. From the vantage point of any reasonable person undergoing this procedure in such circumstances, he would feel as if he is drowning at very moment of the procedure due to the uncontrollable physiological sensation he is experiencing. Thus, this procedure cannot be viewed as too uncertain to satisfy the imminence requirement. Accordingly, it constitutes a threat of imminent death and fulfills the predicate act requirement under the statute.

Although the waterboard constitutes a threat of imminent death, prolonged mental harm must nonetheless result to violate the statutory prohibition on infliction of severe mental pain or suffering. *See* Section 2340A Memorandum at 7. We have previously concluded that prolonged mental harm is mental harm of some lasting duration, e.g., mental harm lasting months or years. *See id.* Prolonged mental harm is not simply the stress experienced in, for example, an interrogation by state police. *See id.* Based on your research into the use of these methods at the SERE school and consultation with others with expertise in the field of psychology and interrogation, you do not anticipate that any prolonged mental harm would result from the use of the waterboard. Indeed, you have advised us that the relief is almost immediate when the cloth is removed from the nose and mouth. In the absence of prolonged mental harm, no severe mental pain or suffering would have been inflicted, and the use of these procedures would not constitute torture within the meaning of the statute.

When these acts are considered as a course of conduct, we are unsure whether these acts may constitute a threat of severe physical pain or suffering. You have indicated to us that you have not determined either the order or the precise timing for implementing these procedures. It is conceivable that these procedures could be used in a course of escalating conduct, moving incrementally and rapidly from least physically intrusive, e.g., facial hold, to the most physical contact, e.g., walling or the waterboard. As we understand it, based on his treatment so far, Zubaydah has come to expect that no physical harm will be done to him. By using these techniques in increasing intensity and in rapid succession, the goal would be to dislodge this expectation. Based on the facts you have provided to us, we cannot say definitively that the entire course of conduct would cause a reasonable person to believe that he is being threatened with severe pain or suffering within the meaning of section 2340. On the other hand, however, under certain circumstances—for example, rapid escalation in the use of these techniques culminating in the waterboard (which we acknowledge constitutes a threat of imminent death) accompanied by verbal or other suggestions that physical violence will follow—might cause a reasonable person to believe that they are faced with such a threat. Without more information, we are uncertain whether the course of conduct would constitute a predicate act under Section 2340(2).

Even if the course of conduct were thought to pose a threat of physical pain or suffering, it would nevertheless—on the facts before us—not constitute a violation of Section 2340A. Not only must the course of conduct be a predicate act, but also those who use the procedure must actually cause prolonged mental harm. Based on the information that you have provided to us, indicating that no evidence exists that this course of conduct produces any prolonged mental harm, we conclude that a course of conduct using these procedures and culminating in the waterboard would not violate Section 2340A.

Specific Intent. To violate the statute, an individual must have the specific intent to inflict severe pain or suffering. Because specific intent is an element of the offense, the absence of specific intent negates the charge of torture. As we previously opined, to have the required specific intent, an individual must expressly intend to cause such severe pain or suffering. *See* Section 2340A Memorandum at 3 *citing Carter v. United States*, 530 U.S. 255, 267 (2000). We have further found that if a defendant acts with the good faith belief that his actions will not cause such suffering, he has not acted with specific intent. *See id.* at 4 *citing South Atl. Lmtd. Ptrshp. of Tenn. v. Reise*, 218 F.3d 518, 531 (4th Cir. 2002). A defendant acts in good faith when he has an honest belief that his actions will not result in severe pain or suffering. *See id. citing Cheek v. United States*, 498 U.S. 192, 202 (1991). Although an honest belief need not be reasonable, such a belief is easier to establish where there is a reasonable basis for it. *See id.* at 5. Good faith may be established by, among other things, the reliance on the advice of experts. *See id.* at 8.

Based on the information you have provided us, we believe that those carrying out these procedures would not have the specific intent to inflict severe physical pain or suffering. The objective of these techniques is not to cause severe physical pain. First, the constant presence of personnel with medical training who have the authority to stop the interrogation should it appear it is medically necessary indicates that it is not your intent to cause severe physical pain. The personnel on site have extensive experience with these specific techniques as they are used in SERE school training. Second, you have informed us that you are taking steps to ensure that Zubaydah's injury is not worsened or his recovery impeded by the use of these techniques.

Third, as you have described them to us, the proposed techniques involving physical contact between the interrogator and Zubaydah actually contain precautions to prevent any serious physical harm to Zubaydah. In "walling," a rolled hood or towel will be used to prevent whiplash and he will be permitted to rebound from the flexible wall to reduce the likelihood of injury. Similarly, in the "facial hold," the fingertips will be kept well away from the his [*sic*] eyes to ensure that there is no injury to them. The purpose of that facial hold is not to injure him but to hold the head immobile. Additionally, while the stress positions and wall standing will undoubtedly result in physical discomfort by tiring the muscles, it is obvious that these positions are not intended to produce the kind of extreme pain required by the statute.

Furthermore, no specific intent to cause severe mental pain or suffering appears to be present. As we explained in our recent opinion, an individual must have the specific intent to cause prolonged mental harm in order to have the specific intent to inflict severe mental pain or suffering. *See* Section 2340A Memorandum at 8. Prolonged mental harm is substantial mental harm of a sustained duration, e.g., harm lasting months or even years after the acts were inflicted upon the prisoner. As we indicated above, a good faith belief can negate this element. Accordingly, if an individual conducting the interrogation has a good faith belief that the procedures he will apply, separately or together, would not result in prolonged mental harm, that individual lacks the requisite specific intent. This conclusion concerning specific intent is further bolstered by the due diligence that has been conducted concerning the effects of these interrogation procedures.

The mental health experts that you have consulted have indicated that the psychological impact of a course of conduct must be assessed with reference to the subject's psychological history and current mental health status. The healthier the individual, the less likely that the use of any one procedure or set of procedures as a course of conduct will result in prolonged mental harm. A comprehensive psychological profile of Zubaydah has been created. In creating this profile, your personnel drew on direct interviews, Zubaydah's diaries, observation of Zubaydah since his capture, and information from other sources such as other intelligence and press reports.

As we indicated above, you have informed us that your proposed interrogation methods have been used and continue to be used in SERE training. It is our understanding that these techniques are not used one by one in isolation, but as a full course of conduct to resemble a real interrogation. Thus, the information derived from SERE training bears both upon the impact of the use of the individual techniques and upon their use as a course of conduct. You have found that the use of these methods together or separately, including the use of the waterboard, has not resulted in any negative long-term mental health consequences. The continued use of these methods without mental health consequences to the trainees indicates that it is highly improbable that such consequences would result here. Because you have conducted the due diligence to determine that these procedures, either alone or in combination, do not produce prolonged mental harm, we believe that you do not meet the specific intent requirement necessary to violate Section 2340A.

You have also informed us that you have reviewed the relevant literature on the subject, and consulted with outside psychologists. Your review of the literature uncovered no empirical data on the use of these procedures, with the exception of sleep deprivation for which no long-term health consequences resulted. The outside psychologists with whom you consulted indicated were unaware of any cases where long-term problems have occurred as a result of these techniques.

As described above, it appears you have conducted an extensive inquiry to ascertain what impact, if any, these procedures individually and as a course of conduct would have on Zubaydah. You have consulted with interrogation experts, including those with substantial SERE school experience, consulted with outside psychologists, completed a psychological assessment and reviewed the relevant literature on this topic. Based on this inquiry, you believe that the use of the procedures, including the waterboard, and as a course of conduct would not result in prolonged mental harm. Reliance on this information about Zubaydah and about the effect of the use of these techniques more generally demonstrates the presence of a good faith belief that no prolonged mental harm will result from using these methods in the interrogation of Zubaydah. Moreover, we think that this represents not only an honest belief but also a reasonable belief based on the information that you have supplied to us. Thus, we believe that the specific intent to inflict prolonged mental is not present, and consequently, there is no specific intent to inflict severe mental pain or suffering. Accordingly, we conclude that on the facts in this case the use of these methods separately or a course of conduct would not violate Section 2340A.

Based on the foregoing, and based on the facts that you have provided, we conclude that the interrogation procedures that you propose would not violate Section 2340A. We wish to emphasize that this is our best reading of the law, however, you should be aware that there are no cases construing this statute, just as there have been no prosecutions brought under it.

Please let us know if we can be of further assistance.

Jay S. Bybee

Assistant Attorney General

Source: Memorandum, August 1, 2002, formerly "Top Secret," for John A. Rizzo, Acting General Counsel of the Central Intelligence Agency, from Jay S. Bybee, Office of the Assistant Attorney General, Office of Legal Counsel, U.S. Department of Justice. (Office of the Assistant Attorney General, U.S. Department of Justice, Washington, D.C. 20530. August 1, 2002.)

Bibliography

Organizations as Sources for Information

The most current sources of information about contemporary war crimes, genocides, and atrocities around the world, are available from organizations such as:

ACLU (http://www.aclu.org/)
Amnesty International (http://www.amnesty.org/)
Armenian National Institute (http://www.armenian-genocide.org/)
Coalition for the International Criminal Court (http://www.iccnow.org/)
Crimes of War Project (http://www.crimesofwar.org/)
Doctors Without Borders/Médecins Sans Frontières (www.doctorswithoutborders.org)
Genocide Watch (http://www.genocidewatch.org)
Human Rights Council (http://www2.ohchr.org/english/bodies/hrcouncil/)
Human Rights First (http://www.humanrightsfirst.org)
Human Rights Watch (http://www.hrw.org/)
International Association of Genocide Scholars (http://www.genocidescholars.org/)
International Committee of the Red Cross (http://www.icrc.org/)
International Institute for Genocide and Human Rights Studies (A Division of the Zoryan Institute) (www.genocidesstudies.org)
Interpol (http://www.interpol.int/public/CrimesAgainstHumanity/Default.asp)
Open Society Justice Initiative (http://www.justiceinitiative.org/)
Reporters Without Borders (http://www.rsf.org/)
United Nations (http://www.un.org/preventgenocide/adviser/genocide.shtml)
U.S. Holocaust Memorial Museum, Washington, DC (http://www.ushmm.org/)
War Crimes, Genocide, and Crimes against Humanity (http://www.war-crimes.org/)
War Crimes Prosecution Watch (http://www.publicinternationallaw.org/warcrimeswatch/)

Books

Allmand, Christopher T. *The Hundred Years War: England and France at War, c. 1300–c. 1450*. New York: Cambridge University Press, 1988.

Amnesty International Report. *Torture in the Eighties*. London, Amnesty International Publications, 1984.

Bailey, Sydney Dawson. *Prohibitions and Restraints in War*. London: Royal Institute of International Affairs, Oxford University Press, 1972.

Ball, Howard. *War Crimes and Justice: A Reference Handbook*. Contemporary World Issues. Santa Barbara, CA: ABC-CLIO, 2002.

Bard, Mitchell. *Forgotten Victims: The Abandonment of Americans in Hitler's Camps*. Boulder, CO: Westview Press, 1994.

Bardakjian, Kevork B. *Hitler and the Armenian Genocide*. Cambridge, MA: Zoryan Institute, 1985.

Bartov, Omer. *The Eastern Front, 1941–1945: German Troops and the Barbarisation of Warfare*. Basingstoke, Hampshire: Macmillan, in association with St. Anthony's College, Oxford, 1985.

Bartov, Omer. *Mirrors of Destruction: War, Genocide, and Modern Identity*. Oxford and New York: Oxford University Press, 2000.

Bauer, Yehuda, and Robert Rozett. "Estimated Jewish Losses in the Holocaust." In *Encyclopedia of the Holocaust*, ed. Israel Gutman. New York: Macmillan, 1990.

Belgion, Montgomery. *Victor's Justice*. Hinsdale, IL: Regnery, 1949.

Bendersky, Joseph W. *The "Jewish Threat": Anti-Semitic Politics of the U.S. Army*. New York: Basic Books, 2000.

Benton, Wilbourn E., and Georg Grimm, eds. *Nuremberg: German Views of the War Trials*. Dallas, TX: Southern Methodist University Press, 1955.

Benz, Wolfgang. *Dimension des Volkermords: Die Zahl der Judischen Opfer des Nationalsocialismus*. Munich: Deutscher Taschenbuch Verlag, 1996.

Bergen, Doris L. *War and Genocide: A Concise History of the Holocaust*. Lanham, MD: Rowman and Littlefield, 2003.

Best, Geoffrey. *Humanity in Warfare*. New York: Columbia University Press, 1980.

Blakeslee, Spencer. *The Death of American Antisemitism*. Westport, CT: Praeger, 2000.

Bloxham, Donald. "Milestones and Mythologies: The Impact of Nuremberg." In *Atrocities on Trial: Historical Perspectives on the Politics of Prosecuting War Crimes*, ed. Patricia Heberer and Jürgen Matthäus, 263–282. Lincoln: University of Nebraska Press, 2008.

Brackman, Arnold C. *The Other Nuremberg: The Untold Story of the Tokyo War Crimes Trials*. New York: HarperCollins Publishers, 1989.

Braeckman, Colette. "Incitement to Genocide." In *Crimes of War: What the Public Should Know*, ed. Roy Gutman and David Rieff, 192–194. New York: Norton, 1999.

Browning, Christopher. "Genocide and Public Health: German Doctors and Polish Jews." In *The Path to Genocide: Essays on Launching the Final Solution*, ed. Christopher Browning, 145–168. Cambridge: Cambridge University Press, 1992.

Browning, Christopher. *Ordinary Men: Reserve Police Battalion 101 and the Final Solution in Poland*. New York: Harper Perennial, 1992.

Bryce, James, and Arnold Toynbee. *Treatment of Armenians in the Ottoman Empire: Documents Presented to Viscount Grey of Fallodon, Secretary of State for Foreign Affairs*. London: Causton and Sons, 1916.

Buchheim, Hans, et al. *Anatomie des S.S. Staates*. Munich: Deutscher Taschenbuch Verlag, 1999.

Buzzell, Colby. *My War: Killing Time in Iraq*. New York: G. P. Putnam's Sons, 2005.
Calvocoressi, Peter, and Guy Wint. *Total War: The Story of World War II*. New York: Pantheon, 1972.
Chang, Iris. *The Rape of Nanking: The Forgotten Holocaust of World War II*. New York: Basic Books, 1997.
Chorbajian, Levon, and George Shirinian, eds. *Studies in Comparative Genocide*. London and New York: Macmillan, 1999.
Chuter, David. *War Crimes: Confronting Atrocity in the Modern World*. Boulder, CO: Lynne Rienner, 2003.
Cigar, Norman. *Genocide in Bosnia: The Policy of "Ethnic Cleansing."* College Station: Texas A&M University Press, 1995.
Cohen, Roger. *Soldiers and Slaves: American POWs Trapped by the Nazis' Final Gamble*. New York: Knopf, 2005.
Cooper, John. *Raphael Lemkin and the Struggle for the Genocide Convention*. New York: Palgrave Macmillan, 2008.
Coram, Robert. *American Patriot: The Life and Wars of Colonel Bud Day*. New York: Little, Brown, 2007.
Crozier, Frank P. *The Men I Killed*. Garden City, NY: Doubleday, 1938.
Dadrian, Vahakn N. *German Responsibility in the Armenian Genocide: A Review of the Historical Evidence of German Complicity*. Watertown, MA: Blue Crane, 1996.
Dadrian, Vahakn N. *The History of the Armenian Genocide: Ethnic Conflict from the Balkans to Anatolia to the Caucasus*. Providence, RI: Berghahn, 1995.
Danner, Mark. *Torture and Truth: America, Abu Ghraib, and the War on Terror*. New York: New York Review of Books, 2004.
De Zayas, Alfred M., and Walter Rabus. *The Wehrmacht War Crimes Bureau, 1939–1945*. Lincoln: University of Nebraska Press, 1989.
Dreschler, Horst. *Let Us Die Fighting: The Struggle of the Herero and the Nama against German Imperialism (1884–1915)*. London: Zed Press, 1980.
Duggar, Ronnie. "To Prevent or to Stop Mass Murder." In *Genocide, War, and Human Survival*, ed. Charles B. Strozier and Michael Flynn, 59. Lanham, MD: Rowman and Littlefield, 1996.
Ehrenfreund, Norbert. *The Nuremberg Legacy: How the Nazi War Crimes Trials Changed the Course of History*. New York: Palgrave Macmillan, 2007.
Etcheson, Craig. *After the Killing Fields: Lessons from the Cambodian Genocide*. Westport, CT: Praeger, 2005.
Fahey, James J. *Pacific War Diary, 1942–1945*. Boston: Houghton Mifflin, 1963.
Finnes, John. "The Ethics of War and Peace in the Catholic National Law Tradition." In *The Ethics of War and Peace: Religious and Secular Perspectives*, ed. Terry Nardin, 20–24. Princeton, NJ: Princeton University Press, 1996.
Gage, Beverly. *The Day Wall Street Exploded: A Story of America in its First Age of Terror*. New York: Oxford University Press, 2009.
Gagnon, V. P. *The Myth of Ethnic War: Serbia and Croatia in the 1990s*. Ithaca, NY: Cornell University Press, 2004.
Gellately, Robert, and Kiernan, Ben, eds. *The Specter of Genocide: Mass Murder in Historical Perspective*. Cambridge and New York: Cambridge University Press, 2003.

Gewald, Jan-Bart. *Herero Heroes: A Socio-Political History of the Herero of Namibia, 1890–1923*. Oxford: James Currey, 1999.

Gillespie, James M. *Andersonvilles of the North: The Myths and Realities of Northern Treatment of Civil War Confederate Prisoners*. Denton: University of North Texas Press, 2008.

Gironella, José María. *One Million Dead*. Translated by Joan MacLean. Garden City, NY: Doubleday, 1963.

Glatthaar, Joseph T. *The March to the Sea and Beyond: Sherman's Troops in the Savannah and Carolinas Campaigns*. New York: New York University Press, 1985.

Gourevitch, Philip. *We Wish to Inform You That Tomorrow We Will Be Killed with Our Families: Stories from Rwanda*. New York: Farrar, Straus and Giroux, 1998.

Graber, G. S. *Caravans to Oblivion: The Armenian Genocide, 1915*. New York: Wiley, 1996.

Grimsley, Mark. *The Hard Hand of War: Union Military Policy toward Southern Civilians*. New York: Cambridge University Press, 1995.

Groehler, Olaf. "The Strategic Air War and Its Impact on the German Civilian Population." In *The Conduct of the Air War in the Second World War: An International Comparison*, ed. Horst Boog, 279–297. Proceedings of the International Conference of Historians in Freiburg im Breisgau, Federal Republic of Germany, August 29 to September 2, 1988. New York: Berg, 1992.

Gross, Jan T. *Neighbors: The Destruction of the Jewish Community in Jedwabne, Poland*. Princeton, NJ: Princeton University Press, 2001.

Grotius, Hugo. *De Jure Belli ac Pacis* (On the Law of War and Peace). Translated by A.C. Campbell. London, 1814. http://www.constitution.org/gro/djbp.htm.

Gutman, Roy, and David Rieff, eds. *Crimes of War: What the Public Should Know*. New York: Norton, 1999.

Haber, L. F. *The Poisonous Cloud: Chemical Warfare in the First World War*. Oxford: Clarendon Press, 1986.

Hafetz, Jonathan and Denbeaux, Mark. *The Guantánamo Lawyers: Inside a Prison Outside the Law*. New York: New York University Press, 2009.

Hamburg Institute for Social Research, ed. *The German Army and Genocide: Crimes against War Prisoners, Jews, and Other Civilians, 1939–1944*. Translated by Scott Abbott. Foreword by Omer Bartov. New York: New Press, 1999.

Hansen, Horace R., *Witness to Barbarism*. St. Paul, MN: Thousand Pinetree Press, 2002.

Hartigan, Richard Shelly. *Lieber's Code and the Law of War*. Chicago: Precedent, 1983.

Hartmann, Florence. "Bosnia." In *Crimes of War: What the People Should Know*, ed. Roy Gutmann and David Rieff. New York: Norton, 1999.

Heberer, Patricia and Matthäus, Jürgen, eds. *Atrocities on Trial: Historical Perspectives on the Politics of Prosecuting War Crimes*. Lincoln: University of Nebraska Press, 2008. Published in association with the United States Holocaust Museum.

Hilberg, Raul. *The Destruction of the European Jews*. New York: Holmes and Meier, 1985.

Hilberg, Raul. *Perpetrators, Victims, and Bystanders: The Jewish Catastrophe, 1933–1945*. New York: Aaron Asher, 1992.

Hirsch, Herbert. *Genocide and the Politics of Memory: Studying Death to Preserve Life*. Chapel Hill and London: University of North Carolina Press, 1995.

Holinshed, Raphael. *Holinshed's Chronicles of England, Scotland, and Ireland. London, Printed for J. Johnson (etc) 1807–08*. New York: AMS Press, 1965.

Holmes, Richard. *Acts of War: The Behavior of Men in Battle*. New York: Free Press, 1985.

Horowitz, Irving L. "Science, Modernity and Authorized Terror: Reconsidering the Genocidal State." In *Studies in Comparative Genocide*, ed. Levon Chorbajian and George Shirinian, 15–30. London and New York: Macmillan and St. Martin's Press, 1999.

Höss, Rudolf, Pery Broad, Johann Paul Kremer, and Jadwiga Bezwińska. *KL Auschwitz Seen by the SS*. New York: Howard Fertig, 2007.

Jeansonne, Glen. "Combating Anti-Semitism: The Case of Gerald L.K. Smith." In *Anti-Semitism in American History*, ed. David A. Gerber, 152–166. Urbana: University of Illinois Press, 1986.

Jensen, Olaf and Claus-Christian W. Szejnmann. *Ordinary People as Mass Murderers: Perpetrators in Comparative Perspective*. New York: Palgrave Macmillan, 2008.

Johnson, James Turner. "Historical Roots and Sources of the Just War Tradition in Western Culture." In *Just War and Jihad: Historical and Theoretical Perspectives on War and Peace in Western and Islamic Traditions*, ed. John Kelsay and James Turner Johnson. New York: Greenwood Press, 1991.

Jones, Adam. *Genocide: A Comprehensive Introduction*. London and New York: Routledge, 2006.

Jones, Adam, ed. *Gendercide and Genocide*. Nashville, TN: Vanderbilt University Press, 2004.

Jones, Adam, ed. *Genocide, War Crimes and the West*. London and New York: Zed Books, 2004.

Jones, James. *The Thin Red Line*. New York: Scribner, 1962.

Jünger, Ernst. *The Storm of Steel: From the Diary of a German Storm-Troop Officer on the Western Front*. New York: Howard Fertig, 1975.

Kaplan, Marion A. *Between Dignity and Despair: Jewish Life in Nazi Germany*. New York: Oxford University Press, 1998.

Karagueuzian, Hrayr, and Yair Auron. *A Perfect Injustice: Genocide and Theft of Armenian Wealth*. Ardsley, NY: Transaction, 2009.

Karsten, Peter. *Law, Soldiers, and Combat*. Westport, CT: Greenwood Press, 1978.

Kiernan, Ben. *Blood and Soil: A World History of Genocide and Extermination from Sparta to Darfur*. New Haven, CT: Yale University Press, 2007.

Kiernan, Ben. ed. *Genocide and Democracy in Cambodia: The Khmer Rouge, the United Nations, and the International Community*. New Haven, CT: Yale University Southeast Asia Studies, 1993.

Kingston, Jeffrey. *Japan in Transformation, 1952–2000*. New York: Pearson Education, 2001.

Klee, Ernst, Willi Dressen, and Volker Riess, eds. *"The Good Old Days": The Holocaust as Seen by Its Perpetrators and Bystanders*. New York: Free Press, 1991.

Klefisch, Theodor. "Thoughts about Purport and Effect of the Nuremberg Judgment." In *Nuremberg: German Views of the War Trials*, ed. Wilbourn E. Benton and Georg Grimm. Dallas, TX: Southern Methodist University Press, 1955.

Knoll, Erwin, and Judith Nies McFadden, eds. *War Crimes and the American Conscience*. New York, Chicago, and San Francisco: Holt, Rinehart and Winston, 1970.

Koenigsberg, Richard A. *Hitler's Ideology: A Study in Psychoanalytic Sociology*. New York: Library of Social Science, 1975.

Koenigsberg, Richard A. *Nations Have the Right to Kill: Hitler, the Holocaust, and War*. New York: Library of Social Science, 2009.

Krammer, Arnold. *Nazi Prisoners of War in America*. 1979. Reprint Lanham, MD: Scarborough House, 1996.

Krammer, Arnold. *Prisoners of War: A Reference Handbook*. Westport, CT: Praeger Security International, 2008.

Krammer, Arnold. *Undue Process: The Untold Story of America's German Alien Internees*. London: Roman & Littlefield, Publishers, 1997.

Kressel, Neil J. *Mass Hate: The Global Rise of Genocide and Terror*, rev. ed. Boulder, CO: Westview Press, 2002.

Kuper, Leo. *Genocide: Its Political Use in the Twentieth Century*. New Haven, CT: Yale University Press, 1981.

Lacqueur, Walter. *The Terrible Secret: An Investigation into the Suppression of Information about Hitler's 'Final Solution.'* London: Weidenfeld and Nicolson, 1980.

LeBor, Adam. *Complicity with Evil: The United Nations in the Age of Modern Genocide*. n.p. 2006.

Lee, Albert. *Henry Ford and the Jews*. New York: Stein and Day, 1980.

Lemkin, Raphael. *Axis Rule in Occupied Europe; Laws of Occupation, Analysis of Government, Proposals for Redress*. New York: Howard Fertig, 1944.

Léon-Portilla, Miguel, ed. *The Broken Spears: The Aztec Account of the Conquest of Mexico*. Boston: Beacon Press, 2006.

Levi, Primo. *The Drowned and the Saved*. Translated by Raymond Rosenthal. New York: Summit, 1998.

Lieberman, Benjamin. *Terrible Fate: Ethnic Cleansing in the Making of Modern Europe*. Chicago: Ivan R. Dee, 2006.

Lipkes, Jeff. *Rehearsals: The German Army in Belgium, August 1914*. Leuven: Leuven University Press, 2007.

Lochner, Louis P. *What about Germany?* New York: Dodd, Mead, 1942.

Loewenberg, Peter. *Decoding the Past: The Psychohistorical Approach*. New York: Knopf, 1983.

Lukas, Richard C. *The Forgotten Holocaust: The Poles under German Occupation, 1939–1944*. New York: Hippocrene, 1997.

Maguire, Peter. *Law and War: An American Story*. New York: Columbia University Press, 2000.

Mamdani, Mahmood. *When Victims Become Killers: Colonialism, Nativism, and the Genocide in Rwanda*. Princeton, NJ: Princeton University Press, 2001.

Maogoto, Jackson Nyamuya. *War Crimes and Realpolitik: International Justice from World War I to the 21st Century*. Boulder, CO: Lynne Rienner, 2004.

Marrus, Michael R. "The Nuremberg Doctors' Trial and the Limitations of Context." In *Atrocities on Trial: Historical Perspectives on the Politics of Prosecuting War*

Crimes, ed. Patricia Heberer and Jürgen Matthäus, 103–122. Lincoln: University of Nebraska Press, 2008.

Masaaki, Tanaka. *What Really Happened in Nanking: The Refutation of a Common Myth*. Tokyo: Sekai Shuppan, 2000.

Martin, Dean. *Collaboration in the Holocaust: Crimes of the Local Police in Belorussia and Ukraine, 1941–1944*. New York: St. Martin's Press, 2000.

Matthews, William, and Dixon Wecter. *Our Soldiers Speak, 1775–1918*. Boston: Brown, Little, 1943.

Mayer, Jane. *The Dark Side: The Inside Story of How the War on Terror Turned into a War on American Ideals*. New York: Anchor Books 2009.

McCarthy, Richard D. *The Ultimate Folly: War by Pestilence, Asphyxiation, and Defoliation*. New York: Knopf, 1969.

Merritt, Anna J., and Richard L. Merritt, eds. *Public Opinion in Semisovereign Germany: The HICOG Surveys, 1949–1955*. Urbana: University of Illinois Press, 1980.

Meron, Theodor. *Henry's Wars and Shakespeare's Laws: Perspectives on the Law of War in the Later Middle Ages*. New York: Oxford University Press, 1993.

Meron, Theodor. "Reflections on the Prosecution of War Crimes by International Tribunals." *American Journal of International Law* 100, no. 3 (2006): 556.

Michael, Robert. *A Concise History of American Antisemitism*. Lanham, MD: Rowman and Littlefield, 2005.

Milgram, Stanley. *Obedience to Authority: An Experimental View*. New York: Harper and Row, 1974.

Miller, Arthur G. *The Obedience Experiments: A Case Study of Controversy in the Social Sciences*. New York: Praeger, 1986.

Miller, Donald E., and Lorna Touryan Miller. *Survivors: An Oral History of the Armenian Genocide*. Berkeley: University of California Press, 1993.

Minear, Richard. *Victor's Justice: The Tokyo War Crimes Trial*. Princeton, NJ: Princeton University Press, 1971.

Monin, Lydia, and Andrew Gallimore. *The Devil's Gardens: A History of Landmines*. London: Pimlico, 2002.

Morgenthau, Henry. *Ambassador Morgenthau's Story*. Garden City, NY: Doubleday, 1918.

Mortimer, Geoff. *Eyewitness Accounts of the Thirty Years War, 1618–48*. New York: Palgrave, 2002.

Nersessian, Vrej Nerses. *Armenia*. World Biographical Series, vol. 163. Oxford and Santa Barbara, CA: Clio Press, 1993.

Neufeld, Michael J., and Michael Berenbaum, eds. *The Bombing of Auschwitz: Should the Allies Have Attempted It?* New York: St. Martin's Press, 2000.

Orenstein, Henry. *I Shall Live: Surviving against All Odds, 1939–1945*. New York: Beaufort, 1987.

Ortiz, Sister Dianna. "Government-Sanctioned Torture and International Law: A Survivor's Perspective." In *Fear of Persecution: Global Human Rights, International Law, and Human Well-Being*, ed. James D. White and Anthony J. Marsella, 177–188. Lanham, MD: Lexington, 2007.

Pakenham, Thomas. *The Boer War*. New York: Random House, 1979.

Papadatos, Petros. *The Eichmann Trial*. New York: Praeger, 1964.

Peskin, Victor. *International Justice in Rwanda and the Balkans: Virtual Trials and the Struggle for State Cooperation*. Cambridge, UK: Cambridge University Press, 2008.

Petermann, Simon. *Guantánamo: Les dérives de la guerre contre le terrorisme*. Edited by André Versaille. Paris: André Versaille Print, 2009.

Piccigallo, Philip R. *The Japanese on Trial: Allied War Crimes Operations in the East, 1945–1951*. Austin: University of Texas Press, 1979.

Prawdin, Michael. *The Mongol Empire: Its Rise and Legacy*. Translated by Eden and Cedar Paul. London: Allen and Unwin, 1967.

Quinley, Harold E., and Charles Y. Glock. *Anti-Semitism in America*. New York: Free Press, 1979.

Reitlinger, Gerald. *The Final Solution: The Attempt to Exterminate the Jews of Europe 1939–1945*. New York: Beechhurst Press, 1953.

Rejali, Darius M. *Torture and Democracy*. Princeton, NJ: Princeton University Press, 2009.

Robertson, Geoffrey. *Crimes against Humanity: The Struggle for Global Justice*, rev. ed. New York: New Press, 2002.

Rosenbaum, Alan S. *Is the Holocaust Unique? Perspectives on Comparative Genocide*. Boulder, CO: Westview Press, 2009.

Rosenne, Shabtai, ed. *6,000,000 Accusers: Israel's Case against Eichmann; The Opening Speech and Legal Argument of Mr. Gideon Hausner, Attorney-General*. Jerusalem: Jerusalem Post, 1961.

Rummel, R. J. *Death by Government: Genocide and Mass Murder in the Twentieth Century*. New Brunswick, NJ: Transactions, 1994.

Runciman, Sir Steven. *A History of the First Bulgarian Empire*. London: G. Bell and Sons, 1930.

Russell, Edward Frederick Langley (Lord Russell of Liverpool). *The Scourge of the Swastika: A Short History of Nazi War Crimes*. London: Greenhill, 1954.

Russell, Edward Frederick Langley (Lord Russell of Liverpool). *The Knights of Bushido: A Short History of Japanese War Crimes*. London: Greenhill, 1958.

Saggs, H.W.F. *The Might That Was Assyria*. London: Sidgwick and Jackson, 1984.

Sands, Philippe, *Torture Team: Rumsfeld's Memo and the Betrayal of American Values*. New York: Palgrave Macmillan, 2008.

Sax, Boria. *Animals in the Third Reich: Pets, Scapegoats, and the Holocaust*. New York: Continuum International Publishing Group, 2000.

Scharf, Michael P., and William A. Schabas. *Slobodan Milošević on Trial: A Companion*. New York: Continuum, 2002.

Schell, Jonathan. *The Village of Ben Suc*. New York: Knopf, 1967.

Schermer, Michael, and Alex Grobman. *Denying History: Who Says the Holocaust Never Happened and Why Do They Say It?* Berkeley: University of California Press, 2000.

Schindler, Dietrich, and Jiří Toman, eds. *The Laws of Armed Conflicts: A Collection of Conventions, Resolutions, and Other Documents*, 3rd rev. ed. Dordrecht: Nijhoff, 1988.

Semelin, Jacques, Michael J. Dwyer, and Stanley Hoffman. *Purify and Destroy: The Political Uses of Massacre and Genocide*. Paris, Editions du Seuil, 2005, London, C. Hurst, 2007.

Shaw, Martin. *What Is Genocide?* Cambridge and Malden, MA: Polity, 2007.

Sheehan, Neil. *A Bright Shining Lie: John Paul Vann and America in Vietnam*. New York: Random House, 1988.

Simpson, Gerry. *Law, War and Crime: War Crimes Trials and the Reinvention of International Law*. Cambridge: Polity Press, 2007.

Slowes, Salomon W. *The Road to Katyn: A Soldier's Story*. Edited by Władysław T. Bartoszewski. Translated by Naftali Greenwood. Cambridge: Blackwell, 1992.

Smith, A. H., ed. *The Parker Chronicle 832–900*. Exeter: University of Exeter Press, 1980.

Smith, Bradley F. *Reaching Judgment at Nuremberg*. New York: Basic Books, 1977.

Snyder, David Raub. *Sex Crimes under the Wehrmacht*. Lincoln: University of Nebraska Press, 2007.

Staubing, Harold Elk, ed. *The Last Magnificent War: Rare Journalistic and Eyewitness Accounts of World War I*. New York: Paragon House, 1989.

Stember, Charles Herbert, Marshall Sklare, and George Salomon. *Jews in the Mind of America*. New York: Basic Books, 2006.

Strozier, Charles B., and Michael Flynn, eds., *Genocide, War, and Human Survival*. Lanham, MD: Rowman and Littlefield, 1996.

Taylor, Telford. *The Anatomy of the Nuremberg Trials: A Personal Memoir*. New York: Knopf, 1992.

Taylor, Telford. *Nuremberg and Vietnam: An American Tragedy*. Chicago: Quadrangle, 1970.

Todenhöfer, Jürgen. *Warum tötest du, Zaid?* Munich: C. Bertelsmann Verlag, 2008.

Tolstoy, Leo. *War and Peace*. World's Classics Series. London: Oxford University Press, 1933.

Trial of the Major War Criminals before the International Military Tribunal, Vol. 2, *Proceedings 14 November 1945—30 November 1945*. Buffalo, NY: William S. Hein, 1995.

Tucker, Jonathan B. *War of Nerves: Chemical Warfare from World War I to Al-Qaeda*. New York: Pantheon, 2006.

Tusa, Ann, and John Tusa. *The Nuremberg Trial*. London: BBC Books, 1995.

Tutorow, Norman E., ed. *War Crimes, War Criminals, and War Crimes Trials: An Annotated Bibliography and Source Book*. With the Special Assistance of Karen Winnovich. Bibliographies and indexes in World History, No. 4. New York and Westport, CT.: Greenwood Press, 1986.

Tyerman, Christopher. *God's War: A New History of the Crusades*. Cambridge, MA: Harvard University Press, 2006.

Union of Soviet Socialist Republics. *Material on the Trial of Former Servicemen of the Japanese Army Charged with Manufacturing and Employing Bacteriological Weapons*. Moscow: Foreign Languages Publishing House, 1950.

Van den Berghe, Pierre, ed. *State Violence and Ethnicity*. Niwot: University Press of Colorado, 1990.

Vietnam Veterans against the War. *Winter Soldier Investigation*. Boston: Beacon Press, 1972.

Wakabayashi, Bob Tadashi, ed. *The Nanking Atrocity 1937–1938: Complicating the Picture*. New York: Berghan, 2007.

Wawro, Geoffrey. *The Franco-Prussian War: The German Conquest of France in 1870–1871*. New York: Cambridge University Press, 2003.

Whitlock, Flint. *Given Up for Dead: American G.I.s in the Nazi Concentration Camp of Berga*. Cambridge, MA: Westview Press, 2005.

Willis, James F. *Prologue to Nuremberg: The Politics and Diplomacy of Punishing War Criminals of the First World War*. Westport, CT: Greenwood Press, 1982.

Wolff, Leon. *Little Brown Brother: How the United States Purchased and Pacified the Philippines*. New York: Oxford University Press, 1991.

Wright, Quincy. *A Study of War*. Chicago: University of Chicago Press, 1964.

Yoo, John. *War By Other Means: An Insider's Account of the War on Terror*. New York: Atlantic Monthly Press, 2006.

Zabecki, David T., ed. *World War II in Europe: An Encyclopedia*. New York: Garland, 1999.

Zamoyski, Adam. *Moscow 1812: Napoleon's Final March*. New York: Harper Collins, 2004.

Periodicals

Akçam, Taner. "The Anatomy of a Crime: The Turkish Historical Society's Manipulation of Archival Documents." *Journal of Genocide Research* 7, no. 2 (2005): 60–86.

Ansen, David. "Spielberg's Obsession." *Newsweek*, December 20, 1993, 112.

Apuuli, Kasaija Phillip. "Procedural Due Process, and the Prosecution of Genocide Suspects in Rwanda." *Journal of Genocide Research* 11, no. 1 (2009): 11–30.

Associated Press. "Ex-Soldier Gets Life in Prison for Iraqi Slayings." *The Wall Street Journal*, June 30, 2009.

Bassiouni, M. Cherif, and Christopher L. Blakesley. "The Need for an International Criminal Court in the New International World Order." *Vanderbilt Journal of Transnational Law* 25, no. 2 (1992): 151–182.

Berkeley, Bill. "Sounds of Violence: Rwanda's Killer Radio." *New Republic*, August 22, 1994.

Borch, Fred L. Untitled Review of *The Tokyo War Crimes Trials: The Pursuit of Justice in the Wake of World War II*, by Yuma Totani. *Journal of Military History* 73, no. 1 (2009): 323–325.

Brady, Brendan, and Keo Kounila. "Khmer Rouge Prison Chief Takes Blame for Killings." *Los Angeles Times*, April 1, 2009, A28.

Chedekel, Lisa, and Matthew Kauffman. "Army Sees Record Number of Suicides in Iraq." *Hartford Courant*, May 30, 2008.

Chigas, George. "The Politics of Defining Justice after the Cambodian Genocide." *Journal of Genocide Research* 2, no. 2 (2000): 245–265.

Cohen, Roger. "C.I.A. Report on Bosnia Blames Serbs for 90% of the War Crimes." *New York Times*, March 9, 1995, A1.

Cohen, Roger. "Where G.I.'s Were Consumed by the Holocaust's Terror; A Filmmaker Helps Thaw Memories of Wartime Guilt." *New York Times*, April 17, 2001, E1.

Comyns-Carr, A. S. "The Tokyo War Crimes Trial." *Far Eastern Survey* 18, no. 10 (1949): 109–114.

Contreras, Guillermo. "Bataan Death March Survivors Hear Apology." *San Antonio Express-News*, May 31, 2009, 1.

Copeland, Libby. "Prison Revolt." *Washington Post*, May 10, 2004, C01.

Dedarbaum, Jonathan. "The Rome Statute of the International Criminal Court: A Commentary." *Journal of Genocide Research* 6, no. 4 (2004): 601–604.

DesRoches, Christian A. "Accounting for Horror: Post-Genocide Debates in Rwanda." *Journal of Genocide Research* 8, no. 1 (2006): 91–94.

DiMento, Joseph F. C., and Geis Gilbert. "The Extraordinary Condition of Extraordinary Rendition: The C.I.A., the D.E.A., Kidnaping, Torture, and the Law." *War Crimes, Genocide and Crimes against Humanity* 2 (2006): 35–64.

Donagan, Barbara. "Atrocity, War Crime, and Treason in the English Civil War." *American Historical Review* 99, no. 4 (1994): 1137–1166.

Donagan, Barbara. "Prisoners in the English Civil War." *History Today* 41, no. 3 (1991): 28–35.

Eltringham, Nigel. "'We Are Not a Truth Commission': Fragmented Narratives and Historical Record at the International Criminal Tribunal for Rwanda." *Journal of Genocide Research* 11, no. 1 (2009): 55–79.

Frederick, Jim. "When a Soldier Murders: Steven Green Gets Life." *Time*, May 21, 2009.

Gillers, Stephen, "The Torture Memo," *The Nation*, April 28, 2008.

Ginsbergs, George. "Laws of War and War Crimes on the Russian Front during World War II: The Soviet View." *Soviet Studies* 11, no. 3 (1960): 253–285.

Hagan, John, and Scott Greer. "Making War Criminal." *Criminology* 40, no. 2 (May 2002): 231.

Hershey, Amos S. "The History of International Relations during Antiquity and the Middle Ages: International Law Impossible before the Rise of the Modern European State System." *American Journal of International Law* 5, no. 4 (1911): 901–933.

Hobbs, Jesse. "Ex Post Facto Explanations." *Journal of Philosophy* 90, no. 3 (1993): 117–136.

Horton, Scott. "An Idea Whose Time Has Come—and Gone?" *The Economist*, July 23, 2009, 58–59.

Horton, Scott. "A Nuremberg Lesson." *Los Angeles Times*, January 20, 2005, B13.

International Herald Tribune. "Research Shows Estimates of Bosnian War Death Toll Were Inflated," June 21, 2007.

Karnell, Aaron. "Justice on the Grass: Three Rwandan Journalists, Their Trial for War Crimes, and a Nation's Quest for Redemption." *Journal of Genocide Research* 8, no. 1 (2006): 89–91.

Kiernan, Ben. "The Demography of Genocide in Southeast Asia: The Death Tolls in Cambodia, 1975–79, and East Timor, 1975–80." *Critical Asian Studies* 35, no. 4 (2003): 585–597.

Law, Helen H. "Atrocities in Greek Warfare." *Classical Journal* 15, no. 3 (1919): 132–147.

Mayer, Jane. "Outsourcing Torture: The Secret History of America's 'Extraordinary Rendition' Program." *The New Yorker*, February 14, 2005.

Menzel, Jörg. "Justice Delayed or Too Late for Justice? The Khmer Rouge Tribunal and the Cambodian 'Genocide' 1975–79." *Journal of Genocide Research* 9, no. 2 (2007): 215–233.

Moffett, Sebastian. "Japan Justice Minister Denies Nanking Massacre." *Reuters*, May 4, 1994.

Neumann, Franz. "The War Crimes Trials." *World Politics* 2, no. 1 (1949): 135–147.

New York Times. "Chirac Urges Turks to Recognize Genocide," October 1, 2006.

New York Times. "Turkey Freezes Military Ties with France," November 1, 2006.

Nizich, Ivana. *War Crimes in Bosnia-Hercegovina*, Vol. 1, *A Helsinki Watch Report*. New York: Human Rights Watch, 1992.

Palombino, Fulvio Maria. "Universal Jurisdiction in Absentia over Genocide: Some Critical Remarks in Light of Recent Spanish Jurisprudence." *Journal of Genocide Research* 9, no. 2 (2007): 243–249.

Parks, W. H. "Crimes in Hostilities." *Marine Corps Gazette*, August 1976, 16.

Peck, Grant. "Ex-Prison Chief Regrets Killing 16,000." *Associated Press*, April 1, 2009.

Phillips, Peter. "Death by Torture: U.S. Media Ignores Hard Evidence." *CounterPunch*, December 2, 2005.

Pickard, Daniel B. "Comment: Security County Resolution 808: A Step toward a Permanent International Court for the Prosecution of International Crimes and Human Rights Violations." *Golden Gate University Law Review* 25 (1966): 435.

Prévost, Ann Marie. "Race and War Crimes: The 1945 War Crimes Trial of General Tomoyuki Yamashita." *Human Rights Quarterly* 14, no. 3 (1992): 303–338.

Rivkin, Jr., David B., and Casey Lee A., "The Memos Prove We Didn't Torture." *The Wall Street Journal*, April 20, 2009, A15.

Rummel, R. J. "Deadlier Than War." *Institute of Public Affairs Review* (Melbourne, Australia) 41, no. 2 (1987): 24–30.

Shane, Scott, and Mark Mazzetti. "In Adopting Harsh Tactics, No Look at Past Use." *New York Times*, April 22, 2009.

Sterngold, James. "Japan Official Forced to Quit over Remark." *New York Times*, August 14, 1994, A5.

Time. "Press: Jew Shoot." August 24, 1936.

Time. "My Lai: A Question of Orders." January 25, 1971.

USA Today. "Cousins Convicted of War Crimes in Bosnia." July 22, 2009.

Webb, Henry J. "Prisoner of War in the Middle Ages." *Military Affairs* 12, no. 1 (1948): 48.

Weikart, Richard. "Darwinism and Death: Devaluing Human Life in Germany 1859–1920." *Journal of the History of Ideas* 63, no. 2 (2002): 323–344.

White, Josh. "Ex-Soldier Charged in Killing of Iraqi Family." *Washington Post*, July 4, 2006, p. A01.

White, Josh. "General Demoted, but Cleared in Abuse Probe." *Washington Post*, May 6, 2005, A08.

White, Josh. "Reprimand Is Sentence for Officer at Abu Ghraib." *Washington Post*, May 10, 2007, A03.

Will, George. "The Last Word: Jedwabne." *Newsweek*, July 9, 2001, 68.

Williams, Carole J. "Different Approaches for Two Men at Center of 'Torture Memo' Controversy." *Los Angeles Times*, April 22, 2009.
Zorbas, Eugenia. "What Does Reconciliation after Genocide Mean? Public Transcript and Hidden Transcripts in Post-Genocide Rwanda." *Journal of Genocide Research* 11, no. 1 (2009): 127–147.

Web Sites

Cohn, Marjorie. "*How the Bush Administration's Opposition to the International Criminal Court Has Put Peacekeepers and Others in Danger.*" FindLaw for Legal Professionals. http://writ.lp.findlaw.com/commentary/20030908_cohn.html.
Crim, Brian E. " 'We Ourselves Are the War:' Understanding the Relationship between the First World War and the Holocaust." *Ideologies of War, Genocide and Terror*, sponsored by Library of Social Science. February 27, 2009. http://www.ideologiesofwar.com/docs/crim_koenigsberg.html (accessed July 3, 2009).
Genocide Watch. "Countries at Risk of Genocide Politicide or Killing 2008." *Genocide Watch*. http://www.genocidewatch.org/images/Risk1_08_11_01_Countries_at_Risk_2008.pdf.
Griech-Polelle, Beth A. "Review of Richard Koenigsberg's Lecture: The Logic of Mass Murder: Hitler the Holocaust and War." *Ideologies of War, Genocide and Terror*, sponsored by Library of Social Science. January 21, 2009. http://www.ideologiesofwar.com/docs/bgp_rk.htm (accessed July 3, 2009).
Japan Times Online. "Okinawa Slams History Text Rewrite." June 23, 2007. http://search.japantimes.co.jp/cgi-bin/nn20070623a1.html (accessed July 4, 2009).
"Murder in the Name of War—My Lai." BBC News, 20 July 1998. http://news.bbc.co.uk/2/hi/asia-pacific/64344.stm (accessed July 4, 2009).
New York Times. "A Guide to the Memos on Torture, 2002–2003." *New York Times*. http://www.nytimes.com/ref/international/24MEMO-GUIDE.html.
Papazian, Dennis R. "Useful Answers to Frequent Questions on the Armenian Genocide." Armenian Research Center, The University of Michigan-Dearborn, 1991. http://www.umd.umich.edu/dept/armenian/facts/answers.html (accessed July 3, 2009).
PEN American Center. "PEN Protests Charges against Turkish Author Orhan Pamuk." Press Release. September 2, 2005. http://www.pen.org/viewmedia.php/prmMID/369/prmID/1331 (accessed July 3, 2009).
Schwartz, Teresa Pencak. *Poland—Hitler's First Target for Annihilation during the Holocaust*. http://www.holocaustforgotten.com/poland (accessed July 3, 2009).
"Turkish-American Writer Shot Dead." BBC News, January 19, 2007. http://news.bbc.co.uk/2/hi/europe/6279241.stm (accessed July 3, 2009)
University of Missouri—Kansas City School of Law. "The Nuremberg Trials—Justice Jackson's Opening Statement for the Prosecution." Famous World Trials Project. University of Missouri—Kansas City. http://www.law.umkc.edu/faculty/projects/ftrials/Nuremberg/Jackson.html#The%20Lawless%20Road%20to%20Power (accessed July 4, 2009).
U.S. Department of the Army. *Review of the Preliminary Investigations into the My Lai Incident. Vol. I—The Report of the Investigation*. Washington, DC: U.S.

Government Printing Office, 1970. http://www.loc.gov/rr/frd/Military_Law/pdf/RDAR-Vol-I.pdf (accessed July 4, 2009).

U.S. Department of the Army. *Review of the Preliminary Investigations into the My Lai Incident. Vol. II—Testimony*. Washington, DC: U.S. Government Printing Office, 1970. http://www.loc.gov/rr/frd/Military_Law/pdf/RDAR-Vol-IIBook8.pdf (accessed July 4, 2009).

U.S. Department of the Army. *Review of the Preliminary Investigations into the My Lai Incident. Vol. III—Exhibits*. Washington, DC: U.S. Government Printing Office, 1970. http://www.loc.gov/rr/frd/Military_Law/Vol_III-exhibits.html (accessed July 4, 2009).

Miscellaneous

Armenian Assembly of America. *Armenian Genocide Resource Guide*. Washington, DC: Armenian Assembly of America, 1988.

Bartov, Omer. "Industrial Killing: World War I, the Holocaust, and Representation." Annual Holocaust Conference, Millersville University History Department, 1997. http://www.millersville.edu/~holo-con/bartov.html (accessed July 3, 2009).

Berberian, Laura J. "Official United States Documents on the Armenian Genocide: An Annotated Bibliography." Master's thesis, University of North Carolina at Chapel Hill, 2008.

International Committee of the Red Cross. *Report of the International Committee of the Red Cross (ICRC) on the Treatment by the Coalition Forces of Prisoners of War and Other Protected Persons by the Geneva Conventions in Iraq during Arrest, Internment, and Interrogation*. February 2004.

Lateline. Transcript: *Serbia Not Responsible for Bosnia Genocide: UN*. February 27, 2007. Australian Broadcasting Corporation. http://www.abc.net.au/lateline/content/2007/s1858837.htm.

Meet the Press. Transcript, December 4, 2005. NBC News.

Price, Isabel B. "Gerald L. K. Smith and Anti-Semitism." Master's thesis, University of New Mexico, 1965.

United Nations. International Tribunal for the Prosecution of Persons Responsible for Serious Violations of International Humanitarian Law Committed in the Territory of Former Yugoslavia since 1991. *Report to the President: The Death of Slobodan Milošević* (The Parker Report). The Hague. May 2006. www.un.org/icty/milosevic/parkerreport.pdf.

U.S. House. Armed Services Investigating Subcommittee of the Committee on Armed Services. *Investigation of the My Lai Incident (Under the Authority of H.Res. 105)*. Washington, DC: Government Printing Office, 1970.

White House. *Humane Treatment of al Qaeda and Taliban Detainees*. Washington, DC, February 7, 2002. http://www.pegc.us/archive/White_House/bush_memo_20020207_ed.pdf.

Ziemke, Earl Frederick. *The U.S. Army in the Occupation of Germany, 1944–1946*. Washington, DC: Center of Military History, U.S. Army, 1975.

Index

About the Author

ARNOLD KRAMMER is Professor of History at Texas A&M University. A highly praised teacher for more than three decades, Krammer has written widely in English and German about POWs, including such books as *Nazi Prisoners of War in America*; *Prisoners of War: A Reference Handbook*; *Hitler's Last Soldier in America* (with Georg Gaertner); *Undue Process: The Untold Story of America's German Enemy Aliens*, and *The Forgotten Friendship*. He has co-edited three volumes on the Holocaust, *Children and the Holocaust*, *Women and the Holocaust*, and the *Holocaust through National Perspectives*, and has written more than 40 articles on subjects including World War I, the Spanish Civil War, World War II, and East Germany and even a seminal article on fuel and the Third Reich.